W9-BCU-011

AMERICANA LIBRARY

ROBERT E. BURKE, EDITOR

AMERICANA LIBRARY

The City: The Hope of Democracy
By Frederic C. Howe
With a new introduction by Otis A. Pease

The Fight for Conservation
By Gifford Pinchot
With a new introduction by Gerald D. Nash

Borah of Idaho
By Claudius O. Johnson
With a new introduction by the author

The Deflation of American Ideals: An Ethical Guide for New Dealers
By Edgar Kemler
With a new introduction by Otis L. Graham, Jr.

Bourbon Democracy of the Middle West, 1865-1896
By Horace Samuel Merrill
With a new introduction by the author

SENATOR WILLIAM E. BORAH
in 1934

BORAH OF IDAHO

BY

CLAUDIUS O. JOHNSON

With a New Introduction by the Author

UNIVERSITY OF WASHINGTON PRESS

SEATTLE AND LONDON

University of Washington Press Americana Library edition 1967

Library of Congress Catalog Card Number 36-8450
Printed in the United States of America

Thou shalt provide out of all the people able men, such as fear God, men of truth, hating covetousness. — Exodus: XVIII, 21.

TO MY NEIGHBORS

THE PEOPLE OF IDAHO

PREFACE

In February, 1934, the preparation of this biography was begun. The reluctance with which Senator Borah gave his consent to the project has been matched only by his generosity in giving the writer unrestricted access to his private correspondence. The only request the Senator made was that his life be written as it has been lived. The writer has attempted to follow the Senator's wishes, permitting the facts to speak for themselves, and refraining, as far as possible, from intruding his own opinions. To pass judgment smugly upon each act of a famous living public man may be as irritating to the reader as it is hazardous for the writer. Yet the writer has not hesitated to draw some conclusions.

Senator Borah has played a large part in many movements. Certain historical events have been briefly sketched in order to aid the reader in estimating the Senator's part in them, but the reader must find the economic, social, and political history of the United States in other volumes. It is obviously impossible because of the limits of space and, in the writer's opinion, inadvisable as a matter of technique to rewrite the history of such events as the League of Nations fight and the Washington Conference in this single volume on Senator Borah. There is less need for rewriting such history in a biography of Senator Borah than there is for doing so in the biography of a different type of man, because, in a sense, Borah of Idaho has always stood apart from the event. He has initiated some movements, he has popularized more, he has given color to many ; but he has seldom been in the inner circle of organizers and promoters. His part has been that of molding and expressing public opinion. Whatever his part may have been in the secret manipulations which led to the rejection of the League by the Senate, his chief contribution, perhaps the most significant of all contributions, was in popularizing anti-League sentiment and making the adverse vote in the Senate politically expedient. He played an even more solitary part in the Washington Conference. Supported by a public opinion which he had aroused, he forced the President against his will to call it, but he was not even a delegate to the Conference. Borah is an independent force. The primary purpose of this biography is to follow the play of that force upon events.

Acknowledgment is due to the State College of Washington for release from teaching during a part of the period in which this research and writing have been accomplished. The writer is grateful to Norman Hapgood, Salmon O. Levinson, and Colonel Raymond Robins for information and suggestions. Professor J. W. Howerth of Greeley, Colorado, who attended Enfield College with Borah, and a number of the Senator's fellow-students at the University of Kansas, including William Allen White of Emporia and Thomas F. Doran of Topeka, were kind enough to give their opinions of the Senator as a college man. Scores of Idaho people have patiently answered the writer's questions and offered information which could come from no other source. Of these Judge Miles Johnson, Mark Means, Irvin E. Rockwell, Benjamin Oppenheim, and Ray McKaig are particularly entitled to gratitude. Newspaper publishers have been uniformly courteous, but the writer is under special obligations to the publishers of the Lewiston *Tribune* and the Idaho *Statesman* who generously placed their files and offices at his disposal.

C. O. J.

Pullman, Washington
February 12, 1936

CONTENTS

Borah of Idaho: His Last Years and a Re-evaluation ... xiii

I. The Middle West ... 1

II. The West ... 23

III. Oratory and Politics ... 39

IV. The Voice of the People ... 57

V. Dynamite and Politics ... 73

VI. Idaho's Dividends ... 88

VII. The National Statesman Emerges ... 113

VIII. Who Is a Republican? ... 135

IX. New Freedom Politics ... 153

X. A Conception of States' Rights ... 174

XI. New Horizons ... 190

XII. A Conception of Americanism ... 204

XIII. The Mirabeau of the Battalion of Death 223

XIV. Swords and Ploughshares ... 257

XV. Conscience and Courage ... 282

XVI. The Chairman of the Committee on Foreign Relations ... 311

XVII. Anti-Imperialist ... 336

XVIII. Borah-Russian Relations ... 354

XIX. "We Have Scotched the Snake" ... 369

XX. A Venture in Idealism ... 386

XXI. The Hammer of Thor ... 408

XXII. Borah and Hoover ... 432

XXIII. The New Deal ... 468

XXIV. Borah the Inscrutable (?) ... 490

Index ... 501

LIST OF ILLUSTRATIONS

Senator William E. Borah in 1934 . . . . *Frontispiece*

William Nathan Borah . . . . . . *Facing page* 6

Elizabeth West Borah 6

Birthplace of Senator Borah, Fairfield, Ills. 10

Cumberland Presbyterian College, Enfield, Ills. . . 10

W. E. Borah, a leader of the Idaho Bar about 1906 . . 26

Mr. and Mrs. W. E. Borah shortly after their marriage in 1895 36

Senators Borah, Lodge, and Smoot, 1920 246

Senator Borah's Press Conference 326

Mrs. Borah 424

BORAH OF IDAHO: HIS LAST YEARS AND A RE-EVALUATION

In the fall of 1936 William E. Borah came before the people of Idaho seeking their endorsement for a sixth term in the United States Senate. I attended his meeting in Moscow and complimented him upon his physical vigor and undiminished talent in holding an audience. He laughingly remarked, "Yes, you will have to write another book." My *Borah of Idaho* had been published in the spring of 1936, and Borah, now Dean of the Senate, continued in his place until his death on January 19, 1940. I am not writing another book,[1] but the time is appropriate for an assessment of Borah's later contributions to public life and for a further consideration of his place in American politics.

Although the Senator liked President Franklin D. Roosevelt—his refreshing liberalism, his courage, and his resourcefulness—and he supported more of the President's measures than he opposed, he was not a New Dealer. Borah was a conservative on the Constitution and governmental power. Even the few who considered him a radical admitted that he was sound on the Constitution and the basic principles of republican government. Humane and compassionate, Borah supported the large New Deal appropriations for relief and its Social Security program, but he was very critical of the ease with which it could find constitutional powers for some of its experiments and its tendency to expand both national and executive power. Thus he objected to the delegation to the President of the power to reduce the tariff under the Reciprocal Trade Agreement Act and of the power to exercise business

1 The Senator's entire career is well covered by Marian C. McKenna in her *Borah* (Ann Arbor: University of Michigan Press, 1961). Her volume has been helpful to me in the preparation of this additional material on Borah. I have drawn also on my own articles on Borah, as follows: "William E. Borah: The People's Choice," *Pacific Northwest Quarterly*, XLIV (January, 1953), 15-22; "William E. Borah: The Issue First, the Party Second," *Northwest Science*, XXVII (1953), 95; "Borah's Bequest to Democracy," *Idaho Yesterdays*, I, No. 4 (Winter, 1957-58), 11-20; and "Borah—His Political Impact," *Borah Foundation Lectures* (University of Idaho, Oct. 22, 1963, and March 26, 1964).

code-making authorized by the National Industrial Recovery Act. Under the Constitution, argued the Senator, such powers may not be delegated to the President.

The political surprise of 1936 was Borah's effort to win the Republican nomination for President. His strongest claim for the honor rested upon his support of a number of the New Deal programs and his discriminating and effective criticism of its other programs. Unshakable in his devotion to the American constitutional system, opposed to monopoly and to special privileges for big business, but also opposed to government control of the economic and social order, this old-style Jeffersonian-Jacksonian liberal, who in his prime had never thrown his hat in the ring for President, saw, at seventy-one, the possibility of support for that office from both the progressive and conservative wings of the Republican party. It is not likely that he had any great expectation of getting the nomination, but he appeared to have strong hope of winning a sufficient number of convention delegates to give him a leading voice in the shaping of the party platform and, more important, in the selection of the presidential candidate. He did not say who would have his support for the nomination if he himself should fail to receive it, but he did declare his opposition to any conservative candidate. Among such conservative possibilities he included Alfred M. Landon, whom he early denounced as a big-business champion, presumably arriving at that erroneous conclusion because of the enthusiastic support Landon was receiving from a large number of business leaders. Although a month or so prior to the convention the Senator appeared to modify slightly his opinion of the Kansan's conservatism, Borah never supported Landon in the convention or in the election campaign.

Borah announced his candidacy for the nomination on February 4, 1936, being the first to enter the field. He went forth alone and perhaps lonely. He had meetings, only fairly well attended, in New York, Ohio, and Illinois, in which he spoke for rank-and-file selection of delegates to the Republican convention, and against monopoly and big business. He was not supported by an effective organization, except in Wisconsin, where he had the aid of the experienced La Follette forces; he was endorsed by no outstanding national party leaders; and he had but little financial backing. He won twenty-two of the twenty-four delegates in Wisconsin, about half of the fifty-seven in Illinois, the uncontested primary in Pennsylvania (but with only twenty delegates pledged to abide by the result), ten delegates in Oregon, eight in Idaho, and a few more scattered about in the West. Altogether he expected to go to the convention with a hundred delegates. But under the pressure and heat of the old guard his support melted away and flowed to Landon. Even the Idaho delegates, after Borah released them, gaily joined the Landon forces. Borah was hurt. Recalling his efforts through the years to make the Republican party more responsive to the needs of the common man, his voice broke and the tears flowed.

But he was not long cast down. Soon he was back in Idaho and staging a vigorous campaign for re-election to the Senate. There is no evidence that Roosevelt desired his defeat. On the contrary, we have the hint from James A. Farley, chairman of the Democratic National Committee, that Borah was among those favorites of the President whom, regardless of party affiliation, he preferred to see re-elected to the Senate. As for Farley, although it was his fixed policy to support all Democratic candidates, he made no special effort to defeat Borah.[2] But the organization Democrats in Idaho thought they had an opportunity to retire Borah at last. The Democratic candidate for the Senate was the popular C. Ben Ross, a folksy type of campaigner, now serving his third term as governor of the state. It was generally agreed that Borah had never faced such a formidable opponent, and that Roosevelt's coattails would certainly give Ross a sufficient boost to carry him to Washington. Many stalwart Republican organization men who had long been decidedly hostile to Borah, because he had almost never worked with them, viewed with complete equanimity, not to say with satisfaction, what they regarded as Borah's fading chance of re-election to the Senate. Such Republicans did not openly oppose Borah, but they smiled when they talked of what Ben Ross could do to him. Ross, they would say, does not pretend to be a statesman; he just talks to the people, and the people go for him. As for Borah, the voters are tired of his learned discourses on the Constitution, monopolies, and so

2 McKenna, *Borah,* p. 338.

on. Thus did these old guard Republicans view the prospects in the coming senatorial campaign and election.[3]

Ross entered the campaign with great confidence. He gave the impression that he was sure that he would win, just as he had won his three gubernatorial races, by talking to the folks, by entertaining them. The Ross candidacy was recognized as a serious threat to Borah by friends of national stature in both political parties. Senators Burton K. Wheeler (Democrat), Robert M. La Follette, Jr. (Progressive), and George Norris (Independent), stood ready to come to Idaho if Borah wanted help. His supporters in Idaho, to answer the charge of Ross (often believed) that Borah had been so busy with national and international affairs that he had done practically nothing for Idaho, distributed a leaflet listing the national legislation which Borah had sponsored that was of importance to Idaho and the West and naming also, and perhaps more important for the immediate purpose, the irrigation dams and public buildings that he had obtained for Idaho. But the Senator himself fired practically all the guns in his campaign. He followed his almost annual practice of motoring over much of the sparsely inhabited state, speaking in many of its widely separated cities, towns, and villages. Almost invariably he spoke to a packed house, for the farmers, laborers, stockmen, cowhands, and lumberjacks would ride or drive for miles to hear him. He made their trip worth while.[4]

Always avoiding personalities and partisan claptrap, he stuck to the issues—monopoly, the monetary system, relief of unemployment, and others. He would begin very quietly and easily, establishing rapport with the crowd. Then he would put a question or name an issue, indicating its various angles and complexities. Following this he would marshal facts and figures (not too many), perhaps quote some authorities, and maybe drop a light comment. He would suggest his solution of the problem, modestly at first, but as he elaborated his views, talking faster and faster, he would seem to become more convinced of the soundness of his solution. Then he

[3] This information the writer gathered from conversations with a number of Republican organization men in the summer of 1934, when it was already understood that C. Ben Ross would be Borah's opponent in 1936.

[4] The writer heard Borah address his constituents in 1930, 1934, and 1936.

would take up another question and run through the same cycle, always with perfect ease and with such casual assurance that he would appear to be feeling his way except in his climaxes. The people would listen intently for an hour, for an hour and a half, for as long as he would talk. Sometimes he would give them a laugh, not by telling a story but with a humorous comment on a matter relevant to the issue. More often he would make them smile, but always they hung on his words, seeming oblivious to heat and poor ventilation and the prospect of later refreshments. Borah talked sense to the people of Idaho. He appeared to assume that they were adults who could understand. From him the voters learned, some consciously and perhaps more subconsciously, that they infinitely preferred thought to hokum. They listened cynically to candidates who gave them cheap entertainment, and they laughed at their antics, but when they had heard Borah they could begin to discuss the issues on their merits. There is no doubt that the Senator contributed to the self-esteem of the people of Idaho as well as to their enlightenment. They loved him because he understood and respected them, was easy to approach, and released them from their verbal inhibitions. They were proud that the Senator from Idaho was a *United States* Senator with an international reputation.

Borah's question period following an address was a pure delight. "Now, I'll be glad to answer any questions [slight pause] if I can." The questions would come, and all that were honestly and sincerely put he would answer—frankly, modestly, courteously.

Question: "Isn't a lot of that New Deal relief money being wasted?"

Answer: "Well, where there is so much money to be handled and it is necessary to act quickly, I suppose there is bound to be some waste. You may know that I voted for those appropriations. I did so because I thought they were necessary."

As the campaign drew to a close, there were probably only a very few people in Idaho who believed that Borah would be defeated. It is doubtful if C. Ben Ross was numbered with them. On election day the Republican slate was wiped clean, except for Borah, who managed to survive the Ross threat by the score of 128,723 to 74,444. Roosevelt received 125,683 votes and Landon 66,232, and the Democrats carried both seats for the national House of Representatives and all state offices. This election affords one of the best examples of ticket-scratching on record.

At the beginning of his sixth term Borah found the opportunity to strike a stout blow for the independence of the judiciary, a safeguard of freedom deeply embedded in the Anglo-American tradition and one which the Senator was ever ready to defend. On February 5, 1937, Roosevelt practically dropped a bomb on Congress with his "Court Packing" proposal. It called upon Congress to authorize the President to appoint a judge to the Supreme Court and any inferior court in which a sitting judge who had attained the age of seventy did not retire. At the time the plan was proposed it would have made possible the addition of six judges to the Supreme Court. The Republicans in the Senate decided to keep quiet and let the Democrats fight it out among themselves. The Democratic opposition to the President's plan was relatively quiet also, but not inactive. Its leader and most determined member was Senator Burton K. Wheeler of Montana. Hardly less active was Borah, who in almost daily meetings with Wheeler planned and plotted the defeat of the President's measure. Presently they had a bipartisan majority of the Judiciary Committee on their side, and that majority's report, written by Wheeler and Borah, was something of a classic on the independence of the judiciary. To be sure, it was probably the shift of the Supreme Court to a more liberal position on constitutional issues that killed the President's scheme—made it unnecessary—but the valiant fight of Wheeler, Borah, and a few others, and the masterly report of the Judiciary Committee remain significant parts of the record.

On the international scene Borah remained steadfast in his belief that the United States was morally and politically superior to any other nation and that its ideals would be lost if it became involved with other nations, even in organizations designed to promote peace. He was not opposed to America being a party to international agreements, but his assent was not forthcoming for commitments which might in any way limit its freedom of action. One of his main themes was that the United States should remain free to work out its domestic problems.

The Senator saw great hopes for peace for his country through strict adherence to neutrality, and he appeared to hold with some others, notably Professor Edwin Borchard, that the United States had been drawn into the First World War because American munitions makers and financiers had, in effect, committed their country to the cause of the Allies. In 1934, in a major Senate speech, Borah designated the manufacturers of arms as "international criminals," and the Senate authorized a committee headed by Senator Gerald Nye to investigate the munitions industry. The committee revealed that enormous profits had been made from the sale of munitions, and it claimed that American bankers had urged our entrance into the war as a means of rescuing their large loans to the Allies. The report of the committee had considerable impact, and President Roosevelt himself was impressed by it. Congress proceeded to pass the Neutrality Act of 1935, which called for an embargo on war supplies whether destined to an aggressor or to the victim of an aggressor. The President and Secretary of State Cordell Hull had favored a bill which would allow sales to a victim of aggression, thus permitting the United States to cooperate with other nations in curbing aggression. But the strongest devotees of neutrality, with Borah near the top of the list, would have none of it.

As Japan and Germany became more threatening, Roosevelt delivered in Chicago his famous Quarantine Speech (1937), in which he said that the peace-loving nations should oppose those that violate treaties and create "a state of international anarchy . . . from which there is no escape through mere isolation or neutrality." Senator Borah and other isolationists accused the President of "warmongering." Borah thought that Hitler was not such a terrible fellow, and in 1938 he was ready to go to Germany if he could be assured of an interview with Hitler. "There are so many great sides to him," he said, "I believe I might accomplish something." The Berlin Foreign Office assured Borah that der Fuehrer would receive him. The State Department had serious misgivings about the trip, however, and as Borah was ill for a short time and busy in the Senate after that, he postponed the journey indefinitely. But even after the war broke out Borah naïvely remarked that if he could have talked with Hilter, "all of this might have been avoided."[5]

In July of 1939 the President had a conference at the White House with key cabinet members and leaders of the Senate, including Borah, in the hope of gaining support for a revision of the arms embargo. The President stated that war might break out any time and that, if and when it came, the embargo would prevent him from acting in the best interest of the United States. Secretary Hull supported the President's position. Borah interrupted to make his often quoted statement, "I do not think there is going to be any war in Europe, between now and the first of January or for some time thereafter." Hull angrily responded that the Senator should come down to the State Department and read the dispatches from all over Europe. "I don't give a damn about your dispatches," Borah retorted. "We all have means of acquiring information," he continued. "I myself have gone to great effort to secure information from different sources." The Idahoan is also sometimes reported as having advised the Secretary that his sources of information were more reliable than those of the State Department. Such heated exchanges did not of themselves thwart the President's hopes for a modification of the embargo, for the Democratic leaders present informed him that they lacked the necessary majority in the Senate. The President then said that if the Senate failed to act it would be his duty to inform the country of that failure. To this Senator Borah responded: "It is no part of your constitutional duty to tell the Senate when to act or how to act."[6] It is well for the Senator's reputation that it has more solid foundations upon which to rest than his record at this particular White House conference. His manner was almost arrogant, and in less than two months Germany's attack on Poland proved that the State Department's information was more reliable than his.

Senator Borah's confidence in the arms embargo was not shaken even by the outbreak of war in Europe. In a futile effort to prevent its repeal he made a speech probably as able

[5] McKenna, *Borah*, pp. 357-60.
[6] *Ibid.*, pp. 361-64.

as any he had ever delivered. He showed realism in his opposition to placing the trade in arms on a cash-and-carry basis (the policy adopted when the embargo was repealed), arguing that the arms would go to the nations that had the shipping facilities, France and England, thus, in effect, putting the United States on their side. But he may have been faulty in his judgment if he believed that, regardless of what precautions might be taken against American involvement, the political officials of the United States and the great majority of American people would stand by and see England and France fall.

On January 16, 1940, a few days after his last Senate speech (against a proposed delegation of power to the President) and vote, the Senator suffered a brain hemorrhage from which he died on January 19. From those who had opposed him no less than from those who had shared his views the tributes flowed in. His funeral service in the Senate Chamber was memorable because of the unmistakable evidence of personal loss on the part of so many in attendance. But it was in his home town in Idaho that he received the most moving testimony to his hold on the common man. As the veteran gravedigger performed his accustomed labor in Boise's Morris Hill Cemetery, he found it not as Hamlet's friend Horatio had phrased it, "a property of easiness." He wept. "I have known him many years," said he, "but this is the prettiest spot in the cemetery; it will be a nice place for him to rest."[7]

The effort to evaluate the Senator in the final chapter of *Borah of Idaho* calls for certain modifications and additions. In many respects he was a liberal of the old school. Like Jefferson and other liberals among the Founding Fathers, he was a staunch and effective advocate of civil liberty. In this he fitted into the twentieth century, and perhaps as well as did his contemporary Mr. Justice Louis D. Brandeis. But his position on the role of government in the economic order was more in accord with that of the liberals of the Jackson period (who held that government should favor no class and that it performed its functions best when it tried to give equal economic opportunity to all) than with that of the New Dealers who favored wide public regulation of the national economy.

If Borah's position on government in the economic order

[7] *Time* (Feb. 5, 1940), p. 15.

was too old-fashioned to suit the majority's views of what the times required, so his position on international relations came to be regarded as inappropriate for the age of the modern dictators. His ideas of conducting an effective foreign policy without making any political commitments and of maintaining strict neutrality in a war which Hitler might win were found to be completely unsuited to the demands of the forties. The Senator may have been too rigid in his opinions, too unmindful of changing conditions.

What was William E. Borah's impact on American politics, on its public life? His influence over the people of Idaho has been sufficiently emphasized above. His impact on the Republican party organization in the state was simply this: he repeatedly scored an unusual personal triumph over it. His remarkable victories he achieved usually with little, if any, organization support, and once he was elected in the face of its active opposition. He had as little influence over the organization as it had over him. In a clear-cut fight with the Republican party for a direct primary law, he lost, and the organization continued to be run by reactionaries. It should not be surprising that he made no dent in the organization, for he was not an organization man. It could hardly be expected that the Senator, who ignored or scorned a political organization, would be instrumental in improving it. His failure in this particular suggests some of the limitations of the essentially lone operator in politics.

In national politics Senator Borah was independent in his speeches and votes on the issues as they came before the Senate, but he bolted the Republican party in an election only twice—in 1896 and 1898, when he was a Silver Republican and before he was elected senator. Indeed, during his long career in the Senate he actively supported Republican presidential candidates except in 1912, 1932, and 1936. It is common knowledge that in 1920 he vigorously campaigned against the League of Nations and therefore in the interest of Harding and that in 1928 he struck smashing blows time after time for Hoover. In the latter campaign he was unquestionably the leading figure in popularizing the party's ticket with the voters.

Despite Borah's independence in the Senate, his legislative

record was not barren, as both the McKenna and Johnson biographies have pointed out. It is true that he did not particularly like committee work, that he was normally a poor compromiser, and no sort of fixer. Yet when he was strongly interested in a measure he could and did follow it into the committee and negotiating stages. Witness his tireless and skillful work in getting affirmative action from the Senate on the constitutional amendment authorizing the federal income tax and the one requiring the direct election of United States Senators, his off-the-floor activities against the Covenant of the League of Nations, his quiet and patient background work which probably saved the Glass-Steagall Banking Reform Bill of 1933, and his skillful cooperation with Senator Wheeler in exposing the demerits of Roosevelt's "Court Packing" plan. It is conceded that his legislative record does not measure up to that of a number of his colleagues, but he is commonly given less than his due as a legislator because his speeches eclipse his other legislative performances.

Everyone concedes that Borah was a superb orator. A few maintain that he was nothing else—just an artist with words.[8] But back of his speeches was much reading and study of the issues. Relating always to the questions and problems of the day, his speeches contained substance no less than form, and sometimes a high moral call. He never came anywhere near being a bore, for he had an uncanny perception of timeliness, and he spoke only when he had something to say and was fully prepared. Whether he spoke in the Senate or out he had a national audience. He championed such causes as pardons for wartime political offenders (early twenties), disarmament (early twenties), justice for Mexico (late twenties), the recognition of Soviet Russia (the twenties and early thirties), and neutrality (the thirties). He denounced, among other things, corruption and betrayal in high places, monopolies, and other interests that would use government for their special purposes, war and the politics that led to it and the profiteering that accompanied it. It is not easy to assess the value of oratory, even of oratory filled with facts, steeped in national tradition, and charged with ethical concepts. But one can hardly deny that

[8] See, for example, John Milton Cooper, Jr., "William E. Borah, Political Thespian," *Pacific Northwest Quarterly*, LVI (October, 1965), 145-53.

it plays an appropriate part in the political process. This writer is convinced that the speeches of Senator William E. Borah informed, stimulated, or inspired millions and that some of his utterances altered the course of events.

CLAUDIUS O. JOHNSON

January, 1967
Pullman, Washington

BORAH OF IDAHO

CHAPTER I

THE MIDDLE WEST

THERE is nothing of the "up Boston way on Beacon Street" in the ancestry of United States Senator William Edgar Borah. The Senator himself has no interest in his genealogy beyond a pleasant insistence that the Borahs are of plebeian stock. He thinks the public has no interest in the Borah family and none in his early life. But the Borahs were more than ordinary people, and one may disagree with the Senator concerning the public's interest in his background.

The original Borahs were Bohemians. There is a story that one was king of Bohemia. Having lost his throne in a revolution, he went to a German state, then to France, where one of his daughters married a French prince. But the former king and his family soon returned to Germany, probably Bavaria, and established permanent residence there. We know that Martin Luther met Catharine von Bora in a convent and that she became his wife. This is about all the information—authentic and otherwise—that we have on the Borahs in Europe.

About 1760, three Borah brothers came to America and settled in Lancaster County, Pennsylvania. Two sided with the Patriots in the Revolution. One, the "Irreconcilable," aligned himself with the Tories, and he returned to the old country after the war. To one of the Patriot brothers a son, Jacob, was born in 1765. This great-grandfather of William E. Borah, young as he was, served two separate enlistments in the Revolution.

Jacob Borah had eight sons. All of them moved to Butler County, Kentucky, about 1810. On one of the Borah farms the little town of "Borah" developed, and a post office was established there. A century later the town had ceased to be, and in 1913 the post office was abolished. But near the head of a tongue of land formed by a horseshoe bend of the Green River, nine miles north of Morgantown and eight miles south of Beaver Dam, still sits Borah's Ferry, named for the grandfather and great-uncles of the Senator, who, some critics say, goes like the ferry from side to side.

One of the eight Borah boys who went to Kentucky was John, whose son, William Nathan Borah (father of the Senator), was born in Butler County in 1818.

In 1820, four of the eight brothers, including John, went to Wayne County, Illinois. Another brother moved to Grant County, Wisconsin, a few years later. Three brothers remained in Kentucky. John left his few slaves there also.

The Borahs who selected Illinois for their permanent home settled in Jasper Township, near Fairfield, on the edge of the region known the country over as "Egypt." It was a section of fairly fertile land with gently rolling, wooded hills. There is still something of freshness and beauty in it. Here the Borahs worshipped God and begat children according to His laws. Here they toiled and earned an honest living. Here they became leaders in every good civic enterprise. In the course of time there were scores of Borahs in Wayne County. Sixty years ago they were much more numerous in that region than at present, for the common, rather depressing situation has come about — the later generations have scattered all over the continent.

William N. Borah married Elizabeth West, a native of Indiana, who bore him six daughters and four sons. She was a retiring, sweet, gentle mother who allowed her children to tease her into granting them many little favors and indulgences frowned upon by a stern father. The Senator describes her as just a dear mother who devoted her whole life to her family to the exclusion of every outside interest save her church. Her change of church affiliation was typical of her. Born and reared a Methodist, she became a Presbyterian in order to worship with her husband, who was ardent in the latter faith. There was Irish blood in the mother of William E. Borah, and through her pleasant moods ran a strain of melancholy. Her famous son was never able to explain this melancholy, nor has he ever been able to explain his own occasional spells of gloom other than to say it is in his blood from his mother's side.

Other traits which the Senator may have inherited from his mother are his retiring nature and his gentleness. That he has such traits will come as a surprise to many readers. His reputation for the contrary has grown out of his boldness in proclaiming issues and attacking shams and frauds. Despite his powerful offensives for or against things, the Senator is personally modest and retiring. Gentleness he has never shown in handling an issue, but gentleness he has always shown in personal relations, even to the point of avoiding personalities in heated political campaigns.

In 1920, while on one of his infrequent visits to the old home, the Senator went to the family burial ground in the yard of the Presbyterian Church. The man who had just defeated the Versailles Treaty in the United States Senate and who was the leading campaigner for Mr. Harding stood beside his mother's resting place and wept as if the shrubs and flowers of many kindly years had failed to obscure the void of an open grave.

Alice, Walter Scott, Oliver, Susan, Harriett, and Sadie took their places in the Borah household before William Edgar (some of his critics say his middle name should have been Versus) came on June 29, 1865. As is often the case with large families, the younger members, in a sense, belonged to a different generation. At least Willie never knew his older brothers as he did his younger brother, Charles Franklin, commonly known as Frank; nor was he ever on terms of fairly complete understanding with his older sisters as he was with his younger sister, Mattie, a favorite also with Frank. The tenth child in the Borah family was Caroline.

The home into which the future Senator was born was one of neither wealth nor want. His father was a fairly successful farmer and stock-raiser. Parents and children worked hard and lived the typical farm life of their section and period.

THE father of William E. Borah was a devout Christian and a careful and constant student of the Bible. The Senator, himself very familiar with the Scriptures, says he has never known a man who knew the Bible as thoroughly as his father did. The elder Borah was a leader in the Presbyterian Church, but, despite repeated printed statements to the contrary, he never preached. A great friend of his was Judge Silas D. Bryan, who lived about seventy-five miles from

Fairfield. The fathers of William E. and William J. met as often as they conveniently could and argued on the Scriptures. When the Senator's father came into court, the Great Commoner's father often adjourned the sitting for greetings. Once the two devout and argumentative men started a discussion on their favorite topic at eight o'clock in the morning, before the court met. Their argument started in the corridor of the court house, but they edged off to a hotel and continued their debate until five in the afternoon. We can only guess the nature of the compliments paid to them by the lawyers and litigants who had business at court that day. The sons of these worthy sires did not meet as their elders did. They went about their tasks at home, each entirely unknown to the other.

Ministers always had a hearty welcome at the Borah farm house. The father liked to entertain any number of ministers attending a Presbytery, much to the disgust of the boys who had to care for their horses. The boys had some compensation, however, for even ministers' horses could be raced. On one occasion the future Senator found to his delight that what appeared to be a "wooden" horse could outrun all the rest, and he tells to this day, with tears of laughter, how he so successfully trained this horse to race that the steed threw the poor old minister when he mounted to return to his home. The father explained to Brother Druinson that there must have been something under the horse's saddle, and Willie, unlike the George Washington of Parson Weems, thought it best to let that explanation go unchallenged.

William N. Borah's religion included charity and tolerance. His appearance reminded one of the old prophets, whose words he could quote by the hour. He could say "Thou hast sinned" in such tones as to bring conviction to the heart of the transgressor; but for all that he could understand the weaknesses of the flesh and make allowances. He had read the New Testament as well as the Old, and he kept them in accommodation. He took no pleasure in the reflection that unrepentant sinners would be punished forever. He really wanted sinners to repent, and he was always ready to help furnish the opportunity. He was never willing to vote for the expulsion from the church of an erring brother, and, what is more to be marveled at, he insisted upon the obligation of the church to continue in membership women who had made what was regarded as the most fatal slip.

There was a breadth of tolerance and a nobility of spirit about the patriarch of the Borah household which made a lasting impression upon his children. That it has influenced the public career of Senator Borah there is not the slightest doubt. The Senator's private correspondence touching matters of religious bigotry, race hatreds, and similar subjects in which passion and prejudice play a large part is replete with references to his father and the lessons in Christian charity learned from his example. When the Ku Klux Klan was reviving after the World War and was showing some strength in Idaho about a year before Borah was to come up for re-election, he wrote to a man in Idaho: "I am a believer in the fundamental principles of religious liberty. It was instilled into me by my father's earliest teachings, although he was a most devout Presbyterian elder. . . If the time ever comes when I shall have to sacrifice my office for these principles, I shall unhesitatingly do so."

The Bible, the church, and the farm were not the only interests of William N. Borah. He was active in support of the public schools and the educational institutions of his church. Politics also claimed his attention. The rugged, lonely, self-reliant Lincoln with his penetrating wisdom, majestic simplicity, and human sympathy was a man after the heart of the farmer of Jasper Township. The Emancipator was a saint in the Borah household. His Republican principles stood not so far below the precepts of Holy Writ. The Senator's father took an active, although wholly local, part in furthering these principles as he understood them. Local politicians were often in consultation with him and occasionally such a well-known figure as Senator John A. Logan was a guest on the Borah farm.

When the news came from Idaho that Will Borah would go to the United States Senate, the Fairfield *Press* (December 13, 1906) proudly announced that he "is the son of W. N. Borah, of Jasper, now hale and hearty at the age of eighty-nine years. His father, as all of our old readers know, was one of the prime movers in every advanced step taken by this county in pioneer days. He is a man of strong mind, possessing exceptional talent as a public speaker for one not specially drilled or educated as an orator. Those of our people who know the father are not astonished at the reputation achieved by the son."

To an older reader familiar with the problem of disciplining a large family of children on a farm, it may seem almost incredible that no corporal punishment was ever administered to the Borah children. The Senator says that their mother would not permit it. His sister says that this was true, but that it was also true that their father could control his children without recourse to painful stimuli. He was stern and exacting but just and fair. He was wise, too, wise enough not to see every little slip or prank for which discipline might be meted out. There was mutual respect and confidence between father and children. Obedience to him was taken for granted.

Once, when Willie went to sleep while driving a complicated piece of machinery and wrecked it on a stump, his father said, "Willie, if Frank had done that, I'd whip him." The whole family laughed at this, well out of Father's sight, for the idea of Frank, a sort of Joseph with his father, being whipped when no other child was ever "licked" struck them all as very humorous.

As the Senator looks back at his childhood, he is inclined to say that he had a rather dismal time of it, chiefly because of his father's puritanical views and exacting discipline. Yet the Senator is quick to admit that this puritanism was tempered with sweet reasonableness and that the discipline was administered without the use of the rod. The only essential difference between the parent and the son is probably explained by the difference in age — forty-seven years. The boy was not irritated by his father's religion, nor did he belittle his virtues. But he was after all a boy and even the boy Willie was not content simply to work in the daytime and to contemplate "good works" at night and on Sunday. He wanted to have a little fun. Some fun he had, but he could never enjoy it with his father, and on occasion the parent frowned darkly upon some form of amusement or even forbade it.

WILLIAM NATHAN BORAH

ELIZABETH WEST BORAH

Willie wanted to go to plays, but his father felt that plays were immoral or at least failed to teach a positive lesson in virtue. Willie loved to read and his father did, too, but the latter thought the Bible, *Pilgrim's Progress,* biographies of Washington, the autobiography (expurgated) of Franklin, a few of Scott's novels, and a paper or two like the Chicago *Inter-Ocean* ought to be sufficient for all reading requirements. The young man liked all of these, but he wanted more variety. He liked to read the Bible, but he wanted to read Robert G. Ingersoll also. Indeed, he once came into possession of Ingersoll's *Mistakes of Moses* and was engrossed in it when his father took it from him with a solemn warning about the wickedness of that brilliant atheist. Willie retrieved the volume later and, to avoid any unpleasantness, finished it in the haymow.

Despite the differences of father and son, Willie was very much like his father, and the Senator, by all accounts, is his father all over again, except that he does not take the Scriptures literally and still enjoys dramatic art and every type of good literature. The Senator now looks like his father, talks like his father, even gestures like his father. One of his sisters says that a great pleasure which comes to her when the Senator delivers an address over the radio is that she hears her father speak again. The sternness, the righteous indignation, the fiery declamation, the firm conviction, the abiding faith, the love of his fellow-men are all there. William N. Borah, Jr., would have been a most appropriate name for the Senator. The father went his own way, could never be forced. The son wanted to go his own way, resented being forced. The differences they had arose over their similarities.

As a boy Will Borah accepted his father's faith without much question. He read all the religious books on his father's shelves. The one which made the strongest impression upon him — and which an old-book dealer finally found for him a few years ago, much to his delight — was by Doctor Daniel March, entitled *Night Scenes in the Bible.* There were such chapter headings as "The Last Night of Sodom," "Saul's Night at Endor," "Jonah's Night at Nineveh," and "Midnight in the Prison at Philippi," each with an appropriate illustration. There were subtitles on such topics as "profligate young men," "luxurious habits," "self-indulgent young men dangerous," "the gay not always happy," "danger of wine drinking," and "sure way to destroy a nation." The book was well written and, quite aside from any religious interest a boy might have, would prove entertaining. The young Senator was quite as much interested in the drama of it, the well-told tales, as in its spiritual lessons. His interest in Ingersoll was very much the same. He cared little for his atheism, but he liked the way Ingersoll wrote. He cared less for Ingersoll after he grew up, but he has always admired the courage expressed in the last lines penned by the great atheist:

> "We have no God to Serve or Fear,
> No hell to shun,
> No devil with malicious leer,
> When life is done."

Will Borah never experienced what the evangelical Christians refer to as "conversion." As a child he was put in great fear of hell for a period, but even as a child he probably despised the idea of being converted for the negative purpose of escaping torment. He soon overcame his fear. He did it not by assuming a fatalistic attitude, or by becoming an atheist, or by carousing, but by reading the New Testament.

He found spiritual peace, but he never felt a conviction of sin to cause him to cry out, "What shall I do to be saved?" He never felt the necessity of joining a church, but he did join the Presbyterian Church as a boy to please his parents. He has never been more than a nominal church member, but he has always been a lover and something of a student of the Bible. For some time during his first term as Senator he taught a men's Bible Class in one of the Presbyterian churches in Washington.

Back in 1924 he wrote to a minister: "If one believes in and accepts the Bible as God's word to his children, so much the better and so vastly more important that its study be encouraged in all proper ways. But even from the viewpoint of literature and moral teaching, from the viewpoint of character building, its study is yet of greater moment than any other single book in all literature. In richness of expression, in imagery, in moral inspiration, in the power to inspire disinterested service, and to direct one along the paths of tolerance and charity, it is the book of all books. . ."

To the earnest Christians who often ask him, "Are you a Christian?" he usually replies that he was brought up by devout Christian parents; that he accepted that belief and still holds it; that he does "not doubt at all the fundamental teachings of the Christian religion. But I want to say that no one realizes more than I do that I do not live up to my belief."

The Senator says that he thanks his Maker every day he thinks of it for his remarkably good eye sight. He believes in prayer, not perhaps as a regular exercise, but as the supreme effort of a man confronted by a situation in which human efforts seem futile. He confidently believes that he prayed Mrs. Borah back to life when she lay at death's door a few years ago.

Senator Borah does not meet the "Fundamentalist's" or sectarian's test of Christianity, but by any liberal standard he is a Christian, a deeply religious man. He believes that a Divine Conscience rules humanity, and that ultimately right will triumph; otherwise life has no meaning.

On Christmas Eve, 1932, the Senator delivered one of his best radio addresses. "This Christmas belongs to the poor, to the needy. . . Laughter and music can not drive from our thoughts the vast number of children who will wait in vain, wan and hungry, for the coming of Santa Claus. . .

"Men may, and do, dispute the divinity of Jesus of Nazareth, science may seek to impeach the authenticity of his inspired mission, but no sane man or woman will undervalue the transcendent beauty or the incalculable worth of the rules of human conduct which he announced during his brief ministry on earth. . . Humanity was the foundation rock upon which the Man of Galilee built his enduring creed, humanity broad enough and practical enough to encompass and administer to all kinds of human suffering and every form of human frailty – 'healing all manner of sickness and all manner of disease among the people.'"

An octogenarian in New York wrote that he had heard many distinguished clergymen of various creeds but that in all the range of his experience he had never heard such a Godlike address. The Baptist minister at Brooklyn Tabernacle wrote : "I have said more than once in public that the sceptre of moral leadership in this nation has passed definitely into your hands. . . How refreshing is a prophetic voice and how it thrilled us." The Senator treasures these letters.

THOUGH the parents of William E. Borah had no education beyond that afforded by the common schools of their day, they wanted to give their children wider educational opportunities. The Borah children received their first training at Tom's Prairie public school, a few miles from the Borah farm. Willie was fortunate in having for a teacher a man who had been a college professor but who had lost several good college positions through drink. He was an inspiring teacher and from him the future statesman got his first taste for literature. The teacher returned to his bottle from time to time and the good people made determined efforts to displace him. The elder Borah, although he yielded to none in his abhorrence of drunkenness, would not allow the dismissal of that rare gem, a master teacher. Study was a pleasure at Tom's Prairie, and so were the opportunities to make little orations and speeches. Willie was good at speechmaking from the start, and he was often singled out to do the honors on special occasions.

Young Borah was a husky fellow and gave a good account of himself in the popular game of "Bull in the Ring." He had the usual number of fights and perhaps more than his share of victories. During these early school days he had much sport with horses. He went to the county fair where Kentucky horses raced, and he developed a delight in fine horses that has never left him. His father, seeing no sin in horseflesh, allowed him to call one of the family horses his own. Will became one of the best horsemen in the community.

Having absorbed what Tom's Prairie school had to offer, Will was sent to Enfield College (in reality only an academy), a Cumberland Presbyterian institution some twenty-five miles

BIRTHPLACE OF SENATOR BORAH, FAIRFIELD, ILLINOIS

CUMBERLAND PRESBYTERIAN COLLEGE
Enfield, Ills., where Senators William E. Borah and Wesley Jones received their secondary education

south of Fairfield. There were not many instructors and each covered several subjects. None stimulated Will as had the tippling ex-college professor at Tom's Prairie. Will was poor in mathematics, but good in Latin. History and literature were his favorite subjects. He wrote an essay on War, inspired largely by stories he had heard his father tell. It was considered so good that it was brought to the attention of the President of the College. The President would not believe Will had written it until he revealed the source of his inspiration. Young Borah belonged to one of the literary societies and loved to debate a subject that interested him, but he never cared at all for formal, scheduled competition. He took delight in the sermons of the Reverend E. T. Bowers of Enfield, because that divine was such a powerful orator. Will did not care particularly for his theology but he appreciated oratory wherever he could find it.

One of Will's fellow-students at Enfield was Wesley Jones, who came there almost a grown man but still a "barefoot boy." The Lincolnesque Jones was very ambitious, fully determined to go to Congress, and was considered something of a prodigy at the College. Long before Borah went to the Senate, Jones was representing a Washington district in the House of Representatives. Later he moved over to the other wing of the Capitol with Borah.

Another fellow-student, Professor J. W. Howerth, of Greeley, Colorado, writes concerning Borah : "I do not remember to have heard him take part in the program of a literary society or in debating. He appeared to me then, as he appears to some now, something of a 'lone wolf,' though I remember no wolfish traits. As was said of another William, William Pitt, he was not especially easy to approach, rather the contrary. His aloofness was probably due to what I thought then and think now, namely, to entertaining company in the parlor of his own thoughts. I remember something of his gallantry, if not with the ladies, with respect to one at least. He was a good student but not especially distinguished as such, as was Senator Jones. Borah, I should say, cared little about asserting himself to make an impression either on students or faculty. He attended to his own business."

Borah remained at Enfield only one year and did not complete the preparatory course. He got into a bit of mischief. For amusement the bolder boys sometimes caught freight trains, rode into Carmi, a few miles distant, and spent the night. Will was one of those adventurous spirits who were detected and the President wrote Mr. Borah that the boy should be sent home. William N. Borah's letter to the President persuaded that gentleman to allow Will to complete the year. The father wrote nothing of the matter to the son, being content to let the matter rest until he should return home.

While at Enfield Borah had a very satisfactory experience at a political rally. Republicans from miles around had gathered in the town to celebrate the election of Garfield. Several well-known speakers were scheduled to talk, but they did not appear. What was to be done? Finally someone suggested that there was a young man in the audience from the College who could speak. He was brought forward. He looked so queer that the chairman hesitated to introduce him, but finally did so. "Mr. Chairman, jubilant Republicans, and disgruntled Democrats," Borah began. His speech was a great success, many in the audience remarking that they had never heard such a good speech from a young man.

This was not the first time Will had attended a political meeting. Once he had played hooky from school to hear a speech by Dick Townsend, Democratic Congressman from southern Illinois. During the Garfield-Hancock campaign (at the end of which he had made the victory speech), he went to hear another Democratic politician, a Mr. Funkhouser, speak for Hancock. Every time he made a point for Hancock a rough man with a red bandana handkerchief tied over his head would shout, "Hurrah for Garfield." Funkhouser finally grew tired of this and said, "I suppose when we have all shuffled off this mortal coil, when the sheep are being separated from the goats, some fool goat will bleat, 'Hurrah for Garfield.'" A great uproar and struggle greeted this remark. Funkhouser jumped out of the window. Borah escaped from the building, but paused to witness a bloody fight in the schoolhouse yard. Another time he went to a night meeting against his father's orders. The boys tied Will's horse to a rail in such a manner that he could not be untied. As they stood back in the dark to watch the fun, they saw Borah take the rail under his arm, mount his steed, and gallop off.

Will Borah had no political ambitions at the time. Unlike Wesley Jones, he was at least not planning to go to Congress. He merely liked political campaigns for the opportunities they presented for oratory. He liked the drama of the thing. He enjoyed going to a Democratic meeting as much as to a Republican meeting. No amount of suggestion will cause him to say that he had ambitions to be a Representative or a Senator.

But in these days he was thinking very much of the law. That had been his consuming ambition from the time he was old enough to know something of a lawyer's business. Even as a very young man he felt that lawyers were independent men, and he wanted more than anything else to be independent, not only financially independent but intellectually independent. He told his father he wanted to be a lawyer. He received no encouragement, for his father put lawyers in the class with the Pharisees and the Publicans. "Besides," argued his father, "you have already shown that you can be a successful stock-dealer." But William the Younger said he was going to be a lawyer.

Partly for financial reasons and partly because he did not want his son to be a lawyer, the father did not send Will back to school the following year. The young man had always liked drama and, with his plans for an education temporarily thwarted, he was about to try his talents as an actor. But the road show failed, and Will never again seriously considered a stage career. His interest in the drama has continued, however, to this day.

"I see by the New York *World,*" he wrote an actor a few years ago, "that you and others are supporting the nomination of Edwin Booth for election to the Hall of Fame at the coming quinquennial election. I was greatly pleased to see this. . .

"I saw Booth but a few times, and of course many years ago. But the force of his acting lives on vividly in my memory as if it were yesterday. Next to the gifted creator of great dramatic characters comes the rare individual who can take the character from the printed page and present it a living, moving being. Booth is entitled to take his place among the truly great."

The answer to Will's prayer for more schooling came from Lyons, Kansas. One of his older sisters, Mrs. A. M. Lasley, whose husband was a lawyer, lived there. They invited Will to come to Lyons, and he left Fairfield with high hopes.

THE Senator says that he has neglected his family since he left Fairfield. This is simply one of the many matters in which the Senator overstates the case against himself. In fact, in this instance, he slanders himself. True, he never did write letters home twice a week nor remember them in other conventional ways, but he was always a loyal, affectionate son and a considerate, generous brother and uncle. Dozens of illustrations of his sympathy and helpfulness might be given, but the instances are for the most part of such a personal and intimate nature that it would be inappropriate to record them. He did not always hear of troubles in his family, for nearly all of the Borahs had pride and independence and did not relish asking favors or having others ask favors for them. They knew of Will's troubles, for they read about them in newspapers and magazines and sometimes wrote letters of concern to him. "Do not worry about the articles in the newspapers," he would reply. "I have been slandered into fame and I cannot feel bitter toward those who have been so helpful in that respect."

Friends of the Senator's favorite sister, Mrs. Rinard, sometimes tell her that the great Senator has no time to think about her or his other relatives, but she smiles tolerantly, for she knows that busy as Will is he always has a little corner in his heart for his family. Equally certain of his continued affection are his older living sisters, Mrs. Alice Heidinger and Mrs. Sadie Mabry.

Professional as well as fraternal ties kept Will and his younger brother Frank in close contact. Frank was a successful lawyer in New Orleans. He died in 1933, but a distinguished name in Louisiana is that of his son, Wayne G.

Borah, appointed Federal District Judge in 1928 on his record as prosecutor, although the record of his uncle probably had something to do with it.

The two oldest brothers — Walter Scott, a physician, and Oliver, a farmer — have been dead for many years. Walter Scott went to Louisiana to practise medicine. He sent his colored janitor out to vote the Republican ticket one election day, but the Negro was chased away from the polls. The enraged doctor took the terrified Negro back to the polling-place and forced him to mark a ballot, which the doctor then deposited for him. An election officer struck Doctor Borah and the doctor shot him. The affair did not increase the number of the doctor's patients, but he managed to escape conviction for crime. When Frank later took up his residence in Louisiana his interest in the Republican party in the South was entirely in making it a white man's party, and he often unburdened himself to Will on the difficulties that Southern Republicans had to face.

The letters which the Senator has received from relatives the country over he has always treated with consideration. Here is one from a cousin in Kansas: "My wife is supposed to be an heir to a large estate maybe you have heard of it it was taken to President Wilson some too years ago they say he appointed a comity to see to it but the league of nations . . . took up all of his time . . . I am enclosing a stamped envelope for quick reply." The Senator wrote him a kindly letter, explaining that the estate proposition was undoubtedly a fraud and advising against spending money on it.

Not only has the Senator kept in affectionate regard members of the Borah family, but his interest in the old town of Fairfield has continued. To the editor of the Fairfield *Press* he wrote in 1924: "I take it up week after week and year after year and old faces crowd my memory, old landmarks rise up before me, I see again as in boyhood days dear old Wayne County, Illinois, and all its wholesome life and sturdy men and women. Those of kin and those of friendship, together with the thousands of incidents which neither change of place nor the flight of years can efface, come trooping in upon me."

And so the ambitious young man left "dear old Wayne County," not long removed from the frontier, left its gently rolling hills and its forests, symbols of loneliness, of strength, and of eloquence; left the State of Lincoln and the oaken virtues of the Borahs. The frontier he found again on the plains of Kansas; he found there again loneliness, loneliness which makes children of freedom, strangers to repression and convention. To this new country he carried the Lincoln tradition and the family virtues. To it he carried his love of literature and his hatred of liquor, an affinity and a revulsion, which he maintains charted him through many of the shoals of youth.

Receiving some help from his sister and earning some money at odd jobs, Will Borah spent a year in the public school at Lyons. After this he taught a country school for a year or so, never forgetting his ambition to become a lawyer and being so engrossed in reading history and law that he felt in later years that he had not put as much energy into his teaching as he should have. But with all his work, he still managed to mingle a little with the young people of the Wabash School neighborhood and to attend protracted meetings, for which he expressed a distinct dislike, at the Prosper Church. After his experience in the country school, he did some teaching in Lyons.

On September 11, 1885, the *Courier* of the University of Kansas announced that W. E. Borah, of Lyons, would enter the University, and concluded its brief line with "he will be a leading man." The Betas, with an eye for a scholar and ever interested in assembling "leading men" under their banner, soon placed their pin on sub-freshman Borah. The Phi Delts, seeking the same general type the Betas sought, pledged freshman William Allen White, son of a pioneer physician of Emporia. In this bit of inter-fraternity rivalry the Phi Delts won a distinct victory. White was the type. The Betas missed their guess on Borah. They regarded him as almost a total loss socially. He went to their small parties with punctiliousness but without enthusiasm. Although he sometimes made a date for himself, and at least one girl on the campus was very fond of him, for the big parties he usually had to be "doled out" to some sorority where a girl of his sort was paired with him. He was not a woman-hater and he was not particularly bashful; he was merely not interested in and lacked the money for much social activity.

He had not the slightest desire to be a "big man on the campus," and the call to go forth into campus activities for the glory of the "dear old fraternity" did not strike a responsive chord. The Betas thought he should at least bring them some honors in debate and oratory, but he would not even do that. He did belong to the Orophilian Literary Society and took some part in its deliberations, but he was not interested in winning banners and prizes. When the time approached for him to get ready for a try-out for an important inter-society debate, he might be found in the library deeply buried in some other subject. He agreed wholeheartedly with Walter Bagehot that "of all the possible ways ever invented by man for separating the faculty of argument from the capacity of belief, the art of debate is probably the most effectual," but even as a student Borah never debated a subject unless he was interested in it.

Borah came to the University not knowing just what courses to take and wishing very much that he had someone to advise him. Indeed, he says that from the time he was about fifteen until he came to Idaho he was simply feeling his way along and always sensed the need of guidance he never seemed to get. Yet his need was probably not so great as he thought, for Professor Sterling (still teaching at the University of Kansas), who helped him enroll, says he noticed at once that Borah knew what he wanted and did not seem to be in need of advice.

As a sub-freshman Borah did most of his work in Latin and English. The next year (1886–1887) he took as many courses as he could get in history and literature, with one course each in elocution and composition. His favorite teacher was Professor Canfield of the Department of History, although Professor Carruth in Literature ran Canfield a close second. Borah says that he was not a particularly good student, that he was more of a reader than a student, sacrificing his class work for general reading, which interested him more. But the serious young man's professors evidently considered his class performances entirely satisfactory, for the

Registrar's Office reports that Borah received the highest possible grade in each subject he carried.

Borah left the University in the early spring of 1887, being threatened with tuberculosis. He soon regained his strength, but he never returned to the University except for a brief visit the next year. The uncompleted freshman year at the University marks his farthest advance toward a formal education. He is largely self-educated.

The Betas may have been somewhat disappointed in him, but Borah left no enemies on the campus. Neither did he leave any warm friends. He has never had an intimate friend, one to whom he would pour out all his hopes and fears, one to whom he would reveal his soul. If a man does not find such a friend in college, he is not likely to find one anywhere else.

Of Borah at the University, his classmate, William Allen White, writes : "He just didn't jell as a collegiate character. He was older than the average member of his fraternity and in the classroom he was a serious man with no 'side,' no quibs and jibes ; an honest, hard-working, substantial, serious student, who smiled easily but rarely laughed. I should say that his outstanding qualities were a studious habit, an obvious indifference to the opinion of others, a desire to get on in the classroom rather than on the campus, not exactly a grind, but a man who had years to make up and a purpose to attain, one of those older students in a group, like a big Newfoundland dog among smaller and more agile pups, who is good-natured so long as he is not disturbed.

"My general impression of him at the time was that he was an earnest person. I was not. I was frivolous. If he noticed me it was because I made him grin. Very soon after college, we became friends. We were not friends in college, merely pleasant acquaintances. He was then as he has been all his life, a bit repressed, preoccupied, restrained in his demonstrations of affection, but still cordial enough and certainly always grateful for favors received. But he never let his gratitude corrupt his soul and turn him from his appointed path. This was true in college where he did not let his membership in his fraternity change his determination to get the most out of his books and the professors. He did not come for the social advantages of college. He did not get them. If he cared for them it wasn't enough to pay the price they required."

The "Borah Paid for the Turkeys" story is a part of Beta lore. Some of his fraternity brothers, carrying out a mischievous fraternity tradition, went to a farm house one dark night and stole four turkeys. The Betas had a great banquet, the "annual turkey pullin'." Here we let a member of the foraging party, Thomas F. Doran, a leading attorney of Topeka, and a Beta Brother of the class of 1888, take up the story.

"Senator Borah condemned the whole proceeding and insisted that the boys go out to the farmer and settle with him and pay him for the turkeys. They were willing to pay for the turkeys, but no one had the courage to take the money out to the farmer. Borah kept insisting that they do this, and finally some of the Senator's friends, who were practical jokers, hired a brawny, tall Kentuckian, dressed him up as a farmer and sent him to the home where Senator Borah lived. . . The farmer said to him, in substance, that he was the farmer who owned the turkeys that were stolen by the 'Beacha Peacha Pie' fraternity and he understood that Borah was a member of that fraternity. . . He also stated that while Mr. 'Bory' did not help to steal the turkeys, he helped to eat them as he had attended the banquet and was therefore equally guilty with the others.

"Mr. Borah asked him not to speak so loudly. The farmer said : 'Why, Hell, there is no secret about it. Unless I get my money at once, I am going to turn them in to the grand jury that is in session.' Mr. Borah asked him what he wanted for the turkeys. He said : '$5.00.' Mr. Borah said he did not have that much money, but . . . he went upstairs, borrowed $3.00 from Professor Dyche and paid the pretended farmer $5.00 for the turkeys. . . The practical jokers then had an oyster supper."

When Borah learned of the joke, he still insisted that the farmer should be paid. Even as a college student, he had a conscience and a sense of honor.

IN January, 1888, the *University Review* carried the news item that "W. E. Borah, now a prosperous attorney at Lyons, spent several days with the Betas last week." The "prosperous" part of the announcement was a characteristic fraternity exaggeration, an implication to the campus that, after all, the Betas felt they had done well to initiate Borah. The "attorney" announcement was no exaggeration, for Borah had read law in the office of his brother-in-law, A. M. Lasley, and had met the easy requirements for admission to the bar. He had made a special study of evidence, hoping to become a great trial lawyer.

His first experience with the law came with cases in the justice's court, cases with which his brother-in-law did not care to trouble himself. Will enjoyed this work from the beginning. He says he did not know much about the law, but neither did opposing counsel.

There is a story that Borah was named by the Mayor of Lyons for City Attorney and that the Council failed to confirm the appointment. The first part of the story is true. The second part is not — the Council *approved* the appointment. The City *Record,* Vol. II, pp. 34, 36, and 55, shows that he was nominated and confirmed, and that he resigned a few months later. Perhaps there was some objection to Borah on account of his youth. At any rate, the position was not an important one, and the Senator has all but forgotten that he ever held it.

A woman was charged with beating her step-child to death. Public opinion was inflamed against her, and when she came to Attorney Lasley he thought here would be a good case to pass on to brother-in-law Will. Will was delighted. He secured a change of venue and managed to get a hung jury, much to the surprise of everyone. The case did not come to trial again until after Borah had gone to Idaho. This time the woman was sent to the penitentiary.

An elderly man living outside of Lyons was last seen alive in a wagon passing through a little valley. He arrived home dead, with the lines in his hands. It was clear that he had been murdered. He left considerable property, and his wife appeared in court, asking for papers of administration. Her step-son protested, alleging that the woman was not his father's lawful wife, that her first husband was still living. The judge advised the woman to consult an attorney. Since she knew no attorney, the judge suggested Borah. It developed that this woman had married her first husband in Illinois many years before. The day after the wedding his hat and coat were found on the bank of a river, and it was assumed that he had drowned himself. The step-son claimed that this first husband was living in an out-of-the-way place in Missouri. After some difficulty the ambitious attorney secured enough money to get there. There he actually found the man described, with a wife and a number of children. Borah showed him the picture of the woman in Kansas and asked him if he had ever seen her before. The man said, "I'll have nothing to do with you." Borah replied, "From that I assume that you do know this woman." The fugitive husband got nervous. Borah explained to him that he was in a ticklish position but that he had nothing against him. He persuaded him to come to the county court house, where he selected as counsel a shabby attorney with a goatee. Borah suggested to the lawyer that the thing for his client to do was to refuse to testify. The attorney was grateful for this advice and passed it on to his client. The judge held that he need not testify. Thus Borah won his case and the woman back in Kansas received some $10,000 from her murdered husband's estate.

The practice of law did not take Borah from his reading. He not only continued his study of law, but he continued to read the works of the great masters in history, government, and literature, including Latin literature in the original. He liked to prepare and deliver orations. One summer day, when a hot Kansas wind was blowing the sand down the unpaved streets and carrying layers of fine dust through the cracks of windows and doors of Lyons offices, a fellow-attorney came to the office of Lasley and Borah for a reference. There sat Borah, sweating and begrimed, with books and papers before him and an expression of satisfaction on his face. "What on earth are you doing at work this terrible afternoon, Will?" asked the visitor. "Oh, I have just finished writing a Fourth of July oration," answered Borah. "Where are you going to deliver the oration?" continued his caller.

"Why, nowhere," replied the strange, earnest young man, "but I just thought I'd like to write one."

The burden of the young man's practice was not so heavy that he did not have some time for politics. He took an active part in a state senatorial campaign in 1888, speaking first in the north end of the county. He spoke so effectively there that the committee brought him back to the more sophisticated Lyons vicinity. This twenty-three-year-old orator did not wave the bloody shirt, a very popular bit of campaign technique for Republicans in those days, and a device which young Albert J. Beveridge in Indiana could not deny himself. Borah spoke on issues and men, chiefly on the issues.

With a little money in his pocket, Borah became slightly more active socially than he had been at the University. He was very popular with the older people and something of a favorite with the younger set. Young ladies were pleased and flattered with his attentions. Elderly people in Lyons recall with great pride their friendship with the Senator when he was just Will Borah.

Borah considered Lyons a poor place for a struggling young lawyer. He knew that lawyers made their reputations from handling important cases and he did not see much prospect for such cases in Lyons. Then, too, Kansas as a whole was not so happily situated in those days. The farmers were not prosperous and "isms" proposed to make them so did not particularly interest Borah. He had a living to make. Furthermore, it is probable that he did not relish the idea of practising law under the tutelage of his brother-in-law. He had a hankering to "Lone Wolf" it. Besides all of this, Borah was restless; he had found no anchorage. He felt that somehow he was not in the right place; consequently, he looked about for a better location.

CHAPTER II

THE WEST

BORAH had the idea that Seattle, Washington, then a small city, would be a good place in which to locate. The Mayor of Lyons, the one who had appointed Borah City Attorney and had remained keenly interested in his progress, suggested that he stop at Boise, Idaho. The Mayor had a relative in Boise who wrote glowing accounts of developments in that city. In the fall of 1890, a few months after Idaho had been admitted to the Union, Borah started west, feeling his way along, uncertain as to where he would locate.

On the train he fell in with S. S. Taylor, a gambler of Nampa, a railroad town not far from Boise. The gambler and the prospecting lawyer became friendly. Borah asked him about Boise, and if there was a serious shortage of young lawyers in that city. The gambler could not say precisely what the prospects for a young lawyer were, but he thought they were good. Moreover, he told Borah that if he located in Boise he could expect some business from the gambler and his friends. With this inducement, plus the negative one that he had only $15.75 in his pocket, Borah decided to remain in Boise for a time at least.

He visited several law offices, but no lawyer or law firm needed his services. He was beginning to be a bit discouraged. He bought some inexpensive furniture, however, rented a cheap office, and started out without a partner. Almost immediately he received a telephone call from Taylor to come to Nampa at once — a telegraph operator had shot a Chinese. The operator had come off duty late at night and had gone into the kitchen of his hotel for food. He and the Chinese cook got into an argument ; the cook took a knife and chased the operator into the dining room where hotel guests are supposed to eat. When the cook turned around to walk back to his domain, the operator shot him in the back, killing him instantly. Naturally, the operator was charged with murder.

The old magistrate before whom preliminary examination

was held, perhaps upon some such flimsy theory as that *Chinamen are not citizens,* said, with some vehemence, "It is not murder to kill a Chinaman." Borah saw that the abominable Justice meant to discharge his client, so he said little, allowing the prosecutor and the Justice to do most of the talking. Presently, Borah's client was permitted to depart. Borah walked out with him, accepted thirty-five dollars, and advised him to keep on going. The lawyer did not know much about Idaho courts; but he knew that in any state where human life is protected, one certainly would be punished for shooting a man in the back and killing him. The operator left Nampa.

After this Borah frequently served as counsel in criminal cases for "sports" and "toughs." He could not afford to be fastidious in his choice of clients. Indeed, few young lawyers can afford this luxury. Besides, Borah was not particularly concerned about the social status of his clients. These men were entitled to counsel when in trouble. They came to him, and he gave them the best he had. This practice he considered to be, and it is accepted as, correct legal ethics. Moreover, Borah liked some of these men personally. He did not gamble and he did not drink, but he enjoyed the company of these easy men, nearly every one of whom had some good qualities.

Not all of Borah's criminal practice was on behalf of the accused. The District Attorney of Ada County was not very successful as a trial lawyer, and he was wise enough to call Borah in to assist in prosecutions. All of this was good experience and excellent publicity for a young man trying to rise in his profession.

Borah's earliest sensational case (1896) as a prosecutor was that of Diamondfield Jack. Jack was a gun-fighting cowboy working for a cattle company in Nevada in the days when cattle men and sheep men were almost at war over the boundary lines of their pasturage. It was a common saying that no line was respected until someone had been killed upon it. Sheep ruin pasture for cattle. Cattle will not eat or drink after them. The cattle men, taking their cues from their stock, scorned sheep-herders as the cattle scorned the pasture which sheep had destroyed. One day two sheep herders were murdered, and the Sheep Owners' Association employed Borah to detect and prosecute the murderer.

Clad in rough attire, Borah proceeded to southern Idaho, visiting ranches as one interested in buying cattle, a business his father thought he had practically mastered as a boy. One night he came to a ranch of which a Negro was foreman. He and the Negro discussed sheep herders, and the Negro told him that Diamondfield Jack had spent the night at that ranch a few days before the murder. Jack, he said, lay in bed and shot at the rafters overhead, and he showed Borah the holes in the rafters. He further informed the detective-lawyer that Jack had carried a .45 caliber revolver and .44 caliber cartridges. Borah dug a few bullets from the rafters. They were the same as those found in the slain men.

The trial brought out cattle and sheep men in full force, the former siding with the accused and spending large sums of money for the defense – the latter crying for the death of the accused and supporting the prosecution. Each day guns were taken from the numerous persons entering the court room. Diamondfield Jack made a lunge at Borah during the trial. The Negro ranch foreman was so frightened because of the threats made by cattle men that he "forgot" everything. Special Prosecutor Borah frightened him so much more that he broke down and gave the testimony. Jack was convicted and sentenced to be hanged. The death march had started when the execution was prevented by a writ of *habeas corpus*. Afterward his sentence was changed to life imprisonment, a pardon following within a few years.

Borah was eager for business (a few of his brother lawyers thought a little too eager), and he gave to it all the energy he possessed. More and more civil suits came his way, so that in time he practically abandoned the criminal practice. His work became very largely that of counsel and attorney for some of the strongest corporations in Idaho. He was often in the State Supreme Court and in the Federal District Court and not infrequently went before the Federal Circuit Court of Appeals in San Francisco. At the time of his election to the Senate he probably had the most lucrative practice in the State. A man, now a Justice in the State Supreme Court, says that, despite Mr. Borah's large, profitable practice, he never refused a man who had a case, whether or not he had money for the fee.

Lawyers and judges all over Idaho emphasize the fact that Borah's power as an advocate was equaled by his skill as an office lawyer, that he was what few lawyers are — what the English would call both barrister and solicitor. They emphasize another fact, that Borah, like all other successful lawyers, was a fighter. They speak further of his wonderful briefs, models of lucid English. They say he was, and is, sound on the Constitution, that he would make a great Justice in the Supreme Court of the United States.

The Boise lawyer continued his reading and study of law, history, government, and literature. He read and read and read. Whether he made a trip to San Francisco or to some nearby town in Idaho, he took books along and read them on the train and during spare moments in stations and hotels. His scrapbooks of this period contain many serious articles on men and issues — articles on silver, trusts, monopolies, railroads, graft, the southern Negro. He is less serious in one on "Drinks of Famous Men," and becomes even humorous in a selection on the *Congressional Directory*. He clipped articles on Bryan and pasted down the "Maxims and Aphorisms" of Theodore Roosevelt. Borah has always been a reader and a student, but never entirely lacking in humor.

Another fact about Mr. Borah's reading is that he read a great deal aloud when alone. This was his way of testing and measuring the brilliance of a "purple passage." He still reads aloud occasionally, and his selection at such times is likely to be some great drama from the Scriptures. Because he has often been heard reading aloud, the report has gone abroad that he rehearses his speeches. The Senator denies that he ever rehearsed a speech aloud or before a mirror. On the other hand, several of his companions of the early Boise-lawyer days smile at this denial, admit that perhaps he was just reading, but say that to them he sounded more like a man speaking to empty chairs. But one may easily imagine that when Borah read aloud a selection from some great parliamentary debate or an impassioned plea by some popular tribune, he read with care to reproduce the effect. It may well be, therefore, that eavesdroppers, not so familiar with

W. E. BORAH
A leader of the Idaho Bar about 1906

the masters of oratory as was Borah, were convinced that he was rehearsing a speech.

WHAT sort of country was this in which the attorney with the Illinois-Kansas background established himself? It was a State of majestic mountains, deep canyons, roaring waterfalls, and placid lakes; a State of forests and minerals; a State the northern part of which was blessed by abundant rainfall and the southern part of which waited for the ingenuity of man to turn the waters upon the land that they might bring forth produce. Nature could have done little more to make Idaho beautiful; it could have done a great deal more to make her productive.

Boise City, as it was called when Borah first established himself there, was the capital of Idaho. It was the second city in population with some 2311 inhabitants, while Pocatello could boast of 2500. These figures are somewhat misleading from the commercial standpoint, for all frontier towns of this type served a fairly wide area and had much more trade and did a greater variety of business than the number of their inhabitants would indicate. Within the spacious Boise Basin were some farms and large cattle and sheep ranches. Within relatively easy access of Boise were valuable silver mines. Railroad connections made Boise a distributing center.

Walking along the street, Borah saw some twenty law offices, perhaps as many doctors' offices; Peter Sonna's wholesale and retail hardware store; the Sonna Opera House, which usually did "capacity business"; the W. E. Pierce Company's offer of "headquarters for speculators and investors," of main street lots for $80.00 per foot, and of residence lots for $75.00 to $225.00 each; the shop of the Coffin Plumbing Company; the location of the Boise agency for Wanamaker and Brown, "the largest tailoring house in America"; Nathan Falk's dry-goods store; Pinney's "mammoth book and stationery store"; the City Boarding Stables; drug stores, furniture stores, jewelry stores, and club rooms. He passed by many saloons, among them the Grotto Saloon — "strictly first class — drinks 12½ cents" — and the Gem Saloon, which offered straight whiskeys served by white bartenders. He may have stopped to rest in the lobby of the Overland Hotel, "well supplied with mountain spring water," or at the Capitol Hotel with 120 rooms, "comfortably equipped with electric lights and bells." This was enough for one evening. It was not a big city, but it seemed much more lively and progressive than Lyons.

There was still much of the frontier in and around Boise. A great many men, the riff-raff of both Union and Confederate armies, had come to the Basin after the War. Vigilantes had been organized to preserve order until the regular authorities were strong enough to maintain it. These days were some distance in the past when Borah arrived, but the spirit of the old rough "individualism" remained. Boise as Borah saw it about the time Idaho was entering statehood was something of a "free" city, although major crimes of violence were not particularly numerous.

If the people of Boise fell a little below the average in righteousness, they probably ranked above the average in intelligence. Ignorant men do not flock to the frontier. If it appeals somewhat to the reckless, it appeals also to the intelligent and the resourceful. Boise's leading citizens were for the most part educated men from the East and Middle West. From these sections came many of its ministers, lawyers, doctors, and teachers. Calvin Cobb, something of an aristocrat, the stalwart Republican editor of the Idaho *Statesman,* came from Illinois. The inhabitants of the Capitol City took a lively interest in the news of their country and the *Statesman* served them in this capacity a little better than might have been expected of a frontier newspaper.

IN the whole State of Idaho there were only some 80,000 souls when Borah arrived from Kansas. They lived for the most part in the irrigated districts of the southeast and of the Boise Basin and in the rainfall counties of the north. The population was essentially rural, no town in the State having a population of more than 2500. Nevertheless, there were other important towns besides Boise and Pocatello. There was Hailey in the south central part of the State ; Caldwell, a short distance northwest of Boise ; Lewiston, on the extreme western boundary and about two-thirds the distance from the southern to the northern boundary; Moscow, just north of Lewiston, the home of the State University and of one of Idaho's leading citizens, William F. McConnell; and still farther north was Wallace, growing to be one of the chief mining centers.

The population of Idaho doubled between 1890 and 1900. It doubled again during the next decade. It increased by about 33 per cent from 1910 to 1920, but the total of 445,032 in 1930 was only slightly in excess of the figure for 1920. The cities grew in population somewhat more rapidly than did the State as a whole, but Idaho remains a rural state with only about 30 per cent of its population residing in cities of more than 2500.

Idaho has never had a high percentage of foreign-born inhabitants. When Borah came to the State less than 20 per cent of its residents were of this class. In 1930, only about 7 per cent were foreign-born. Moreover, the great majority of Idaho's immigrants were of what Americans generally consider the most desirable nationalities — English, Canadian, German, Norwegian, and Swedish. There were not many from southern Europe and very few Orientals, although there was a sufficient number of the latter to excite some prejudice.

Never disturbed by racial or nationality groups, Idaho from time to time allowed itself to get very much excited about a religious sect, the Mormons. These earnest and industrious people did the greater part of the pioneering in the south-eastern part of the State, where they came to hold the balance of political power. Of 24,000 church members in Idaho in 1890 nearly two-thirds were Mormons. When they seemed inclined to support Democratic candidates, Republicans railed about the sin of polygamy; when they swung toward the Republican column, the Democrats became concerned about the "purity of the American home." Let it be said, however, that there were always in both political parties strong minorities which deplored the dragging of this question into politics, and as tolerance advanced apace, the Mormon question came to be less of an issue, although it has never entirely disappeared as such.

No doubt Borah soon learned that the earliest (in the '60's) business in Idaho had been gold mining in the areas about the north central part of the State and the Boise Basin; that lead-silver mines had become more profitable as the Territory approached statehood; and that the richest lead-silver belt in the world was in the Cœur d'Alene Mountains, well up toward the north end of the State. Mining has always been one of the chief interests in Idaho.

Soon after the gold discoveries, cattle men came into Idaho with their great herds. There was good grazing for cattle on the open plains from early spring until well on in the summer. The lands about the mountain ranges furnished better grazing in the summer and fall. The cattle business increased rapidly for some years and became one of the dominant interests of the State. It is still a major occupation, but, relatively, not as important as it was in 1890. Sheep men followed the cattle men to Idaho and grazed their flocks in the same general area of the State, the large section running from the center to the southern border. The conflict between the two types of stock raisers has already been noted. The sheep industry, like the cattle industry, remains one of consequence in Idaho.

Another large industry of Idaho, developed principally since 1900, is that of lumber. Some of the great lumber mills are located near Boise, but the greater number of them are in the area beginning with Lewiston and running on to the north. Something over a third of the total area of the State is true forest land, the greater part of it being in national forests.

Yet another large force in the economic life of Idaho is its railroads. When young attorney Borah reached Boise, there was a transcontinental line through southern Idaho, the Union Pacific, entering the State from Granger, Wyoming, passing through Pocatello, Boise, and other Idaho cities, and finally reaching Portland, Oregon. Through the Panhandle of the north the Northern Pacific had been constructed, and through this same Panhandle the tracks of the Great Northern and the Chicago, Milwaukee and St. Paul were later laid. These great railway systems and the local railroads in Idaho have not only played a large part in her economic development, but they have played a part in her political history as well.

The chief industry of Idaho is agriculture. It was not the first, but for forty years or more it has been in the lead, and during the second half of this period it has exceeded all other occupations in the number of persons engaged in it, capital invested, and output. The northern part of the State, where rainfall is plentiful, was the first section to develop agriculturally. In some sections of the south, where rainfall is light, dry farming — cultivation in such a manner that the maximum amount of moisture is conserved — has long been practised.

But the greater portion of farm lands in southern and eastern parts of the State have been made productive only by irrigation. Water was first brought to the land in the 'fifties and 'sixties by individual farmers or by small groups of farmers. Around 1880, corporations took an interest in irrigation and constructed ditches, furnishing the settlers with water somewhat as they supply farmers with electric power in our time. There was complaint about these corporations, and the State provided that irrigation districts might be constituted as school districts are and that these districts might undertake the task of irrigation. Then, in 1894, Congress passed the Carey Act which made possible the irrigation of unsettled lands. A few years later, Congress passed the Reclamation Act by the terms of which money was advanced to the states for the construction of irrigation projects. Idaho profited handsomely by both the Carey Act and the Reclamation Act. One of the first services Borah rendered Idaho as Senator was to secure more funds for completion of irrigation projects. One of the projects for which he secured funds is the Boise project, which supplies water to about 300,000 acres. Irrigation was the salvation of Idaho. Were the farmers of southern Idaho more primitive, they would worship the Snake River.

Among Idaho's principal crops may be mentioned wheat, oats, barley, corn, and hay. Southern Idaho is famous for its potatoes. Since about 1920 Idahoans have been fond of saying that Borah and their potatoes are their chief advertisements. Another important crop in the south is the sugar-beet, a beet that grows best on irrigated land. This beet has sometimes figured in the politics of the State. To the list of agricultural products may be added peas and beans.

Fruit-growing developed in Idaho in the course of time, and during the favorable years in the past decade perhaps as many as 10,000 carloads of apples, prunes, and peaches left the State. Dairying is another of the more recent industries, fine herds of pure-bred dairy cattle now being a common sight for the motorist.

With an economy predominantly agricultural, Idaho has never been a State for great fortunes. Some of its citizens made money in mines, lumber, cattle, and sheep, and a few men entered the class of the wealthy, but all in all Idaho has been a State of small incomes — one of "Joe" Grundy's backward states.

BORAH looked upon Idaho and liked it. It grew upon him, and he loved it. His professional relations were largely with the mine operators, the timber barons, the sheep and cattle kings, and a few other big interests, but his sympathy was largely with the farmers. The larger business interests which Borah represented as a lawyer in the decade preceding his election to the Senate were hostile to the interests of the farmer. Like a Jefferson, Borah stepped out of his economic class and championed the cause of the farmer and the mechanic, and as Jefferson found these people most numerous in America, so Borah found them most numerous in his frontier State of Idaho. Like Jefferson he was hated for deserting his class and becoming the mouthpiece of the inarticulate masses, and like Jefferson he appreciated the compliment. As Jefferson fought for religious liberty in Virginia, so Borah fought for religious liberty in Idaho, for the religious liberty of the Mormons. It seemed intolerable to him that these people, industrious, thrifty, tenacious, honest, temperate, and chaste, all after the best American traditions, should be singled out for persecution. Some of his earliest political efforts were on behalf of fair play for the Mormons.

The farmers and the Mormons, the greater number of whom were farmers, responded to Borah. They have acknowledged their debt to him over and over again. With characteristic generosity, Borah has time and again expressed his debt to them, saying that all he has ever accomplished he owes to the plain people of Idaho. It is quite true that the obligation is mutual. But this has taken us ahead of our story.

MR. BORAH made friends in Boise, friends among the robust men. He was never exclusive in his friendships, including in that category practically all of the younger business and professional men of the city. But, it must be repeated, he never had an inseparable companion nor a friend with whom he shared his innermost thoughts. Boise friends always speak of Borah as likable, lovable, manly, genteel, a good conversationalist, witty, but not of the "have you heard this one?" type. He is never vulgar, and never holier than thou. In the earlier days there were quite a few who called him "Bill," "Billy," or "Will."

Older men were fond of him and gave him their assistance and friendship. One of these, not many years older, was Calvin Cobb, editor of the Idaho *Statesman*, who helped establish Borah politically, but who walked with him no more after the Senator displayed his determined purpose to be the judge of his own Republicanism. Another friend was James H. Hawley, an attorney, a leading Democrat since territorial days, and Governor from 1911 to 1913. He and Borah were often on opposite sides of important lawsuits, but this never interfered with their friendship. Between the two men there was a genuine affection, ever increasing with the passing of the years. When the Governor died at an advanced age in 1929, the Senator wrote a friend: "It is difficult to realize that that tremendous vitality, that restless, resistless force, which you and I have known for so long, is at rest for all time.

"What a friend he was! I count it among the richest of instructive experiences of my life to have been associated with him and pitted against him in important court trials. . . The last visit I had with him we talked over those days, and when I said to him: 'Governor, I have always been proud of our long friendship,' he replied with deep feeling of emotion: 'Will, — I will not call you Senator — did we ever have any angry words?' I replied: 'Not outside of the courtroom.' And he laughed heartily as the tears rolled down his cheeks." The Christmas before, the Senator had presented the pioneer lawyer with a volume entitled *Kit Carson, the Happy Warrior of the Old West.*

Governor Hawley was only one of the many friends of early days whose affection was spanned by the decades and unfathomed by any test of association. Over and over again the Senator's correspondence reveals his unremitting concern for old friends in Idaho. In 1915, a gentleman wrote with much enthusiasm of Borah's chance for the presidency. Near the end of his letter he told of the death of one pioneer and the breakdown of another, Mr. Richardson. "I do not want to write about other things today," replied Borah, "I only want to send a word to Mr. Richardson."

To a dear friend and strong political supporter he wrote: "When I heard of your illness it was like hearing from one of my own kith and kin, yes, even more so." Of the same man he said to another: "If ever I should come home and not find John Hart, there would be a feeling of sadness which no language of mine can describe. I not only have a deep affection for him for the thousand and one unselfish acts of friendship of which I have been the recipient but because of his magnificent character as a man."

Some friends of other days are now friends no more. The vicissitudes of politics account for the greater number of these tragedies. Borah early recognized that one of the prices he had to pay for his public life was the loss of a few friends. He paid the price with great agony of spirit, although the toll was not heavy in terms of numbers. Occasionally a wavering friendship was restored. One friend had heard from several sources that Borah had not favored his candidacy for the United States Senate. He wrote the Senator that he was forced to believe these stories and that, having regarded Borah with the affection of a son for a father, his confidence in human nature was practically destroyed. The Senator replied that he knew about the stories, the "devious and devilish" ways employed by "deceitful bands of hell-hounds" to undermine him with his friends because he would not take orders. The friend was convinced and replied that he had always counted the Senator his dearest friend and would doubt him no further.

Fifteen years later this friend wired Borah that he had dreamed about him the night before and was worried when he read in the morning paper that Borah had had his tonsils removed. He begged the Senator to be careful. The Chairman of the Committee on Foreign Relations was immensely pleased and wired his thanks, concluding with – "We are kids yet."

This story of Idaho friendships might continue almost indefinitely, but it must close with the statement that one who has been privileged to turn through the correspondence files and see something of the virile affection existing between these men has taken a lesson in friendship.

As an ambitious and hard-working lawyer, Borah did not waste much time, but he was not a grind or a book-worm. He took time for an occasional ride, or an occasional lark. He liked to drop into a friend's place of business for a short chat. He was asked to join a number of organizations, secret orders for the most part, and almost invariably accepted. He did not care particularly for the organizations, but he joined to avoid giving offense and because he considered the purpose of such organizations worthy. He felt no obligation to attend their meetings, although he was regular in the payment of dues. His interest in his Beta brothers was probably as strong after he left the University as it was while he was there. He has always tried to meet with the Boise Betas at their dinners, and he has helped several "locals" secure Beta charters.

THE leading young attorney of Idaho's capital city was never a society man. He preferred the company of men, but he was very fond of Mary, commonly called Mamie, the daughter of Governor William F. McConnell. She was intelligent, diplomatic, and very witty. "What are you doing now, Miss McConnell?" asked a newspaper reporter. "Oh, just writing extemporaneous speeches for the Governor," she replied. She met Borah when he was making campaign speeches for her father. They took horseback rides, buggy rides, and strolls, and presented themselves one Sunday morning (April 21, 1895) at the home of Mr. and Mrs. C. Jacobs, where they were quietly married.

The *Statesman* notes that "the marriage was a complete surprise to the many friends of the contracting parties; but the well wishes for their future happiness are none the less heartfelt." The Borahs took the morning train for Caldwell, Idaho, where the groom had a case to argue the next day. The ardent suitor had been saying that he had to go East soon, and that they should be married at once and thus combine the wedding trip with the business trip. Anyhow, "William and Mary" had a royal reception at Caldwell. The Cornet Band gave them a serenade. Mr. Borah treated the boys generously and made a felicitous little speech to the assembled crowd.

W. E. Borah as a married man did not neglect his work. He was usually too busy to go out in the evening. Sometimes he would promise to go, with every intention of doing so; then something would come up which, in his opinion, made a social evening impossible. Again, he would promise to have an evening free, to be home at a certain time, only to become engrossed in a point of law and find he had overstayed his time at the office. It is quite probable that the young wife resented this. It is equally probable that the husband, always ready to concede his faults, said that he could not blame her for resenting it, a form of generosity which sometimes adds irritation to resentment. But in the course of time, the Borahs came to understand each other thoroughly and to realize that their qualities were complementary. Seldom seen together outside the home, their affectionate companionship, based upon understanding, has never been questioned by those who know them. If further proof of this is wanted, it is found in the Senator's acute distress when Mrs. Borah lay at death's door in 1932.

There is a story to the effect that when Senator Borah became Chairman of the Committee on Foreign Relations, he said to Mrs. Borah: "Now, we can go into society as much as we like, or we can follow the course we have been following — you making the social rounds as far as you can without me and I devoting myself to my work." The lady known to intimates in Washington as "Little Borah" did not hesitate

MR. AND MRS. W. E. BORAH

Shortly after their marriage in 1895

for a moment: "You must have time for your work," was her reply.

The Senator insists that Mrs. Borah is a better politician than he is. This is doubtful, but it is true that she is much more versatile than the Senator in personal relationships. She has an easy cordiality, a delightful flow of conversation on many topics, and a lively, at times almost rollicking, sense of humor. Her statesman sometimes refers to her as his "vaudeville." Always one of Idaho's most popular ladies, she is no less a favorite in Washington. "The perfect wife for a public man," attending a dinner in the hectic days when President-elect Hoover was selecting his Cabinet, answered a question which was in the mind of each guest but which no one dared ask directly. "I feel perfectly sure that I am in the hands of my friends, so I am going to tell you all. The Secretaryship of State has been offered the Senator — by everyone except Mr. Hoover."

Mrs. Borah has always been a great friend of the unfortunate and the underprivileged. Orphans, disabled soldiers, and socially maladjusted persons have often heard her cheering voice and almost as often received from her material aid. In 1924 she was so busy with disabled veterans and other unfortunates who called her at practically all hours, week days and Sundays, that the Senator had to insist that she go to Idaho and take a rest.

In the Chinese of Boise the Borahs took a joint interest. It started when they engaged a Chinese cook. He and all his friends came to the Borah home with their troubles. For sympathy, suggestions, and legal advice the Chinese were ever faithful and grateful to the Borahs. For years after Mr. Borah was elected to the Senate, the Chinese remembered Mrs. Borah each Christmas with some beautiful token of their friendship. One Christmas happened to find Mrs. Borah in Boise, and her Oriental friends came out in a carriage and made their presentation with great formality. There were a number of presentation speeches which revealed the fact that the committee had spent many anxious hours over the question as to whether the Senator's Lady should have a pink or a blue shawl. They finally compromised on a cream-colored one which Mrs. Borah wore with great pleasure.

The Senator's friendship with the Chinese – gardeners, laundrymen, and restaurateurs – is worthy of a paragraph. When Yee Yin, long a friend, died in 1914, the busy Senator wrote a letter to his voteless Chinese friends, taking especial precautions to make sure that the letter would be appropriately delivered at the Chinese Temple. A few years later, the Senator had occasion to write his agent in Boise about a mortgage on the Temple. "I guess we will permit the matter to stand at $5500," he wrote. "I rather think that I cheated myself in some way when I sent them these figures. According to my investigations now it is $6500 and if they were white people I would undertake to explain how the mistake was made. . . But . . . they [the Chinese] would never feel but that I had cheated them."

This is a picture of W. E. Borah, the Boise lawyer, of his Idaho, and of his Idaho friendships. The next chapter presents another picture, that of the emergence of the public man.

CHAPTER III

ORATORY AND POLITICS

1776 1891

GRAND CELEBRATION OF INDEPENDENCE DAY

at

Boise City

July 4, 1891

at

Miller's Grove

President of the Day

GOVERNOR NORMAN B. WILLEY

Orator of the Day

W. E. BORAH

THESE headlines the Idaho *Statesman* carried, July 1, 1891. Perhaps the oration Borah delivered was the same one he had prepared in Lyons a year or two before. Be that as it may, "his oration was listened to with the closest attention. . . His eloquent address was admirably delivered."

"I think," he said, "it is something more than the hollow mockery of custom or the superficial and meaningless parade of tradition which gathers together this vast throng of jubilant people." This sounded slightly like a college boy's oration, but the other parts were better.

"It is said of a famous Roman statesman that before going forth to the Senate Chamber to combat the alluring corruption of his people he would visit the tomb and study the life of the elder Brutus, whose sturdy virtues nourished anew the patriot's manhood. This is the real worth of today's celebration. . . We should upon this occasion view as intelligently as we can the questions of the present."

He then discussed the question of the distribution of

wealth, ever a favorite topic with him, and said that Americans could meet and solve this problem. Against monarchies founded upon force he placed democracies founded upon intelligence. "The republic which neglects the education of its subjects is the monarchy which disbands its standing army and leaves its men-of-war to rot upon the sea.

"Civilization is not a flower of Eden, it blossoms amid the storms and tempests of life, where men have been made noble by affliction, independent by toil, brave by the thrill of conquest, where brain and sinew wrestle with the realities of existence."

There was no bloody shirt, little spread-eagleism, little bombast. It was, in all probability, a much better Independence Day oration than the people of Boise were accustomed to hear.

This was Borah's first noteworthy speech in Boise, but he would not have had this opportunity had he not already demonstrated his competence. He had hardly arrived in Boise when he delivered a political speech so full of vigor and with words flying so rapidly that the boys gave him the obvious nickname of "Kansas Cyclone," a name which Idahoans later gave to another acquisition from Kansas, Walter Johnson.

This young fellow liked this kind of speaking much more than he did the college-literary-society variety. This was real ; that was artificial. He was not at all backward about putting himself forward, and, as he was a very stimulating speaker, his forwardness was not resented.

HAVING established a local reputation as a lawyer and a speaker during his first year in Boise and having shown a taste for politics, he was nominated by acclamation for City Attorney on the Republican ticket, June 20, 1891. The Democrats had their ticket and the Fusionists had theirs. The Fusion candidates, for the most part, ran well ahead of the others, although Republican Borah lost by only three votes. A few years later the local boss told Borah that he had actually won the City Attorneyship, but that he had had him counted out because he was a new-comer in Boise. Borah did not care, really. He had gone into the fight largely for the fun of it. He never wanted a public office until he ran for the Senate in 1902, and for that very reason his services were much sought after and greatly appreciated in every political campaign.

He was Chairman of the State Central Committee in 1892, a position he felt forced to resign for lack of time to give to it. But he went to the State Convention, which chose the Idaho delegates to the National Convention in that year. After the delegates were chosen and a platform favoring "the free and unlimited coinage of silver" and approving the tariff was adopted, old line Republican leaders made "stirring" or "interesting" speeches on the importance of the silver question and what the tariff had done for Idaho, but when the young man from Boise was called upon "he responded with an eloquent ten-minute speech that aroused great enthusiasm." [1]

A few months later, he made the tedious trip to Moscow, up in the Palouse country, to attend the convention called to nominate Republican candidates for State offices. "The brilliant young attorney from Boise was the unanimous choice of the convention" for temporary chairman. The committee on organization reported in favor of nominations by secret ballot. Borah called someone to the chair and took the floor to ask for a roll call by counties and a right for any member to challenge the vote of his county and ascertain how each individual voted. Because the old Republican war horses opposed this with vigor, it was finally voted down.[2]

Borah was more fortunate in his efforts to liberalize the party's attitude toward the Mormons. The Mormon suffrage plank was in the minority report of the platform committee, but Borah took the floor and won a victory for the people whose Church had recently abandoned polygamy and declared for the separation of church and state. The plank adopted pledged the Idaho Republicans to remove all the political disabilities of the Latter Day Saints.[3]

The convention also went on record for free silver, a Federal department of mines, postal savings, the right of labor to

[1] *Statesman,* May 6, 1892.
[2] Lewiston *Teller,* August 25, 1892.
[3] *Statesman,* August 20, 1892.

organize, and expressed its opposition to compulsory company stores. The platform was thus fairly liberal, the Populists having made their influence felt in the Republican ranks.

Borah went to many parts of the State carrying the Republican gospel. At Blackfoot, the home of Republican United States Senator Fred T. Dubois, his "eloquent and unanswerable argument in favor of perpetuating Republican principles aroused the audience to the highest pitch of enthusiasm. The fame of this incomparable orator had preceded him, and the audience dispersed with expressions of admiration for the speaker." At Pocatello, two evenings before, he had held "his audience spellbound for the greater part of the time. He showed by the record that Cleveland, while Governor and President, vetoed bills which were intended as a relief to the laboring classes and never failed to approve of those in the interest of capital." He pointed out to the Populists in his audience that a vote for their candidate, Weaver, was a vote for Cleveland and therefore against their own interest.[4]

But the Populist party, the flower of agrarian distress in the 'nineties, advocating the direct election of Senators, direct legislation, woman suffrage, postal savings, income taxes, severe curbs upon corporations, was being heard from. Its ringing declaration that "the fruits of the toil of millions are boldly stolen to build up colossal fortunes for the few, unprecedented in the history of mankind" was a saying which the many small-income Idahoans kept and pondered in their hearts. Effecting a combination with the Democrats in 1892, they carried the State for the Populist presidential candidate. The vote was Weaver, 10,520; Harrison, 8599. The Republicans were successful, however, with their state ticket, the vote for governor being: Republican, 8178; Democratic, 6769; Populist, 4865.

The Republicans of Idaho assembled with enthusiasm in Boise in 1894 to draft a platform and nominate candidates for the next campaign. Borah was there and was on the resolutions committee. The significant planks of the platform were those calling for silver at the ratio of 16 to 1 and for woman suffrage. The Democratic platform had the same

[4] *Ibid.*, September 29 and 27 respectively.

provisions, but added the direct election of United States Senators. The Populists included these three items and asked for much more. Woman suffrage was voted by the next legislature.

In this Republican convention a move was made to prevent the reëlection to the United States Senate of Idaho's Grand Old Man, Colonel George L. Shoup. The plan was to get the convention to nominate a candidate, for the convention was supposed to have a majority favoring the candidacy of Willis Sweet. "Gentlemen," shouted Borah, after the matter had been before the convention for some time, "the most contemptible methods have been resorted to here today to force this resolution down the throats of the convention by traducing the coming legislature. That alone should be enough to defeat it." [Prolonged cheers.] Borah objected to the resolution that the convention make the nomination, thus binding Republican members of the legislature to vote for the nominee, on the primary ground that the movement for a convention nomination had come not from the people, but from the scheming resolutions committee. Borah's substitute motion — that the convention make no nomination — finally carried the day.[5] It is quite probable that this resolution saved Colonel Shoup, for, even with the legislature free to make the choice, he barely won his reëlection the next winter.

Fighting for the Grand Old Man further endeared the "brilliant young orator" to the people of Idaho ; but in making the fight Borah fought against the very thing he himself was able to advocate ten years later. There was this important difference, however : the convention nomination idea was trumped up *in the convention* of 1894 ; but when Borah later made his fight for it he went directly to the people and had them pledge their delegates to make such nomination.

Borah's speech, in this same convention, nominating Edgar Wilson for Congress, was not only commented upon by Idaho papers as a masterpiece, but such out-of-State newspapers as the Salt Lake *Tribune* gave it notice. His opening sentence was, "In a few more days we will not be speaking to the chosen representatives of our party, but, standing in the fierce light

[5] *Ibid.*, August 9, 1894.

of public scrutiny, exposed to the relentless test of public opinion, amenable to the stern demands of Idaho's voters, we will be called upon to render an account for all we have done and are to do here."[6] He did not soar above or slump below this level. It was a simple, short speech in good, pleasing English. It was better than at least ninety per cent of the speeches which placed in nomination candidates for the presidency in that period.

THE Republicans won a rather easy victory in Idaho in 1894, but the signs of the times were unpromising for the future of the party in that State. Silver was the chief cause. Before the great silver mines of the country had been developed, silver and gold had been coined at the ratio of 16 to 1, a ratio which because of the scarcity of silver in the early 'seventies had made a silver dollar worth slightly more than a gold dollar. Little silver was brought to the mints, and in 1873 Congress stopped the coinage of the silver dollar, an action which, though hardly noticed at the time, came to be designated in our history as "the Crime of '73." Shortly thereafter silver became abundant and its value as compared with gold steadily fell until by 1890 the ratio was something like 32 to 1. Debtors, farmers, and other advocates of easy money joined in urging the restoration of the silver dollar at the old ratio of 16 to 1. Silver and lead-silver mining interests, though less numerous, were perhaps more influential in forcing the issue. Silver was in politics for twenty years before 1896.

From time to time, a few concessions were made to the silver people but in the economic crisis of '93 President Cleveland, supported by "sound money" men in Congress, had the silver purchase act repealed. There was much misery in the land at the time, and the silver forces were greatly augmented and became decidedly militant. In the West, and even in the Democratic South, President Cleveland became one of the most unpopular men in the United States. Free silver, that is, the coinage of any amount which might be brought to the mints, at the 16 to 1 ratio became the rallying cry of those sections.

The silver question did not agitate Idaho internally —

[6] *Ibid.*, August 10, 1894.

practically everyone in the State was for free silver. The big lead-silver mining interests wanted it, for silver coined at 16 to 1 would yield them double its actual market value. The farmers, sharing the distress of other farmers of the West, wanted it because it would make dollars cheaper, give them more dollars for their produce, and more dollars with which to pay their debts. Other groups in Idaho were simply drawn along by these two most powerful interests. From the poorest debtor farmer to the heaviest investor in mining properties, from the most radical Populist to the least liberal Republican, Idahoans were vigorous champions of unlimited coinage at 16 to 1 long before 1896.

Idaho, with its mines, cattle, and sheep, with its population drawn largely from the Middle West (except the Mormons who came from Utah), and with its foreign-born citizens of those nationalities which usually venerated Lincoln, should have been a fairly safe Republican State. Its people were not unanimous in their belief in the tariff myth, but they believed most ardently in the magic of silver. If the national Republican party should show a decidedly unfriendly feeling for silver, it might mean party disaster in Idaho. The Democratic Populist combination had given the Republicans a good warning by taking Idaho, Kansas, and two or three other normally Republican states away from the Republicans in 1892. Moreover, the people of Idaho had some advanced ideas on other questions of the day — for example, woman suffrage, the direct election of senators, postal savings, the income tax.

Borah's position in the campaign of 1896 may be introduced by shifting the scene to the Senate floor. The time is June 8, 1934, and the debaters are Senators Borah and Fess. Senator Borah said that he favored going back to the gold standard and restoring silver to a ratio of 16 to 1 with gold.

"This is the first time I have heard the Senator from Idaho stood on the 16 to 1 platform," retorted the Senator from Ohio. "He didn't do it in 1896."

"You are mistaken, I did," replied the Idahoan. "And if it had not been for the discovery of gold in Alaska and Australia, silver would have won."

When the Ada County (Boise's location) Republican convention of 1896 completed its work, it was suggested that W. E. Borah be sent for to warm the delegates' hearts with oratory. A committee was sent to inform that gentleman of the desire of the convention, but he could not be found. Other speakers filled in, among whom was Governor McConnell, father-in-law of Borah. He said that no man had any business in a Republican convention who did not endorse the protection of American industries and favor the free coinage of silver.[7] Borah would have said the same, with the emphasis on the latter. Up in Nez Perce County the Republican convention declared for silver and for the reëlection of Senator Dubois, long a Republican leader in Idaho, although a few delegates said that they were more for McKinley than they were for silver and did not want to embarrass him. County after county made a strong declaration for silver.

The Lewiston *Tribune,* the leading Democratic paper in the State, commended Dubois for his declaration against "a gold-bug or straddle candidate" for the Republican nomination and praised him for his statement promising to bolt the convention if it nominated such a candidate. The *Tribune* accurately prophesied that the astute politician would have to leave the Republican party.[8]

The *Tribune* also printed with approval a prophecy of the Boise *Mail,* which was that the National Republican convention at St. Louis would "taffy up the silver Republican with another international agreement plank [on bimetallism]. The dose will be swallowed, as usual." [9]

The state convention at Pocatello was to be a great affair. At the head of the Ada County delegation was W. E. Borah, "the young giant of oratory, whose voice will make the echoes around the Gate City ring." The *Statesman* lists as a further achievement of the Ada County leader the fact that he had arranged for a Pullman car to take the delegation to Pocatello.[10]

The Pocatello convention was a Dubois and silver affair. Dubois and men equally strong for silver were chosen as delegates to the national convention. The state platform

[7] *Ibid.,* May 10, 1896.
[8] *Tribune,* May 13, 1896.
[9] *Ibid.,* May 20, 1896.
[10] *Statesman,* May 14, 1896.

condemned "the action of the Democratic party for its efforts in attempting to demonetize silver," a reference to the repeal of the Silver Purchase Act by the Cleveland Administration. The delegates heartily endorsed "the action of Senator Dubois in joining with his associates named in the fearless position taken in behalf of the free coinage of silver, protection in American industry and reciprocity, one and inseparable." [11]

"Idaho not only needs a new deal, but a new deck, a new shuffle and a new cut," the Lewiston *Tribune* editorialized. "And all these Idaho will have." [12]

The Idaho delegates at St. Louis were discouraged even by the opening prayer of Rabbi Sale. When he got to the "golden ring," a Jewish colleague whispered to one of Idaho's leading delegates, Willis Sweet, "My God ! the Rabbi is praying against us." Senator Teller of Colorado made the concluding speech for silver, and when he had finished, he walked out with the other delegates from Colorado and those from Idaho went along.[13] "Sound money" had won. The expected break had occurred.

Back in Idaho there were mixed feelings. The majority of Republicans were ready to desert McKinley, but the real organization men said little, the greater number of them preparing to support him. Even a few of the rank and file of Republican voters said that, while they were still as strong as ever for silver, they would have to vote for McKinley. One said, "If my party nominates a yellow dog, I am going to vote for him." Another said, "I am for silver but don't know exactly where I am at."

As for W. E. Borah, the *Statesman* said that he was "one of the ablest and cleanest men," but that his threat to bolt the Republican party was wholly bad ; that Republicans should stand by McKinley for tariff protection.[14] But Borah went on his way. On legal business at Silver City, he attended a Democratic meeting, was called upon to speak, and did so. He said he was speaking only because of his interest in silver, and, if the *Statesman's* report is correct, he said he was a Re-

11 *Tribune,* May 20, 1896.
12 *Ibid.,* June 3, 1896.
13 *Ibid.,* July 1, 1896.
14 *Statesman,* July 11, 1896.

publican and did not think he could leave that party.[15] But a few days later the *Tribune* reported that "Boise's silver-tongued orator" would not only speak for the metal, the name of which was used to characterize his tongue, but would actively support Bryan. At the same time it announced that Republican State Senator Dewey, with large silver interests, had said he would "vote the Democratic ticket from Bryan electors to constable." [16]

Senator Dubois, who had led the Idaho delegates out of the St. Louis convention, visited Boise in triumph on July 29. There was a great procession headed by a band, followed by carriages of notables, marching clubs, torches and "transparencies," another band, more "transparencies," yet another band, still more "transparencies." Some of the "transparencies" read: "Hanna put the kettle on, McKinley wants tea," "No crown of thorns; no cross of gold," "Money can't buy the people," "Silver has no politics this year," "William Bryan, the idol of the people," "Cleveland and Sherman are for McKinley," "Palouse Bill will now lay still" (reference to Governor William McConnell of the northern Palouse hills, who was standing by McKinley), "Subsidized newspapers cut no ice" (reference to the *Statesman,* also standing by). Then there was a portrayal of a man turning a somersault, which was a pointed reference to a number of former silver advocates and leading administration politicians who had suddenly deserted silver for McKinley.[17]

Around the first of August the silver Republicans of Ada County had an indignation, protest, and "ways and means" meeting in Boise.[18] Attorney-General Parsons said that the Republican officers of the State had betrayed the party in Idaho because they hoped Hanna and McKinley would share the loaves and fishes and "pie" with them. Parsons ridiculed Governor McConnell, who a few months before had said that no one had any business in a Republican convention who did not favor free silver, for going over the State now and telling the people that free coinage would not leave enough gold in Idaho to open a jackpot. The audience enjoyed this, for the

[15] *Ibid.,* July 14, 1896.
[16] *Tribune,* July 18, 1896.
[17] *Statesman,* July 30, 1896.
[18] *Ibid.,* as reported in the *Tribune,* August 5, 1896.

Governor was known to have some familiarity with the game in which the jackpot holds the center position.

Former Chief Justice Joseph Huston doubted whether America was the free country she was supposed to be. "Even Queen Victoria and the Czar of all the Russians and the jack-anapes who rules the German Empire are not as tyrannical as is King Caucus of this country." He had left the Democratic party in 1860 and would leave the Republican party now. Lincoln was the last President the people had had, he said, and they would have their next in Bryan, who would not be controlled by the gold sharks of Wall Street or Lombard Street. "Does not the face of every American tingle with shame as he witnesses America, like the bastinadoed elephant, bowing down to the British rider?"

As usual, W. E. Borah carried away the honors. There was just one class of Republicans, he said, those who maintained that the party had fought for the free coinage of silver. He compared the Republicans of the State who were supporting McKinley with the "grinning monopolistic gold-bugs of England." He was hissed. Then he told the hissers that they did not have a spoonful of brains and defied any McKinley man in the house who could raise his voice above a whisper to contradict his statement. As for W. B. Heyburn, a regular of the regulars, who had suddenly dropped his advocacy of silver after the St. Louis convention, he queried, "If he was sincere at the Pocatello convention when was it he received this new inspiration?" He said that this Ada County Republican meeting was based "upon the principles upon which we have stood for years. . . We are here in accordance with the declaration of every platform for which Idaho Republicans have fought since my acquaintance in this State." Borah's position could not be challenged on that point. He even suggested that McKinley be read out of the Republican party, and added that to support him and silver at the same time was duplicity and a blunder. Idahoans, he said, should stand by silver and "that brilliant leader, William J. Bryan."

This speech reveals a great deal of Senator Borah's attitude toward his party. The real Republicans of Idaho were the silver Republicans who would not follow McKinley. They were the Republicans because they had a majority and because they continued to adhere to the policy all Idaho Republicans advocated prior to the St. Louis convention. The fact that this policy was rejected by the national convention did not make Idaho Republicans any less Republican. Even if free silver was now supported by only a minority (it was in fact supported by a large majority) of Idaho Republicans, they still had a right to claim to be Republicans. This is the essence of Borah's Republicanism — that a minority, no matter how small, has a right to be the judge of its own Republicanism. As it was, the situation was quite simple. With such a large proportion of Republicans in Idaho staying by the silver banner, Dubois and Borah and their followers could say that they had not left the Republican party but that the Republican organization of Idaho had left the party.

Idaho was on the warpath for the unlimited coinage of silver at the ratio of 16 to 1. "Gold-bugism" was anathema, and the Boise *Sentinel*[19] gave the best popular description of that "bug." "It is a headless thing, as it thinks not of the wrath to come. It is a heartless thing and cannot feel as is witnessed by the suffering it causes without remorse ; when it moves it is in wrath ; when it pauses it is amid ruin ; its prayers are as curses ; its god is mammon ; its communion is death ; its vengeance is eternity ; its decalogue is written in the blood of its victims ; . . . it is as seductive as the vampire, as poisonous as the serpent, as destructive as the tiger, yet as cowardly as the jackal."

The silver people in Idaho got busy during the month of August and mixed the poison for the regular Republicans. The Democrats, silver Republicans, and Populists united in support of Bryan for President and Frank Steunenberg (Democrat) for Governor. For Congress there was a three-cornered race. The stalwart Republicans, the Populists-Democrats (Popocrats), and the silver Republicans each had a candidate. "The sorriest spectacle ever witnessed in Idaho or in any other state," lamented the *Statesman,* "was that presented in the bolters' [Silver Republican] convention yesterday when a ticket was put in nomination composed partly of

[19] As quoted in the *Tribune,* June 24, 1896.

Democrats, partly of Populists, and partly of men calling themselves Silver Republicans." [20]

Borah was chairman of the Silver Republican convention. He did not want to be nominated for any office and was not nominated for any at this convention. But later, when it was decided that a Silver Republican should run for Congress, he yielded to the earnest entreaties of Senator Dubois and agreed to be a candidate. Borah was a strong supporter of Dubois and Dubois was not satisfied with the Populist-Democratic candidate. The editor of the *Statesman* wrote sarcastically of the "Comedy of Errors." "Mr. Borah, who has been looking on enviously at the reputation Mr. Bryan has been making as a 'Willie Boy,' could resist the temptation no longer, and accepted the nomination for Congress with the understanding that he should be allowed to make seventeen speeches a day from now until November and be billed as the boy candidate who has never been old enough to accept a nomination." [21]

The Democrats, Populists, and Silver Republicans had all the fun in the campaign. As the Republicans were on the defensive, they would not meet any of the silver crowd in debate. Everyone knew that the regular Republican organization in Idaho was in for a terrific drubbing. When the announcement was made that so-and-so would run for such-and-such minor office on the G.O.P. ticket, it was greeted with some such remark as "another lamb for the slaughter."

Because the silver votes were split in the Congressional race Borah had little hope of winning, but he had his share of the pleasure of the campaign. He went all over the State telling the people not to trouble about him but to make certain that men were sent to the legislature who would vote for the return of Dubois to the United States Senate in 1897. He denounced the "Crime of '73," that is, the repeal of the Silver Coinage Act, and insisted with all the ardor of the young statesman who headed the Democratic ticket that the solution of our currency ills lay in coining unlimited quantities of silver at the ratio of 16 to 1 with gold. This was his leading argument everywhere, but it was not his sole argument

20 *Statesman,* August 28, 1896.
21 *Ibid.,* September 27, 1896.

any more than it was the sole argument of Mr. Bryan. He paid his respects to the money power, to trusts, to monopolies, and to any group which seemed to fatten too much at the expense of the people as a whole.

While William Edgar Borah was furnishing "oratorical treats" for the silver people of Idaho, one of his classmates at the University of Kansas, William Allen White, now the young and very conservative publisher of the Emporia *Gazette,* was serving an editorial treat to the stalwart Republicans of the East. In his "What's the Matter with Kansas" of August 15, White in colorful language proceeded to say what he thought of the "Popocrats" in that State. The two Wills were as far apart as the poles, for the Will who remained in Kansas had not yet met Theodore Roosevelt to receive his baptism of liberalism. Mark Hanna used a million copies of the editorial in promoting McKinley's campaign, and when the election was won he offered White a job, which he wisely declined.

Borah went back to his law practice after the election. The regular Republican candidate for Congress had received 6000 votes, Borah, the Silver Republican, nearly 9000, and the Populist-Democratic candidate, 13,500. Bryan carried Idaho easily and practically all the candidates for State and local offices on the McKinley ticket were completely snowed under. It seemed that there were hardly enough "regulars" left in Idaho to man the post offices.

Despite the fact that the silver forces won a complete victory in the contest for seats in the legislature, Dubois was not returned to the Senate in 1897. He needed Populist and Democratic votes for election and there were too many Democrats who had hardly recovered from the torture Dubois as a Republican had inflicted upon them. The Democrats made a fusion agreement with the Populists by the terms of which a Populist was to be elected to the Senate. But the Democrats would not agree upon anyone the Populists nominated. Finally a Democrat, Henry Heitfelt, a member of the legislature and a substantial farmer of Lewiston, agreed to be called a Populist, and he was duly elected to the Senate.

Economic conditions improved somewhat, the Spanish-

American War came on, and there was talk of expansion, but the friends of silver in Idaho were not ready to speak much of other things. On the other hand, the regular G.O.P. in Idaho had managed to keep an organization in which W. B. Heyburn, a mining lawyer of Wallace, and former Governor McConnell, now Indian Inspector, were leading figures.

The *Tribune* maintained that these Republicans stood for "pure Hannaism," and that it was reliably informed that their state platform in 1898 would be of the "Mark Hanna-Cleveland-Carlisle-Wall Street variety." [22] Their convention did endorse the financial policies of the national administration. As for the *Tribune,* it insisted that "the vital, imperishable principle of bimetallism will have to be settled before the Republican party will be allowed to shift the campaign to questions of less consequence." [23] The Silver Republicans, the Democrats, and the Populists agreed with the *Tribune.* The time was not quite at hand when the printer's error — "a true and *tired* friend of silver" — could be allowed to pass as correct.

W. E. Borah attended the Silver Republican convention and was made chairman of the committee on platform. He said that the platform could be prepared in an hour and that he was opposed to waiting to see what the other silver people might do in their conventions. The Silver Republicans, he said, stood for the white metal and for protection of American industries and labor. If the other friends of silver did not endorse the protection principle, that was unfortunate, but the principle should not be bargained away. The convention added another plank — it declared for the annexation of all territory over which the United States had acquired control in the Spanish-American War.

The Democrats and the Silver Republicans perfected an agreement upon candidates for governor and Congress, leaving the Populists and the regular Republicans with their own candidates. The fusion candidates won another victory, but the Republicans staged a remarkable comeback. The Populist candidates were poor thirds.

[22] *Tribune,* July 29, 1898.
[23] *Ibid.,* August 5, 1898.

IN 1900, the Spanish-American War had come and gone, but its glories lingered. Imperialism appealed to the imagination. Senator Hoar, who opposed it, was now considered something of a dodo. The expansion extravagancies of young Senator Beveridge were more in the popular key. Moreover, prosperity was returning; even the West was feeling it. Bryan was still a fine figure, but a little out of date, both in opposing imperialism and advocating silver. Gold discoveries were increasing the quantity of money, thus doing what he had hoped to accomplish with silver. Even the *Tribune* found that the silver question was not exactly an imperishable one, and turned its penetrating editorials to other topics.

A few Silver Republicans became regular again in 1898. Two years later there was a general movement back to the regular columns, and W. E. Borah was of the group which came back. The combined strength of Democrats, Populists, and the remaining Silver Republicans was just sufficient to carry Idaho for Bryan in 1900. The same group combinations managed to squeak through to victory in the State and Congressional elections. It was clear, however, that the revolt in the Gem State had spent its force. After 1900 Populism was dead.

In the campaign of that year Borah agreed to make eight speeches for the Republican committee. The *Statesman* explained that his business prevented him from accepting a lengthy itinerary, and by its compliments clearly indicated that it forgave Borah, fully and freely, for his waywardness of 1896 and 1898.

Preceding Borah's speech at Pocatello there was a grand torchlight parade headed by a "magnificent flambeau club under the leadership of Joe Duckworth, the blacksmith." [24] As for the speaker, he "was at his best and he was frequently applauded. . . He neatly replied to a hoodlum who attempted to interrupt him. The hoodlum, with reference to nothing, asked: 'Do you believe in 16 to 1?'

" 'Yes, I do,' replied Mr. Borah, 'and, I apprehend, a great deal more than you do.' " He declared that he was as much

[24] *Statesman,* October 26, 1900.

for free silver as ever, but that he knew he could not get it through Dick Croker and Bryan.

Then he spoke of prosperity under McKinley and said he wanted to see it retained. If prosperity is due to natural causes, "there have been times in the history of this country when even the Lord seemed powerless to help the party in power, and until I have some notice that the Lord has deserted the Republican party I shall assume that he is still with us."

One of the best lawyers and speakers in Idaho, Borah held the popular interest by his continued presentation of public questions during the period preceding the next election. Not obviously seeking office, he was nevertheless placing himself in line for a seat in the United States Senate. He made a splendid address at the state convention in 1902. His hand was seen in the anti-monopoly plank of the platform and his candidate, John T. Morrison, received the nomination for governor. It was understood that Borah was a candidate for the Senate, but the convention took no action on this matter since it was the practice of the Republicans of Idaho to leave the choice of a Senator entirely to the discretion of the state legislature.

In the campaign of that year, the politically astute Senator Fred T. Dubois — once a Republican, now a Democrat — quickly recognized Borah as the Republicans' greatest threat and directed most of his fire at him. The young attorney gave a good account of himself and it was largely through his efforts and the return of prosperity that the Republicans won all the state executive offices and a substantial majority in the legislature. They were thus assured of the senatorship.

If the party was assured of the senatorship, Borah was not. Other and older men wanted the place. The leading rival of Borah was W. B. Heyburn, a very conservative lawyer of Wallace who had done more than any other man to hold the Republican remnant together in the sad days of Populism. Heyburn was backed by the moneyed interests — the railroads, the mines, and other business enterprises of the State. It was clear that he could give Borah a strong contest in the Republican legislative caucus.

On the first ballot in the caucus Borah had 18 votes, Heyburn 15, and two other candidates had 17 votes between them. The next day Heyburn's managers made a deal with the other candidates under the terms of which they threw their support to Heyburn, who won the caucus nomination with 28 votes. Borah received 22. Some men, six or seven, were bought for Heyburn at $750 per head. One such individual came to Borah, confessed it, and wept. Borah's supporters wanted to bolt the caucus, but he dissuaded them, accepted the situation with good grace, and made a firm resolve relative to 1906.

Thus Heyburn, who had held the old guard of federal office-holders together for six years while the other Republicans of Idaho had been seeking false gods, became United States Senator. Borah returned to his law office, where he continued to be happy and unusually successful.

CHAPTER IV

THE VOICE OF THE PEOPLE

WITH no election for the United States Senate in Idaho for four more years, Borah pursued his practice of law vigorously, happily, and profitably. Timber companies and banks sought his services. His income was around $30,000 a year. These were his last and best years as a lawyer.

But he was always ready to give some time to a political campaign. In 1904, he went as a delegate to the Republican national convention. Back in Idaho, it was rumored that he would support Frank Gooding for governor, and that Gooding and Senator Heyburn would then back Borah for the Senate in 1906 and 1907. The talk was that Borah would not work for Governor Morrison for a second term; that those who said he would based their statement upon the report of a man who had seen Borah and Morrison meet on a street corner; that Borah was not such a fool as to jump on a hearse being driven to the graveyard. At the Republican state convention at Moscow (August 9) he was very much in evidence and very much with Gooding, who was the choice of the convention for governor.

The Republicans had an easy time of it in Idaho in 1904. There was prosperity in full bloom, and Roosevelt was a man after the heart of every rugged Idahoan. Parker, the Democratic nominee, with his "gold-bugism," aroused a degree of enthusiasm among Idaho Democrats which resembled nothing so much as one lone clam giving a cheer for chowder.

"Why, oh, why, does not the Democratic party have the vision to see and the candor to admit that it is dead?" asked Colonel Thomas Fitch, in a speech at Lewiston.[1] "Why does it not go to its grave like a gentleman instead of walking around trying to save its funeral expenses?" He said that political economy was an abstruse science and that he feared that some Democratic leaders understood it but little better than the bookseller who placed in his shop window a sign reading: "For sale, Mill on Political Economy, Price, one dollar. Ditto on the Floss. Price, one twenty-five."

[1] *Tribune,* October 12, 1904.

Lacking a good issue for the state campaign in 1904, the Democrats, under the leadership of Senator Dubois, made one from the Mormon question. It seemed that the time might be ripe for another moral storm about the Mormons. Roberts of Utah had been elected to the House of Representatives a few years before and had been denied his seat because he was a polygamist. Smoot, no polygamist, was elected to the Senate by the Utah legislature in 1903. The efforts of some United States Senators to keep this immoral (?) Mormon from contaminating them and the Republic was one of the biggest laughs of the first third of the twentieth century. To be fair with the Senators, however, it should be recorded that their objections to Smoot were laid on the technical ground of his position in the Mormon church hierarchy. The question whether or not Smoot should have his seat in the Senate was not settled for several years and it was much discussed throughout the country. That part of rural America in which few Mormons resided became greatly exercised over the "Mormon menace" during the Smoot controversy and remained excited for several years after Smoot was given full title to his seat.

Readers who lived in small towns about 1904 may recall that anti-Mormon lecturers were sometimes given a few minutes on the program at the local "opera house" to tell of the horrors of polygamy, show pictures of a few polygamous families and the Mormon temple at Salt Lake City, and declare that the Mormons would like to locate a temple like that in Ruhicksville. And let it be recalled that President Roosevelt displayed strong prejudice against the Mormons in his opposition to the election of Senator Smoot. Other Republican leaders were more cautious, and they left it to the Democrats assembled in national convention (1904) to denounce polygamy and demand a separation of church and state.

Idaho was not particularly perturbed about the Mormon issue in 1904. It was an issue only because Dubois had dragged it in. Between one-fifth and one-fourth of the voters of the state were Mormons. They had leaned toward the Democratic party, but when Dubois left the Republican party and entered the Democratic he met great flocks of

Mormons coming out. This was too much. He insisted that the strong Republican tendencies of the Mormons were brought about by undue pressure from high officers of their church. Such pressure began to be exerted about 1900, but figures from the Mormon counties of Idaho do not prove that Mormons were leaving the Democratic party any more rapidly than the Presbyterians and Baptists. The fact is that Idaho was growing more solidly Republican because of good times and Theodore Roosevelt, whom Dubois very much admired.

With Mormon voters in the minority in the State, it seemed safe to Senator Dubois to make their sins an issue, probably with the hope of getting votes for Democratic candidates from the gentiles (non-Mormons) of both parties. The Democratic state platform demanded "the extermination of polygamy and unlawful cohabitation within the State of Idaho, and the complete separation of church and state in political affairs." [2] A great many Democrats saw the folly of this issue. The State's leading Democratic newspaper, the Lewiston *Tribune,* deplored the fact that Dubois made this the main issue when there were so many important questions to discuss. On the floor of the state convention Judge S. S. Denning of Latah county spoke his mind. "The matter of all this high moral tone standard plank in the platform against polygamy, whereby all the voters in the Republican party would flock to vote the Democratic ticket on that account, is a chimera and a dream. You may bait the Democratic political hook with beatitudes, and the whole Republican party will go to hell before it will take a nibble." [3] Frank Gooding, the Republican candidate for governor, publicly scoffed that the Democratic party had fallen into the hands of the pinks of morality, and the votes in November revealed a further decline in Democratic strength since 1902.

Much as Borah deplored the injection of the Mormon question into the campaign of 1904, he had to answer Dubois. Borah got sarcastic and entertaining on the issue as the campaign progressed. In Lewiston,[4] "I say to you tonight, not-

[2] *Ibid.,* August 17, 1904.
[3] *Ibid.,* August 16, 1904.
[4] *Ibid.,* October 26, 1904.

withstanding they declare I am a bishop in the Mormon Church, I am in favor of punishing any man guilty of violating the laws of this State. . .

"He [Dubois] says there are no laws in the State to cover these offenses. Well, if there are no laws in this State to cover these offenses, what in the name of all the gods at once has Senator Dubois been doing for eighteen years? Is there a friend of Senator Dubois in the audience? (From the audience, 'Guess not.') Is it a fact that this man has been in this State for eighteen years, holding the senatorship for twelve years, and hasn't got a friend? If there is a friend, stand up; I want to ask a question. [No friend of Dubois had the audacity to rise.] If he has got no friends, I will ask his enemies. What law has Senator Dubois suggested in eighteen years covering a single one of these offenses? . . . What has he suggested to the legislature to cover these matters in the eighteen years he has lived in the heart of Mormondom?"

Referring to the story that certain Mormon members of the legislature tried to get him to agree to vote for the seating of Smoot in the United States Senate in return for their support in the Idaho legislature, in 1903, and that they voted for Heyburn when he (Borah) would not promise to support Smoot, Borah said: "Now I hate to say some things in public that I would like to say in private, but I am going to say this: That the man who circulated that statement is a willful, deliberate and industrious liar. . .

"These three men [Mormon members of the legislature] visited me in my rooms when I was a candidate for United States Senator and they asked me in substance if I was prejudiced against Senator Smoot and I said 'No.' I said, 'I shall examine the evidence and vote in accordance with my conscience.' They said, 'That is perfectly satisfactory,' and instead of those three men going back and voting for Senator Heyburn they went into my caucus and voted for me until the close of the voting."

With Dubois polygamy was the unpardonable sin. In 1890, President Woodruff of the Mormon Church had had a revelation and all Mormons had been told to cease contracting plural marriages. While all plural marriages were, of course, technically illegal, with the issue of this manifesto, the civil authorities, recognizing that great hardships would be forced upon many Mormons if the law were enforced, refrained from applying the rigors of the statute to persons who were married to more than one wife prior to October 6, 1890, the date of the manifesto.

But Dubois insisted that Mormons in Idaho had contracted plural marriages since the manifesto. He insisted further that there were no adequate laws in Idaho by which this offense could be punished. Borah answered:[5] "If Senator Dubois will file a complaint against any one or more living in polygamy in the State of Idaho by reason of marriages contracted since the manifesto, in a court of competent jurisdiction and furnish me the evidence . . . I . . . agree to find the court in which to try the case, the law under which punishment could be had and assist in the prosecution without charge or cost to anyone."

A Mr. Owen, not Senator Dubois, then sent Borah a list of some thirty names of Idahoans whom he charged with polygamy. Borah said that it was the same old list which they had been "hawking" about for months. "There is not a single new name on it. I presume every leading Republican has seen that list many times and knows where it came from. All of the persons therein named, as far as I have been able to investigate, are instances of marriage prior to the manifesto." Borah declared at Lewiston, the day before he gave out this statement in Spokane, that one man on the list was eighty-four years of age and had married his last wife in 1849. Yet doubtless there were a few men living in Idaho in polygamous marriages contracted since the manifesto.

Borah did not give all of his time to answering Dubois on the Mormon question. In his speeches in every part of the State he took plenty of time to praise the Republican party and ridicule the Democrats. He said that Lincoln was the greatest man who ever lived and strongly implied that Theodore Roosevelt was a close second.

He said that political parties "have character — reputations

[5] *Statesman,* October 27, 1904.

built up the same as the reputations of men. . . Every grand deed, every pledge fulfilled, every promise kept, make up that character. . . The party that struck the shackles from the slave, released a people from the clutches of Spanish tyranny, and gave a new flag to the sky, the party which married the Atlantic and Pacific with the trans-continental railway and is now linking the seas with the isthmian canal ; the party which found American industries prostrate and in ruins and placed them at last in competition with the world and is standing guard over them still, is the party which appeals to you tonight for your vote and support. It is a party with a creed, with a faith and the power to do." [6]

What did he have to say of the Republican candidate for governor? A few paragraphs from Borah's speech at Weiser,[7] where Walter Johnson won his early fame at baseball, will serve as the answer. "Frank Gooding is a man from the ranks. . . He is of that class who open and work the mines, clear the sagebrush, plant homes and pay the taxes. He has the bluntness of honesty, the directness of conviction, the resolution and determination of courage. . . His indomitable will power, his tireless energy, his open, outspoken disposition as shown by the fearless, open method with which he has met the issues of this campaign, stamps him as a man of force, one of that class of men who make states and open up new countries while the more fortunate wait upon the dancing master and keep open the pawnshop."

Borah may not have had an agreement with Gooding whereby the latter was to support Borah for the United States Senate in 1906 and 1907, but the manner in which Borah campaigned for Gooding might well have led people to believe there was such an understanding and have given Borah reasonable expectation of receiving Gooding's support. Not only did Borah support Gooding but he was entirely regular in supporting the national administration and in his expressed faith in the Republican party. By all the rules of the game he had every reason to hope that he would have no opposition within his party for the next vacancy in the Senate.

[6] *Ibid.*, November 6, 1904.
[7] *Ibid.*, November 1, 1904.

HAVING lost the election to the United States Senate in 1903, an election to which he and the great majority of fair-minded people thought he was entitled, and having lost it because of a combination against his nomination in the Republican legislative caucus, Borah was determined to have nothing to do with a caucus in his next race. His plan in 1906 was to secure the election of delegates to county Republican conventions who favored his candidacy, get the county conventions to pass resolutions demanding the nomination of a candidate for senator by the state convention, and have the state convention make such nomination, thus taking the place of the legislative caucus and obligating all Republican members of the legislature to support the convention nominee for senator.

It was characteristic of Borah that his opposition to nomination by the state convention in 1894 did not embarrass him in his support of the plan twelve years later. He did not even take the trouble to explain why he was opposed to it at one time and for it at another. But the *Statesman*, strong for the convention plan and equally strong for Borah, reconciled his opposing views in the editorial "Wise Men Change." [8] The proposal in 1894 "was a trick to beat Senator Shoup; but now we have a situation in which it is necessary to have the candidate selected at the convention in order that the interests of the party may not be sacrificed." Furthermore, continued the editorial, it made no difference whatever how Mr. Borah "may have stood on the abstract question twelve years ago; he is now in favor of this line of reform, in company with such a large army of sincere people in every state and every section, and it is worse than baying at the moon for any one to call up his position in the convention twelve long years since as a reason why the plan of making a nomination in state convention should not be endorsed by the people."

Senator Heyburn, who mortally feared and hated any change that might place him within reach of the people, wrote from Washington that he opposed Borah's scheme. Replying in a letter [9] both impish and caustic, Borah stated:

[8] *Ibid.*, July 21, 1906.

[9] Found in an old newspaper clipping. Date unknown, but very probably about June 1, 1906.

"I observed that you deemed it necessary to turn aside from your arduous duties at the capital long enough to give us the benefit of your ripened wisdom on the subject of endorsing a candidate for United States Senator at the state convention." Then, after answering Heyburn's objections in the same vein, he concluded: "I should be exceedingly glad if your duties at Washington end in time to enable you to enter upon a public discussion of this matter before the people of this State. . . I expect to find time to discuss this matter before the people in the different counties of the State before the state convention meets and will accommodate myself to your convenience in the matter of time and place that we may jointly discuss the same." The joint discussions did not take place.

Governor Gooding, who desired a second term, Judge James H. Beatty, who very much wanted to be United States Senator, J. H. Brady, chairman of the state central committee, who also had ambitions to represent his State in the Senate, in fact, practically all of the Republican regulars were opposed to Borah's plan. But he did have the powerful support of Calvin Cobb, able editor of Idaho's leading Republican paper, the *Statesman.* Furthermore, the younger men and the rank and file seemed to be with Borah.

He gave to the press a masterly argument for his proposal.[10] "Those who advocate the plan of endorsing some one at the state convention," it begins, "do so because they believe in the selection of a United States Senator by direct vote of the people. And they believe the convention plan to be the nearest approach to an election by popular vote to be had under present conditions. . .

"When we think of the effort made through all these years [to secure an amendment for the direct election of senators] and of the result, we can see at once the insincerity of those who say, 'Let us wait until we get an amendment to the Constitution.' Methuselah was an infant at the time of his demise compared to the age which the learned advocate of this Fabian policy would attain should he live to see that amendment submitted to the people. . ." Borah was the Sen-

10 *Statesman,* July 8, 1906.

ate leader in the fight which resulted in the submission of this amendment only six years later.

He recalled the fact that Lincoln had been nominated for the Senate by a Republican convention at Springfield and pointed out that Republicans in a number of states were now following the plan used to nominate Lincoln and the plan advocated for Idaho — and Borah.

He then showed how the system of election by the legislature, after nomination by party caucus, took time, sometimes months, from the regular legislative business, how trades were made on appropriations, laws, appointive jobs, and what not, facts perfectly familiar to those who have studied the old system. He was not on such solid ground when he stated that "the legislature is the place where corporate interests can exercise absolute control in the matter of election of United States Senators and that such influences are wholly without power before the people." He continued, "No one would contend for a moment that the State of New York would at any time have dared to put for popular approval either Tom Platt or Chauncey M. Depew. . . Nevertheless they are there, the representatives of the greatest state in the Union, men utterly devoid of character or standing, the truckling representatives of the worst element in American politics. . .

"It has been suggested that we wait until we have a primary election law. This suggestion resembles very much the suggestion that we wait until we have an amendment to the Constitution of the United States. . . If those who say let us wait until we get a law were not trying to thwart every effort to get one, we might consent to wait. . .

"In conclusion I wish to say there may be many reasons why this or that particular person should not be nominated or endorsed for Senator at Pocatello. There may be, and in the minds of some no doubt there are, conclusive reasons why the writer should not be endorsed, but there can be no reason why the Republican party should not take the step in favor of election of a Senator by direct vote of the people and nominate someone. Our party has twice in this State declared in favor of election of Senators by direct vote of the people. Why should it, if sincere, decline to take the first step? It has since defeated the primary election law. Shall we now oppose the convention plan? . . ."

Borah's efforts began to tell after a few weeks and a great many Republican leaders who opposed his plan ceased to make any more objections in public. As for Borah, he declared that if the convention failed to nominate a candidate for the Senate, he would not be a candidate before the legislature the following January. "That matter has been gone over many times with friends who have urged me to change my attitude, but there has been and will be no change. I am always willing to yield on mere matters of policy, but on this matter the course to be pursued is plain, and I believe my friends are all coming to see it that way." [11]

Borah and Brady, his leading opponent for the nomination, made bitter fights in the primaries in nearly every county in the State, but particularly in the south and southeast, Borah for delegates to county conventions who were for nomination by the state convention and Brady for delegates who would vote to adhere to the old legislative caucus plan. The earlier county conventions following the primaries showed that opponents and proponents of the Borah plan were about evenly matched, but later conventions swung decisively for Borah. The Fremont county convention was reported as the most exciting ever held in that part of the State. Borah attended this convention and made a rousing appeal. It voted 77¼ to 66¾ for the Borah plan, and instructed the 36 delegates it selected to attend the state convention to support Borah.[12]

The Fremont convention did not do what every good Republican county convention was supposed to do — it did not endorse the administration of Governor Gooding. There was a strong and probably correct rumor that Gooding and Brady were allied against Borah and that the Borah forces pointedly neglected to endorse Gooding as a warning to him to stop fighting Borah. Counties continued to swing into the Borah column, and the rumor persisted that Gooding and Brady had combined against him. William Schuldt

[11] *Ibid.*, July 16, 1906.
[12] *Tribune*, July 19, 1906.

wired Gooding that the Brady forces were fighting Borah through Gooding and ended with the cryptic words: "Suggest you have this stopped." Gooding replied: "Have wired along lines suggested by you." [13]

In Borah's own county he had no opposition for delegates in the primaries. The county convention instructed its delegates "to vote as a unit in state convention in favor of a resolution providing for the nomination of Senator.

"For this high office, Ada county presents a favorite son in the person of Hon. W. E. Borah. . . We commend him to the convention as the united and unanimous choice of his friends and neighbors who know him best and who have learned thoroughly to appreciate his magnificent equipment for the responsibilities of this great trust." [14]

This county convention "forgot" to endorse Governor Gooding. When the *Statesman* representative asked leaders about this omission they stated that it was an oversight. Borah agreed over long distance telephone that the failure to endorse Gooding was "regrettable." [15] A few other county conventions having failed to commend Gooding, it was fairly plain that if Borah wanted to do so he could prevent him from receiving another nomination for governor.

Despite the fact that, after about July 20, it was perfectly obvious that Borah would have a good majority at the state convention, a few of the later county conventions refused to approve his plan. In Nez Perce, for example, the anti-Borah forces had control and the convention "endorsed and commended and pointed with pride to the magnificent record" made by Senator Heyburn, who hoped that Idaho would never become a "crank state" and ask for such things as tariff reform. But Judge R. S. Anderson of Lewiston wanted to know why the Republicans of his county were so foolish as to "undertake to oppose Mr. Borah, who is recognized as the most able lawyer and orator of Idaho." [16]

The delegates gathered at Pocatello and proceeded to reach agreements on all important matters before they assembled in state convention. The delegates from Kootenai,

[13] *Ibid.*, July 26, 1906.
[14] *Ibid.*, July 27, 1906.
[15] *Statesman*, ed., July 27, 1906.
[16] *Tribune*, July 26 and 27, 1906.

Latah, Idaho, and especially from Nez Perce counties came down fully determined to vote against the convention nomination plan, but they finally yielded in the interest of party harmony. Borah worked with the delegates from the south and Gooding with those from the north, each where he was strong, and it was agreed in caucus (July 31) that Gooding should again be nominated for governor and have the final word on some other names to go on the state ticket, that the convention should nominate a senator, and that Borah should be the nominee. Borah called his delegates together and explained the caucus agreement and said that if any of them thought he had done anything dishonorable he would withdraw from the race.

Brady expressed his satisfaction with the "outcome of the peace negotiations." Judge Beatty, a poor third in the race for Senator, was very bitter. Fifty or sixty delegates of the 399 held a protest meeting, but they could not agree upon a plan of action. The next day the convention nominated Borah for the Senate by acclamation. Thus ended, for the time being, Borah's fight with the Idaho Republican machine, a fight which some of the Idaho papers likened to La Follette's fight in Wisconsin.

THE campaign which followed the nominations need not detain us long. The state Democratic convention met at Coeur d'Alene and, after ousting some Mormon delegates, nominated Senator Dubois to succeed himself. Borah and Dubois, long friends and political co-workers, but having taken different directions politically since 1900, now faced each other as candidates of opposing parties for the United States Senate. They campaigned very much as they had in 1904. Borah praised the Republican record, state and national, and Roosevelt, inveighed against the trusts, and ably argued for a direct primary law for Idaho. Dubois held that the Republican party for which he had worked until 1896 and which had honored him so many times had outlived its usefulness, although he had little to say against Roosevelt. It is not easy to convict Dubois of insincerity in changing parties, for there were many and persistent rumors that McKinley had offered him a place in his cabinet if he would return to the Republican fold and that Roosevelt had held out strong inducements to him as late as 1905. Dubois was in many respects a very lovable man, and he had many friends in Washington.

Dubois laughed at Borah's Republicanism, never allowing anyone to forget that Borah had followed him out of the regular Republican party on the trail of free silver in 1896 and 1898. He said that he was just as good a Republican as Borah. Then Borah asked an audience : "If he is as good

Courtesy of the Idaho Statesman

a Republican as I am, where do you get off? I think it must be some town near Buffalo. (Laughter.) I think perhaps, under these conditions the Democratic battle song in Idaho should be 'Put Me Off at Buffalo.' " [17]

Dubois declared that the only real issue in 1906 was the Mormon question. Since the issue seemed petty to Borah, he gave it less attention than he had given it two years before. Dubois said that he was fighting against polygamy and for decency. "I am honored everywhere that people believe in one wife and the purity of the American home. If I go down to defeat . . . I want the people of Idaho to continue to vote to keep the home pure." [18] He went down to defeat, but for some years Dubois continued to bring the Mormon

[17] *Statesman,* September 15, 1906.
[18] *Tribune,* September 23, 1906.

question into Idaho politics. Democrats became disgusted and nowhere was that disgust better expressed than in the editorials of the Democratic *Tribune* under such titles as "More Polygamy Rot" and "When Will the Mormon Idiocy End?"

From the date of the organization of their Church the Mormons had been off and on a persecuted people. If the leaders sought to influence the rank and file to support a particular party or candidate, what was more logical? Their persecutions naturally built up a strong central organization within the Church and made of them a "clannish" people.

As for Borah's relationship with the Mormons, that is a simple story. His attitude toward them has never changed. In reply to a question asked about them by a Pittsburgh minister, in 1915, he wrote: "No honest, candid, sincere man would for a moment impeach them in their citizenship, their loyalty and devotion to the State, if he knew them as I know them." He praised them for their industry, frugality, and temperance. With reference to the matter of plural marriages, Borah admitted, off the political platform, that there might be some such unions even in Idaho. President Joseph F. Smith of the Mormon Church in a sermon in Salt Lake City, April 6, 1911, deplored the fact that there had been eleven hundred such marriages the year before, and again warned his people that plural marriages had ceased to have the sanction of the Church. While President Smith's sermon technically sustained the charge of Dubois it also illustrated another fact – that the Mormon Church as an organization was acting in good faith upon its promise to stamp out plural marriages. Borah was well toward the head of that tolerant group of people who recognized that a practice of generations could not be reversed without recurrences in sporadic instances. He was satisfied with the pledges and efforts of the Mormon Church.

Borah's spirit of tolerance, which he always insisted came from his father, and his sense of fairness made him strong friends among the Mormons. He was asked to go to Washington as counsel for Senator Smoot in the contest over his seat, and failed to go only because he and the Church could not agree upon the financial value of his legal services. The

Mormons supported Borah politically not because they expected special favors from him, but because they believed he would give them a square deal.

There was one issue that the Republicans presented with some success which they had not had in 1904. That issue was "Law and Order," an issue which had grown out of labor troubles, culminating in the assassination of former Governor Steunenberg. This story is reserved for the next chapter, but it should be stated here that William D. Haywood and others were in an Idaho jail, during the campaign of 1906, awaiting trial for the alleged crime of plotting the murder of Steunenberg.

The whole country got excited about the Haywood case, and, as might be expected, President Roosevelt took a hand in it. About the first of November he sent Secretary of War Taft to Idaho to make some "law and order" speeches. Taft explained that Roosevelt was as indignant at mine owners as he was at miners' unions, since both had been guilty of many acts of violence. This was Borah's position. He never was anything but a friend of organized labor, but he could not condone any kind of murder.

Prosperity, Roosevelt, Borah, "law and order," and *Dubois* gave the Republicans an easy victory in Idaho. When the legislature met, the Senate vote for United States Senator was Borah, 15; Dubois, 6. In the house the vote was Borah, 38; Dubois, 12. "There was no turmoil, no bootlicking, no guerilla warfare, no trades or jobs, no barter or sale of men's honor. There was no excitement. It was as calm a proceeding as a vote to pay a bill to a man who had earned a dollar for his day's work, and they knew the dollar was his. No frills or feathers, no waste of words or money or temper. There were no promises of jobs, no hopes of rewards to come, in the vote as cast. It was the voice of the people of Idaho speaking." [19]

A great reception was given for Borah at the Idanha. "Dress suits jostled coarser garments, cutaways rubbed elbows with well frayed sacks; Paris gowns and home made frocks were in line. . . It was a citizens' reception, and all

[19] *Statesman*, January 16, 1907.

classes took part. Any man, especially a man of the real people, might feel pleased at such an outpouring of enthusiasm. And Mr. Borah was pleased. He showed what he thought of the matter. He appeared without a dress suit. . . He don't really like dress suits, anyway. He is common ; he is of the people." [20]

But Borah was to go through some very strenuous months before he entered upon his duties in the United States Senate in December, 1907.

[20] *Ibid.*

CHAPTER V

DYNAMITE AND POLITICS

IF you ask practically anyone who is over forty years of age and is not a resident of Idaho how Mr. Borah came to be elected Senator, he will tell you that he was a struggling young prosecuting attorney who won fame and a seat in the United States Senate through his successful prosecution of Big Bill Haywood. Yet Borah was never a prosecuting attorney except in a few cases in which the State retained him as special counsel. Furthermore, he was elected to the Senate six months before he assisted as special prosecutor in the Haywood case. And Haywood was acquitted. Borah did win national fame for his part in the prosecution, but Darrow won the case. Yet Borah's part in prosecuting labor leaders for alleged crimes of violence forms a chapter of such interest that it must not be omitted. It carries what might at first appear to be a strange contradiction — that Borah, recognized always, even by Labor itself, as a friend of Labor, should appear as the prosecutor of its leaders.

The trail of labor-capital violence in Idaho began almost with the opening of the rich silver lead mines in northern Idaho in the 'eighties. This area of beautiful wooded hills and narrow valleys is known as the Cœur d'Alenes. Here the struggle continued intermittently until 1899. It ended with the assassination of former Governor Steunenberg at Caldwell in December, 1905, and the trials following from that crime. The history of this struggle cannot be reviewed here. Furthermore, it would be impossible to write an impartial account. Practically all of the sources are grossly prejudiced. Senator Borah is one of two persons with whom I talked who showed a disposition to recognize both sides of the controversy. This fight between the mine operators and the miners was one in which both sides applied the old law of an eye for an eye, a tooth for a tooth, a life for a life.

In 1892 there were riots in the Cœur d'Alenes. The companies' armed guards and non-union men fought the union men. The union men blew up one plant and were ready to blow up others if the non-union workers were not sent away. The union's terms were met, and when the scabs arrived at Lake Cœur d'Alene from the mines, one version is that the union forces drove them up Fourth of July Canyon. Another version is that which is commonly captioned "The Massacre of Fourth of July Canyon," and it is elaborated with such gruesome detail as "they opened the abdomens of their victims and removed the intestines, so that their bodies would not rise to the surface when thrown into the lake."

Following these riots there was relative quiet in the Cœur d'Alenes until 1899, when the question of union recognition brought another clash. The Bunker Hill and Sullivan Mining Company at Wardner was most determined in resisting the claims of the militant locals of the Western Federation of Miners. There was no contest about wages, the rates of $3.00 and $3.50 per day having been agreed upon. The sole question seems to have been that of recognition of the miners' union.

On April 29, several hundred armed men, presumably union men, at the little mining town of Burke, took possession of a train, procured 3000 pounds of dynamite, and forced the train crew to take them to Wardner. There they blew up the Bunker Hill and Sullivan plant and killed one or two persons. They then boarded the stolen train and rode back to Burke.

As the civil authorities of the county were wholly unable to handle the situation and as the greater number of them were in open sympathy with the miners, Governor Steunenberg, himself the holder of a card in the printers' union, declared the area under martial law, and requested Federal troops. When the soldiers arrived, hundreds of union men were arrested and thrown into "bull pens." There was, of course, some injustice and some brutality in such procedure.

The prosecuting attorney of Shoshone County, Mr. H. F. Samuels, was an excellent man but a poor lawyer. As he had many friends among the miners he asked to be freed from the duties of prosecutor. The Governor named James H. Hawley, one of Idaho's best lawyers, and W. E. Borah, fast coming to be recognized as having ability equal to Hawley's, to head the prosecution. Despite his friendship for Labor, Borah was perfectly willing to take this part. He regarded the excesses of the Western Federation of Miners as having no rightful place in the program for Labor's advancement. With him murder was murder whether committed in the "class struggle" or in accomplishing a robbery.

Among those indicted for murder, arson, and conspiracy was Paul Corcoran, secretary of the miners' union at Burke, at which point the train was stolen and converted into the "Dynamite Express." Corcoran had witnesses to testify that he was in Burke while the crime was being enacted at Ward ner. One such witness was a butcher of Burke who said that Corcoran had bought a chicken on that day. Borah had the butcher's book brought into court, and it revealed that the chicken purchase was on another day.

The most dramatic incident of the trial arose from the efforts of the prosecution to prove that Corcoran had actually ridden the stolen train from Wardner back to Burke. A witness who lived not far from the railroad testified that she had recognized Corcoran sitting on the top of a box car, with his legs hanging over the side and a gun across his lap. Some railroad men testified for the defense that no one could have sat in such a position because of the crooked track and the speed of the train. The story of how Attorney Borah rode the same train, sitting in the same position Corcoran was alleged to have held, to prove that it could be done, has been told thousands of times. It was a resourceful act and a courageous one on Borah's part, but some of the stories have the train darting around mountain curves at the reckless rate of fifty or sixty miles per hour. As a matter of fact, Borah and his four riding companions were carried at the rate of some fifteen miles an hour, the rate of speed of the dynamite train, quite fast enough for comfort considering their perch on the box car and the crooked track.

In his closing speech for the prosecution,[1] Borah stated that labor unions were not only desirable but necessary. "But we have now to deal with no such orders. We must fight an organization in which its members drink the blood of their latest victim from the skull of the murdered man.

[1] *Spokesman-Review,* July 27, 1899.

We must fight a union which makes its members social Ishmaelites and drives them from the State to avoid a just punishment. We have to deal with a union which uses the American flag as a mask, and has as its cry 'to hell with America.' " These words constitute Borah's most extreme utterance in the case.

The greater part of his speech he devoted to the evidence tending to prove Corcoran's guilt, not to the miners' union. The speech was forceful but fair to the accused. "It is not necessary for us to prove that Corcoran's was actually the hand that fired the shot which killed James Cheyne. When the Jesse James gang surrounded a town to rob a bank the robber sitting on the hillside holding the horses was no less guilty of murder than the man who actually killed the cashier. If Mr. Corcoran at Burke gathered together that mob and sent it on its mission of crime to Wardner, then he was no less guilty of James Cheyne's death than was Mrs. Botkin of murder when she sent the box of poisoned candy to her sweetheart's wife.

"But we do not merely claim that Corcoran was a member of the conspiracy and therefore liable for the death of Cheyne. We contend, and by our witnesses we have proven that not only did he ride down, armed, on the stolen train, but he was in the crowd that actually shot down the victim in cold blood. We do not claim, but without straining the evidence, we could claim that it was none other than Corcoran himself who fired the shot."

Paul Corcoran was found guilty of murder in the second degree. The Judge could have sentenced him to the penitentiary for life, but Corcoran had a good reputation, a wife, and four children. Consequently he was given seventeen years, which by good behavior he might reduce to ten. Corcoran heard the sentence manfully and left for the penitentiary in good spirits. A year or so later he was pardoned by Governor Hunt. It is very probable that this was a political move to win the miners of the Cœur d'Alenes for the Democratic party, but Corcoran was in many respects a good citizen and deserved clemency.

Mary A. Hutton, in a volume most partial to the miners' cause, has this to say of Borah's part in the Corcoran trial :

"Mr. Borah is called the William Jennings Bryan of Idaho, and is a gentleman of extended popularity. He possesses a master mind, and gave one of the most resourceful and eloquent pleas ever given to a jury in the far West." [2]

As has been intimated, Borah's interest in the Corcoran case was due in no sense to any anti-labor sentiment, for he had none, but solely to his interest in restraining violence of any type. His reaction against another type of lawlessness is well illustrated by his vigorous conduct in preventing a lynching only a few years after he had prosecuted Corcoran. One of the few Negroes in Boise happened to be mascot of the baseball team. After one of the games in Nampa, a railroad town twenty miles from Boise, he shot and severely wounded a policeman, claiming the officer had kicked him off the sidewalk. The Negro was jailed, and the "big, strong men" about Nampa wanted to get him out and lynch him.

The word came to Borah, and he persuaded a train crew to take him at once to Nampa. Besides the crew there were on the train only Borah and Ras Beamer. Ras had been something of a tough character, but he had reformed sufficiently to be made United States Deputy Marshal, yet not so thoroughly that the "he-man" element had lost respect for him. He was tall and powerful and usually got what he went after.

Borah and Ras rushed from the train to the jail. Borah leaped to the steps and shouted, "You should not disgrace this State with a lynching." He was jeered. He tried again, without success. He repeated his effort. The crowd showed signs of yielding, at least to the point of hearing him, for after all Borah was well and favorably known in Nampa. They listened as he told them of the glories of Nampa and the grandeur of Idaho. They made sporadic interruptions when he vigorously outlined the necessity of following orderly processes and questioned the courage of a mob. They showed some concern when he spoke of the risk they were running at the hands of "enough men" (glancing in the direction of the car) he had brought along to protect the Negro. While he was upbraiding the mobsters and at the same time appealing to their sense of fair play, Ras Beamer was getting

[2] *The Coeur d'Alenes* (1900), p. 190.

the jail keys from the constable and unlocking the cell. Presently Ras appeared with the boy. "Stand aside," he commanded, and he took the trembling darky through the crowd to the train.

ON the night of December 30, 1905, another crime of violence, one which shocked the whole country, caused Borah to take another special train at Boise. This time he was in the company of Governor Gooding, with Caldwell as the destination. Here Governor Steunenberg, who had declared martial law in the Cœur d'Alenes in 1899, had lived after his retirement from office a year later, and here he had just been blown to pieces by a bomb attached to his front gate.

Borah delivered the eulogy at his friend's funeral. "In the midst of this awful tragedy, let us strive to be just. This crime when fastened upon its author will place him or them beyond the pale of human forgiveness or pity. Therefore, let us not place it unjustly or upon suspicion."

A real-estate man in Caldwell told Borah and others to check up on a man registered at the hotel under the name of "Hogan." Borah looked him over and decided that if he were not the man who had committed the murder he was the sort of fellow who would. When a group walked down to the Steunenberg residence the next morning, "Hogan" followed, walking alone. A former Lieutenant Governor of Idaho broke into his room and found dynamite, lead, and other materials for making bombs. "Hogan" was arrested and grilled. He gave his name as Harry Orchard and finally made a most remarkable confession.

He said he had been employed over a period of years by Haywood, Moyer, and Pettibone, but especially by Haywood, all of the Western Federation of Miners, to murder mining bosses and others who happened to be enemies of the Federation. The twenty-six murders to which he confessed had all been planned by these men. He was the killer, not the planner. About the time of this confession Orchard became religious.

The problem then was to get the men who were the brains of the crime from Denver, Colorado, to Idaho, where they could be put on trial. It was not a simple problem, for

Haywood and the others implicated were not in Idaho when the crime was committed and they were therefore not fugitives from Idaho justice. But perhaps a way could be found. First, it was necessary to keep Orchard's confessions secret. Idaho authorities went to Colorado with the evidence against Haywood and his associates and a request from Governor Gooding for their extradition. The Governor of Colorado was more than glad to coöperate, and in order to prevent the accused from resisting extradition by *habeas corpus* proceedings, the method by which alleged fugitives regularly contest the legality of such requests, the men were arrested one night and put on a train the next morning and sent to Idaho. There they remained in prison for eighteen months while preparations for their historic trial were under way.

It should be stated here that Borah did not come in as one of the lawyers for the prosecution until after the accused men had been brought to Idaho. The case offered him no financial inducement, and there was the danger that his participation in it would antagonize Labor and thus weaken him in his campaign, now getting under way, for the United States Senate. But certain friends, particularly members of the Steunenberg family, persuaded him to enter the case as a civic duty.

The actual trial did not take place until the summer of 1907. From the early spring of 1906 until after the November election, which assured Borah a seat in the Senate, the legality of the manner in which the men had been forcibly taken from Colorado was before the courts. In December, the Supreme Court of the United States decided (Pettibone v. Nichols, 203 U.S. 192, 205) that "No obligation was imposed . . . upon the agent of Idaho to so time the arrest of the petitioner and so conduct his deportation from Colorado, as to afford him a convenient opportunity, before some judicial tribunal sitting in Colorado, to test the question whether he was a fugitive from justice." The Court added, significantly, that "In England, in the case of one arrested for the purpose of deporting him to another country, it is provided that there shall be no surrender of the accused to the demanding country until after the expiration of a specific time from the arrest, during which period the prisoner has an opportunity to institute *habeas corpus* proceedings. There is no similar act of Congress in respect of a person arrested in one of the States of the Union as a fugitive from the justice of another State."

In his dissenting opinion, Justice McKenna said, "Kidnaping is a crime, pure and simple. . . All of the officers of the law are supposed to be on guard against it. . . But how is it when the law becomes the kidnaper, when the officers of the law, using its forms and exerting its power, become abductors? . . . The foundation of extradition between the states is that the accused should be a fugitive from justice from the demanding state, and he may challenge the fact by *habeas corpus* immediately upon his arrest." Borah admits that the manner in which the accused men were snatched out of Colorado was unfair; but he maintains that it was not illegal.

Nearly everyone took sides on the Haywood case. Large sums of money were raised for the defense. President Roosevelt denounced Moyer, Haywood, and E. H. Harriman, a capitalist, as "undesirable citizens." Haywood replied from his prison that the President ought to know he was assumed to be innocent until proven guilty. Maxim Gorky, visiting in the United States, wired his greetings to the famous prisoners in Caldwell jail, and was forced to leave the country *because he had a common law wife*. Conservative newspapers denounced the criminal dynamiters who posed as friends of Labor, and Debs in the *Appeal to Reason* ran the gamut of extreme emotions from Y to Z. There were monster proletarian demonstrations in the cities, and Debs suggested that their armies march to Idaho and free those for whom capital had already erected the scaffold. But calmer men and women, including Mrs. Debs, thought it wiser to leave the matter to Clarence Darrow, who, now in his prime, had traveled through a desert waste and arrived at what he was pleased to call "the Athens of the Sage-Brush" – Boise, Idaho.

From all over the country, and even from abroad, hundreds of newspaper reporters, special writers, and photographers gathered in Boise. Thither came representatives of employers' associations, labor leaders, idealists, young lawyers who wanted to see a battle of the century, and people on vacation. But the inhabitants of Boise and of the fruitful territory spreading toward the north were hardly more excited about the trial, aside from the dramatic interest it offered, than were people in New York, Chicago, and Washington. Idahoans felt that there might be more assassinations before the trial ended, but they were calm. The pioneers knew no hysteria.

The trial started on May 9, and lasted until July 28. James H. Hawley, soon to be elected Governor, and Senator-elect Borah were the stars for the prosecution. Harry Orchard was their star witness. But under the Idaho statute the testimony of a witness who had turned state's evidence was not sufficient for a conviction unless such testimony was corroborated by another witness. The prosecution thought it had such a witness in Steve Adams, who at one time was supposed to have made a confession corroborating Orchard's story. But the defense lawyers stiffened Adams' backbone so that he refused to testify. The State's case was thus considerably weakened.

Darrow spoke for eleven hours in his concluding speech. He spoke not so much for Haywood as for the cause he represented. "Wherever men have looked upward and onward, forgotten their selfishness, struggled for humanity, worked for the poor and the weak, they have been sacrificed. . . If at the behest of this mob, you should kill Bill Haywood, he is mortal, he will die, and I want to say to you that a million men will take up the banner of labor at the open grave where Haywood lays it down. . ." Darrow said he had never had a better opportunity for a courtroom speech, and that when he had finished he was satisfied with his effort. Haywood thought it was superb.

Borah followed in the closing argument for the State. "His presentation of that side was forcible and scholarly," says Darrow.[3] "It was worked out with care and understanding. Few men that I ever met in a courtroom contribute so much industry, learning, and natural ability as Mr. Borah."

[3] *The Story of My Life* (1932), p. 153. Mr. Darrow has several good chapters on this case. See also Louis Adamic's *Dynamite,* Bill Haywood's *Book,* and various magazine articles of 1906 and 1907.

Courtesy of the Idaho Statesman

The Senator emphasized the facts that the Western Federation of Miners was not on trial, and that Haywood should not be convicted because of his general reputation in Colorado. He stated that the only question was – Had Haywood participated in a conspiracy to murder Governor Steunenberg? There was no personal arraignment of Haywood. Borah simply marshaled the evidence presented by the prosecution. "Terrific, crushing, destroying," wrote O. K. Davis,[4] "these are the words that come nearest to describing the tremendous power of the man in argument." Davis was swept off his feet with Borah's wonderful gift of speech and the astonishing rapidity of his flow of words, which always went straight to the mark. "Endowed with the highest dramatic powers, he seizes unerringly the telling point, rushes along with tremendous energy and deadly precision to the climax, and with a burst of eloquence drives home and clinches his conclusion."

"Well, I have heard the best of them in the country," said Haywood, "but Borah beats them all." Perhaps Haywood was not thinking so much of Borah's industry, learning, and ability as a lawyer. Perhaps he was thinking of Borah the

[4] *The New York Times,* July 27, 1907.

Fair. "When," he may have mused, "until this trial, has a leader of a hated cause been tried for murder that he was not prosecuted for leading the cause, and usually convicted for leading it? Borah was fair. He stuck to the indictment for murder. He did not try to convict me by arousing prejudice against the cause I lead."

This was indeed a most remarkable trial of its kind. Not only was the prosecution considerate, but the Judge was fair. Darrow made this statement. It is true that Judge Fremont Wood's career was practically ruined in Idaho after Haywood was acquitted. There was some nasty talk to the effect that he had been unduly influenced for the accused because his former law partner had been of defense counsel, but Borah always stoutly maintained that Judge Wood presided with strict impartiality.

The trial was remarkable in that the jury brought in a verdict of acquittal. It has been said that the jurors returned such a verdict in fear of their lives. Possibly this is true. When the trial had been in progress for about two months, when the jury had heard story after story of how the Federation of Miners had dynamited its enemies, a discharge of a gun at Fort Boise caused half of the jurors to jump out of their chairs. One juror, whom Borah had fought to keep on the list because he knew him for a man of courage, told the Senator a few months later that he "had the guts" to risk his own life in voting for a conviction but that he had a wife and children to think of. However, if all the jurors had believed that Haywood was guilty of murder, it seems extremely likely that some of them would have reported inability to agree. My own opinion is that at least some members of the jury realized with the Judge and the prosecution, that Haywood was being tried only for murder, and they were not convinced that he was guilty.

During this trial, as was the case in the trial in the Cœur d'Alenes in 1899, Borah was frequently threatened with violence. The notes read: "We'll get you"; "You will not get to court tomorrow"; "We let Steunenberg live six years"; and so on. He read a few at first, and then told his secretary not to bring them to his desk. He did not care for a bodyguard, for that would only invite attention to his importance.

He did not go armed, for he had sense enough to know that this was no protection against an assassin. Always courageous, something of a fatalist, too, Borah probably thought very little about any personal risks he might be running in prosecuting these cases.

Concluding the Haywood case, one might say that it was in most respects a credit to Idaho. Compare this trial in a frontier commonwealth with some other state trials — the anarchists' trial in Illinois, the Mooney-Billings trial in California, and the Sacco-Vanzetti trial in Massachusetts, to mention just three other cases!

THE general public is much less familiar with the story of Borah's own indictment and trial than it is with the Haywood story. Yet it is hardly less interesting.

In March, 1907, Senator Borah and a number of officers of the Barber Lumber Company were indicted by a Federal grand jury for timber frauds. It seems that the Company had engaged men to enter public land, put up the price of the land for them, paid them an extra sum, and had taken assignment of the land to itself. The Senator was attorney for the Company and it was alleged that he was party to the crime in that these assignments had passed through his hands.

It has been said that this timber fraud indictment was the plan of the Haywood defense to weaken Borah in the murder trial which took place soon after Borah's indictment. There is no truth to this report. Darrow did tell Borah later that the Haywood defense felt some satisfaction over the indictment, for it had reason to think that such a charge would embarrass the Senator in his prosecution of Haywood. But Borah was not visibly embarrassed or weakened. He was the only member of the prosecution who did not break down in the course of the trial.

The men behind Borah's indictment were the leaders of the Republican party machine in Idaho. Some of these had aspired to the place in the Senate to which Borah had just been elected by the Idaho Legislature. Others disliked him for temperamental reasons. Nearly all of them were jealous of him. All of them had learned what the country was to learn much later — that Borah was a Lone Wolf and would not run with the pack.

Whatever one may think of the ethics of the practice of the Barber Lumber Company, and the gifted editor of the Portland *Oregonian* did not hesitate to condemn the acts of the Company and its attorney,[5] the hypocrisy of the Republican machine in bringing about the indictment is manifest.

The indictment was carefully drawn, carefully drawn to reveal a technical flaw on its face. It was the great hope of its authors that Borah would take advantage of this flaw and avoid standing trial, thus damaging his reputation. If the Senator neglected to take advantage of the flaw, his enemies could hope to do no more than smear him at the trial. No one thought he could be convicted.

A friend in the northern part of the State, Avery C. Moore of Kootenai, predicted that Borah would not only be acquitted, but that he would be in the Senate the rest of his life and achieve a fame equal to that won by Clay and Webster.

Clarence Darrow said: "I firmly believe Senator W. E. Borah to be guiltless of complicity in Idaho timber frauds with which he is charged. . . I have been convinced of the integrity and enormous mental capacity of the Senator."

The Senator refused to take advantage of any technicality, but with several of his enemies in charge of the enforcement of Federal law in Idaho he was not so sure he could get a fair trial. The manner in which he made a fair trial reasonably certain brings out some interesting relationships.

In the Senator's old correspondence files in the penthouse of the Senate Office Building, there is a letter from William Allen White to his "Dear Billy Borah." It was written just after Borah had announced, in 1917, that he would not stand for reëlection to the Senate. White expressed his great regret at Borah's decision and added: "I have always felt that the best single day's work I ever did in my life, was that day I put in for you down at Oyster Bay." Some correspondence with Mr. White brought the explanation of what this day's work was.

This old classmate of Borah's at the University of Kansas,

5 Editorials from October 1 to 8, 1907.

one who had occasionally succeeded in making the serious Borah laugh at his antics, was at Manitou, Colorado, where he was writing *A Certain Rich Man.* "Will" and "Billy" were now good friends. Ten years before, White had met Roosevelt. They became friends at once, and White ceased being a reactionary Republican. Immediately after the Haywood trial Borah went to Manitou and asked White to go to Washington and request President Roosevelt to send from the Department of Justice a special prosecutor for Borah's timber fraud trial. The President arranged for a meeting at Oyster Bay.

Senator Spooner, of Wisconsin, also an attorney for the Barber Lumber Company, met White in New York. They discussed some of the legal points preparatory to White's conference with the President. White went on to Oyster Bay to have lunch with the President and Attorney-General Bonaparte. A writer of sea stories was also present. White presented the case as Borah saw it and made the request which Borah suggested. It seemed entirely reasonable to the President that the Senator-elect should be given every facility for a speedy and fair trial. He was therefore more than willing to send a special prosecutor to Idaho.

Borah's trial opened on September 23 and lasted for ten days. Practically the entire time was taken up by the prosecution. Counsel for the defense, our old friend James H. Hawley, did not take the trouble to cross-examine the witnesses. After this had gone on for about a week, the Judge said : "Great latitude has been allowed here. It is now time for the court to control the order of the testimony. I will let you finish with the one witness on the stand and then I shall call for your proofs connecting the defendant on trial." The only witness the defense offered was Borah. The prosecution took nearly two hours to sum up the case. The defense simply said, "We submit the case, your honor." The jury was out fourteen minutes. Its verdict was "Not guilty."

There was a great celebration in Boise. The Portland *Oregonian,* which had looked upon the ethics of the timber transactions with grave disfavor, stated (October 3) that it should be a matter of general rejoicing "that one United

States Senator, of all who have been put on trial, has been acquitted. On the testimony the verdict was right."

The Government later brought civil suit to cancel the titles to the lands in question on the ground of fraud and conspiracy to defraud. The court found that there was no fraud and no conspiracy to defraud. Consequently, the Senator was doubly vindicated. Borah's refusal to take advantage of technicalities in order to avoid trial, the failure of the prosecution to make a case against him, and his defense tactics should be sufficient to convince the skeptical of his innocence.

On June 15, 1908, President Roosevelt removed the District Attorney and the Marshal, the Federal officials who were responsible for the "persecution" of Borah. In naming their successors the President relied solely upon the recommendations of the vindicated Senator.

It seems appropriate to conclude this chapter with a letter Borah wrote White in 1935: "Will, in all the vicissitudes of the last forty years, there has been laid up in my memory an affectionate and unselfish act upon your part which will never be forgotten as long as I live. In a crucial situation you came effectively to my support. It was of tremendous moment to me at the time and it had much to do with my entire work thereafter. I have never said a great deal about it to you and I have sometimes wondered if you knew how much I appreciated it. But I did appreciate it and I do still think of it beyond any words of mine to express."

CHAPTER VI

IDAHO'S DIVIDENDS

Borah went to the Senate at exactly the right time. Had he been elected in 1903 he would have been absolutely dependent upon his salary. The four years that elapsed until he was elected were the most profitable ones of his law practice, and he went to Washington with approximately a hundred thousand dollars.

In the second place, he took his seat at the right age. He was old enough for mature statesmanship but he was not by any means old enough to look upon the Senate as a place of honorable retirement for a veteran lawyer. Furthermore, he had not served men of wealth and corporations long enough to have the notion that their interests and the public interests were identical.

In the third place, he was fortunate in going to Washington while Theodore Roosevelt was President. They were friends from the first. Each regarded the other as a fighter and a man of courage. They could agree on nearly every subject and they could disagree on the others without irritation. Borah spoke frankly to Roosevelt. He told him what uncomplimentary things he thought of one of his favorites in the Department of Justice. He disagreed with the President on his ship-building program, stating that there was no cause for preparing for war with Japan.

Another disagreement between Roosevelt and Borah arose over the rights of settlers on irrigated lands. The President's Secretary of the Interior, Mr. Garfield, had ordered settlers who could not pay their water rent off the irrigated lands in Idaho. Borah went to the Secretary, who said he could not cancel the order. Then he went to the President, and as soon as the Senator saw him he knew that Garfield had already called him. "I'll have to stand back of my Secretary," said Roosevelt. To which Borah replied : "Well, I am going to wire my people to resist being put off their land, even with rifles." Roosevelt then called the Secretary and asked him not to put the order into effect until they had further conferences. The President and the Senator understood each other thoroughly. Borah could coöperate with Roosevelt, despite occasional differences, to a degree he never reached in working with any other President.

In the fourth place, Borah took his oath of office at a time when he was in tune with growing political sentiment in the country. The progressive era was dawning. By his own test of what constituted Republicanism Borah was always a Republican, but he was usually progressive and sometimes insurgent. The measures he championed during his first term marked him out as a leader in this new era of liberalism (Chapter VII).

To be sure, in 1907, the Senate was still largely the Senate of Aldrich and Penrose. That was to the advantage of Idaho's Junior Senator; for the statesmen who lead the popular cause before major victories are won receive more popular acclaim than those who hold the high places after the cause has triumphed. Borah was fortunate, then, in coming to the Senate in the springtime of the progressive movement, when Senators Beveridge, Cummins, Dolliver, La Follette, and others of their group were growing in popular favor.

In the fifth place, Borah was fortunate in that Senator Aldrich had misconceived his real character. When the Senate Boss had checked up on the Boise lawyer, he had found that Borah had probably the best practice of any lawyer in the Northwest and that he was counsel for leading banks and great lumber companies. This was enough to convince Aldrich that Borah would make a safe and sane Senator. But there was even more in Borah's favor—he had taken time from his profitable corporation practice to prosecute militant labor leaders. Consequently, the Senator from Rhode Island gave the Idahoan some very good committee assignments. Borah also drew an assignment to the Committee on Education and Labor, an unimportant committee on which Aldrich was sure he would do nothing rash and almost equally certain he would do nothing at all. Borah's achievements on this committee (Chapter VII) were not at all in accord with Aldrich's ideas.

Perhaps it might be said that Borah reaped certain advantages by the contrast he presented to his colleague, Weldon B. Heyburn, who had defeated Borah in the Senate fight in the Republican legislative caucus in 1903. Both were lawyers by profession, and both were by temperament honest and industrious. Furthermore, they had about the same theory of their duties in the Senate — that they represented the State with their conscience and talent, thus justifying an occasional vote contrary to the popular will, and that they represented the United States as well as Idaho. There the common characteristics ended. Heyburn was an ultra-conservative Quaker Republican of the Joe Grundy type. In fact, Heyburn was born and reared in Pennsylvania. He said that the men in the press gallery of the Senate should consider themselves as guests and that it was entirely unbecoming of them to criticize the Senate and make fun of Senators. He was opposed to all progressive measures, including, of course, the amendment for the direct election of Senators. Liberals in Idaho hoped that Heyburn would live long — long enough to see the direct election amendment in the Constitution and to learn just what the Idaho electorate, acting under that amendment, thought of him.

Representing a school of political and economic theory that was becoming increasingly unpopular and having temperamental traits that sometimes made him ridiculous, Heyburn was very unpopular with the masses and in fairness to him it must be said that he was seldom judged according to his real worth. Even the considerate Borah could not always resist the temptation to tease his colleague in the Senate Chamber.

Riding the crest of the progressive wave, very much a man of the people, Borah, in contrast to his colleague, was the ideal of the masses of his State and popular throughout the country, even in the South. After Borah had been in the Senate a few years, the Senior Senator from Idaho became "the other Senator from Idaho."

The Junior Senator from Idaho did not plunge immediately into participation in debate on the floor of the Senate. Nor did he enter into the social life of the Capital. He continued the studious habits he had formed long ago. Always a student of history and government, he intensified his studies in these fields. He spent no time whatever *acting* the part of a United States Senator. The time not spent in the Senate Chamber he divided almost exclusively between his two workshops, his study at home and his study in the Senate Office Building. After thirty years in the Senate he had not changed this habit of reading and studying. No one can hope to have any sort of understanding or appreciation of Borah who fails to take note of the fact that he has been first, last, and all of the time a reader and student.

BORAH had little to say during his first session. During the first few months he occasionally made a remark or asked a question in the way of "finding the range" in Senate debate, but he showed a restraint sufficient to satisfy the convention that a new Senator should hear rather than be heard.

It is of some interest to note that in this first session Borah introduced his favorite bill which would prohibit members of Congress from practising before the Federal courts in cases in which the United States is a party. The existing law prohibited members of Congress from practising before the Departments. The new Senator thought (and he has never changed his opinion on this point) that in comparison it was worse for a member to practise in the Federal courts than it was to practise before the Departments. It was not merely the inconsistency of a member of Congress opposing in court a statute he had helped enact into law. The important consideration was that a congressman who has a retainer with a firm is expected by that firm *to help it in legislation.* When the firm goes to such a man about a bill before Congress, it goes to him expecting special treatment. It goes to him with the expectation of profiting by the lawyer-client relationship, the closest of business relationships. The Senator felt that congressmen would not be human if they were not influenced to the detriment of the public by this relationship.

Why, asked the Senator, should firms be paying fancy retainer fees to members of Congress who were notoriously poor lawyers? How did it happen that men who had never practised law were able to find clients after their election to Congress? Borah was sure that fees were paid such men for their legislative influence and not for their ability as attorneys.

Although there was some favorable press reaction to

Borah's proposed legislation, it was not as strongly favorable as might have been expected. The great Webster had practised law while a Senator and so had practically all other lawyer-Senators. If the practice of law in cases in which the United States had an interest was incompatible with the duties of a member of Congress, it seemed strange that some high-minded congressman had not pointed it out long before. At least, this seems to have been the general conclusion. In the Senate, the proposal naturally met with a cold reception.

But Borah's observations and experiences only strengthened his convictions that such legislation was needed and he reintroduced his bill from time to time.

Twenty years after he first introduced his bill a former client sent a representative to Washington to solicit Borah's vote for a particular tariff. The Senator voted against it. A few weeks later he met his old client in the lobby of an eastern hotel. He opened with, "I am opposed to everything you do in the Senate."

The Senator remarked in the same vein : "I take that as a testimonial that I have been right most of the time."

"Your colleague, Senator Thomas, is worth ten times as much to Idaho as you are," continued the disgruntled business man.

"You certainly find me in accord with you there," replied the Senator. "But come to the point. Why don't you say you are angry with me because I voted against that tariff you wanted ?"

The gentleman admitted that that was it.

But Borah was not through yet. "Why don't you come still closer to the point and say that you are angry because you think that as a former attorney of yours I should have considered your interest and voted for the tariff ?"

On April 17, 1934, Borah's bill was actually taken up in the Senate. The vote for taking it up was 31 to 31, but the Vice-President impishly cast the deciding vote for the affirmative. The bill was not considered at length, however, and even Senator Long, who showed some signs of wanting to consider Borah his political uncle, was recorded in the opposition. The Dean of the Senate still hopes to live to see his bill pass that body.

There are those who say that Borah never follows through, that he takes up issues and drops them, forgets them. More will be said on this point later, but this seems to be an appropriate place to record that before he had been two months in the Senate he introduced and argued for a bill he is still sponsoring.

There is a story that Senator Aldrich once tried to have pressure brought upon Borah through his leading clients in Idaho, and found to his great surprise that the Idaho Senator had given up his law practice upon entering the Senate. In reply to a question asked him at Cul de Sac while campaigning in 1906, Borah had declared his purpose to cease the practice of law if elected.

The Senator considered that even practice in the State courts was incompatible with his position as Senator. Both were perfectly honorable; they were simply mutually inconsistent. Besides, he soon decided that one job was enough — that he could not take care of one without slighting the other. He chose the career in the Senate. Only once was Borah about to break his pledge and take a law case. This was in the suit of the Associated Press v. International News Service (1918). Because he was particularly interested in this case, he at one time agreed to join Samuel Untermyer and argue the case for Mr. Hearst in the Supreme Court. However, he later asked to be relieved of his promise.

The offer of a retainer by a large business concern in New York he considered only until he had the answer to this question: "Suppose I have information, which I have acquired as a Senator, concerning prospective legislation of interest to your company, would I be expected to divulge it to the company?" The answer was a gentle "yes." The Senator declined the retainer.

Although Borah practised no more law he continued to be a lawyer. The people, the inarticulate masses, were his clients. As a lawyer he had seen that business was never without an advocate because it could find the price to retain the best legal talent. The people had few advocates. He was proud to be one of them. It will aid materially in understanding Borah's career in the Senate if we consider him as an advocate, an advocate for those in the lower economic strata, an advocate for free speech for despised minorities, an advocate of the recognition of Soviet Russia, an advocate of justice for Mexico, an advocate for the plain people (as he saw it) in the League of Nations and World Court fights. This is another key to an understanding of the Senator's career.

FITTINGLY enough, the Senator's first important speech was a lawyer's plea *par excellence.* On August 13, 1906, there had been some rioting by Negro troops at Brownsville, Texas. A number of them had been disciplined and nearly everybody in the country had a decided opinion on the matter. It was generally agreed from the President down that the soldiers had been justly punished, but some Old Guard Republicans were in a panic for fear of losing the Negro vote. Consequently, the question of whether the Negro soldiers had been too severely dealt with was dragged into the Senate from time to time. Senator Foraker had just reopened the question, much to the President's annoyance. Roosevelt asked Borah to review the case in a speech in the Senate, justifying the action taken against the Negroes. He said he wanted Borah to do it because a speech from a new Senator on the subject would bring more publicity.

Borah's speech was a careful and critical summary of the evidence in the case. Evidence was always one of his specialties in law and he performed this task in a masterly manner. His conclusion was that the evidence proved guilt and that the punishment had been just.

In the Senator's scrap book of the period is pasted an article by Savoyard in the Washington *Post,* under date of December 2, 1907. "Solomon admitted that there were three things too wonderful for his intellectuals ; yea, four for which he knew not : the way of an eagle in the air, the way of a serpent on a rock, the way of a ship in the midst of the sea, and one other that it is not now absolutely necessary to recall. It is possible, barely possible, that if Solomon had been an American and had lived in our day he would have understood the way of the G.O.P. with a nigger, and here is how he would have interpreted it: 'Such is the way of an adulterous woman; she eateth and wipeth her mouth, and saith, I have done no wickedness.'"

It may have been that the Senator had some such matter in mind when in his concluding sentence he said: "I can not imagine a more cowardly act, a more pusillanimous act upon the part of a great party than to undertake to connive at a crime so thoroughly proved as this because of anticipated political exigencies." [1]

Borah was congratulated right and left. Senator Lodge, who was a member of the military committee which investigated the Brownsville affair and who had heard all the evidence, said Borah brought out two strong points he had overlooked. Senator Knox, often rated the leading lawyer of the Senate, congratulated Borah upon the "perfect" legal trend of his argument. Even Foraker said it was "a great speech." Senator Bacon of Georgia, the brightest legal light on the Democratic side, remarked: "I do not know whether you are a statesman or not, but you are a lawyer." [2] Incidentally, this speech pleased the South and it marks the beginning of Borah's popularity there, a popularity in which he has never had a rival among Republican leaders, with the possible exception of Hoover, whom he, more than anyone else, popularized in that section for a brief period.

Before the national conventions of 1908 met, Borah was recognized as more than just a new Senator from the West, and before the campaigns of that year were over he was recognized as one of the chief Republican assets on the stump. Borah was for Taft from the beginning because he thought he would carry out Roosevelt's policies. For Taft's running mate he much preferred Senator Cummins to Sherman, who received the nomination. Borah was booked for several speeches in New England and he made a decided hit at the Republican round-up at Point of Pines (September 14), where he declared: "Bryan is the greatest living authority on things that never happen." A heckler asked him the

[1] *Congressional Record,* April 20, 1908, p. 4970.
[2] *Statesman,* April 21, 1908.

difference between Republican hard times and Democratic hard times. The Senator's audience was well satisfied with his reply, which was : "One is a reality and the other only a fiction of your mind."

From the East Borah was sent to Indiana, Illinois, and Wisconsin. He made a good impression with his speeches at Northwestern University and the University of Wisconsin, perhaps a much better impression than he made in the German communities of Wisconsin when he was campaigning for La Follette's return to the Senate a few years later. In this latter campaign the teetotaling Senator found that the custom was to go to saloons after the meetings. The local politicians would politely wait for Borah to place his order. Invariably it was for a soft drink. The politicians thought that good form required that they follow suit. The eye-witness who relates this incident was not convinced that the Idaho Senator was any particular help to La Follette.

In the 1908 campaign Borah made speeches also in Kansas, Colorado, and Utah. Back in Idaho, he gave a good strong endorsement of the Republican ticket, national and state, and put in some good licks for the enactment of a state direct primary law. After the election he received a letter from the Chairman of the State Central Committee reading, in part, as follows : "I wish you to know that the loyal Republicans of the State fully understand that no small part of our victory is due to your efforts in the field. . ."

Even this early in Borah's career in the Senate the Democrats of Idaho were showing a very decided interest in him, and often crowded Republicans out of their seats at his meetings. From first to last Borah has had as many friends in one party as in the other.

In the State campaign two years later Borah again took a prominent part. True, he talked a great deal of national questions, such as the income tax, but he took time also for state issues and candidates. His good Republicanism was manifest when he came out in support of Governor Brady, who had had a land scandal in his administration, against his old Democratic friend James H. Hawley whom he "loved, honored, and respected." There is no truth in the statement that Borah has never aided his party in Idaho. It is true, however, that he has refused to aid it when its actions were clearly venal or when it declared for a policy absolutely contrary to Borah's public declaration.

In 1934, when Senator Borah was doing his level best to help the Republican candidates for Congress and State offices, he stated that a Democratic candidate for Congress from one of the Idaho districts was unfit to sit in Congress because of his position on Idaho beet sugar. The Democratic candidate's reply was that it mattered not if he failed of election, since he had succeeded in getting the great Borah to take his eyes off Russia, the Polish corridor, and Irak long enough to take a glance at Idaho. This was considered a clever retort, a neat rebuke, even by a great many Republicans, for the general opinion is that Borah has given Idaho but a little corner in his program in the Senate.

But, notwithstanding his interest in national and international affairs, there is rather abundant evidence to prove that he has, even while chairman of the Committee on Foreign Relations, found time to look after the interests of his own State.

During his first term he took a very lively part in four issues which vitally concerned the people of Idaho and the West generally. These issues were: conservation, reclamation, homesteading, and reciprocity.

In 1910 more than half the area of Idaho was included in various types of United States reserves. The total forest reservation was larger than the State of South Carolina; the coal reservation larger than Maryland; the railroad reservation equal to the area of Connecticut; and the phosphate lands reserved occupied a larger area than Rhode Island. There were a few other types of reserves making the total reserved areas almost equal to the area of New York State.

At that time the people of Idaho were somewhat restive under this conservation system. Like the great majority of Americans in other states, they wanted to see their communities grow. They wanted more settlers on the land, more lumber mills on their streams, and more mines in their hills. Some of their leading newspapers, but not all of them, carried such headlines as, "ROOSEVELT POLICIES RE-

DUCE OIL AND COAL PRODUCTION ONE-THIRD" and "PINCHOT BLIGHT ON U.S. MINING," and glowed in editorial satisfaction over the "GROWING REVOLT AGAINST PINCHOT." [3]

One of the first problems to which Borah turned his attention as Senator was this problem of conservation. His first utterances on the subject indicate some impatience with the whole system, but he soon declared that he was a firm believer in conservation and was opposed only to inefficiency and waste in the name of conservation. Incidentally, this is one of the few issues on which Borah and his colleague agreed whole-heartedly. In their criticisms of the administration of the conservation laws they frequently found opposition from Senator Smoot, one of the strongest conservationists of the West.

While Borah made a number of speeches in the Senate indicating his position on conservation, his vigorous address (January 4, 1911) before the Brooklyn Institute of Fine Arts gives a very satisfactory summary of his conception of true conservation.

First, he sought to impress his audience with the character of the Western settlers. "The criminal does not seek the desert and tie himself to a barren tract of land for five years — the criminal hunts for New York and Brooklyn, where the job is easy and where, if successful, he can become a great political power. . . The sturdiest, most home-loving people in the country today are found in the great north-western states. . ."

Did the West believe in conservation? "The vast majority of our people accept in full faith all the underlying principles of the great movement. . . The West, in my opinion, will gladly favor any policy which will prevent waste of these resources, their extravagant exploitation or which will prevent their being gathered into the hands of a few monopolists. . ."

But "the present system for want of practical application of sane principles is one of waste and one entirely to the benefit of monopolists. Mind you, I do not say this is intentionally so. . . But I do say without fear of successful contradiction that there should be many changes in the pres-

[3] *Tribune,* September 26 and 27, 1910.

ent policy, in order to prevent waste and extravagance, in order to serve the small man and not favor the monopolist."

An outstanding example of this waste : "There are at least 3,000,000 acres of lands in the forest reserves in my State which are as good agricultural lands as are now untaken. . . These lands can serve no good purpose in the reserves and it is a waste to withhold them from production. . . What is true of Idaho is true in other states to an even larger degree. . ."

But is it not possible for homesteaders to take up agricultural land in the forest reserves? "Yes, under the law he may. But under the rules and regulations of the Department he cannot as a practical proposition. . . If I say to you that if you go upon that land and work upon it for two years and if I like your work I will give it to you, you will not go unless you are blessed with far more credulity as to human nature than most people are. Especially you will not go if you know I am not going to give it to you if I can avoid it when the question of avoidance rests solely within my own discretion. That is the effect of these rules and regulations. . ."

Then the Senator objected to making the natural resources of the West a source of revenue for the national treasury. He held that the West was thus being taxed for the benefit of the East. In a speech in the Senate [4] a few months before, he had argued at some length that the State was entitled to the benefits of its natural resources. He cited Clay, Benton, and others as authorities for the proposition that lands within a state were for the benefit of the people of that state and should be administered with that in view.

Borah has always been a Jeffersonian on the matter of local self-government. He has always been opposed to "bureaucrats" in Washington or from Washington regulating the local affairs of the people in the states. He has been opposed to it, if for no other reason, because it weakens the fiber of the people. In the matter of conservation he felt that the people of the several states could conserve many of their resources much better than could the national government. This government, he thought, was conserving them for decay

[4] *Record,* June 20, 1910, p. 8509.

and retrogression. For example, he said:[5] "I believed in the regulation and control of power plants for the development of our power sites, and the only question which I desire to present is the question which sovereignty shall do the work. . . The state alone, in my judgment, can deal properly with the subject-matter both as a practical proposition and as a legal proposition." Perhaps this was true with reference to this particular matter. Perhaps the Senator was correct in reaching a conclusion favorable to the states in other conservation questions. But there were many wise men who did not share the Senator's faith in the willingness and capacity of the states to conserve their natural resources. They cited the examples of waste on the part of the older states to prove their point. Indeed, the Senator himself, in his Brooklyn speech, had demonstrated the hopeless failure of the State of New York to conserve her agricultural lands.

At any rate, opinion in the West was generally on Borah's side, and deplored with him the "hounding" of Ballinger from public life.[6] The Senator's efforts were not crowned with any great success, although from time to time some agricultural lands in the forest reserves were restored to settlement. In May, 1910, about 115,000 acres, more than half of them in Idaho, were so restored.

"Borah is a Republican," read an editorial in the Democratic Caldwell *News*. "If we did not feel that Borah is doing good work for his constituents" in trying to keep the country open to settlers, "we would not use these columns to commend and endorse his work."[7]

At the time Borah went to the Senate there were a number of uncompleted irrigation projects in Idaho and other western states. The question was where could the funds to complete them be found. Although the Senator was on the Committee on Irrigation he did not go with other members of the Committee in the summer of 1909 on their junket to visit every irrigation project in the United States. He re-

[5] *Ibid.*, p. 8512.
[6] *Statesman*, March 13, 1911.
[7] January 5, 1910.

mained in Boise studying reclamation problems, particularly that of reclamation finance.

Within a few months he had prepared a plan which called for a $30,000,000 bond issue, the bonds to be redeemed out of the reclamation fund. On November 20, he presented this plan to Secretary Ballinger and won his support for it. On January 4, 1910, the papers carried the news that Borah had won the cordial and earnest support of President Taft.

A month later President Taft told Congressman Hamer (Idaho) that he was still supporting Borah's bill despite that Senator's opposition to nearly all administration measures.[8] Then the President called Borah to the White House and gave him assurance that he was for the $30,000,000 bond issue. He also told him how much he wanted enacted into law a certain conservation bill. Borah agreed to work for this measure.[9] On June 15 the conservation bill, carrying the reclamation bond issue provision as an amendment, passed the Senate.

Borah then went to see Speaker Cannon. Cannon's proposal was that Borah agree to eliminate the $30,000,000 from the conservation bill and he would see to it that a bill providing for a $20,000,000 bond issue passed the House. The Senator asked the Speaker what guarantee he gave. It is reported that the Speaker swore some of his strongest oaths. But the Senator smiled and stuck to his guns. An agreement was reached through President Taft who promised not to sign the conservation bill unless he signed also a bill carrying a provision for at least $20,000,000 for irrigation.[10] This arrangement was carried out.

Senator Borah was cartooned as the "Man with the Hoe" in the Denver *Times,* and one of the leading bankers of South Dakota, a Democrat, said: "Senator Borah is considered one of the brainiest and strongest men in the Senate. . . As a spokesman for the interests of the West, Borah has made a national reputation." [11]

Immediately after the bill was passed, the hard-working

[8] *Statesman,* May 27, 1910.
[9] *Ibid.,* editorial, June 11, 1910.
[10] *Ibid.,* June 21, 1910.
[11] *Ibid.,* May 12, 1910.

Senator went to the President urging prompt allotments of the money for Idaho projects. The *Statesman* expressed the opinion that Idaho should get $4,000,000 of the $20,000,000. Idaho actually received $7,000,000. When the Senator returned to Boise that summer there was a great crowd at the station to welcome him, for he had "made good for Idaho." When they told him to get into the special car which had been provided to take him to his hotel, he laughed like a youngster, and said, "Oh, I'm just a common man – I'll walk to the hotel with the boys." [12]

Idaho had every reason to be satisfied with Borah, and it did not immediately forget his achievement. Two years later, when Borah was a candidate for reëlection, the *Eagle* of Meadows reviewed his record and concluded with this question to the voters: "Have you forgotten the $7,000,000 appropriation he secured for the State of Idaho two years ago?"

The *Spokesman-Review* [13] in eastern Washington praised Borah for his work in getting the irrigation bill through Congress, and the fine old Portland *Oregonian* praised him, albeit with mixed feelings, for his ability to get such a large part of the total for Idaho. It should be stated here that the original reclamation act (1902) provided that the states contributing to the reclamation fund should in due time receive a return benefit of a proportionate expenditure on irrigation enterprises within their respective limits. On this basis Oregonians calculated that their share of the $20,000,000 amounted to $9,000,000. But Senator Borah and some other congressmen of influence succeeded in having repealed the "proportionate expenditure" provision of the original reclamation act before the $20,000,000 bill was passed. Consequently, Oregon received less than $1,000,000 of the fund.

This is the *Oregonian's* "mixed feelings" editorial: [14] "Senator Borah . . . is a representative of whom Idaho may well feel proud. While Oregon may feel wroth over his success in getting away with about $9,000,000 of Oregon's reclamation fund while our own Senators were asleep or cir-

[12] *Ibid.*, July 3, 1910.
[13] July 3, 1910.
[14] January 9, 1911.

culating political buncombe, we cannot but admire the fearless, independent manner in which he stands up for the West. Senator Borah is not seeking to impress the East with any crazy political theories, but he is telling some pointed truths about the land which so many others have lied about and which finds no defenders in the Oregon Senatorial delegation. The Pinchot-Roosevelt Conservation Congress at St. Paul last fall Senator Borah characterizes as a 'cruel and brutal farce.' In a speech before the Brooklyn Institute of Fine Arts and Sciences he attempts to disabuse the minds of his audience of the idea that 'the people of the West should be either in the penitentiary or in the asylums.' What the West needs is more Borahs and fewer Bournes and Chamberlains [Oregon's Senators]."

BUT Borah did not rest on the reputation he had established by his work for the irrigation bond issue. He next turned his efforts to the matter of improving the homestead laws. By an act of February 19, 1909, qualified entrymen were permitted to take up 320 acres of arid, non-mineral, non-irrigable, unreserved, and unappropriated surveyed public lands which did not contain merchantable timber. For some reason such lands in Idaho had been excepted from the provisions of this bill. The Senator introduced a bill removing this exception. The bill became a law on June 17, 1910.

His most significant achievement for homesteaders and possible homesteaders was in his three-year homestead bill. The original homestead law (1862) required the homesteader to reside for a term of five years upon the land before he was eligible for a patent. Western people considered this law entirely too severe in its requirements. They wanted the total period of residence reduced and they wanted a provision which would permit the settler to absent himself from his land for about half the time each year.

Idaho's Junior Senator introduced his measure and pushed it through during the second session of the 62nd Congress. In a brilliant speech ranging from a summary of Ferrero's account of the decline of Roman agriculture in the first century B.C. to a quotation from the report of the American

Consul in Winnipeg relative to Americans coming to Canada to take advantage of her liberal homestead laws, he showed the need for improving the American homestead laws. After quoting from a letter of a forest supervisor explaining to a prospective settler how agricultural land in a forest reserve might be taken up, the Senator said : [15] "Mr. President, in my leisure hours of life I have found pleasure in reading the satires of Juvenal, the letters of Junius, and later the humor of Mark Twain and Dooley ; but I never have seen concentrated into so brief a space such a combination of irony and grim humor as is found in this letter."

Two weeks after this speech (February 5, 1912), while Secretary Fisher was before the House Public Lands Committee making an argument against the Borah-Jones three-year homestead bill, Senator Borah called this very measure up before the Senate and secured its prompt passage without a dissenting vote. The Secretary was in favor of remodeling the homestead laws, but he thought the Borah-Jones bill was entirely too liberal with the settlers.

With his bill through the Senate, Borah went to see Speaker Clark (February 20). The Speaker had very decided presidential ambitions at this time, and he was impressed with Borah's account of the hardships now suffered by settlers and with the Senator's statement that the West was behind his measure. Mr. Clark promised to see the House Committee on Public Lands before the bill was reported and gave other assurance that he would support the bill. The Speaker actually took the floor and made a speech for the bill when it was up for consideration in the House. Borah and Jones were successful also in getting the President to urge the passage of their measure. With such strong backing the bill passed the House unanimously on March 27. The *Statesman* headlined an editorial, "PASSAGE OF HOMESTEAD BILL MAKES IDAHO SAY : 'THANKS.' "

There were some amendments to the bill in the House and it was therefore necessary for the bill to go to conference, that is, to a joint committee of the two houses, where an agreement respecting its final provisions could be worked out.

[15] *Record,* January 17, 1912, p. 1017.

Courtesy of the Idaho Statesman

Secretary Fisher went before the conference committee and practically won the conferees over to his way of thinking. Borah then went to work with each of the conferees to hold them to the essential provisions of the Borah-Jones bill. Here again he was successful. "I hope I never have to work as hard on any other bill," he said.

The day after the House passed the three-year homestead bill, Speaker Clark called the Senator on the telephone. "I have a lecture date at Newark, New Jersey, next week," he said. "You can realize my predicament. I don't want to deliver a lecture over at Wilson's home because it might lead to unpleasant comment."

The Senator said he had no appropriate lecture. The Speaker insisted that anything the Senator had ready would be all right. Borah still refused to accommodate him.

"By the way, Senator," said the Speaker, about to play his

last trump, "how do the people of Idaho like that three-year homestead bill we passed through the House yesterday?"

"I'll fill your date," laughed the Senator.[16]

With the three-year homestead measure on the statute books, Borah quickly secured the passage of two other bills designed to relieve the settlers. One of these gave the homesteader the privilege of determining for himself whether he would prove up under the old or the new law. The other provided for the issuance of patents to homesteaders and desert land entrymen on reclamation projects at the end of the residence period.

In 1911 President Taft proposed reciprocity with Canada. The idea behind it was to lower the cost of living in the United States by an agreement between the United States and Canada providing for free trade in many raw materials and food products, and for substantial reductions on some manufactured articles. Since the progressive Senators (not including Borah) had opposed the Payne-Aldrich tariff with all their energy, there was some hope that they would support the Taft proposition. But the progressives, with the notable exception of Senator Beveridge, were most actively opposed to reciprocity. It seemed to them to sacrifice the interest of the farmers, whom they represented, to the manufacturers of the East, whom the gilded standpatters represented.

There is no conclusive proof of the state of the farmers' mind on this question. The *Statesman,* always a supporter of the policies of a Republican President, repeatedly said that the farmers favored it by a large majority. The Chicago *Tribune's* canvass of the editors of the State showed a majority in favor of reciprocity. The poll of the *Spokesman-Review* in southern Idaho showed 60 per cent of the farmers voting in the poll in favor of the President's reciprocity agreement.

Senator Borah thought the farmers were opposed to reciprocity — or, at least, that they would be when it had been explained to them. In any case, he was sure it would ruin their domestic markets. He plunged into the fight against the agreement with all the energy that he possessed.

[16] *Statesman,* April 7, 1912.

Perhaps the bitterest speech made against the President's plan was that made in the Senate by Borah, June 27–28, 1911. He contended, among other things, that the idea of reciprocity originated with James J. Hill who wanted to increase the business on his railroad running into Canada ; that it provided free trade in the things the American farmer produced and protection for the things he had to buy ; and that the bill threw the markets of this country open to the Canadian farmer to the injury of the American farmer. "Mr. President, if there is one cardinal principle in the protective system more permanent and distinctive than all others it is that the American market place belongs to the American producer so long as he is able to supply that market. With one half of the agricultural lands in the United States untilled, with millions of acres of lands yet to be cultivated, what reason is there for American statesmanship to turn from the encouragement of the American farmer to produce and fill the American market place, to barter and trade with the foreign producer ?"

The reciprocity measure passed the Senate (July 23) by a vote of 53 for and 27 against. But the American farmer never had to take his chances with reciprocity, for on the Canadian side it was defeated by a large majority on September 21. The next day, in Chicago, foodstuffs advanced all along the line.

The defeat of the measure may have been in the interest of the farmer, but it was a decided set-back to the program of removing tariff barriers and lowering the cost of living.

WHILE it is probably true that Borah has not secured as much legislation of special interest to Idaho during any other term as he did during his first, he has never lost interest in legislation of concern to Idaho, certainly not in agricultural legislation. Here is one example. When he was at the very peak of his activity as Chairman of the Senate Committee on Foreign Relations, he took a great deal of time for work on the Perishable Agricultural Commodities Bill. Farmers who had to ship such commodities a thousand or two thousand miles to market often received word that their products were badly damaged upon arrival. Sometimes they were and sometimes they were not, but the farmers had to take the middle-man's word for it. The Senator heard complaints about this from time to time. On more than one occasion he had written to a commission merchant or to a dealer who had reported the receipt of spoiled products. Some of these middle-men, upon further inspection and reflection, decided that the goods were not so badly damaged as they had at first thought and they sent the farmers checks for first-class produce! Borah first introduced a bill to cover this sort of fraud in commerce in December, 1927. He met with producers and middle-men in Omaha, Chicago, and other places, and revised his bill as a result of these conferences. He put it through the Senate in 1929, but it did not come to a vote in the House. The next year it passed both Houses and was signed by President Hoover. It has two features: it lays down rules of fair conduct for middle-men buying perishable agricultural products and it places them under a Federal license, a license which may be canceled by the Secretary of Agriculture under certain conditions. Producers and specialists in agricultural economics join in praising this piece of legislation as one of the most significant achievements of the Coolidge-Hoover era for the farmer.

Let us now take a broad general view of the Senator's activities on behalf of his State. His correspondence with its executive officers, its legislators, its newspaper men, its business men, and its citizens and residents generally reveals his continued and lively interest. The great bales of letters in his files deal with everything concerning the people of Idaho from silver and beet sugar to an amateur benefit performance and the matrimonial plans of Louie Lai.

It is frequently said that Senator Borah pays little attention to the wants of his constituents. This assertion is wholly false. A person in Idaho with a problem has always been able to get a hearing from the Senator. A man in Jordan Valley, Oregon, wrote the Senator in 1924, making the old charge. The Senator replied:

"If you have any neighbors who claim to have written to me and who have not had answers, as your letter indicates, I wish you would send me the names of the gentlemen who claim that fact. If there is anything I try religiously to do, regardless of the hours of service it takes, it is to answer letters from my home State. . . And if all the people to whom I write were my friends, there would be no question about the size of my vote in Idaho."

His interest in Idaho and its citizens can be easily demonstrated by random selections from his correspondence. He established a debate prize at the State University in 1907, the prize to go, not to the winning debaters, but to the University Library for books on argumentation. An Idaho boy at Yale wants to win a place on the "Board" and asks the Senator for an article for the Yale *Daily News,* which he gets. A young man fails his examination for admission to Annapolis. The Senator writes him a fatherly letter. A young woman in desperation writes in 1934 of her great love for a German Jew, and asked if she should go to Germany and marry him. This time the answer was both fatherly and firm. It was "no."

During the World War his correspondence reveals very aggressive action toward the Food Administration in the interest of the disposition of Idaho crops. In one letter he writes: "I have not had the pleasure of meeting Mr. Hoover." In the same period the mail is closed to *The Golden Trail,* a liberal publication in Boise. The Senator sees the proper authorities and the publication has the mailing privilege restored. A young man says that the Draft Act is unconstitutional and is having serious trouble with local patriots who have not as yet entered military service. He writes to Borah, and receives in reply the assurance that he has a perfect right to say it is unconstitutional although he (the Senator) thinks it is constitutional.

He secures public buildings for Boise, Nampa, Twin Falls, Idaho Falls, and many other cities and towns. He has an item added to the appropriation bill for an agricultural experiment station at Jerome. He manages to get a potato expert from the Department of Agriculture to attend the Pocatello potato convention and a dairy man from the Bureau of Animal Husbandry to test Idaho cattle. He interests himself in hog cholera and in the markings on potato sacks.

A mining man writes a letter of complaint about the application of the depletion provision of the income-tax law to mine discoveries and asks the Senator to send the letter to Secretary Mellon over his own signature. This request is complied with. A friend and political supporter has bought considerable oil stock in 1930, and he writes to the Senator in 1933 requesting him to wire, confidentially, what the prospects are for the passage of the oil conservation bill. He suggests that the Senator need not mention oil in his wire. The Senator wires his advice, but uses the word "oil."

But he does not grant the request of a Washington farmer that he read to the Senators his three-page letter. "Man does not live of his self alone," explains the farmer, and he thinks that the "stirring of stagnant waters makes them pure."

The physical limitations of a book make it desirable to leave out further proof, at this point, of the Senator's interest in his State. Let us turn to the question : Why does he have the reputation of lacking such interest ?

First, who gives him that reputation ? It comes chiefly from party organization men and standard Republican newspapers, sources which are usually hostile to the Senator and which sometimes privately dub him "William the Promisor." The general public picks up the statement from these sources, and, hearing it reiterated time and again, begins to wonder if it isn't true.

Second, among politicians a Senator or member of the House who does not get jobs for them is worthless – he has no interest in the organization, none in the state. But Borah has always tried to get places for his particular supporters and for other worthy men of his party. He is not irritated when he is requested to find a place for a man who has the integrity and capacity to fill one. He is glad to do his best for him. But he learned during his first term in the Senate that a Senator was often allowed to name candidates for appointive positions in return for the Senator's support of a particular legislative measure or measures. He swore he would never make any such concession for an appointment.

Senator Borah early told Republican leaders in Idaho that he could not be expected to find places for very many men, that he wasn't that kind of statesman. The organization took him at his word. As a matter of fact, he has been fairly successful in securing appointments because from time to time Republican Presidents have tried to please him. His high standing with Bernard M. Baruch and other leading Democrats has given him some influence even in the selection of Democratic appointees. But the Senator has the reputation of securing few appointments because he himself says he can not deliver them and because his appointments do not always satisfy good organization men.

Third, a Senator is expected to get appropriations for public buildings and other purposes for his state. Even business associations which scorn the pork barrel expect this of him. The business men of a particular town vigorously oppose the general distribution of a whole barrel of pork, but they are more than pleased when their own town gets a good strip of bacon. The Senator has worked for appropriations where he could see the need of them, but he has never been in any sense a pork-barrel man.

Fourth, organizations of business, labor, and so on often expect a Senator to support their interest, even though it may be bad for the state or country as a whole. Senator Borah has often supported the requests of such groups in Idaho. But he has refused in very plain and vigorous language to support a program for a group which he has believed detrimental to wider interests. The aggrieved minority has then said the Senator pays no attention to Idaho's needs.

Fifth, as the Senator became more interested in national and international problems and was frequently a leading spokesman on these matters, these were his only activities to receive much publicity, even in Idaho newspapers. It was not difficult for the Idahoans to persuade themselves that he was no longer a good representative of the State, especially since there was often some impatience with his views on nation-wide and world-wide questions. But nearly all of them will agree that the Senator has continued to give them supreme satisfaction in one particular — in the publicity the State has in having him in the Senate.

To the question "What has Borah done for Idaho?" one might very properly turn the interrogation table. "How could a United States Senator serve only his own state?" and "Does he not serve his state in serving the nation?" Appropriations for public buildings and local appointments are about the only purely home state matters with which a United States Senator has to deal. All other problems demanding his attention are sectional, national, and international. His state must simply take its chances with the others. As "The National Statesman Emerges" in the following chapter, the Idaho statesman does not disappear. Indeed, the record reviewed under "The National" caption runs simultaneously with the record of state and sectional achievement which has just been summarized.

CHAPTER VII

THE NATIONAL STATESMAN EMERGES

THE Junior Senator from Idaho embarked upon his career as a national statesman in the summer of 1909, just eighteen months after he had taken his seat in the Senate. He not only became a statesman in that short time, but he became one of the leading figures in the Senate. Considering the age and experience of many other Senators, this was indeed rapid progress for the young Senator from the West. How did it happen? A partial explanation is found in the Senator's native ability and indefatiguable industry. But there is a broader explanation. The period happened to suit Borah's political philosophy.

This was the progressive period, and Borah was in essentials a progressive. The country was ready for an income tax, a form of taxation Borah had advocated for years. On practically every hand it was being said that Senators should be elected, not by state legislatures, but by the people. The Junior Senator from Idaho could not remember the time when he had not endorsed popular election of Senators. The Woman Suffrage movement was growing. Borah came from a pioneer Woman Suffrage state and had sat in the state Republican convention of 1894 which had without a qualm endorsed this innovation. The masses were asking for postal-savings banks and parcel-post service. The vigorous young solon was in entire accord with these demands. Trust and monopolies were being looked upon as the supreme enemies of the people, a rôle in which Borah had cast them for ten years. Labor was getting more consideration for its demands for shorter hours and better working conditions. Borah could support Labor in all sincerity. In short, the measures for which the great body of the American people were asking were the measures in which Borah whole-heartedly believed. Since the established leaders of the Republican party in the Senate were not in tune with popular sentiment the Progressives often assumed unofficial leadership. Borah came to the post of leader on the income tax, the direct election of senators, and labor legislation.

Senator Borah was a member of the platform committee of the Republican party in 1908, and he helped draft the tariff revision plank which he understood to be a pledge for revision downward. The country as a whole shared this view, but high-tariff Republicans refused to give any such meaning to the revision declaration. Their position was frankly stated by a Senator who could usually be counted upon for frankness, if not for good judgment, the Senior Senator from Idaho, Weldon B. Heyburn. In the special session President Taft had called for the purpose of revising the tariff, Heyburn denounced the platform committee for proposing the revision plank, declaring that in doing so they were actuated solely by fear. He undertook to say that the people did not expect the party to live up to a revision-downward pledge, if one had been made. "The people know the Republican party well enough to know that even though inadvertently, it might make expressions that sounded badly, it could be trusted in the hour of its responsibility." [1]

The Junior Senator from Idaho resented his colleague's slurs upon the progressives, and arose to say once more that he was one of those "who believe that the Chicago platform meant an honest and faithful revision of the tariff, and that that revision was understood in the public mind to be revision downward, but always within lines of sufficient protection to American industries and American labor." [2]

However, Borah's record on the enactment of the Payne-Aldrich tariff (1909) falls between progressive and regular Republican, but much nearer the latter. The ninety votes recorded for Borah on this tariff measure showed his Republicanism to be 74 per cent. (The method of calculating this percentage will be explained when we come to the mathematics of Republicanism in Chapter VIII.) The very best Republicans of the Aldrich-Penrose-Smoot variety rated only about 83 per cent. Republicanism struck rock bottom with La Follette, whose percentage was 25. Clapp's (Minn.) score was 29, Bristow's (Kans.), 30, Cummins' (Ia.), 37,

[1] *Record,* May 24, 1909.
[2] *Ibid.,* p. 2316.

Beveridge's (Ind.), 39, and Dolliver's (Ia.), 44. Bourne (Ore.) and Nixon (Nev.), generally ranked with this progressive group, each made 83 per cent. On the other hand, some regular Republicans strayed from the fold. Thus McCumber (N.D.) and Smith (Mich.) dropped to 75, and Nelson (Minn.) to 43. On the final vote (the vote on the conference report) Borah stood with the regulars. Beveridge, Bristow, Clapp, Cummins, Dolliver, La Follette, and Nelson were the only Republicans voting against the bill. On the whole, the fight within the Republican party against the Payne-Aldrich bill was made by Senators from the Middle West. Far Western liberals like Borah and Bourne stayed fairly regular on this measure.

The explanation for Borah's position on this tariff measure is three-fold. First, he was still a relatively new Senator, and he had not had time to make a deep study of the question. Second, he found Eastern Senators unwilling to vote for reductions on products of their section unless the West took what he considered ruinous reductions on Western products. Third, the largest industries of Idaho were mining, lumber, and live stock and they brought the strongest pressure to bear upon the Idaho representatives in Washington.

Idaho was mining about one third of the lead produced in the United States. Borah stated that he was concerned, and concerned alone, as a representative of his State in making effective the tariff upon ore, and to that end he addressed his remarks.[3] "I want to be fair, and I want the Senators from the middle states to appreciate that the western miners, the men engaged in that great industry in our State, are paying their states more today for that upon which they have to live than they ever paid in the history of the mining regions of the West. A steer standing upon the hoof in the State of Nebraska or Iowa or Minnesota, notwithstanding all the arguments here, will buy more lead than ever before. . .

"The distinguished Senator from Indiana (Beveridge) passed through out region of the country last fall and we yet can hear the cadence of song and poetry in the mountains, but he never mentioned reducing the rate upon lead. . ."

Senator McCumber of North Dakota, practically a treeless

[3] *Ibid.*, p. 2322, May 10, 1909, pp. 1879 ff.

State, was arguing for free lumber. His argument was, in effect, that there was no point in protecting lumber because, since there were just so many trees, it could not be a growing industry. To protect lumber meant that the American lumber industry would have a temporary spurt and that the American supply would be exhausted sooner than it would be without protection. He said further that a number of good Republican states had asked emphatically for free lumber.

Coming from a State in which millions were invested in timber and in which sawmills were employing, at three dollars per day, some 20,000 men (a large group for a thinly populated State), Senator Borah arose to defend the two-dollar duty on lumber.[4] He said that trees could be planted and were being planted. He ridiculed the statement of Senator Nelson (Minnesota) that a tariff on lumber fostered the lumber trusts. He quoted with approval Speaker Reed's characterization of anti-monopoly speakers, which concluded: "The royal man-eating tiger in his native jungle; nay, the very bull himself, the strong bull of Bashan, as he uplifts his bellow over the rocky deserts of Palestine, are all but pale reminders of one of these majestic creatures." The Senator himself had often talked against monopolies and was to continue to do so, but here he was advocating a tariff on lumber for Idaho and the other great lumber states of the Northwest. Incidentally he got his tariff on lumber, lead, hides, and wool.

The tariff, of course, has always been a local issue. Far Western Senators saw their industries threatened. Middle States progressives could vote against the high rates because their states were not particularly concerned. But even among these Senators there was some weakening — for example, in voting for the tariff on hides. Senator Taliaferro, a Florida Democrat, was almost beside himself over his trouble about pineapples. He had managed to get a satisfactory rate for them in the Senate, but the conference had knocked it out. "Mr. President," he said, "surely you are not going to sign that bill with that pineapple paragraph in it?" "Shall I strike out pineapples altogether, or just write in a rate to suit you?" asked Mr. Taft laughingly. "Good-bye, old pine-

[4] *Ibid.*, May 22, 1909, pp. 2288, 2323–2324.

apples, take care of yourself," said the President to Senator Fletcher, the other Floridian, who also had a hankering for a good stiff pineapple tariff.

While Borah stayed very near the regulars on the tariff, he was an out-and-out progressive, a leading progressive, on the issues of the corporation tax and the income tax, issues which were presented along with the discussion of the tariff. On these questions Senator Beveridge became a knight of the old order. Senators Bristow, Clapp, Cummins, and La Follette stood with Borah. Dolliver did also on the corporation tax, but he trailed them badly on the income-tax proposition.

After Justice Sciras had changed his mind, the Supreme Court, in 1895, decided by a five to four majority that the income-tax provision of the Wilson bill of the previous year was unconstitutional. Bryan and his followers continued to advocate an income tax. President Roosevelt recommended to the Congress (1907) both income and inheritance taxes. The Democratic party officially announced its approval of an income tax in 1908 and, to prove its good faith in making the announcement, nominated Bryan for the presidency. The Republican party had not declared for the tax, but Mr. Taft, its candidate, still consulting with Roosevelt in those days, announced his conversion to it, thereby pleasing the progressives of his party and stealing Mr. Bryan's thunder.

With all this pledging for the income tax, the Democrats and insurgent Republicans thought the time had come for action. Consequently, they proposed to write an income tax into the Payne-Aldrich tariff bill. Senator Bailey (Texas) was the chief spokesman for the Democratic Senators, while Cummins (Iowa) and Borah did the honors for the insurgent Republicans. The Idahoan was easily the leader in the fight on the floor of the Senate.

His first great effort was on May 3–4, 1909. La Follette sat in front of him and passed him books and papers from time to time. Borah was unwilling to allow the income-tax decision of 1895 to stand as the final interpretation of the Constitution, just as Lincoln was unwilling to see the Dred Scott decision stand. He believed that the majority erred in the tax case and he frankly wanted to give the Court another opportunity to pass upon the question. To maintain his argument that the majority of the Court was mistaken in ruling that the tax on the income (rents) from real property was a direct tax, he assembled American and British authorities covering a period of two hundred years. "I ask the lawyers of the Senate to present from American jurisprudence or from English jurisprudence a single case which has ever held that a tax upon collected rents is a tax upon real estate." As for the necessity of the income tax, "I say to you that if the Pollock case be the correct interpretation of the law, there is no exigency by which this Government can call upon the great property and wealth of this Nation to meet a portion of its burdens, even if it involves the very life of the Nation itself.

"Those who believe that to be a policy of my party are welcome to that belief. I will not accept it. . . I read an interview the other day by that distinguished American, always interesting and sometimes amusing, Mr. Carnegie. He said that it was not Republican, that its only result was to incite men to perjury. Well, Mr. Carnegie did not make the Republican party. I wish I was just as sure that the Republican party did not make Mr. Carnegie."

In concluding he said that the income-tax matter should be resubmitted to the Supreme Court "upon two propositions, and with all due respect and consideration for that high tribunal : first, upon the facts of history, which have been revealed as to the intent and purpose of the framers of the Constitution, which did not appear to be presented to the Court at that time ; and, secondly, in the light of decisions which have been rendered by the Court since the income-tax decision. . ." [5]

All the great newspapers gave considerable space to this speech. They commented upon Borah's ability, logic, dignity, and power as an advocate. Senator Root thought it was a very admirable and able argument, but he intimated that Borah's experience as an attorney might have caused him to exaggerate his argument somewhat.

Two months later, on two dreadfully hot days, Senator Borah made another income-tax speech.[6] This time he was

[5] *Ibid.*, May 3–4, 1909, pp. 1682 ff.
[6] *Ibid.*, June 30 and July 1, 1909, pp. 3985 ff.

not so much the constitutional lawyer as he was the tribune of the people. He was fiery (some thought bitter) in his charge that Senator Aldrich had allowed the corporation-tax proposal to be brought in for the purpose of defeating the income tax. He read the record of the session of 1898 in which Republican Senators now advocating the corporation tax had then opposed a similar one. He did not call them hypocrites — that would have been superfluous. The Idaho Senator opposed the corporation tax because he said the tax would simply be passed on to the consumer. He had twenty-four telegrams from twenty-four Idaho corporations urging him to support the corporation tax and to vote against the income tax.

Returning to his plea for an income tax, he declared : "It is all unjust and unfair, tyrannical and to my mind, brutal, to hold on to a system of taxation which continues to put all the burden, the ever increasing burden of government . . . upon what we must eat and upon what we must wear and nothing upon the great incomes which fools so often flaunt in the face of the poor and which lead to all kinds of extravagance and public demoralization. There is no possible justification for such a system except the bias and stubbornness of custom and precedent on the one hand, and the viciousness of greed on the other."

The insurgent Republican and Democratic combination apparently had enough votes to get the income tax in the tariff bill. At this point President Taft rescued the regular Republicans with the suggestion that the income tax be proposed in the form of a constitutional amendment and that the agitation for putting it in the tariff bill be dropped. This strategy of the Republican leaders brought temporary defeat but ultimate victory to the advocates of the tax. The resolution for the amendment passed the Senate without a dissenting vote on July 5.

The insurgents and all but two Democrats wanted the amendment submitted for ratification to state conventions rather than to the state legislatures but the regulars would have none of it, and they had the votes to prevent it. Senator Borah explained that the convention had advantages over the legislative method in that the convention would be chosen for the single purpose of considering the amendment while the legislature is concerned with a multitude of affairs which might prevent the amendment from being properly considered.[7] He said that in the legislature it would be possible to logroll other important measures against the amendment and defeat it. This was precisely the reason a number of regulars who had put themselves on record in the Senate for the amendment preferred to have it referred to the legislatures. They knew the habits of state legislatures as well as the Senator from Idaho did, and there was some justification for their ardent hope that the amendment could be defeated in those bodies.

EARLY in January, 1910, Governor Hughes of New York advised the legislature of that State to vote against ratification on the ground that the authority to levy taxes on incomes "from whatever source derived" would permit the national government to levy taxes on the incomes from state and municipal bonds (instruments now exempt from Federal taxation), and thus force the state and its local governmental agencies to pay higher rates of interest on their obligations.

With these words from Governor Hughes an expression of pleased surprise spread over the pages of the conservative metropolitan dailies. "As unanswerable as twelve o'clock noon," "The Governor has given the amendment a deathblow," and similar comments were made. Advocates of the amendment did not deny Mr. Hughes' contention; they simply said his objection was trivial and asked why holders of state and local bonds should not pay a tax on income derived from them.

For a month the Idaho Senator said nothing. Then, on February 10, he arose and made one of those speeches which, even during his first term, stamped him as one of the great constitutional lawyers of the Senate.

He opened with the courteous statement that since "one of our most distinguished and justly celebrated of public men" had recommended against the ratification of the amendment "it has been assumed by the public press . . . that it would be impossible, in view of his declaration, to secure the

[7] *Ibid.*, July 5, 1909, p. 4114.

enactment of the amendment. So firm a hold has the Governor of New York upon the public mind and so high is the esteem in which he is held as a lawyer that it is regarded as in a nature conclusive against the amendment." But "it occurs to me that there are at least two sides to the controversy, and, in my own opinion, the grounds stated for the rejection are not such as should prevail against the amendment." [8] This was a very restrained and modest beginning for the Senator who was to pulverize the Governor's contention.

The Senator remarked that one of the original objections to the Constitution was that it gave Congress plenary powers of taxation. Hamilton had not denied but vigorously defended this power in number XXXI of the *Federalist*. The taxing "power of the National Government at the present time . . . is full, complete, unlimited, and unfettered, save as to exports from the states," continued the Senator. He explained that the two rules Congress was required to observe in taxation — the rule of apportionment by population as to direct taxes, and the rule of uniformity as to duties, imposts, and excises — had reference only to the manner in which the power was to be exercised, and was not a limitation on the taxing power.

The income-tax amendment "does not propose to deal, and was not intended to deal with the question of power. It intended to deal, and does deal, alone with the manner of exercising that power which is already complete. . . The sole obstacle to be removed by those who sought to change the Constitution was that of apportionment. No one has ever contended that it was not within the power of Congress to lay a tax upon incomes. That power has belonged to Congress from its organization . . . whether apportioned or unapportioned was a matter of discussion, and concerning which courts and lawyers differed ; but the power to impose an income tax upon all property, 'from whatever source derived,' has never been doubted, so far as I know, by either court or lawyers in this country."

The Senator stated that the Congress did not tax instrumentalities and agencies of the states under the existing Constitution, not because of any particular provision of the

[8] *Ibid.*, Feb. 10, 1910, p. 1694.

Constitution, but because the courts had rightly held that such a tax would be incompatible with our dual system of government. Since the proposed amendment does nothing more than remove the requirement of apportionment as to direct taxes, how would its adoption enable Congress to tax state instrumentalities? From a constitutional standpoint it opens up no new sources of income; it simply abolishes the rule of apportionment in taxing incomes.

This was the essence of the Senator's argument. It was convincing to the great majority of intelligent people who had taken any interest in the question. Nearly three weeks later the Chicago *Tribune* pronounced it a clear-cut, logical argument "which Governor Hughes had not tried to answer." The Salt Lake *Telegram* declared "it had something of the ring in it of the old days when Webster and Calhoun and Cass and a few others addressed the Senate, a kind of an organ tone of intellect which put to shame the effervescence of the ordinary Senator." To be sure, opposition to the income tax was not silenced by Senator Borah's argument, but when Senator Root sided with Senator Borah against Governor Hughes, friends of the amendment took heart.

After Governor Hughes had become Associate Justice and after the amendment had become a part of the Constitution, the Supreme Court of the United States, in Brushaber v. Union Pacific R. R. (240 U. S. 1, at p. 17), made this statement concerning the purpose of the amendment: "It is clear on the face of this text that it does not purport to confer power to levy income taxes in a generic sense — an authority already possessed and never questioned — or to limit and distinguish between one kind of income taxes and another, but that the whole purpose of the Amendment was to relieve all income taxes when imposed from apportionment. . ."

A few weeks after his speech in the Senate, Borah was asked to speak on the income tax before the Economic Club of New York City. In the heart of the opposition to the tax, he made an energetic defense of the amendment from a practical standpoint. "Someone has said that such a tax would bear unduly . . . upon New York for here in this great city are the great incomes. It is true the great incomes are here. Here live the captains of industry, and here is the city which revels in the splendor and wealth of Babylon of old. We are all proud of New York. The country, the near east, the middle and far west, the south, have a just pride in this great and growing metropolis. Why should we not be proud of you? We made you what you are. . ." [9]

Back in Boise, he delivered a Fourth of July oration [10] "that played upon the emotions of his great audience as a harpist strikes the strings of his instrument, himself raised to an ecstatic pitch by the very momentum of his sweep of thought. . . It was a speech that fairly lifted the people out of themselves and swept them with glowing fires of patriotism. As an example of flawless action and comprehensive scope of subject, it will long live in the memory of those who heard it."

He did not swing into the stride that reached "the inmost feelings of the people" who "responded to climax after climax with waves of applause" for about half an hour. He laid the groundwork by tracing the history of buried republics, pointing a warning finger at the chief causes of failure. Then, he recited from the thirty-first chapter of Job: "If I did despise the cause of my man-servant or my maid-servant when they contended with me, what then shall I do when God riseth up and when he visiteth, what shall I answer him? Did not he that made me in the womb make him and did not one fashion us in the womb? If I have withheld the poor from their desire, or have caused the eyes of the widow to fail, or have eaten my morsel myself alone, and the fatherless hath not eaten thereof." This is one of the Senator's purple passages of Scripture. He spoke it softly and in subdued tones, but with a tensity that held his audience breathless.

"That is all there is to the Constitution," he said, thus putting the government charter in terms of human duties and sympathies blended with religion. Then he told his audience about the income-tax amendment: how the Supreme Court had reversed itself on the income-tax question, and how Senators hypocritically stated that it would be an affront to the Court to refer the same question to it again; and how they had fifty-three votes in the Senate to put the tax in the

9 *Statesman*, March 26, 1910.
10 *Ibid.*, July 5, 1911.

Courtesy of Chicago Record-Herald

tariff bill, and how the special interests got busy and advocated the amendment as a substitute so that the imposition of the tax would be prolonged and perhaps defeated. He concluded with the rather startling prediction that, if the income-tax question was not settled right, "the greatest war in history will be fought around the wreck of the Supreme Court."

DESPITE the fact that there had been agitation for direct election of Senators since the time of Andrew Jackson, the amendment establishing this method of election was not submitted to the states until 1911. Agitation for it had greatly increased since the Senate, in 1894, had broken the tariff pledge of the Democratic party. The amendment resolution had passed the House of Representatives several times, and more than two thirds of the states had declared for it, but the Senate had refused to consider the proposition. Consequently, the press regarded as a significant event the Senator's achievement in getting a favorable recommendation for the amendment from a sub-committee of the Senate Committee on the Judiciary. Still more significant was the fact that the full Committee permitted the amendment to be brought to the floor of the Senate (December, 1910).

On January 13, Senator Borah asked for unanimous consent for January 22 as the date for a formal vote on his resolution. His colleague, Senator Heyburn, objected, thus defeating the effort to fix the date. Senator Cullom of Illinois then asked Senator Borah to allow him to move an executive session. The Idahoan reluctantly agreed to yield, but before he did so, stated that he would, in a few days, ask the Senate to fix a date for the vote, and that if no date was agreed upon, there would be a very small amount of business done until the matter was disposed of.

The *Christian Science Monitor* and some other newspapers joined the Republican regulars in saying that Senator Borah was trying to rush his resolution through the Senate before anyone had time to consider it.[11] In view of the fact that the proposal had been considered (nearly always favorably) everywhere except in the Senate for some twenty years the criticism had little merit.

There was another parliamentary fight on February 3. Senator Nelson moved to take up the bill regulating the leasing of Alaskan coal lands. Senator Borah moved to lay that motion on the table. He lost 36 to 41, some half dozen Senators who favored direct election voting with Nelson because they considered his bill more important at that time. Later, when adjournment was moved, Senator Borah demanded a roll call. This test vote resulted in a victory for the direct election group. The Senator then demanded that his resolution be made the unfinished business of the Senate. Senator Penrose, fearing success of this motion, moved an executive session. Senator Borah demanded a roll call on Penrose's motion, and the executive session was denied 40 to 36. Since it was clear now that Senator Borah had the votes, his resolution was made the unfinished business of the Senate.

11 January 16, 1911.

Old guardsmen tied to their parliamentary strategy the Negro question. If they could irritate the South, Senators from that section upon whom the progressive Republicans were counting would vote against the resolution. Senator Depew had proposed in the Judiciary Committee that the resolution be submitted to the Senate with the following provision attached: "The qualifications of citizens entitled to vote for United States Senators and Representatives in Congress shall be uniform in all the states, and Congress shall have the power to enforce this article by appropriate legislation and to provide for the registration of citizens entitled to vote, the conduct of such elections, and the certification of the result." This would clearly deal a great blow at southern election laws which discriminated in fact, if not in theory, against the Negro. The provision was not recommended by the Committee.

On the floor of the Senate, Senator Sutherland offered an amendment to the resolution giving Congress the power to make rules or to alter state rules as to the manner of electing senators, a power given to Congress by section 4, Article I of the Constitution. This amendment carried a hint that Congress might attempt to do something to give the southern Negro his franchise privileges. It was commonly believed that it was offered only for the purpose of inducing southern Senators to vote against the resolution.

On February 16, Senator Borah spoke against the "Sutherland amendment." [12] He said that the resolution as prepared by the committee was sufficient; that the National Government now had ample power to protect the franchise of all persons qualified to vote in congressional elections; and that the Sutherland proposal was designed to defeat the amendment by drawing the Negro question into the discussion. He made his strongest effort on this last point, replying to Senators Root, Depew, and others who had introduced the race question in their speeches.

"I do not know, Mr. President, how long the North is going to play the hypocrite or the moral coward on this Negro question. . . The Northern States have exhibited the same animosity, the same race prejudice and race hatred that has

[12] Pp. 2656–2657.

been developed in the other parts of the country. . . We burn the Negro at the stake ; our northern soil is cursed with race wars ; we push the Negro to the outer edge of the industrial world ; we exhibit toward him the same intolerance in proportion to his number in our part of the country as they do in every other part of the land, and in the same way. . .

"I want to ask my friends who have raised this question of protecting the Negro in the South, and who assert we have the power under section 4 of Article I — ["The times, places, and manner of holding elections for Senators and Representatives shall be prescribed in each state by the legislature thereof ; but the Congress may at any time make or alter such regulations . . ."] — to deal with the subject, why we do not exercise the power if we have it ? . . .

"It is a fine situation, Mr. President, in which the great Republican party finds itself in this debate. . . It has been asserted upon the floor of the Senate that under section 4 of Article I we can deal with what is called the 'grandfather clauses' of state constitutions. Then the question arises, When are we going to deal with them ? It is my deliberate opinion that we have not an iota of power under section 4 to deal with the question. . .

"We have used the Negro as a political football about as long as our own sense of decency or the Negro's developing intelligence will permit. If we have a constitutional power which may be used to his advantage, we ought to use it whenever and wherever he is being wronged. If we have not such power, we ought to cease to mislead him and have the courage to state to him the truth. We ought at least to cease surfeiting the Negro on these soporific applications of rhetoric, these tender and moving protestations embalmed from year to year in the *Congressional Record*. . .

"Let me say to the Negro from my place in the Senate — although I know my voice will not be heeded nor carry weight with others, but I wait for time to make good — after the exigencies of this debate are over, after this resolution has again been killed, if they should succeed, you will never again hear anything about the virtues or the power of section 4. No measure will be offered here, no bill passed under it for the substantial advantage or benefit of the Negro. Let me say to the black man of the South and to his black brother in the North, do not permit the anxious and restless and hopeful spirit to call you from the path you are pursuing of working out your own salvation."

No Republican had ever made such a frank and courageous speech on the Negro question. It received big headlines all over the country: "BORAH'S GREAT SPEECH," "SENATOR BORAH'S FRANKNESS," "THE VOICE OF A STATESMAN," "MR. BORAH'S HONEST WORDS," "BORAH'S SOUND SPEECH," "BORAH KILLS THE RACE QUESTION," "BORAH BARES SCHEME," "CROCODILE TEARS," "HYPOCRITES UNMASKED," and "A SPEECH EVERY SOUTHERNER SHOULD READ." It did even more to spread his poplarity in the South than his speech on the Brownsville affair, and it was probably almost as pleasing to Southerners as his justification of a statue of Lee in the Hall of Fame.

But speeches rarely change votes, and the Sutherland amendment was adopted. And then, as had been predicted, a sufficient number of Southern Senators voted against the resolution to prevent its receiving the necessary two-thirds vote (February 28). Even so, it lacked just four votes, and Senator Borah was immensely pleased with the progress that had been made.

"The young man from Idaho is by no means a quitter," said the Pueblo *Chieftain,* expressing the general belief that he would force his resolution through at the next session.

There were new faces in the 62nd Congress. The prophecy which La Follette had made, that Senators who had emptied their seats to show their contempt for his outlandish doctrines would some day be permanently deprived of them, was beginning to be fulfilled. Senator Borah proposed his resolution in the special session on May 1, 1911, just thirty minutes after the Committee on the Judiciary had been organized. Six weeks later, the resolution passed the Senate by 64 to 24. It passed the House also, but with a different provision, and this difference failed to get ironed out in the conference. But in the next session the matter was settled, and the amendment was referred to the states for ratification. As the day of the New Freedom was dawning in 1913, the 36th state approved the direct election plan.

Thus the system of election which had made it possible for business combines like sugar, lumber, mining, and railroads in Idaho to say who would be United States Senator and relatively easy for them to say who would *not* be Senator gave way to the system of popular election, the superior merit of which is not open to question save by those who question democracy itself.

While the fight was on for the direct election of Senators, the Lorimer scandal was laid on the Senate's doorstep. There was strong evidence that he had secured his election to the Senate by bribing certain members of the Illinois Legislature. The Senate resolved to investigate the Lorimer case. Senator Borah wanted to amend the resolution by adding the word "immediately," but his motion was lost.[13] However, the investigation was made without unnecessary delay. As soon as the evidence on Lorimer was available, Senator Borah declared for unseating him, being one of the first Senators to do so. Senator Burrows, Chairman of the Elections Committee, opened the case in the Senate with a set speech in which he said Lorimer was not proved guilty because some of the witnesses, having taken bribes, were not credible. Borah leaped up "unexpectedly and without preparation save for the references to the testimony taken by the investigating committee which he had tabulated. . .

"The most sensational moment of the day came at the close of Mr. Borah's speech, when, facing the member whose seat is in question, the speaker depicted the stream of corruption flowing ever since the day Mr. Lorimer declared his candidacy for the Senate. . ."[14] The Senator put the country-wide feeling into words, yet the Senate vote was 46 to 40 for Lorimer. But this vote was taken as the 61st Congress was expiring. Another vote was taken in the first session of the 62nd Congress, in which, since some of the old stalwarts had not been returned to Congress, Mr. Lorimer lost his seat.

The case of Senator Stephenson of Wisconsin was quite different. The legislature of that State recognized the moral obligation of electing to the Senate the candidate who received the highest popular vote in a primary election. Mr.

[13] *Record,* June 20, 1910.
[14] Chicago *Record-Herald,* January 18, 1911.

Stephenson spent something over $100,000 to win in the primary. The legislature then elected him to the Senate. Although then, as now, an ardent supporter of the primary system, Senator Borah vigorously championed the unseating of Mr. Stephenson on the ground that he had corrupted the electorate. To those who said, "This is just what the primary system makes men do," Mr. Borah replied with biting sarcasm : "What a pathetic scene ; how it moves the very bowels of pity to see this law operating upon these men of wealth, driving them against their wishes into all the ecstacies and excesses of reckless spendthrifts. . . If a man represents money in the race, it will cost money to run. If he has nothing to give the people but money, then money he must give them. But if he represents some question of great moment, if he has something to say to the people upon a subject worthy of their attention, if he deals in ideas and issues instead of patronage and checks, he will win over all the money you can put into the fight. . ." [15]

SENATOR BORAH was in high favor with the liberals of the Senate and of the country in his fight for the income tax, the direct election of Senators, and the exclusion of Senators who had purchased seats in whole or in part ; but he parted company with them on the recall of judges, a proposal which, along with the recall of judicial decision, was gaining wide popular acceptance toward the end of Taft's Administration. Arizona was seeking admission to the Union with a provision for the recall of judges in its constitution. An able lawyer, always a believer in stability, Borah made a Senate speech against this provision. This address on the necessity of an independent judiciary is commonly rated among Senator Borah's best efforts.[16] It was delivered in a fine spirit, giving no offense to the liberals and winning unstinted praise from men who had been opposing nearly all the other issues for which Borah had been fighting. The New York *Sun* printed the speech with "sincere admiration. . . We believe that this speech will take high and permanent rank among the great efforts of philosophical statesmen, not only for the dignity of

[15] *Record,* March 26, 1912, p. 3823.
[16] *Ibid.,* August 7, 1911, pp. 3681 ff.

its thought and expression but also for the quality of the patriotism shown by the conspicuous leader of the so-called progressives who dares thus to expose and rebuke the dangerous error of purpose so prevalent among his associates.

"To Senator Owen, to Governor Woodrow Wilson, to Colonel Roosevelt, to Oklahoma, to California, to every person promoting this insidious movement for the overthrow of the established system, to every state wherein the poison is progressively operating, Senator Borah says: 'We owe it to ourselves and to posterity, to the institutions under which we live, and above all to the common people of this country, to see to it that the judiciary is placed, as nearly as human ingenuity can do so, above the reach of influence or of any of the things which may cloud the mind with passion or dull the conscience to the highest demands of even handed justice.' "[17]

In December, 1910, President Taft had discussed with Senator Borah a vacancy in the Supreme Court, and Borah suggested that Justice White, whom he regarded as one of the ablest men in the legal profession, be made Chief Justice. A year later, a few months after the Senator's speech on the stability of the judiciary, there was another vacancy in the Supreme Court. There was considerable discussion of the Idaho statesman for this place, but the President did not offer it to him. Nor did President Harding offer the Senator a place in the Court after having mentioned it to him. As for the Senator, he has never wanted to be a judge. Too much of an advocate, a fighter, he thinks he lacks the judicial temperament. But the eminent Senator from Virginia, Mr. Glass, says Senator Borah would be an outstanding success as a judge. Had Mr. Taft nominated Senator Borah for a place on the Bench in 1911, and had the Senator accepted, the history of this country might have been quite different, following 1918, from what it has been.

In opposing the establishment of the Commerce Court and in guarding against any relaxation of the anti-trust laws, Senator Borah was back with the progressives again. In his opposition to the broad range of subjects which might be arbitrated under treaties which President Taft proposed (1911), he stood

[17] August 8, 1911.

against Senators Lodge, Root, and Burton, and gave some indication of his brand of Americanism with which the country was to become very familiar eight years later.

It has already been pointed out that Senator Aldrich, because he entirely misconceived his character, put the Junior Senator from Idaho on the Committee on Education and Labor. But the Senator from Rhode Island could not have investigated the Senator from Idaho as thoroughly as the latter has investigated the greater number of his problems, for, if he had, he would have learned that this Senator, despite his close association with the most powerful business interests of Idaho, had recommended an eight-hour law for underground mines some years before he was elected Senator. The new Senator in a short time began administering surprises to the Senate Boss by championing the cause of Labor. Long before the end of his first term he was recognized as one of Labor's staunchest supporters in Congress.

As early as December, 1908, he declared that for some years he had favored a government guaranty of bank deposits. In 1910, in advocating the postal-savings bill, he took "strips of hide from Grandpa [Senator] Carter of Montana." Still later, on June 23, 1910, he introduced his resolution directing the Bureau of Labor to investigate labor conditions in the steel industry. This investigation resulted in a significant report. He continued his efforts for Labor in 1912 by putting through the Senate the law establishing the eight-hour day on all government contracts. His service in fighting off hostile amendments was a matter of special comment.

As the campaign of 1912 was coming on he put through the bill to create an industrial commission and the bill to establish the Children's Bureau. The latter was his special concern. He was genuinely interested in abolishing child labor and he believed the facts to be gathered and published by this Bureau would lead the states to prohibit such labor. The idea of a Federal Bureau as a fact-finding agency, with no power to impinge upon the rights of the states, fitted exactly into his theory of the part the Federal Government might play in matters over which it is given no direct constitutional authority.

In the "interregnum" between the election and inauguration of Wilson, the Senator's bill to establish the Department of Labor became a law. Another of his measures of this period to go on the statute books was the prohibition of "time and motion" studies of Government employees.

SINCE about 1925 the statement has been made occasionally that Senator Borah and the big potatoes give Idaho all the advertising she needs. But neither the Senator, despite his first-term record of constructive achievement, nor the potato gave Idaho her national advertising in 1912. In December of that year, Senator Perky, Borah's colleague for a short time, was asked by a Washington barber where he came from. Receiving the reply "Idaho," the barber said: "Well, Idaho has a famous man in Washington now." "Yes, Senator Borah," Perky volunteered. "Not not Borah – Walter Johnson," the barber corrected.

Yet among those who followed the progress of makers of history, Borah was well known at the end of his first term. Idaho was satisfied with him and very proud of him. The *Statesman* (September 1, 1912) headlined Senator Borah's "GREAT RECORD IN THE SENATE" and proclaimed "his achievement for his State, the West, and the nation unparalleled in Congress." It was a record of which any Senator might be proud, not only for the number of measures put through but also for the character of those measures. It was a record of affirmative achievement, little of the Senator's time having been devoted to opposing the measures of others. This was true largely because the Senator was in nearly every respect in step with the spirit of the times.

The period from 1907 to 1913 was the golden age for Idaho's most famous son. Long before that period opened he had preached its ideas and ideals. Long after its close he still proclaimed them. He has them even now. He has always hated trusts and monopolies; he has always feared the money power; he has always favored taxing the rich in proportion to their ability to pay; he has always believed in the direct election of Senators and in the nomination of candidates for all elective offices by direct primaries; and he has always been a friend of Labor. Others have wavered on these points ; some have turned back. But Borah has never turned back, seldom if ever wavered. He has remained the liberal of the first decade of the twentieth century.

CHAPTER VIII

WHO IS A REPUBLICAN?

DURING the Taft Administration the trend of the country was definitely progressive, not only in the West but also in the East. The movements for the income tax, postal savings, parcels-post, more stringent trust regulation, the direct election of senators, direct primaries, woman suffrage, the initiative and the referendum, the recall, and social legislation generally made rapid strides.

Despite the President's reputation for conservatism, he endorsed a number of these progressive proposals and signed the bills enacting them into law. Thus he helped put on the statute books the postal-savings act (over the protest of bankers) and the parcels-post act (over the protest of express companies). He shared some of the credit for the income-tax amendment, awaiting ratification at the hands of state legislatures in 1912. He signed two significant conservation measures, one separating the surface of public lands from the mineral rights beneath and the other withdrawing waterpower sites from entry. But nearly all of the conservation publicity the President received was adverse, arising out of his removal of Chief Forrester Gifford Pinchot, a warm personal friend of Roosevelt. Having the best intentions of revising the tariff, the President finally accepted the Payne-Aldrich document which was very generally condemned as not a true revision but a step backward. He made a genuine effort to enforce the law against restraining trade, but his work was partially blocked by the Court's ruling that only combinations which unduly restrained trade were banned under the law.

A very poor publicity man, unfortunate in that the best showman who had ever been in the White House was still very active, unlucky in the sequence of events, temperamentally unsuited for the rôle of Chief Executive, the President usually failed to get credit for his best achievements. He appeared to be much more out of step with the times than he really was.

The Republicans were definitely divided into progressive and conservative factions in 1910, and the Democrats were decidedly aggressive. After their victory in the Congressional elections of that year, the Democrats became jubilant; the Republicans became more factional; the President's unhappiness increased. The Senate ruined the arbitration treaties he had negotiated with England and France, and his Canadian reciprocity project, which he had pushed through Congress at the cost of increasing party dissension, was defeated by the Canadian Parliament.

Progressive Republicans were determined to prevent the renomination of Taft in 1912. They rallied for a time around Senator La Follette. They considered Roosevelt one of their number, but there was uncertainty as to whether he would support La Follette or seek the nomination himself. La Follette thought Roosevelt had agreed to support him, but as weeks and months passed, the Colonel gave La Follette less and less encouragement. La Follette says in his *Autobiography* (p. 521) that Senator Borah was favorable to his candidacy, but that the Idahoan said he could not declare himself openly on account of political conditions in his own state. He did, however, continued La Follette, give assurance that the Idaho delegation would support La Follette at the national convention. But this conversation took place before February, 1912, when Theodore Roosevelt announced that his hat was in the ring.

In April, 1912, the Colonel asked Senator Borah to come to Oyster Bay. They talked at length of the approaching campaign for the nomination for the Presidency. The Senator, also national committeeman from his State, assured the Colonel that he would give him any assistance within his power in securing the Republican nomination.

The conversation turned to the possible effect of the campaign upon the party, the split which seemed to be impending, and similar matters. This discussion led to the question of whether the dissension would lead to a third party or a third ticket.

The Senator stated: "I hope it will not result in a third ticket or a third party. I am very much opposed to any such movement. A third party would get nowhere. We have got to fight it out in the convention and abide by the results."

Colonel Roosevelt said, in substance: "Our friends should not think or talk about a third party. Any such talk would weaken us in the fight and we want no third party. That would only result in the election of a Democrat." These continued to be the views of the Colonel, so far as the Senator knew them, until a few hours after Taft was nominated.

Back in Idaho the *Statesman* was equally strong for the reëlection of Taft and Borah. The Republican organization in that State was for the renomination of Taft, and, finding no weakness in Borah's armor which might make him vulnerable before the electorate, supported the renomination of the Senator also.

Nevertheless, the Senator used all his influence to line up Roosevelt delegates for the state convention. In Boise, because of the *Statesman* and conservative influences generally, Taft delegates were chosen 2 to 1; but in the rural section of Borah's home county Roosevelt led. The majority of the delegates to the state convention were for Roosevelt, but it cannot be said that the sentiment for the Colonel was overwhelming. Taft had many and strong supporters in Idaho.

The state convention at Lewiston (May 16) praised Taft weakly and Roosevelt warmly. It selected Roosevelt men as delegates to the national convention, but as a concession allowed two Taft men to go along with the understanding they would vote with the majority for Roosevelt. La Follette was the second choice of the Lewiston convention. The Idaho Senators, busy at their posts in Washington, received due praise from the convention, Senator Borah being especially mentioned for his successful efforts in securing for submission to the states the constitutional amendment providing for the direct election of senators.

The *Statesman,* always championing Taft and Borah, said it was madness to attempt to nominate Roosevelt. In Washington, Idaho's Senior Senator, Heyburn, shouted to the progressive senators: "If you believe in the principles of the Democratic party, then go there. Do not use the livery of heaven in which to serve the devil."

M. F. Cunningham (Nora Marks), writing from Boise for the *Tribune,* believed that Borah was in a dangerous position, that Roosevelt might bolt, and that Borah would have to declare himself for Roosevelt or Taft. He went on to say that a number of Taft organization men in Idaho were angry at Borah now and that they would not vote for him for Senator. He admitted, however, that Borah was stronger than his party in Idaho, and considered as well-founded the rumor that the Senator would work quietly for the reëlection of Governor Hawley, his old Democratic friend, and that the Governor would in like manner assist the Senator in his campaign for reëlection.[1]

We move forward a few weeks and gather with the delegates at the national convention in Chicago. Would Senator Borah bolt if Roosevelt was not nominated? The New York *Times,* of June 10, said that Borah, Frank B. Kellogg of Minnesota, and William Flynn of Pennsylvania have told their friends in so many words that they are Republicans and that the Colonel must expect no support from them if he should choose to run on a third ticket. Five days later, Borah is quoted as saying: "So far as the question of bolting is concerned it has never entered my mind."

At the convention Senator Borah was a very prominent figure. He was intensely popular with newspaper men, being interviewed, photographed, and caricatured (his long hair was responsible for this) as few other leaders were.

He was one of Roosevelt's leading supporters, certainly his most eloquent supporter, for the nomination. One of the principal speakers at the Roosevelt forces' strategy meeting on the eve of the convention, he was making great headway when the Colonel rushed in and took the platform, which Borah yielded with good grace. At one time the Senator was understood to be the Colonel's choice for temporary chairman of the convention, but McGovern of Wisconsin was nominated for that honor, perhaps because the Senator had made such positive statements against any bolting tactics.

As the two leading contestants for the nomination showed a firm desire to kill each other off, threatening to wreck the party, Borah was suggested as a compromise candidate. His candidacy seems to have been suggested first by the New York

[1] Lewiston *Tribune,* May 30, 1912.

Post as early as March 14, 1912. As he was reasonably progressive, but not definitely lined up with either faction of the Republican party, the *Post* said he ought to be acceptable to both factions. The suggestion of the *Post* was not taken seriously, certainly not by Senator Borah. At the convention there was again some talk of Borah as a candidate, and one morning the Idaho delegates came down with "Borah for President" hatbands which they distributed in the lobby of their hotel until Borah heard of it. Embarrassed, the Senator ordered them to collect the hatbands at once and get them out of sight. He told them that he appreciated the compliment but that he did not want to be the laughing stock of the convention. William Barnes of New York, no particular friend of the Colonel's, wanted Borah to take second place on a ticket with Hughes. Barnes went to see Borah three times, but the Senator said he simply would not be a candidate.

The story of those hectic days at Chicago need not be prolonged. It is a matter of common knowledge that the regular organization was composed of Taft men and that they were thus able to seat about fifty Taft delegates although the Roosevelt delegates had a better claim to the seats. This gave Taft a small majority and he was nominated.

Senator Borah went to Roosevelt's suite at his hotel, where the Colonel was having his lunch all by himself. Mrs. Roosevelt was sitting by a window in an adjoining room doing some needle work. This was the conversation:

The Senator: "Well, I have come to tell you good-bye. I guess I have done all I can do. The thing is over."

The Colonel: "I am glad you came in. I had a man out hunting for you. I do not know how you feel about it by this time, but if you feel that you can, I should like to have you join my friends in this meeting at the theater tonight."

The Senator: "Well, Colonel, I am sorry, but I have gone as far as I can go. I have always been opposed to a third party movement. I think it is a great mistake. I not only can not go but I would not like to see your friends go over there and commit you, practically nominate you, on a third ticket."

The Colonel, with considerable irritation: "Well, what

would you have me do? These men are in earnest. If they do not nominate me, they will nominate La Follette. The movement can not be stopped."

The Senator: "Colonel, those men will do just as you tell them to do. Call in some of the leaders and tell them that you do not want any such action, and they will not take any such action."

The conversation continued for a few more minutes. Borah told Roosevelt that he would have nothing behind him if he accepted a nomination from this group, that he had been ready to accept the Republican nomination with the platform upon which Taft had been nominated and that, consequently, his group would be just a wing of the Republican party. He told the Colonel further that if he must have a third party, to go home and organize it from the ground up. The Colonel, his temper not improving, told Borah that he could break the Solid South. Borah replied that he would not on any such program as that now contemplated. Then Roosevelt's bolting supporters came running in with bundles of telegrams and shouted: "The country will not stand for it; the country is afire; you must lead us." The Senator edged out of the room.

The Senator has always been of the opinion that had the meeting been postponed until the next day, the nomination might not have been made, but because it came on the day of excited indignation over Taft's nomination, Roosevelt's nomination at the theater was inevitable. To be sure, Roosevelt was not officially nominated at that meeting, but for all practical purposes he was. The later convention was only a ratifying assembly.

A great deal has been said and written about Borah's desertion of Roosevelt in 1912, about the "rabble-rouser" who, performing characteristically, "turned his back on the rabble just as it was ready to charge the gates." Mrs. Alice Longworth, a warm friend of the Borahs, writes of the enemies and deserters who crowded the train on which she rode back East after the convention. She classed Borah with the deserters. As a matter of fact, the Senator's conduct in the Roosevelt-Taft fight was entirely consistent (not that it would have bothered him had it not been consistent) from the time he told the Colonel he would support him for the regular Republican nomination and expressed his opposition to any third ticket until he told Roosevelt to call off the progressives who were about to nominate him at a Chicago theater. The Senator not only never agreed to go into any third-party movement with the Colonel, but he also stated privately and publicly a number of times during the pre-convention campaign that he was opposed to any such movement. It seems fairly clear that it was the Colonel, not the Senator, who did the deserting.

ALTHOUGH he refused to go with Roosevelt on his Pentecostal political crusade, Borah, on the other hand, advocated Taft's reëlection so silently that it hurt. His first statement after the nomination was that he would stand by the ticket but that he did not care to discuss the matter. He never did care to discuss it; nevertheless, he did explain his position fully and frankly when he came back to Idaho. It was that he could not support Roosevelt because he had bolted and that he could not support Taft because of the manner in which the nomination had been made.

Every conceivable effort was made by both Taft and Roosevelt forces to win Borah over, but he stuck to his position of neutrality. Roosevelt said that he would not interfere with Borah in Idaho, and that he would regard his defeat as a national calamity. Yet the Colonel had his manager wire Borah repeatedly that he had better declare for the Colonel before that candidate reached Idaho. Finally Borah replied to one of these wires: "THE COLONEL NEEDS ME IN IDAHO MORE THAN I NEED HIM."

While both parties were tugging at Borah, the Republican state central committee resolved that it could not "too strongly endorse" the Senator who had "reflected the highest honor upon his constituency at home and at large." [2] And on July 30, the Republicans of Idaho went to their first senatorial primary and gave Borah their endorsement for reëlection. A few Democratic papers even came out for Borah,

[2] *Statesman,* July 11, 1912.

and several Democratic candidates for the legislature said that they would vote in the legislature for the return of Borah to the Senate.

When it seemed clear that Borah would not come out for either Taft or Roosevelt, the *Statesman* printed an editorial "We Always Walk with Bill." [3] "If he does not like the first party nor the third party we will, if necessary, start a fourth one — the Mountain Goat party of Idaho — and we will make Bill the Bull Goat. Bill is certainly as sane as the rest of them in knowing positively that he is for himself."

On September 10, the Bull Moose party in Idaho endorsed Borah for the Senate. On the next day the Colonel himself was in Boise for a speech. Borah gave him an "I do not cease to respect and admire" introduction and side-stepped any commitment. The Colonel plunged into his speech denouncing the Republican "steal" at the Chicago convention. When he had detailed a particularly villainous theft, he would turn to Borah with an "Isn't that true, Senator?" or request his audience, with a nod toward Borah, to "Ask Senator Borah." The Senator would smile or nod, but that is all the Colonel could get from him either in public or in private.

Borah's full, frank, and fighting explanation of his position in the Taft-Roosevelt fight was made at Meridian, a little town not far from Boise, where he usually opened his campaigns.[4] "In one day this week," he began, "I received communications from two candidates for the legislature, both on the Republican ticket. One of these gentlemen informed me if I was not a Taft man he would not vote for me. The other said he was a Roosevelt man and if I was not for Roosevelt he would not support me. I did not answer either one of these letters, but I answer them now openly and publicly.

"These men seem to be hunting for an intellectual slave. They seem anxious to bestow their favors and their votes upon some personal menial of some particular individual. They do not ask me whether I am a Republican or a third-party man. They do not ask me whether I believe in this

[3] *Ibid.*, August 28, 1912.
[4] *Ibid.*, September 15, 1912.

policy or that. They do not say 'Your record as a Senator has not been to the credit of your State and, therefore, I must oppose you.' They do not say 'You are unfit to be a Senator, therefore I shall campaign against you.' One of them, in fact, was very complimentary about my work in the Senate. But they do say 'Unless you declare your allegiance to one or the other of these men you must go down to defeat.'

"I reject their standards, I reject their rules, I repudiate their test before the people of this State openly and publicly. If you ask me if I am a Republican I answer, 'Yes,' as I understand Republican doctrines I am. If you ask me if I am a third-party man I answer 'No,' I have not joined the third party. I am a Progressive, but I want to fight inside the old party. But inside or outside I propose to urge the Progressive measures for which I, with others, have stood."

Then he reviewed his record in the Senate during the Taft Administration and expressed the opinion that it was a good Republican record, despite the fact that he had felt compelled to oppose the President on several matters.

"I ask those who say I am not a Republican to meet me upon the record. Where is the Republican who will defend upon the rostrum free trade for the farmer and protection for the manufacturer, free trade for all your grain and farm produce and protection for the blanket which you buy to protect you from the winter's cold? Where is the Republican who will oppose in the open the election of Senators by popular vote? Where is the Republican who will meet me in debate in defense of the commerce court? Is the three-year homestead bill, which gives to the settler a chance to overcome adversity and win a home, un-Republican — the first homestead law was signed by Abraham Lincoln. Is the dry homestead bill, which enables man to reclaim these vast areas of desert and make them habitable and fruitful, un-Republican? Is the Children's Bureau bill, which uncovers the fiendish greed of Eastern manufacturers and rescues from industrial slavery the girls and boys coming to the responsibilities of citizenship, un-Republican? Is the bill that I now have pending to create a department of labor and make the secretary thereof a member of the cabinet un-Republican? Is the title bill which gives the settlers on reclamation projects a chance before they are driven off in adversity and despair un-Republican? Is the eight-hour law I urged through Congress un-Republican? What bill have I advocated that they will condemn? . . ."

He had been nominated for the Senate in the Republican primary, and Republicans elected to the legislature were thus morally obligated to vote for him when the legislature should choose a Senator the following January. He explained how they might free themselves from this obligation, if they did not approve of his stand in the presidential campaign.

"As to the candidates for the legislature, if there are any of them who feel that they cannot conscientiously vote for me as Senator, there is a manly and honorable way to be released from their obligation to do so. I have been nominated at the primary on the Republican ticket. It does not legally bind the members of the legislature, but unless repudiated before the election it becomes a most solemn moral obligation. But I think that the candidate for the legislature who would openly and clearly state to his people before the election that he did not intend to vote for me would in all fairness be released from doing so. I think he has that right. Let him settle it with the voters. If he states to them he will not be bound by the primary and they nevertheless elect him it would constitute a clear exception from the obligation in the present state of our primary law as to United States Senator. If he does not so state it would be dishonorable and cowardly not to stand by the obligation expressed by the primary vote. I know practically all the candidates for the legislature. I haven't a particle of doubt but they will speak plainly on the subject before the election and be bound by whatever statement they make to the voters."

As to the charge that he was a "trimmer," he said: "If they say to you that Borah is trimming, that he does not take a stand, ask them upon what question, upon what issue, upon what measure in Congress or this campaign he has failed to take an open and decided and positive stand. Ask them if they have any doubt as to what his position will be on all these questions in the coming Congress. What policy which touches the interest of the people of this State have I not met openly and candidly? If so, state them. What question is there tonight that touches your interest or your welfare or the welfare of the people of this State about which you entertain any possible doubt as to my position? It is because I am positive upon all these questions that the opposition is coming from certain sources to my reëlection. It is because I refuse to yield my views or modify my position on certain public questions that they are dissatisfied with me. If I were more uncertain they would be far more certain as to their support of me. If I were a little more unsteady they would be more steadfast. Do you people want a representative in the Senate who is uncertain as to policies and well hitched up to individuals who would yield his views and modify his opinions to harmonize with the views of those whom you do not elect to represent you? A man who will not stand for what he thinks is right at home regardless of individuals or candidates at the head or tail of the ticket will not stand up for them at Washington, and God pity the miserable creature sailing upon that turbulent political sea at Washington without convictions for a compass. I have seen them and there is nothing more despicable in all the world besides. Men without poise and purpose, without convictions and determination, who do not stand ready to fight for their views regardless of who opposes them upon all these great questions are the miserable instruments by which men of sinister purposes accomplish their design. There is not a public question, not a public issue that I am not ready to discuss with men or before the people in this campaign. I am for measures, not men, and I will make my campaign on that line regardless of political consequence."

Using an opportunity offered for questions, a man in the audience arose and asked the Senator if he believed President Taft had been honestly or honorably nominated.

The Senator answered: "I think 78 delegates were seated for Taft that any fair tribunal would have given to Roosevelt, and 52 delegates were seated for Taft that no honest tribunal could have denied Roosevelt."

It is worth noticing that Borah made no extreme claims concerning the 252 seats in dispute when the convention assembled. Some weeks after his Meridian speech he explained more fully his position relative to the disputed seats. Speaking at Cœur d'Alene, he said: [5] "I find that some of my political and some of my warm friends are criticizing me for stating that President Taft was not fairly nominated in Chicago. Well, I will repeat it. I sat in that convention as a national committeeman from Idaho. I voted against the seating of 164 Roosevelt delegates. I voted against the seating of 78 Taft delegates – I was not crooked when I cast my votes, and I'll not be a liar in this campaign. . . I cannot change the record and I don't want to. Let that be settled in your minds forever, and if I am defeated let it be so."

ALTHOUGH Borah's Republicanism did not satisfy the old line Republicans in Idaho, even these Republicans knew that the rank and file of Idaho Republican voters were so well satisfied with Borah's record in the Senate that they could easily excuse him from supporting Taft. Republican leaders knew more – they knew that the Progressives were so well satisfied with Borah that they could forgive him for not declaring for Roosevelt, and that many personal friends in the Democratic party and liberals of that party would support Borah. Consequently, after the Senator's Meridian speech, a number of Republican candidates for the legislature, some with enthusiasm, others grudgingly and of necessity, declared their intention, if elected to the legislature, of voting for Borah's return to the Senate.

In a little town in southern Idaho in which Borah was to speak he met a Republican who was on the legislative ticket. Borah said, "How about it?" The candidate said that he could not make up his mind as to whom he would support for the Senate until after he had been elected to the legislature. Borah said: "Tonight either you will declare for me from the platform or I will tell the people you are against me and you can take your chances of election on that." The man declared for Borah that night. The Progressives named no candidates for the legislature. A few of the Democratic candidates declared for Borah.

Borah had no organization support in the campaign. He

[5] *Capital News,* October 5, 1912.

had his own headquarters, sent out his own literature, and arranged his own meetings. He had none of the larger Republican newspapers on his side. Although they did not oppose him, they would not actively support him because he would not declare for Taft. The Progressive press was inclined to be friendly — but not too friendly, because he would not support Roosevelt. Some of the smaller papers, even Democratic papers, gave him whole-hearted endorsement, and the leading Democratic paper, the Lewiston *Tribune*, gave him what amounted to support by paying him compliments.

The Salt Lake *Tribune*, widely read in Idaho, ran an editorial (September 17): "Senator Borah is Manly." "He is not a man to trim, or hedge, or to straddle the fence on any political question. . . He declared his position so openly, so manfully, and with such complete candor, that those who would like to charge him with evasion or trimming are utterly put to shame."

The *Argonaut* of San Francisco (October 19) declared that it would be a shame for Idaho not to reëlect Senator Borah and that his absence from the Senate would be a stupendous loss to the country. It praised him as a great progressive and commended his wisdom in staying by his party, even if he was not staying close by.

Rabbi Wise, tremendously interested in Borah's candidacy, wrote to a friend in Boise: "The failure to return Senator Borah to the United States Senate would be far from honoring Idaho and would, moreover, deprive the Senate and the nation of the services of one of its most gifted leaders. Surely this cannot be."

Without a great deal of effort Borah secured the endorsement of Labor. N. P. Alifas, President of District Lodge No. 44 of the International Association of Mechanics, wrote to many labor organizations in Idaho, praising Borah as a friend of labor and citing concrete examples. Later, replying to a letter from Borah, Mr. Alifas wrote: "The cities you mention as demanding special attention, all have quite a number of organizations which were on my mailing list. . . You will note that among other things I asked them to do, is to put their candidates to the state legislature on record as to their attitude on your candidacy. . . I did not want to make my letter so long that it might not be read so many of the commendatory things that I would like to have said about your record in Congress, I had to omit."

But Samuel Gompers, President of the A. F. of L., was willing to risk a long letter (October 11) to officers and members of all local and central bodies in Idaho. "From information received, it is quite evident that the 'interests' are endeavoring to defeat the Hon. Wm. E. Borah for reëlection to the United States Senate. The working people and all liberty loving citizens of Idaho should rally to his support. As proof of Senator Borah's work and worth I give herewith his record upon all measures which have come before the United States Senate since he was elected, January 15, 1907 in which the interests of labor have been involved." He then gave twenty-two instances in which Borah had championed the cause of labor. "His great humanitarian impulses" had long since appealed to Mr. Gompers. Not only was the Senator glad to have this letter for his campaign, but he was also very proud of this manifestation of labor's friendship.

As the campaign drew to a close it was perfectly clear that the "paramount issue in Idaho was the reëlection of Senator Borah." Those who were bitterly opposed to him (chiefly Taft Republicans) were so sure that this issue was uppermost in the popular mind that they dared not oppose Borah openly. As for the "Moosevelts," they told the voters to be sure to vote the regular Republican ticket for the state legislature (the Roosevelt people made no nominations for the legislative offices), as that was the only way to make sure of Borah's reëlection. Even so, the extent of Borah's victory was something of a surprise.

Borah's failure to declare for Roosevelt, Idaho's lukewarm sympathy with Roosevelt's conservation policies and its appreciation of Taft's support for irrigation projects, the Mormon influence, and the tariff almost carried Idaho for Taft, but Wilson finally nosed him out. Roosevelt received approximately two-thirds as many votes as Wilson. John M. Haines (Republican) won a narrow victory over Borah's friend, James H. Hawley (Democrat), for governor. The

Progressive candidate for governor was slightly behind Roosevelt in the number of votes. How did Borah fare? Since the people could not vote directly for Senators, they could express their preference for Borah only through choosing a legislature favorable to his election, a Republican legislature. This they did with a vengeance. Of the 24 senators chosen, 22 were Republicans; of 60 members of the house, 56 were Republicans. This was the largest Republican majority the Idaho legislature had ever had. And two of the six Democratic members of the legislature were pledged to vote for Borah if their votes were needed. Senator Borah sometimes says he put Idaho to the test in 1912 and that she measured up.

It seems fitting to close this chapter with a further discussion of Borah's Republicanism. In Lewiston, where he held his audience "for two hours in rapt attention," he said:[6] "Any mistakes which I have made in the Senate are my mistakes. I do not and never have undertaken to hide behind a party caucus or a party organization." He explained that because his Republicanism had been challenged so often in the campaign he would ask for the privilege of being personal. He felt that the people of Lewiston would forgive him this one time, "as I have the advantage of a great newspaper [the *Tribune*] of this city and I can reach a great many people by one reference to it." The Senator then stated that President Taft in his letter of acceptance had listed as achievements of his Administration, among other things, the child-labor law (the one establishing the Children's Bureau), the eight-hour law, the homestead law, and the reclamation law. He suggested that, since he was the author of these measures, President Taft at least must consider him a good Republican. Borah made a good case.

Following the subject of his Republicanism still further, we go back into the Senate record for his votes. In estimating the party fidelity of members by their votes we simply take the members where we find them. We take their own word for their party affiliation, but the degree of their fidelity is determined by the company they keep. Thus, without

[6] *Tribune,* October 15, 1912.

going into technicalities, if 25 Republicans vote on one side of a question and 25 other Republicans vote on the other side, each Republican has a party fidelity of 50 per cent. If 30 vote on one side and 20 vote on the other, each man in the 30 group has a fidelity of 60 per cent and each one in the 20 group has a fidelity of 40 per cent. This may not be the most satisfactory method of measuring party fidelity, but it is a way and it has the virtue of simplicity. Perhaps a word is needed to prevent a shock. By this method of measurement no Republican senator will get 100 per cent on fidelity, because that would be possible only when all Republicans vote together. This almost never happens. The man who associates with the greatest number of Republicans in voting gets the highest rating; the man who associates with the smallest number gets the lowest rating. Consequently, the reader must not be surprised to find that Aldrich, Penrose, and Smoot are rated at less than 100 per cent, nor may the good Republican be resentful when he reads that La Follette's fidelity to the Republican party was well above 1 per cent.

Taking the first Congress in which Borah sat, the Sixtieth, we find that the Aldrich-Penrose-Smoot variety of Republican averages around 80 per cent in fidelity. Borah stood well down the list with 60 per cent, La Follette alone being lower with 50 per cent. On the question of Employers' Liability which should have differentiated regulars and progressives, Borah indicated the extreme of progressivism, having a Republican fidelity score of only 30 per cent. La Follette's votes were not recorded on this measure.

In the Sixty-first Congress good Republicans like Aldrich made fidelity scores of around 90 against the income tax, while those who favored the income tax (Borah, Bristow, Clapp, and Cummins) scored only 28 per cent on Republican fidelity. On the corporation tax (introduced to defeat the income tax) about the same difference in scores obtained. Stalwart G.O.P. men made scores of 83 per cent on the Payne-Aldrich tariff. Borah's score of 74 per cent was not far behind, while progressive senators from the Middle West ranged between 50 and 25 per cent. In opposing the postal savings bill the conservative Republicans made a fidelity score of about 85 per cent; in favoring it progressives made a fidelity score ranging from 40 per cent on up. Borah's score was 53 per cent. On ship subsidies the regulars had a fidelity of 77; the most consistent progressives went only 20 per cent of the way, while Borah reached the 43 per cent mark.

Coming to the Sixty-second Congress, that which marked the end of the "Progressive Era," we find Borah more of a progressive than a regular in his tariff votes. It should be stated, however, that regular and progressive sentiments on this question were much more evenly balanced than they were over the Payne-Aldrich tariff. On the American Seamen Act regulars stood at about 62 per cent; Borah voted with the progressives with the lowest Republican fidelity — 38 per cent. An interesting trend was noted in the votes on the Children's Bureau. Regular Republicans, for the most part, along with the progressives, supported it, with the result that Borah, La Follette, and other progressives suddenly found themselves with a Republican fidelity of about 80 per cent. The few die-hards who opposed it dropped well toward the bottom of the scale in party fidelity!

In summary, measured by the votes of all senators who called themselves Republicans, Borah falls distinctly in the progressive group on all important matters save the tariff, where he was not far below regular. But Borah was not interested in the progressive organizaton as an independent organization. He regarded himself as a progressive Republican rather than as a *Progressive*. His interest was in making the Republican party progressive. He could not see what could be accomplished by a Progressive party beyond assuring victory to the Democrats.

The Senator knew that the greater number of those who shared his social views were in the party of Roosevelt in 1912, but he knew also that nearly all of them would come back to the Republican party sooner or later. He remembered 1896.

The Senator had another reason for not leaving the Republican party. It was that he was as free in it as he would be in any other. That Borah has been free in the Republican party is a statement which he can always make "without fear of successful contradiction."

But there are still hundreds of thousands of people who ask why Borah, a Republican, would not support Taft, the Republican nominee. The answer is that Borah was a Republican with a conscience so acute that he could not endorse a political steal. This answer brings only irritation and the defiant question, "Then why wouldn't he support Roosevelt?" He didn't support Roosevelt because he felt that revolt was futile. This reason satisfies few people. They insist that a man must support someone. Most men do, but Borah did not and does not. He supports issues. In 1912 he battled for reëlection on progressive Republican issues. This fight for issues rather than men, this carrying an issue rather than wearing some other man's collar or some organization's halter, is what the country at large simply cannot understand. That is why the public, even the great majority of the enlightened people, cannot understand Borah. But the Idahoans have understood him fairly well since 1912.

CHAPTER IX

NEW FREEDOM POLITICS

SENATOR BORAH had been reading Wilson's works for years and he regarded him as "a ripe scholar" and "a profound student of American institutions." [1] In addition, the Senator had a very high appreciation of Wilson's literary style. In the published views of the President-elect, the Senator found as a basis for dissent only enough ground to maintain that minimum of difference which a Senator of one party feels duty bound to hold toward a President of another. The Senator awaited the inauguration of Mr. Wilson without misgivings. He was anxious to see how far the President would push the New Freedom program.

Only a few weeks after Mr. Wilson's nomination there was debate in the Senate upon the question of the single six-year presidential term. The Idaho Senator said he wanted to read something from "an acknowledged leader in public affairs." Senator Cummins yielded the floor after Borah admitted that he desired to read from Dr. Wilson's *Congressional Government.* After the reading Senator Bacon of Georgia said he hoped the author would continue to hold those views after March 4, 1913. Borah made this pertinent observation : "I have no doubt they will all be entertained, because everyone knows that Dr. Wilson has well-settled views and convictions." [2]

A month later Mr. Borah was again reading Dr. Wilson's *Congressional Government* to his colleagues. Senator John Sharp Williams remarked that Theodore Roosevelt had accused Jefferson of cowardice and that Wilson had never been so unjust. Senator Borah replied to his friend : "The Senator ought not to touch too heavily upon the subject of what Roosevelt said about Thomas Jefferson. Governor Wilson has said about Thomas Jefferson practically the same thing Colonel Roosevelt said about him. He said he was a negative character touching a philosophy in which he did not

[1] *Congressional Record,* July 16, 1912, p. 9126.
[2] *Ibid.,* 9127.

believe because it was popular. That is the substance of his statement."

Mr. Williams: "Ah, that is the substance put upon it by the Senator from Idaho."

Mr. Borah: "I can read it." The Senator immediately turned to the place and read: "The difference between Mr. Jefferson and General Jackson was not a difference of moral quality so much as a difference in social stock and breeding. Mr. Jefferson, an aristocrat, and yet a philosophical radical, deliberately practised the arts of the politician and exhibited oftentimes the sort of insincerity which subtle natures yield to without loss of essential integrity." [3]

Still another time Borah read from Wilson. Senator Williams, slightly deaf, had understood Senator Borah to say he was reading from Hamilton. The Senator from Mississippi arose to denounce what the Idahoan had just read. A colleague gave a strong tug at the Mississippian's coat sleeve and told the embarrassed Senator that Borah had read from Dr. Wilson.

ABOUT the first of December, 1912, Senator Borah suggested that the Republican party would do well to propose a program which would include a proper system of national taxation, the rehabilitation of our financial system, and an effective solution of the trust problem. A number of Democratic papers thought these suggestions good for the Democrats, and their party did deal with these questions.

The income tax, now possible under the amendment which Senator Borah had so ably championed, was enacted at last. Borah was heartily in favor of it because it was a tax which the rich could not easily pass on to the poor, and because he felt that this form of tax would make the people more conscious of the fact that the government was spending their money, thus increasing their interest in governmental economy, ever a favorite subject with Borah. The Senator insisted upon wording the law so that corporations might not escape the tax or wealthy estates escape by incorporating themselves. He introduced an amendment providing for rates slightly higher on the large incomes than the very

[3] *Ibid.*, August 19, 1912, p. 11262.

modest ones called for in the original bill. Senator Lodge said the rates proposed showed a malicious attempt to brand the wealthy as criminals. To this Borah replied: "I seek to punish no man because of his wealth. . . But I would count myself recreant to the public service if I did not seek to so shape the laws of my country as to mete out to him the same obligations as rest upon the unsuccessful or penniless. It is not demagoguery; it is the fundamental but forgotten principle upon which this government was established." [4]

The Senior Senator from Idaho (Senator Heyburn had died late in 1912) took considerable interest in the Federal Reserve Bill. He had studied the central banking systems in Great Britain, France, and Germany, and he had read the none-too-reassuring history of such institutions in the United States. He was opposed to any revival of the earlier American type of central banking, not because these institutions had not been business successes, but because all of them had become entangled in politics. He favored the central banking systems in the European countries named because the governments of those countries controlled the issue of currency and made such currency legal tender. He was in favor of establishing a central banking system in the United States — but a system in which the government, not the bankers, would initiate the issue of currency. To allow the bankers to expand and contract the currency "takes from the people a sovereign right and parcels it out to those whose prime interest must be that of gain, and, not satisfied with giving over to private interests the sole use and monopoly of currency and credits, it gives them the astounding privilege to say how much we shall have or how much we shall not have." [5]

Trusts and monopolies have always been arch-demons with Borah. He wanted the Sherman law made more specific. "To my mind it is just as impracticable to try a man for the crime of restraint of trade as it would be to try a man who had committed murder for having retarded the development of the human race." [6] But the Senator gave very little sup-

[4] *Ibid.*, August 28, 1913, p. 3841.
[5] *Ibid.*, December 12, 1913.
[6] *Ibid.*, August 9, 1913, p. 3220.

port to the Wilson anti-trust legislation. He viewed the proposed Federal Trade Commission with the gravest misapprehensions. He considered the proposal as a scheme for regulating monopoly, a plan under which the monopolies would make a supreme effort, with every prospect of success, to regulate their regulators. The Sherman Act had the right principle, he said ; it set out to abolish trusts and monopolies. That – not regulation – was what Borah wanted. As for the Clayton Anti-Trust Act, designed to bolster up the Sherman Act and exempt labor and agriculture from prosecution as combinations in restraint of trade, he voted against it as a whole, because he looked upon it, he wrote a constituent, "as a vicious deception and a fraud, inconsistent, incongruous, duplicitious, and ambitious, purely a political makeshift to mislead the people into the belief that something tremendous has been done on the trust question." He received many letters listing objections to this bill. His stock reply was that the Republicans had nothing to do with it, that Congress had nothing to do with it, and that all legislation was by the Democratic caucus under the control of the President.

Borah took his usual position on the tariff, arguing that the farmer should have more protection than that provided for in the Underwood bill, that free trade for the producer and protection for the manufacturer meant ruin to the former, that the country could not prosper unless agriculture prospered. He wanted goods manufactured by convicts and by women and children working an excessive number of hours barred from the United States. He lashed out at American manufacturers employing child labor, and stated that "every law which a republic writes should have in it not only a principle of economy, but it should have in it also the principle of humanity." [7]

This principle of humanity has always been strong with Senator Borah, and during this same period he gave other evidence of his adherence to it. It was reported that the miners in the Paint Creek Coal Fields in West Virginia were being tried by military courts when the civil courts were open, a process involving the "most vital principle of per-

[7] *Ibid.*, October 2, 1913, p. 5342.

sonal liberty." The West Virginia Senators argued, of course, that an investigation as proposed by Senator Borah would constitute an invasion of states' rights. But Borah's resolution passed (May 27, 1913). Early in January of the next year Borah reported the findings of his committee — that parts of West Virginia had been without the republican form of government which Congress was supposed to guarantee to each state. The Springfield *Republican* said that if Senator Borah reported facts which discredited the authorities of the State, "that's pretty near the last word." [8] The Idaho Senator was then urged by letters and wires to get similar investigations in Michigan and Colorado. He agreed that such investigations should be held, but replied that the majority party should take the initiative. About this time a Boise labor union wired him to support a certain labor bill without amendment. He wired back that no true representative should ever make such a promise.

One of two votes cast in the Senate by William E. Borah which he now regrets is that cast in 1916 against the confirmation of Louis D. Brandeis as Associate Justice of the Supreme Court. It is inappropriate to enter into a detailed discussion of the reasons which impelled Borah to vote in the negative. In the first place, he was afraid Brandeis believed in the theory of regulating trusts and monopolies rather than in the good straightforward plan of abolishing them. In the second place, and this was his chief objection to Mr. Brandeis, the Senator's ideas of legal ethics differed somewhat from those which he understood Mr. Brandeis held as a practising attorney. But the Senator hastens to explain that he has long since been satisfied in his own mind that the conscience of Mr. Justice Brandeis was at all times clear in the matter of legal ethics.

"Your vote was certainly a severe disappointment to your friends in the East," wrote a man from New York. "For this reason I think it is due your friends to take them into your confidence on the subject." The Senator replied that Justice Brandeis was now on the Bench and that the subject

[8] Springfield *Republican,* January 6, 1914.

was closed to discussion. He stated, however, that "It is wholly immaterial to me whether anybody in the world approves of my course if I am individually convinced that I am doing the right thing."

IN Chapter VI the point was emphasized that the Senator continued his interest in Idaho and her affairs after he became a national statesman. But it is appropriate to return to that subject, for during his second term there arose a situation which shows the limit the Senator places upon that interest and reveals a reason for the belief that he has lost it. The rivers and harbors bill of 1914, reeking with and almost sinking under its cargo of pork, carried an appropriation to deepen and clear the channel of the upper Columbia River. Since Lewiston on the Snake River stood to benefit by this improvement, the Commercial Club of that city asked the Senator why he opposed the rivers and harbors bill.

The Senator replied, August 13, 1914: "It is indefensible both as a matter of policy and by reason of the notoriously bad items or projects covered by the bill. Anxious as I am to see a rivers and harbors bill passed, I find myself unable to compromise upon a measure which to my mind is indefensible from the standpoint of official decency and public morals. . ." He then gave examples of proposed improvements which would cost the Government more than the value of all freight moved.

"But I am told in the face of these facts through letters and telegrams that the corps of engineers have made these recommendations and they seem to think I should excuse myself by falling back upon the recommendations of the engineers. When the engineers are criticized they say, we were simply trying to carry out the policy of Congress. . . I would consider it a distinct act of moral cowardice, a signal betrayal of duty to the people whom I try to represent if when confronted with such a condition as this bill presents I should cowardly fall back upon a recommendation of the engineer," who, after all, did not recommend some of the worst projects called for by the bill.

"I would like to feel that I have the support and endorsement of the people of Lewiston. . . But whether I have the support of the people at home or not, I must oppose this bill in its present form."

This is another quality in Borah which many people, especially politically-minded people, cannot understand. How on earth could a man in Congress have the unadulterated nerve defiantly to throw a piece of pork, for which his constitutents are clamoring, back into the barrel? Taking it makes no trouble; rejection brings endless explanations. "Official decency" and "public morals," these are not mere catch words with Borah.

As a matter of fact, in this particular controversy, Senators Borah, Burton, and Kenyon forced many of the worst items out of the river and harbors bill, and because the projects in which Lewiston was interested were fairly worthy ones, appropriations were finally made for them.

Another Idaho incident of the same year throws a great light upon the reason for Senator Borah's being considered such an indifferent Republican. The Republicans and the remnant of the Progressives in Idaho were still angry with Borah because he had hoed a middle row in 1912, but everyone who hoped to get on the Republican ticket in 1914 wanted his endorsement because his name was potent with the voters. Imagine the chagrin of the Republican organization in Idaho, when Borah, after reading that the State Treasurer, a candidate for reëlection, was short in his accounts, wrote that the Treasurer should get off the ticket if the charge was true or substantially true.

The party's executive committee held a meeting and the chairman wrote the Senator that they had "finally decided that if the Treasurer would see that the State was secured that they would continue to support him, and that is the way the case now stands."

The Senator replied (October 5): "It is an indefensible principle of public morals to seek to impose upon the public for another term the service of a man who confesses by his settlement that he was guilty of the original charge. . . You say that he was determined to stay on the ticket and that the matter, as I understand you, is beyond the control of the Committee. . . It is not beyond the control of the voters and it is not only the duty of the voters to defeat Mr. Allen but it is the solemn duty of the Republican organization to see that he is defeated. So far as I am concerned, I simply will not overlook such matters. I shall not bother you or the committee again about this but I shall adopt my own course with reference to dealing with such matters. . . I want to say in conclusion that I am writing under as much restraint as I can put upon myself. . ."

Borah supported the Idaho Republican candidates for Congress in the campaign of 1914, even being so regular as to support Senator James H. Brady for reëlection, although Borah's old friend, James H. Hawley, was running for the Senate on the Democratic ticket. Governor Hawley wrote Borah (October 8), jollying him along and begging him not to come to Idaho for the campaign. The Senator made no reply to this letter. A few days later he wired the Republican organization in Idaho that there was no plot to defeat Brady and that he would win by 10,000 majority. At another time he said he would come to Idaho if the Congressional ticket was in danger. But Borah would do absolutely nothing for the state ticket because of the scandals in the administration.

Brady and the two Republican candidates for the House of Representatives won by comfortable margins. The Republican candidate for governor lost because of State House corruption and Borah's denunciation of it. Republican organization men in Idaho continued to scowl at Borah's failure to support the state ticket while the State Treasurer and the Deputy State Treasurer were being tried, convicted, and sent to the penitentiary. It was also proved that other state officers had been guilty of the grossest neglect of duty.

Two years later the Republican national committee wanted Borah to spend all of his time in the national campaign, leaving Idaho to look after itself. The Senator said he would have to spend all of his time in Idaho if the national committee did not contribute a good sum for the Idaho Republicans. It finally allotted $20,000 for the State. Then the committee wanted to limit the Senator to one night in Idaho. Borah would not stand for this and he made six night speeches and two day speeches in his own state.

PERHAPS the chief interest of Senator Borah between 1912 and 1916 was in the reorganization of the Republican party. His liberalism as a regular Republican and his refusal to go off with the Progressive movement marked him as a man who might be expected to bring the separate factions back together. His constructive career as a statesman and his power on the platform made this a most reasonable expectation. Borah had stayed by the G.O.P. because he hoped the party would become liberal. His efforts between 1912 and 1916, therefore, were in the direction of reorganizing the party along liberal lines.

He gave many interviews and made many speeches advocating reorganization with anti-monopoly as the corner-stone of the new structure. In a Lincoln Day speech at Baltimore, in 1913, he said: "Monopoly is at war with Democratic institutions and the conflict is as irrepressible as was the contest between freedom and slavery."

He thought the states might provide the fundamental remedy for monopoly, and he quoted from a Supreme Court decision the statement that the state has "a right to forfeit every corporate charter for misuse or abuse of power."

But Congress has the power to block monopoly effectively. "If Congress itself should declare that no corporation should engage in interstate trade so long as it held or sought to vote the stock of another, the trust question would near the beginning of the end."

He would not repeal the Sherman Anti-Trust Law, but he would make it more specific. "If a corporation lowers the price of a product in a certain territory in order to injure a competitor, make that specific act a violation of the law and a basis for action, civil and criminal. If an agreement be made limiting the output of an article, if there is a division of territory, if one company foments strikes in another, make these and similar acts specific offenses."

He said that monopolies were here "largely by the fault of the whole people," that neither their origin nor their suppression was a matter of economics alone, and that an awakened conscience was the one thing essential for their destruction.

In the fall of 1913 the Senator was in New Jersey assisting the Republicans in their triennial campaign for state offices. In December, although not a member of the national committee, he had a proxy and was reported to have been easily the dominant figure at the meeting, successfully opposing the calling of a convention for 1914. "Senator Borah," stated the Boston *Transcript,* "is deserving of Republican congratulations and appreciation for the service rendered by him at the committee meeting in reconciling conflicting views, eliminating personalities, and pointing the way to that reorganization which must precede any hope of Republican restoration." [9]

The next Lincoln Day found Borah in the very heart of conservatism, at the Republican Club of New York City, where he spoke on "The Republican Party." It was a harmony dinner and the Senator reviewed some of the recent manifestations of a Republican rebirth. But he did not hesitate to criticize a convention system under which southern delegates were the pawns in the hands of the national organization. Nor did he "pussyfoot" on his favorite topic – monopoly. Progressive Republicans, he said, "ask for nothing more and will be reconciled with nothing less than the free, full expression, and the full flow of opinion, in party organization and party affairs among its voters and members, to the end that this great code of humane and progressive laws [he had just reviewed progressive legislation of the past ten years], of wise and permanent institutions, may be extended, that the work may go on until political freedom shall be at the beginning and industrial freedom at the end of the party story, until monopoly, ten thousand times worse than black slavery, shall understand that between it and republican institutions there is eternal war – Mexican war where all the captives are slain without the benefit of clergy."

Republicanism, as the Senator understood it, meant "that the supreme question of the hour is not alone the making of wealth, but also its fair and equitable distribution. It believes with its first great seer and prophet that 'capital has its rights which are worthy of protection,' but that 'labor is prior to and the superior of capital.' That life is more than

[9] Boston *Transcript,* December 17, 1913.

riches and humanity more than machinery. It rejects the Draconian code based on modern materialism that human suffering and social misery are the natural fruits of human progress. It repudiates the doctrine of let well enough alone as the maxim of intellectual cowards and entrenched privilege, concealing beneath its gloss of peace and contentment the elements of class domination and national decay."

The press in the East did not play up these parts of Borah's speech, and for that reason many people got the idea that he lacked the courage to denounce monopolies and special interests in New York. At a less formal harmony meeting in Columbus, Ohio, on February 26, he restated what he had said in New York and paid his compliments to Mr. George W. Perkins, the "angel" of the Progressives. The press gave these phases of the Columbus address wide publicity.

He attacked former Senator Beveridge for his kind words about large business combinations and he ridiculed the statement of a president of one of the largest trusts to the effect that he would like to be regulated a little. "Mr. Perkins, the most persistent and powerful voice in the United States now of the third party, says that is the thing to do, that these monopolies are the proper thing and all they need is a little regulation. . . But I pay to Mr. Perkins the tribute of consistency. He refuses to turn his back on the method by which he made his great fortune."

This brought a wrathful letter from Mr. Perkins (February 27). "You say I am at least consistent in my position. Thank you; I believe I am. I wish I could say as much for your position in politics. You . . . chose to remain with the Republican party so that you could 'reform it from within' and, incidentally, by straddling the Progressive and Republican parties, secure your own reëlection as Senator from Idaho. You succeeded in achieving your personal desire, viz., your reëlection as Senator, but up to date you have not made a brilliant success of reforming the Republican party from within. You attended the recent 'confessional' held by the Republican national committee at Washington, when all of you who were there admitted by your words and acts that Taft's nomination . . . was secured by fraud; but you went into that 'confessional' with the same men in charge.

So that your efforts at reforming the Republican party from within do not seem to have met with any success up to date. . .

"On the trust question the country knows that the Progressive party believes that large business units are necessary in this day of interstate and international communication and trade ; that there is a mighty difference between a large business concern in a given line of trade and a concern that is a monopoly in a given line of trade. . . The Progressive party recognizes that there have been and are evils existing in the industrial corporate affairs of this country and it believes that these evils can be eliminated and hereafter prevented precisely as evils have been eliminated in the railroad and banking world by governmental regulation of railroads and banks. In short, the Progressive party has a perfectly definite program and policy on the so-called trust question. . . What is your Republican party's program in regard to it? . . . What is your program? . . ."

Borah made immediate reply. "I have just read your letter and I regret to have come under your displeasure. . . I did not undertake to state the attitude of the third party on the question of monopoly. In the first place, I do not know its exact attitude. I had heard upon what seemed to be good authority that an accident happened to one plank of its monopoly platform between the time the platform left the convention hall and the time it reached the telegraph office. I am not sure, therefore, in the face of this most unexpected accident that the platform was full and complete upon this subject. Secondly, I felt that the voters of the third party were not in favor of monopoly. I therefore chose to take its most active and prominent leaders, Mr. Beveridge and yourself, and judge somewhat of the situation by your views."

The Senator then discussed "cruel and brutal monopolies" in which Mr. Perkins had had a hand. He did this because Perkins had stated that if the Senator had proof of the charges against him he should give such proof to the public. Then he concluded : "According to your view there is not a monopoly in the United States and never could be, and according to your view, whatever they [monopolies] may be, the attempt of the government to destroy them is outrageous, and results, as I understand you, in compelling monopolies to pay women five dollars a week. . ."

In reply Perkins wanted to know whether the country was "to accept the pussy-footed speech you made when you sat at the speaker's table with Wm. Barnes, Jr., at the Lincoln Day banquet of the Republican party held in New York on February 12, or is it to accept the attack on big business you made at Columbus, Ohio, two weeks later? Does what you believe depend on the section of the country in which you are speaking?"

At about the same time Borah received the second Perkins letter he also received letters from Charles D. Hilles and Franklin Pierce, both of New York. These gentlemen supplied the Senator with more ammunition to use against Perkins. But Borah decided the controversy had gone far enough, and, although he had written Perkins another letter, he did not mail it.

The press of the country enjoyed the Borah-Perkins affair immensely, giving it full publicity and extended editorial comment. The consensus of opinion seems to have been that the Senator had come out first in the argument, but that Perkins was not far behind. Perkins' charge that Borah had straddled the Republican and Progressive forces in 1912 to win reëlection to the Senate was weak. Borah did not ride two horses. He rode only one horse and that was his own. On the other hand, Perkins' jibe about the Senator's lack of success in reforming the Republican party from within hit the mark. Wise political observers saw long before February, 1914, that the Republican party would not stand for Borah's type of reforming. The Republican party was being revived because Progressives were coming back to the fold, not because Republicans were becoming progressive. The meeting in Columbus at which Borah spoke and aroused the ire of Perkins was in the hands of old regulars. Former Senator Joseph B. Foraker and Senator Theodore E. Burton were there. As the *News* of Joliet, Illinois, ironically put it, referring to Borah's declaration against monopoly: "The reporter neglected to add that this sentiment was vigorously applauded, or that Foraker and Burton in their enthusiasm attempted to carry the speaker around the hall on their shoulders!" [10]

As for Perkins' challenge to Borah to declare himself on the trust question, the Senator had done so long ago. He would abolish the trusts by a few quick sharp strokes of legislation. But Perkins hit the mark again when he asked Borah the position of the Republican party on the trust problem. He knew the party would never accept Borah's solution or anything like it.

Invitations to speak to young Republicans, old Republicans, women Republicans, and just plain Republicans continued to accumulate in Borah's office. He accepted as many as he could. In the meantime Perkins was reported to be putting aside a tidy sum of money for the purpose of retiring the Senator to private life in 1918.

In the fall of 1914 Borah went to Indiana to help the Republican candidates. Will Hays, known locally as Live Wire Hays, the Republican state chairman, was already demonstrating that talent for political organization that later won him the chairmanship of the national committee. "He held organization meetings at every point where the Senator spoke," says the Indianapolis *News*. [11] He "talked up organization, and on the trains and trolley cars and everywhere he went he was busy with politics. The rapid pace set by Mr. Hays fatigued Senator Borah so much that the Senator, in order to get a little sleep, decided he would forgo the Princeton meeting. He was, as he expressed it, 'all in.'" But Hays took care of the situation. He chartered a sleeper at his own expense so that the Senator could have more sleep before he reached Princeton.

The Senator said to the people of Indiana: Beveridge, the candidate for the Senate on the Progressive ticket, "has been telling you what a wonderful career he had in the Senate – all of which I agree to – but he had it as a Republican and he has never had any career since he ceased to be a Republican. Every one of those laws which he had passed and which he tells you were essential to the welfare of the Amer-

[10] Joliet *News*, February 27, 1914.
[11] Indianapolis *News*, October 26, 1914.

ican people and of the utmost importance to the human race generally, and having right smart to do with omnipotence itself, was passed by a Republican Congress, of which Mr. Beveridge was himself a member, and yet he turns around and in the next breath tells you that the Republican party was so bad that he couldn't stay in it any longer!" [12]

The Senator was carrying and showing to select individuals in Indiana a letter he had from Colonel Roosevelt [the Senator later lost the letter] in which the Colonel conceded in effect that Borah had acted wisely in not leaving the Republican party in 1912. Early in 1914 the Colonel told William Allen White and others that he would go through that year but that he realized that it was an uphill business. After the extremely poor showing the Progressives made in the fall elections, Roosevelt said he did not propose to go out and whip a dead horse again.

One might easily maintain that the Progressive party never was a party. Seventy-five per cent of its members were merely personal followers of Theodore Roosevelt who had supported him in 1912 because of their indignation over the action of the Republican convention. They had no great interest in a social reform program. They were not organization men. They were of Mr. H. G. Wells's great company of "God-sakers" — people who could assemble in holy wrath and say, "For God's sake, why doesn't somebody do something?" but who were helpless to do anything. The Progressive party was devoid of the essential elements of persistence.

In May, 1913, Colonel George Harvey, who had picked Wilson as a winner, predicted that Senator Borah would be the Republican candidate in 1916. Even before this time, a few others had suggested Borah as the logical candidate. After Colonel Harvey's prediction, discussion became more common. But Borah, wishing to avoid any long-distance run for the presidency, followed the correct formula — "I am not a candidate."

At a banquet in Baltimore in January, 1914, which Senator Borah attended, Speaker Clark stated that Borah would

[12] *Ibid.*

be the next Republican candidate. The Senator laughed and said he was not accepting any after-dinner nominations for the presidency. But the talk went on. The Senator was praised as a great harmonizer, a man with many friends among both Republicans and Progressives, a man who "has a positive genius for making friends of those he antagonizes." (Even Perkins later relented.) Newspaper men treated the insurgent leaders with good-natured raillery, but they were usually serious when they wrote of Borah. A Boston *Transcript* man wrote him down as able, solid, independent, conservative, quiet, and patient.

Alfred Henry Lewis gives a characterization of him at this period: "Broad, self-centered as the Pyramids, of positive dignity, with a genius for the taciturn. . . Orator though he is, Borah never gives the impression of gabbiness. He speaks in the Senate for the most part with no gesticulations, no raising of his voice above the conversational tone, with deliberation but no hesitation — taking interruptions with an unruffled good nature, standing as solidly upright as a monument. He has a round, boyish face, a rich, musical voice, a clear enunciation, and the air of ease and good comradeship of the West and none of its spread-eagle qualities." Even at this period his colleagues would fill their seats when he was to speak.

"An interesting comparison is afforded between Borah and La Follette," continues this writer. "Each one has been a vigorous champion of progressive ideas and yet has remained steadfastly in the Republican party. Each one has courage and power and constructive ability. But whereas Borah has remained on good personal terms with radicals and stand-patters, La Follette has rendered himself *persona non grata* not only to the conservatives but to a large section of the radicals. Borah is a friend of both Taft and Roosevelt. La Follette is a friend of neither. Borah gives the impression always of being master of his ideas. La Follette gives the impression of being mastered by his ideas. Borah runs on a low gear most of the time. La Follette always runs on a high gear and seems unable to observe either the speed-limit or the time-table." [13]

[13] *Current Opinion,* April, 1914.

The *North American Review* of December, 1914, carried another comment on Borah by Colonel Harvey. He declared that he "stands forth by contrast with the Smoots, the Knoxes, the Penroses, the Cannons, and the Paynes, the foremost liberal Republican of the present day. Intellectually the peer of Mr. Root or Mr. Lodge, he surpasses either in comprehension of the public will and public hope, and has imbibed more freely from his environment the moving spirit of the times."

Borah was picked by his Republican colleagues in the Senate to answer President Wilson's Jackson Day speech (January 8, 1915) at Indianapolis in which the President had said that the Republican party had not had an idea in thirty years. The Senator's political effort was highly successful. The Springfield *Republican* said that "Borah was brilliant, partisan, and unfair — but so was the President." Republican organizations used 300,000 copies of this speech. A few months after the speech was delivered, the *Transcript* ran an editorial — "The Call for Borah."

Later on in 1915 Theodore Roosevelt had C. C. Connolly, Robert J. Collier, and Henry J. Wigham to lunch at Oyster Bay. It was just after Barnes had sued Roosevelt for libel. The conversation turned, of course, to the question of a Republican candidate for 1916. Roosevelt said, according to Connolly, that he had all he could ever get out of the presidency, and that Borah was the man to lead the party to victory against Wilson. He said that the party should dispose once and for all of its foolish fear to nominate a man from a small state in the West. This seems, however, to be as far as the Colonel ever proceeded in the matter.

The Senator's office was flooded with letters asking him to run for the presidency and offering him aid. The majority of these letters went unanswered. Borah stated that a candidate was a slave and he wanted be free. When a group of friends in Kansas started a "Borah for President" movement, he wrote thanking them, but stated positively that he was not a candidate. "Please accept this as covering and conclusive of the whole subject both now and later," he urged. He wrote an Idaho group to the same effect. His brother Frank wrote from Louisiana that he was trying to line up a

Courtesy of Berryman and the Washington Star

delegation for him at the next convention, a white delegation. The Senator told him to forget the "presidency business." But the Senator did make this public statement in April, 1915: "If by any chance the party should nominate me, I, of course, should accept. To pretend or intimate otherwise would be absurd. But I shall not seek the nomination nor strive in any way, directly or indirectly, to obtain it. Nor have I the slightest expectation of it coming my way." [14]

This is the whole story of Borah and the presidency to

[14] New York *Sun,* April 18, 1915.

1935. He always had many friends in all parties who would like to see him President. He knew this and appreciated it deeply. But he also knew that the people who wanted him for President were not the people who controlled conventions. He had never had an organization and did not want one. Yet he knew that without organization no one could get the nomination. He felt, therefore, that the cause was hopeless. Besides, he had always wanted to be free, not only free in a presidential season, but free all the time, free to say what he wanted to say in the Senate and in the country without hearing the charge that he was speaking with an eye on the presidency. Furthermore, he wanted to be free to read and study, study and read. He wanted to be President, but he would rather read a book. But, to repeat, although he has not the slightest expectation of its coming his way, if in some future time the rank and file in the Republican party should force his nomination, he will take it, gladly.

As 1916 drew near, Borah continued to say that the Republicans should adopt a liberal platform and that stand-patters should have little influence in the convention. He said he did not want any business man's campaign, that that would be too narrow. He said further that President Wilson was stronger with the country than he was with his party and that he would be a foeman worthy of Republican steel. "I differ with President Wilson on most of his policies but I have a very high admiration for him as a man." [15] In the summer of 1915, Borah was saying that Hughes would get the Republican nomination unless he refused to accept it.

The Republicans and the Progressives advanced on Chicago again in June, 1916. Borah was there as one of the leading harmonizers of the two conventions. Roosevelt had announced in May that he would not accept a nomination on the Progressive ticket but he indicated that he might take a Republican or a fusion nomination. Nevertheless, all the old left-wing Progressives decided to hold a strong convention. Perkins was not of this group, but he had his reasons for coming to the convention. The Progressives believed that if they would nominate Roosevelt at once, on Thurs-

[15] *Capital News*, April 25, 1915.

day, and leave the place for the vice-presidency unfilled, they might get a coalition with the Republicans. The Perkins group in the Progressive convention forced an adjournment before Roosevelt could be nominated. This they did because they did not want Roosevelt for President. They preferred Hughes.

Borah went before the Progressive convention as the representative of "another convention." He was given a great demonstration which was led by George W. Perkins. Borah's speech was short, consisting of praise of Roosevelt and the importance of agreement between the two conventions. Perkins said Borah's visit was another sign of the friendly spirit between the two conventions. Harmony was in the offing. While the Progressives nominated Roosevelt the same day the Republicans nominated Hughes, Roosevelt signified his intention of withdrawing if Mr. Hughes proved satisfactory. Roosevelt did come out for Hughes a few weeks later. Nearly all of the Progressives followed him. The revolt was over.

Had the Republican party been liberalized along Borah's lines? Perhaps not, but it was liberal enough to suit the Progressive George W. Perkins! In fact, he felt so well about it that he tacitly forgave Borah for the things he had said about him and written to him two years before. He even asked Borah to come up to New York, meet a few leaders, have dinner, and talk things over.

In fairness it should be said that the crisis in our relations with Mexico and with the Central Powers, bringing up the question of preparedness, might well have caused leaders to forget domestic reform. The planks on the subjects mentioned were of tremendous interest to Borah, and he and Senator Lodge practically wrote them. A domestic plank which Borah wrote was that dealing with woman suffrage; the party endorsed it, but recognized the right of each state to settle the question for itself.

Republicans were grateful for Borah's help in healing the breach in the party. The lack of interest in Borah's liberal ideas on the part of nearly all the other leaders may have made them somewhat less grateful than they would have been otherwise, but they recognized the value of having a liberal like Borah speak for the Republican party. He could give it a liberal stamp before the people and the party could reap the benefit without itself becoming liberal. The story has continued. The Senator has always tried to reform, sometimes to purify, the party from within. The party leaders have used him to great advantage on various occasions, but to date the party has not adopted many of his ideas. Borah has performed this labor of love for thirty years. The cynic might say that love suffereth long and is kind, that hope clingeth like a leech.

CHAPTER X

A CONCEPTION OF STATES' RIGHTS

BEFORE we enter upon the complex crises in our Mexican and European relations, we must turn to a consideration of some questions of states' rights. The original states' rights men had debated and shed their blood over the slavery question. The neo-states' rights men shed their coats and debated Prohibition and Woman Suffrage. To his good friend, Senator Glass, Borah is a modern states' rights man after his own heart. Indeed, the Jeffersonian from Virginia regards the Lone Lion from Idaho as the greatest living exponent of states' rights.

Although Borah has always hated liquor, he has not always advocated Prohibition. His original position on liquor was purely personal. He would have nothing to do with it himself, but if his friends and neighbors wanted to muddle their heads with it, that was no particular concern of his. Consequently, he took little part in the earlier "local option" fights in Idaho. His own county went through such a campaign in 1909, but, although he was in Boise toward the end of the contest, the newspapers do not indicate on which side he stood.

In Idaho the fight for statewide Prohibition began in earnest in 1910. The Anti-Saloon League followed the strategy it was using in other states, the policy of endorsing dry candidates in the primaries and dry candidates for the election campaign, regardless of party affiliation. The *Statesman* viewed this procedure with alarm. "Such tactics as those fathered and followed by the Anti-Saloon League," it declared, "will very soon destroy all party organization, and the Republicans and Democrats may as well get ready to turn the entire field over to the manipulators who are handling the politics of that organization. No objection could be made to putting out an Anti-Saloon League ticket or a statewide Prohibition ticket, or any other kind of reform ticket, but for a few manipulators to worm themselves into the political parties and organize a party within both parties is just a little too assumptive to be accepted by Republicans and Democrats generally, at least without protest." [1]

At Grangeville the Senator is reported to have said that the question of statewide Prohibition could be handled satisfactorily only by an amendment to the state constitution. But he did not say whether he was for or against such an amendment.[2] In a speech a few days earlier he had explained the position the two parties in Idaho took on the question. "The Republican says that it intends to submit fully this question as it is generally and popularly understood among the people, and as it is generally and popularly understood by those who demand it. The opposition, as I understand it, takes the position that it proposes, if given power, to deny the people the right to vote upon that question. That is the square, open issue upon this subject. We need not dwell upon technicalities." [3] But the voters of Idaho gave no clear opinion on the question in 1910.

The Senator's first genuine interest in the regulation of the liquor business arose out of the efforts of Congress to protect the Dry states. It had been held that a state had no authority to prohibit the admission into its jurisdiction of liquor shipped from other states on the ground that such prohibition interfered with interstate commerce, a subject upon which the national government alone was empowered by the Constitution to legislate.[4] As President Taft was ending his last winter in the White House, Congress passed the Webb-Kenyon Act, prohibiting the shipment of liquor into a state in violation of its Prohibition laws. In discussing this measure, Senator Root said that, although Congress could prohibit the shipment in interstate commerce of all liquor, it had no authority to prohibit the shipment of liquor under conditions laid down by the states.

Senator Borah : "Mr. President, we fix the rule in this act of Congress. Congress does not leave it to the states to fix the rule. Congress fixes the rule, and says that whenever liquor is being shipped in violation of the law of a state, it itself declares that it shall be prohibited. In other words, it

[1] *Statesman,* August 27, 1910.
[2] Lewiston *Tribune,* October 9, 1910.
[3] *Ibid.,* October 2, 1910 (quoted from *Statesman*).
[4] Leisy v. Hardin, 135 U.S. 100.

establishes the rule, although the operation of the rule depends upon certain conditions. When those conditions exist, the rule operates and applies to all shipments coming within that rule. Congress itself, however, selects the conditions which must exist, and Congress classifies the commodity and Congress itself establishes the rule." [5]

Four years later the act was before the Supreme Court of the United States. Mr. Chief Justice White delivered the Court's opinion, the material part of which reads: "It is true the regulation which the Webb-Kenyon Act contains permits state prohibitions to apply to movements of liquor from one state to another, but the will which causes the prohibitions to be applicable is that of Congress, since the application of state prohibitions would cease the instant the act of Congress ceased to apply." [6]

Early in 1914 the Superintendent of the Idaho Anti-Saloon League wrote Borah, urging him to make a declaration for statewide Prohibition. The Senator replied that he did not want to make a statement just now, that his views were generally known anyhow. He added: "But the truth is that just at present I do not feel like taking on the work which an expression of public opinion upon this subject would necessarily entail in the way of correspondence and answering criticism. I believe in following up the fight when you once start it." At that time the Senator was busy with the sub-committee of the Judiciary which was studying the question of a national Prohibition amendment. Soon his files were full of mail from ardent Prohibitionists who sometimes subscribed themselves in some such fashion as "Your co-worker for a Dry Idaho and a saloonless nation."

A correspondent of Soldier, Idaho, urged the Senator to do something for Prohibition and to do it soon. The Senator agreed that the "fearful traffic" should be abolished, but stated that "it is a difficult thing as a practical proposition to handle. Upon this subject I am open to instruction." The Prohibitionist of Soldier was keenly disappointed. "I had hoped," he wrote, "to hear your clarion voice leading the hosts of temperance on to victory and was depressed to hear

[5] *Congressional Record,* February 10, 1913, p. 2920.
[6] Clark Distilling Co. v. Western Maryland R.R. Co. 242 U.S. 311.

its faltering uncertain tone." Then the Senator sent his second letter, the first, as Borah sarcastically put it, not having been "sufficiently jammed with adjectives." "Now, Mr. —, not all who cry Lord, Lord, shall enter the Kingdom of Heaven, and I have found out that not only in Washington but elsewhere the most effective services done for the human race are by those who reflect very seriously upon the best way to accomplish it and who use their brains instead of their tongues exclusively. . .

"I was one of the majority of the sub-committee voting to report it [the Prohibition amendment] but it was after I had rewritten the resolution myself, which rewriting is conceded by all, so far as I know, to make it much more effective and desirable than it was originally. A little reflection and a little thought does not hurt even in a good cause."

The Senator was now (1914) definitely committed to state Prohibition by amendment of the Idaho Constitution and to national Prohibition by amendment of the Federal Constitution. The provision in the latter amendment that the states should have concurrent jurisdiction in enforcement was one for which the Senator fought valiantly.

The 1914 Prohibition campaign in Idaho was not without interest. The Superintendent of the Anti-Saloon League wrote Borah *very confidentially* that the League was doing all it could to defeat Republican Governor Haines in the primaries and was throwing its support for the Republican nomination to a Mr. Lewis. He added, moreover, that the League was generally favorable to the election of Republicans since all the anti-liquor legislation the state had ever enacted had come from Republicans.

The League's program was statewide Prohibition, first by statute (because this could be had more quickly), and then by constitutional amendment. As a last resort, the Wets in Idaho were saying that if Idaho wanted Prohibition it should come, not by statute, but by amendment. A Boise brewer, a friend of the Senator, asked him if he did not agree that the only fair way to get Prohibition was by amendment. The Senator agreed entirely, saying that "to have legislative statewide Prohibition would leave the matter constantly in politics." The brewer showed this letter to others.

The Superintendent of the League, Mr. William J. Herwig, wrote the Senator a very courteous letter, explaining the use which was being made of his letter to the brewer and asking him to declare for statutory Prohibition, pending the adoption of an amendment. The Senator made this explanation of his position : "If we have legislative statewide Prohibition it will not be regarded as a settled matter. Those who are opposed to Prohibition will still remain camped on the field and those who are opposed to Prohibition and connected with the liquor interests upon the outside of the State will still look upon it as a territory for their possible recovery. And it will make the matter a living issue behind which will be organized a vast amount of public sentiment in certain localities. On the other hand, if we secure the adoption of a constitutional amendment it will be regarded as settled for a number of years at least and will give Prohibition an opportunity to prove itself. The opposition will necessarily withdraw from the field and the people will have an opportunity to observe the actual workings of Prohibition.

"Another thing we ought to take into consideration, Mr. Herwig, is this. The change which comes from statewide Prohibition will in the very first instance almost exclusively prove unpopular. The readjustment which has to take place and the rehabilitation of society, as it were, leads to criticism and objections and for a time almost invariably as a history of Prohibition shows weakens the Prohibition cause. If you have statewide legislative Prohibition and undertake to secure an adoption of a constitutional amendment two years thereafter, you will weaken the Prohibition forces in your fight. All the unpopularity of the cause which comes from the first changes without the advantage of the permanent effects of Prohibition will rise up to confront you. In other words, you will make the fight for a constitutional amendment in two years from now under very adverse circumstances if you get legislative statewide Prohibition. My judgment in these matters, I find, is confirmed by almost all the leading advocates of Prohibition here in the City, I mean the representatives of the cause.

"Patience and courage, Mr. Herwig, will win any cause for righteousness that was ever initiated and we can afford to be patient and afford to be courageous in so tremendous an enterprise for you must remember that thousands and thousands of good citizens and well meaning people are still opposed to Prohibition and believe that it will prove a failure. So far as I am concerned, therefore, Mr. Herwig, I cannot support legislative statewide Prohibition. . . I know of course that thousands of good men and women will criticize my position but I am willing to wait for time to justify the wisdom of my course. . ."

But in Idaho in 1914 all of the parties were more or less Dry. By the next year statewide Prohibition was obtained by statute, and in 1916 the state Prohibition amendment was adopted.

Turning now to the national Prohibition question, we find William E. Borah again giving a national amendment his strongest endorsement in a letter to the Anti-Saloon League of Oregon in November, 1915. The movement grew apace and the War came on to help put it "over the top." In June, 1917, Frank Knox, still of the Manchester (N. H.) *Union*, wrote Borah that the Republicans had won in the last election in New Hampshire because his papers had insisted, and held the candidates to it, that the principal plank in the Republican platform should be national Prohibition. This had won rural counties solidly and had offset the pro-Administration majorities in the cities.

The amendment resolution was submitted to the states in December, 1917. It contained one provision, that "Congress and the several states shall have concurrent power to enforce this article," which Borah had insisted upon. But it also carried a provision which Borah had declared to be unconstitutional, namely, that "this article shall be inoperative unless it shall have been ratified as an amendment to the Constitution by the legislatures of the several states, as provided for in the Constitution, within seven years."

The Senator considered the seven-year limit unconstitutional because Article V of the Constitution stipulates that amendments shall be effective "when ratified," not that they shall be effective if ratified within a time limit fixed by Congress. But the Supreme Court in 1921 (Dillon v. Gloss) rejected this contention with the observation that "as a rule the

Constitution speaks in general terms, leaving Congress to deal with subsidiary matters of detail as the public interests and changing conditions may require ; and Article V is no exception to the rule."

On February 21, 1910, Senator Borah introduced a resolution for a constitutional amendment which would prevent any citizen of the United States from being disfranchised on account of sex. The Senator made no remarks in favor of his resolution, but Mrs. May Arkwright Hutton, President of the Washington (State) Political Equality League, thanked him "in the name of American womanhood." "Mr. Borah was my choice of men for the Senate," she said, "and I suggested that the matter be taken up with him. I also had considerable correspondence with him, which led me to believe he would introduce the amendment." [7]

Four years later, the Senator had reached a decision on the national amendment proposal. He was opposed to it. Although he was still one of the leading advocates of woman suffrage, he was opposed to the national amendment. The reasons for his opposition were stated in a remarkable speech in the Senate, March 17, 1914.[8]

First, he was opposed to woman suffrage by national amendment because that was the "most impracticable, impossible way," to get woman suffrage. The amendment must be ratified by thirty-six states and it was obvious to him that there were more than twelve states which would vote against ratification, thus setting back indefinitely the movement for equal suffrage.

Then came the fireworks. "There are sixteen states in the Union that will never ratify the amendment so long as the Fifteenth Amendment [the so-called Negro suffrage amendment] is in the Constitution. . . We may just as well be candid and open and fair about this proposition The Fifteenth Amendment to the Constitution of the United States is a dead letter." He stated that it was circumvented in the South with the consent of the whole nation. To add to the

[7] Quoted in the *Statesman,* February 26, 1910 (from the Spokane *Chronicle*).
[8] *Record,* March 17, 1914, p. 4959.

Constitution another suffrage amendment, purporting to enfranchise two million Negro women, would simply mean more evasion on the part of the South. He considered it morally indefensible to submit an amendment which, if ratified, would be ignored in a number of states.

Yet the Senator did not criticize the South. "I am one of those, Mr. President, who has never hesitated to say that the writing into the Constitution of the United States of the Fifteenth Amendment at the time it was written there was a mistake. It was a serious mistake. It came before the hot passions of the Civil War had cooled and judgment had time to resume its sway. . . It came in a large measure as a sort of retaliation and revenge. The idea of taking a people and lifting them out of a thousand years of savagery and barbarism, of three hundred years of slavery, and placing them in a position where they are required to perform all the duties and obligations of citizenship of a highly civilized Republic!" This was the part of the Senator's speech which the press played up.

"But there is another reason [for my opposition] — and it is even a more controlling reason to me because it goes to what I conceive the very foundation principles of the Republic — and that is the old doctrine, discarded and worn, but vital and indispensable — the doctrine of state rights for local affairs. I can not conceive of a state . . . which has lost the right to say who shall vote for its state officers."

Then the Senator praised Hamilton, who would have given the central government too much power, and Jefferson, who would have given it too little, and remarked that their opposing views had brought about a fair balance of power between the nation and the states. He also referred to Lincoln, and toward the end of his speech indicated his disapproval of a book by a "highly educated professor" who had left the unmistakable impression that the "Fathers" did not trust the people.

Reasonably satisfactory to the anti-suffrage people, this speech thrilled the South, where Borah was already very popular for having boldly proclaimed several years before that the Republican party had played the hypocrite on the

Negro question. Congressman Glass's Lynchburg *News* commented :[9] "The most detestable feature of the incident is that the Idaho Senator spoke the words of verity — that he stated propositions which, however prejudiced to the woman suffrage campaign, are unassailable — far beyond the pale of successful challenge." Some Negroes liked the speech. The *Bee,* published by that race in Washington, D. C., extended its thanks to the Senator in an editorial.

In 1921 William L. Marbury of Baltimore asked the Senator to join in the case of Leser v. Garnett (258 U. S. 130) as *amicus curiae* and repeat and amplify the theory he had advocated in the Senate that a state was no longer a state when it had lost its right to control the suffrage. He added : "You are one of the few who seem never to take counsel of your fears and yet never to have lost anything because of having the courage of your convictions." Mr. Borah replied that he had long since ceased the practice of law and deemed his appearance in the Supreme Court in this case inadvisable. But in presenting the case, counsel gave the substance of the Senator's argument. The court passed over this contention with the observation that if the Nineteenth Amendment destroyed the autonomy of the states as political bodies, the Fifteenth, which had been in operation for fifty years, did the same, for the phraseology of the two amendments was "precisely similar." The only difference was that the Fifteenth Amendment used the words "race, color, or previous condition of servitude," while the Nineteenth used the word "sex."

But the Senator continued to be an earnest advocate of woman suffrage — by action of the individual states — after his speech of March 17, 1914. He wrote a few articles on its behalf and when he could do so he gave his time to state campaigns. In a long letter Mrs. Carrie Chapman Catt wrote him that he could help with addresses in the New York State campaign of 1915, and Frank A. Vanderlip urged him to come to New York for what turned out to be the victory campaign in that State in 1917.

The plank adopted by the Republican national convention

[9] Lynchburg *News,* March 19, 1914.

in 1916, favoring "the extension of the suffrage to women," but recognizing "the right of each state to settle this question for itself" was, as has already been indicated, Borah's own plank.

Favoring the extension of woman suffrage by states and vigorously opposing the national amendment was a distinction which many suffragist leaders could not appreciate. The Idaho Senator not only was attacked in their speeches and publications in the East, but they even sent a brave contingent to Idaho in 1917 and 1918 to build fires behind the Senator. "If the Extreme Left of the suffragists can have its will," said the New York *Times* in October, 1918, "Mr. Borah will be succeeded by some mediocrity who is sound on the one and supreme question in the world of these enthusiasts. Senators of the first rank are so rare that Mr. Borah's continuance in the post which he fills with such brilliancy and fruitful achievement is a matter of concern to the whole country." [10] A considerable portion of the population of Idaho seemed to resent this windmill-fighting expedition of the suffragists. At any rate, the election figures in 1918 indicate that the Idahoans could consider Borah in somewhat the same light as the *Times* considered him.

But there is not the slightest doubt that the people of Idaho wanted their Senator to support the national suffrage amendment. Writing him on this point in May, 1918, Ray McKaig, of whom we shall hear more, told the Senator that he had saddled Pennsylvania, New York, and other states with Prohibition and asked him why he was now unwilling to impose woman suffrage upon the Southern states. The "ablest constitutional lawyer in the Senate" explained that the two amendments were wholly dissimilar: a state could have woman suffrage and no other state or any group of states could disturb it in the peaceful enjoyment thereof; on the other hand, a state might vote for Prohibition and then not be able to enforce the law because liquor would be shipped in from other states despite all precautions. In other words, since the states which did want woman suffrage could have it without the national amendment, the Senator was more than

[10] New York *Times,* October 17, 1918.

willing to oppose the suffrage amendment for the benefit of the states which did not want it ; and since the majority of the states, wanting to be dry, could not be dry unless the whole country was dry, he was willing to force all the states to be dry.

Viewed from the standpoint of policy, the Senator's argument may be followed without difficulty. Viewed from the angle of Federalism, it may still be followed, since the suffrage could easily be handled by the individual states while liquor, a commodity of commerce, could not be so easily dealt with by local action.

From Idaho came another letter to the Senator on the suffrage question. It was from E. A. Burrell, a leading Republican of his State, who disagreed entirely with the Senator's stand on the suffrage question. He said the Senator should support the amendment whether he liked it or not, since the people of Idaho were undoubtedly for it. In his reply the Senator rewrote a forgotten chapter from Edmund Burke on representative government. "You say: 'As our representative you have no moral or legal right to set up your individual views against the collective judgment of the people.' Yes, I have and then the people have the greater right to retire me.

"But, Burrell, to say that because a man is a Senator he is to have no views of his own, no convictions, no conscience is to advocate a doctrine which upon reflection you will be ashamed of and which you yourself as a Senator would never accept. If I go before the people and pledge myself to certain policies I am bound to carry them out . . . but if questions arise here, as this question does, I have a right, and am in honor bound, to respect my convictions and my own views, and then submit my case to the people, and if they approve they will keep me here and if they disapprove they will retire me. But now, Burrell, there is an easy way out of this. I dislike to give up my friends . . . but . . . I am prepared to give up both friends and party. I suggest, therefore, in perfect sincerity, that you go to Boise, ask [S. D.] Taylor to call the state central committee together, and if the committee . . . feels that my position will jeopardize the success of the party and will pass a resolution to that effect, I will tender my resignation as a candidate, and you can fill my place on the ticket. . . All I ask is that this action be taken prior to the 5th day of September so that I may adjust my own future conduct in time to test this question and my position on these public matters before the people of my state.

"You said in your conclusion that if I should change my attitude the people from coast to coast would applaud my action. They would denounce me in their hearts if not in words, as they should, as a miserable, cringing coward who changed a life-long conviction in order to get an office. I would have their contempt, and, what is even worse for me, my own."

Mr. Burrell answered by return mail that he was for Borah, with or without woman suffrage.

As the people of Idaho were preparing to give Mr. Borah a triumphant return to the Senate, the Montgomery *Advertiser* was saying that the people of Alabama, whose rights Borah had championed, would "gnaw a file" if they did not succeed in electing a legislature which would reject the amendment when it was submitted to the states.

At this point it is appropriate to digress from the Senator's conception of states' rights and interject a matter which reveals a characteristic of William E. Borah. His position on the suffrage and Prohibition had pleased the South immensely, where he was looked upon as the outstanding example of a Republican who understood and respected the South. Many Southerners thought he had their view of the Negro question. Imagine their dismay, therefore, when in 1921 the Senator held up the appointment of a nominee for United States Attorney for a district in North Carolina until a charge of race discrimination, made against him by some Negroes, could be investigated. "I am a southern man . . . of high standing in the business and social world . . . a son of the late Senator ——, a man of power and ability in our State," a North Carolinian wrote. "I can say to you truly and frankly, with all due respect to you and to your position and to your honest opinion that you have simply thrown

North Carolina's chances of ever going to the Republican party to the winds."

The Senator gave this answer: "Is it really proposed by certain men of North Carolina to organize a political party whose cardinal tenet is Negro disfranchisement and call that party the Republican party? . . . The Constitution guarantees the same rights to the Negro that it does to the white man. Are we going to leave the Constitution unchanged, the great charter unmodified, and seek to build up a political party whose fundamental principles are: thwarting the enforcement of these constitutional guarantees and of denying to one class of our people rights which we take an oath to give them. Can you imagine a more cowardly, lawless and immoral proposition than that. . .

"But suppose we consider it in another light. If I have not read politics in vain, that which is politically immoral is politically inexpedient. If the Republican party is opposed to the Negro voting in the South, what will be its position in the North? What will the Republican party say to the Negro in Illinois, Indiana and New York? That which we step on in North Carolina will sting us in Illinois. To advocate disfranchisement in North Carolina and enfranchisement for the same class of people in Illinois would be a piece of political debauchery which would leave us 'without the slightest fig-leaf of decency.'"

Of course, North Carolina Republicans were planning in 1921 to do precisely what the Senator's letter intimated—establish a White Republican party in the State.

Southerners who knew of the Senator's action probably argued to this effect: "We thought Borah was for us. Now we find he is against us. Oh, well, they say, though, that he is inconsistent and now we have an example of it." This is the type of criticism so frequently made of the Senator. His reply to it is that he is for the Constitution, the laws, and honest principles of government, as he understands them. His loyalty is to these, not to men, nor to particular interests, nor to special sections of the country. Sometimes he pleases, sometimes he displeases; but the Constitution, the law, and honest government must prevail.

But within a year the Senator was "solid" again in the Solid South. It was his conception of states' rights which restored him to favor. When the anti-lynching bill of 1922 was before Congress, the Senator wrote a letter (June 12) to the Boston *Transcript* on that effort and similar ones in and out of Congress to force the national government to take jurisdiction over what the Senator considered state affairs.

He stated that in his opinion the anti-lynching bill was unconstitutional. Even if it were constitutional, he argued, it would not cover more than one case of lynching in five, since the measure would apply only in those cases in which a state or municipal officer failed to protect from lynching a person in his custody.

He considered also the broader question as to whether the police power of the states, including control over hours of labor, child labor, etc., should be taken over by the national government. He pointed out that the tendency was very definitely in that direction and that weak congressmen were voting for measures which they knew to be unconstitutional in order to satisfy their constituents in these matters. If the nation is to invade the domain of the states, he said, it should at least wait until the Constitution had been amended to permit it. At this point he quoted from Washington's Farewell Address the warning that the Constitution should be changed only by amendment in the manner provided in that instrument.

Similarly, he has consistently opposed all plans to increase the national government's authority over education. When the Towner-Sterling education bill attracted considerable interest in 1922, a number of "patriotic" organizations urged Mr. Borah to support this measure. A man of some consequence grew very insistent. He wrote: "In view of the fact that every enemy of the American Public Schools is actively opposing this bill . . . I trust that you will pardon my blunt frankness when I state that it has reached the point where the real Americanism of any one opposing this bill is seriously in question and I trust that the rumor concerning you is entirely erroneous."

The Senator had no difficulty in formulating his reply.

It was : "I do not make up my mind upon these matters previous to hearings or upon threats of outsiders. You will duly and unmistakably be informed as to my position after I shall have arrived at a conclusion. I observe your statement in the last paragraph of your letter in which you say, 'You will pardon my blunt frankness,' etc. and then you observe that the Americanism of any one opposing this bill is seriously in question. I beg to state to you, my friend, with equal bluntness that you are not the gentleman who passes upon my Americanism. I pass upon that myself and I am perfectly willing to take the consequences of my position."

"The eyes of Idaho are upon you. You have one last chance," wrote a voter from that State in 1924 in an attempt to frighten the Senator into supporting the Child Labor amendment. "Your letter will not have the slightest effect upon me," replied the Senator. "I do not vote down here for or against questions under threat or out of political fear. . . Those who do not like it can make their views known at the polls."

To a woman who wrote more politely, he answered : "Here you are, a Jeffersonian Democrat, the cardinal principle of which doctrine was the integrity of the states, urging me, a Hamiltonian Republican, to support a constitutional amendment enabling the national government to deal with the children of the states. Strange times, these are. But I think I can encourage you to expect favorable action, as the women always get nowadays what they ask for."

In another letter concerning the same amendment, he said : "I regard it as the most pronounced invasion of local self-government that has ever been proposed. I think it changes the whole structure of our government. We place 40,000,000 human beings under the absolute control of Congress. And all this seems to be so utterly unnecessary in view of the fact that only two states now really are behind in child legislation."

The Senator has the view of Jefferson and other early Americans that local government is, or should be, the vital unit, and he is unwilling to see state powers transferred to the national government simply because the states may be neglecting their duty. He believes the state governments are equal to their task when the public is sufficiently interested and alert. Besides, he has always abhorred Federal bureaus, which have nine lives, each as hard to take as that of the turtle. "Bureaucratic administration" he considers wasteful, inefficient, and destructive of that popular interest in government without which democracy cannot survive. On the subject of states' rights the Senator is a hopeless reactionary or a valiant defender of the Constitution, depending upon one's point of view.

CHAPTER XI

NEW HORIZONS

PRIOR to his election to the Senate, Borah's interest in foreign affairs was no greater than that manifested by the typical frontier lawyer with an Illinois-Kansas background. By instinct and training he was an ardent nationalist, ready at all times to assert the greatness and self-sufficiency of his country. When he gave this nationalism a broader meaning after the World War, however, there was something fine about it. It was of such a pure quality that what he asked for his own people he insisted upon for others. He stood for untrammeled independence for every homogeneous group that wanted it. This broad nationalism was not entirely absent from his political philosophy of the formative years, but his attitude toward Mexico and Colombia during the New Freedom era was so severe at times as to obscure a philosophy which was never obscured after 1920 — namely, that each nation should be allowed to solve its own problems in its own way.

The Wilson period brought Borah face to face with serious foreign problems for the first time. These problems were: the Panama Canal tolls question, the proposed settlement with Colombia, intervention in Mexico, and neutrality in the World War.

The proposal to repeal the law exempting American coastwise vessels from the payment of Panama Canal tolls "brought out the fighting blood" in Senator Borah. The Hay-Pauncefote treaty stipulated that the Canal should be open to the vessels of all nations on equal terms. Under the pressure of patriotic sentiments and American coastwise shippers, Congress passed a law in 1912 exempting the American ships. Great Britain protested vigorously, a protest which probably strengthened the political force of the Democratic platform declaration that American vessels should enjoy such exemption. Great Britain grew more insistent against the exemption of American vessels, and President Wilson, despite his party's pledge to the American people, asked Congress to repeal the exemption provision. Legal talent was divided on the question of our right to exempt our own ships with the preponderance of opinion seemingly against it.

When it was suggested that the President was to make "short horse" of having the Senate repeal the Canal tolls, Senator Borah hotly replied: "Not by a damn sight. I will fight it to the last ditch and so will others." Borah made several speeches against the repeal bill, his argument being that the treaty had not expressly granted away the right of the United States to exempt its own vessels and that no such conclusion should be reached by implication.[1] But the repeal was voted, nevertheless, although the question of the right to exempt American vessels from tolls was reserved. Senators Root, Lodge, and a few other Republicans voted against Borah on this question. Borah, however, has never lost interest in the matter and he has actually put an exemption bill through the Senate twice.

On the long-standing question of a settlement with Colombia for our rather hasty action in recognizing the independence of Panama and in arranging with the latter Republic for the construction of the Canal, Senator Borah sided with Theodore Roosevelt. Secretary Bryan submitted to the Senate a proposed treaty with Colombia under the terms of which the United States was to express regret for its actions and pay Colombia $25,000,000 as an indemnity. Colonel Roosevelt denounced this treaty as an attack upon the honor of the United States, and his influence was strong enough to prevent the Senate from consenting to its ratification. The Senator wrote to an old friend in Boise whom he called "uncle": "It might be a wise thing as a mere matter of grace to give something to Colombia in order to avoid the bad feeling which exists in Central America by reason of that and other things which we have done. But I would not want to give her $25,000,000 or anything like it and I would not want to apologize for Panama's rebellion." On the other hand, in the very same letter, he demonstrated that fine spirit of anti-imperialism which was to come to full fruition after 1920. He referred to the pending treaty with Nicaragua as "out-

[1] *Record*, May 22, 1914, p. 9024.

rageous. We took some battleships and went down to Nicaragua and put a certain faction in power and now we are making a treaty with that faction, in other words making a treaty with ourselves. Uncle Sam gets some queer twists in his mind when he goes to deal with small powers." In short, the Senator was much opposed to doing again the sort of thing that had been done to Colombia, but he was not willing to admit the wrong done to Colombia.

Writing to another friend in the same city, in 1919, the Senator observed: "As the Colonel said, he took the Canal. He is certainly entitled to have it named after him, for nobody else, perhaps, could have 'took' it just that way."

In 1921, when the settlement with Colombia was being made, Senator Borah still opposed the payment of money, despite the fact that such payment was not to be accompanied by an apology from our Government. A. H. Vandenberg, editor and publisher of the Grand Rapids *Herald*, later Senator from Michigan, wrote (March 17) to Borah that he agreed with him entirely. The president of a syndicate "largely interested in Colombian petroleum lands" wired the Senator that he would be pleased to come to Washington to give him information. The Senator wired back: "If you could help me to defeat the Colombian treaty I would be glad to see you." But the Senator was perfectly willing to see Professor Shepperd of Columbia University, who was known to favor the treaty, for his advocacy was not flavored with oil.

While the Senator was feeling "very deeply about this matter" because Colonel Roosevelt was no longer living to take care of himself in the discussion, he received a letter (April 15) from Frank Knox, then of the Manchester *Union*. It read, in part: "Any concession to the group of high binders who control Colombian affairs, will be properly interpreted down there, as a display of weakness on our part, and is sure to be followed with fresh demands. Our State Department, at this very moment is engaged in a controversy with Venezuela, in which our contention is thoroughly sound. Presumably, if we set up the Colombian precedent, we will be presented with a bill to salve the feelings of injured Venezuela."

In addition to opposing the treaty because he regarded it

as an unworthy means of purchasing oil concessions for American interests in Colombia, the Senator opposed it as "a great wrong to at least two great American characters." The Senator was even willing to make a fight to prevent the money from being appropriated after the treaty had been ratified. As a matter of fact, the Senator's opposition to a settlement with Colombia grew largely out of his personal loyalty, 1912 to the contrary notwithstanding, to Theodore Roosevelt. When asked if he defends the Colonel's actions in "taking" Panama, he says that he does, smiles a bit sheepishly, and offers no further explanation. The Senator's position on this matter may reveal the rare instance in which principle was overcome by personal loyalty, loyalty to a great dead American.

SENATOR BORAH's position on the Mexican crisis is not easy to follow, no easier than that of President Wilson. President-Dictator Diaz had been overthrown after his forty-five years of "brutocracy." Francisco Madero, the liberal who succeeded him, was murdered after two years. General Huerta came into power with every indication that he would go back to the policies of Diaz. President Wilson refused to recognize his regime. Huerta was then deposed by Carranza and Villa, who proceeded to fight each other for control. Despite the fact that Wilson had announced his intention of allowing Mexico to work out her own problems, Americans had so many interests in Mexico that he found it impossible to keep his hands off.

When the President decided to send the Atlantic fleet to the Gulf, Senator Borah said: "We have started on a march to the Panama Canal and we will not stop until we get there. Once the flag of the United States is raised in Mexico it will never come down." [2] The Senator was simply stating, in bolder language than a great many statesmen are willing to employ, that demonstrations such as that to be undertaken often led to permanent occupation of weaker countries. Yet the Senator said in reply to the question, "What would you do if you were President?" — "If I were President I would say to the Mexican people, 'We want you to settle your own

[2] *Ibid.*, April 23, 1914, p. 7122.

internal affairs, and we will never interfere for the purpose of acquiring territory.' Secondly, I would say to them, 'You will respect American lives and property or the United States will see to it that they are protected.' "[3] Borah and Wilson agreed in their opposition to acquiring Mexican territory. They disagreed only on the point of how far our Government should go on the "lives and property" formula. Wilson had the responsibility.

A friend in Boise wrote the Senator in 1915 that something should be done by the United States to protect the Catholics in Mexico. Borah replied : "To talk of protecting the Catholics as Catholics is to put the proposition upon too narrow a basis. . . I would place the duty and invoke the obligation of the United States to act upon a broad and sane foundation : first, the right and duty to protect American citizens, and second, the right and duty of this Government, especially in view of the Monroe Doctrine, to shield humanity from those revolting and shameful cruelties regardless of creed or nationality. My Bible and my religion teach me that there may be times when it is the duty of Christians to fight." This was something new as an interpretation of the Monroe Doctrine, and despite Borah's anti-imperialistic sentiments, imperialists could find in it just the sort of cloak for which they were looking.

Senator Borah had considerable correspondence on the Mexican problems with Henry Lane Wilson, former United States Ambassador to Mexico. In a letter of January 1, 1916, Wilson wrote : Unless Congress insists upon "a joint committee of investigation the whole matter will disappear in showers of diplomatic dust and reports prepared *ad hoc,* while the lyrical and amorous gentleman who presides over the destinies of this nation will go on his way rejoicing."

A few days later the Senator received a letter from a Republican editor in Ohio. "Here only in this month's issue . . . I have advocated you as one of the two strongest Republican preferences. Then to hear such small utterances as those from you in trying to block the appointment of Ambassador Fletcher [to Mexico] merely in order to cast reflection upon the President, not only convinces me of my error

[3] St. Paul *Dispatch,* January 15, 1915.

but that, after all, Woodrow Wilson is about the only man in the United States right now who is big enough to occupy the Presidency. . . We have a large circulation and I think it my patriotic duty to express my disappointment."

This is the kind of letter to which Mr. Borah delights to reply. He wrote: "Let me assure you that you have made a mistake in the gentleman to whom you have written if you suppose for a moment that at any time through the threat of any newspaper or magazine I shall hesitate to express myself precisely as I feel. I am opposed to the confirmation of Mr. Fletcher. I do not believe in accrediting an ambassador to a man who has been either directly or indirectly instrumental in the murder of a great number of American citizens, until such time, at least, as he signifies his willingness to make reparation for these murders. . . During the short time I may be in public life I shall never hesitate to express my views upon public questions regardless of threats or im plied denunciation, and if I should ever reach that contemptible and cowardly attitude in public service wherein I fail to do so I trust I will have a spasm of virtue sufficiently extended to enable me to tender my resignation to my State."

When the German submarines sent the British liner, the *Lusitania,* carrying many Americans, to the bottom of the sea in May, 1915, Senator Borah declared in Boise (May 9) that the deed would not bring any decisive action from this Government — that we were taking much worse things from Mexico without going to war. He stated further that he did not believe in peace at any price although he understood that such a policy was popular. Senator Lodge wrote from Nahant: "I read your excellent statement in regard to the *Lusitania.* Wilson's letter made the right demands on Germany and caused an outburst of popular approval, but in my opinion he is not going to do anything. . . In other words, he is going to repeat his Mexican performance." Borah's reply was: "Just how long rhetoric will suffice it is rather difficult to say."

At the time Lodge and Borah were exchanging notes, the Grand Rapids *Review* presented its readers with an interesting comment. "If it were not for the fact that this capable

Westerner seems to take his cue from William Randolph Hearst when it comes to discussing the Mexican question and is far from sound on the tariff, he would look better to most people." [4] In truth, the Senator has always seen some good in Mr. Hearst. That gentleman, he says, always stands for America.

Borah continued to give attention to the Mexican situation, more attention than he was giving to the frightful affair in Europe. In January, 1916, he reviewed the Mexican "outrages" since March, 1911, and concluded that he did not believe anything was to be gained in the long run "by this policy of waiting for a nation like Mexico to settle its difficulties when those difficulties involve the rights of our own people. Retribution, in my judgment, moves swiftly for the nation which forgets or abandons its own." [5] When the President sent the punitive expedition into Mexico after Villa in March, 1916, Borah approved this as an act well within the constitutional authority of the President and as a matter of policy.[6] Perhaps he had decided to put away his fears that the American flag once up in Mexico would never come down.

Two months later Borah was venturing to say that "you will not find in the pages of history an instance in which a strong, powerful nation, a nation professing service toward all mankind and assuming to be the guardian of the rights of humanity, has ever submitted as we have" [7] to such indignities as those heaped upon us by Mexico. At the Republican national convention he made an "Americanism" speech, understood to have reference primarily to the Mexican situation. "Make our position strong for America first, for the protection of American rights here and abroad," he declared.[8]

Senator Borah's impatience with Mexico during the Wilson Administration stands out in striking contrast with his friendly and considerate attitude toward that Republic following the World War (Ch. XVII). Probably, the truth is that during Wilson's term Borah did not think the matter

[4] Grand Rapids *Review,* May 25, 1915.
[5] *Record,* January 12, 1916, p. 943.
[6] *Ibid.,* March 13, 1916, p. 4003.
[7] New York *Times,* May 9, 1916.
[8] *Ibid.,* June 9, 1916.

through. His information did not seem to go far beyond the fact that American "life and property" were in danger in Mexico. Ten years later he understood very fully what was provoking the agitation against Mexico and took the lead in an enlightened policy toward that country.

SENATOR BORAH took little interest in the European struggle which started in July, 1914, beyond an insistence that all neutral rights under international law be strictly accorded to America and Americans. He offered no suggestions as to how to harmonize the legal rights built up in past centuries with the modern commerce in the means and implements of war. Borah was in the same situation in which the great majority of our public men found themselves during the period of our neutrality — he had no new ideas with which to meet the new international problems.

Senator La Follette was the trail-blazer in trying to devise a method for keeping the United States out of the European war. His first efforts were directed toward bringing about a cessation of hostilities. As early as February, 1915, he introduced a resolution calling for a conference of neutral nations for the purpose of considering means for stopping the war. "Who can say," he asked, "at what moment the dark curtain that veils so much of this struggle may be swept aside by uncontrolled forces that will fasten upon the peaceful nations and draw the whole world into the vortex of war?" Then he referred to the profits our munitions people and other business interests were drawing from the war and to the peril those profits might bring the nation. "It is repugnant to every moral sense that governments should even indirectly be drawn into making and prosecuting a war through the machinations of those making money by it." Why pray for peace and supply arms? he asked. He referred to the agitation for American preparedness and stated the fact of which the country as a whole understood little at the time, that behind every appropriation for the Army and Navy were those who wanted fat contracts, "with attendant opportunity for graft and easy money."[9] Some very substantial newspapers treated La Follette's statements with respect and ex-

[9] *Record*, February 12, 1915, p. 3632.

pressed the hope that public authorities would follow up his suggestions.

In 1914, Secretary Bryan advised bankers that loans to belligerents would be inconsistent with our "true spirit of neutrality." But two months later our Government announced that it would not approve or disapprove credits made by American banks for the purpose of facilitating belligerent purchases in the United States. At the same time the State Department advised the bankers that it would object to the sale of foreign war bonds to the public. So much prosperity arose from the purchases made by the Allies in the United States that in August, 1915, the Government of the United States agreed that the belligerents might float public loans in this country.[10] La Follette assailed these loans to the Allies as a violation of American neutrality.[11] In other words, he believed the policy originally announced should be continued.

Early in 1916, La Follette developed his ideas more fully on the shipment of munitions to the Allies. "It is conceded," he said, "that the manufacture and shipment of arms and munitions of war is within the accepted precedents and principles of international laws as heretofore construed and maintained by this country and by most of the other countries of the world. But . . . never before in history has traffic in arms with belligerents had the significance that the shipments of munitions of war by us to Europe has today. . . In the face of such a struggle . . . precedents must yield to the appeal of a common humanity." [12]

What was Borah saying at this time? He was saying that Americans should insist upon their rights. Thus when Senator Jones, admitting the right to travel on belligerent ships, argued that American citizens should refrain, as a patriotic duty, from such travel, Borah arose to say that since they had a perfect right to travel on unarmed ships of belligerents they had a perfect right to look to the Government of the United States for protection.[13] Two months later he

[10] Hearing of the Senate Committee on the Investigation of the Munitions Industry, January, 1936. Walter Mills, *Road to War*.
[11] New York *Times*, September 20, 1915.
[12] *Record*, January 27, 1916, p. 1619.
[13] *Ibid.*, January 5, 1916, p. 506.

said: "I have had but one rule to guide my conduct since this unfortunate conflict in Europe began . . . and that was whenever I conceived an American right to exist, and it was challenged upon the part of any country or nation, to meet that challenge without vacillation or compromise. . . I should therefore, had I been permitted to do so, have voted for the principle that an American citizen has a right to travel upon a merchant ship armed for defensive purposes. . . It is a right which has been established for these five hundred years, and in my judgment this is not the time for the great American Republic to begin to temporize and compromise. . . I am not afraid of war if it is necessary to protect American rights." [14]

On February 3, 1917, President Wilson announced that diplomatic relations with Germany had been severed. A resolution was introduced in the Senate approving the President's actions. La Follette was opposed to the resolution because he believed with four other Senators that the United States had not been neutral in its conduct. Borah spoke for the resolution. Yet he may have had the feeling that we had not been thoroughly or consistently neutral, for he reiterated that we should be neutral, utterly neutral. He believed in absolute neutrality. He said that this severance of diplomatic relations certainly should not mean that we were then on the side of the Allies. We should stand out alone for neutrality, he said, and have no part in any alliance or league.[15]

Soon the President asked Congress for the authority to arm merchant ships for their protection. Borah was not of the "little group of willful men, representing no opinion but their own," who are supposed to have filibustered as Congress was approaching adjournment in March, 1917, against authorizing the President to arm our merchant ships against German submarines, thus rendering "the great Government of the United States helpless and contemptible." On the contrary, he joined the great majority of the Senators in signing the statement announcing support of that bill.

Perhaps this was a pure case of filibuster, but an examina-

[14] *Ibid.*, March 3, 1916, p. 3470.
[15] *Ibid.*, February 7, 1917, p. 2749.

tion of the *Record* reveals that those who were favoring the bill did much of the talking. La Follette complained bitterly that he could not get the floor, when Senator Hitchcock, leader of the forces favoring the bill, was recognized for a second speech. Senator Norris pointed out that the opponents of the bill had confined their remarks to the subject at hand and had not made use of quorum calls, neither of which limitations would have been observed had they been engaged in a genuine filibuster.

Although it necessitates a brief digression from the subject at hand, this seems to be an appropriate place to record that Senator Borah has never participated in a filibuster. Once, when trying to bring the resolution for direct election of senators to a vote, he intimated that he might filibuster against some measures desired by the opponents of direct election ; but he did not. Even so, he is opposed to a cloture rule in the Senate. He says he has never seen a bill killed by filibuster or discussion which was not defeated in the public interest. Perhaps the bill just mentioned constitutes an exception in his mind, but in that particular case the President later discovered that it was not necessary to get authority from Congress for this action.

In March, 1925, Clinton W. Gilbert of the New York *Evening Post* wrote : "If government is to be conducted in the open under the eyes of men, the Senate must be preserved as it is." He went on to say that the House was a mere machine and that newspaper men seldom went to its galleries ; that the executive departments were simply propaganda institutions. The Senator wrote to Gilbert : "You have stated in a single paragraph the whole proposition with reference to cloture in the Senate."

About a month after the famous "filibuster" against the armed merchant ship bill, the President asked Congress for the declaration of war. Norris, La Follette, and several other Senators opposed it. La Follette made a four-hour speech against it. He said that America had not been impartial in its dealings with the belligerents ; that England had violated our rights as neutrals and that we had condoned it ; that we were now going to war with Germany because we would not condone her violations of our rights, although her actions were less reprehensible than those of England, the Mistress of the Seas having been the original offender. How can we in sincerity, asked the Senator, say we are going to war to make the world safe for democracy when several of our allies have the most autocratic forms of government? Then he wanted to know why the American people had not been asked for their opinion in the matter. (He had introduced a resolution calling for a referendum on war on April 29, 1916.) He said that they would vote against it ten to one, and that the espionage bills, conscription bills, and other forcible measures the Government now had in preparation were proof of the fact that the Government agreed with his conclusion as to popular opposition to the war.

Senator Norris said that he was opposed to the "useless and senseless" war raging in Europe and that he was going to vote against our participation in it. He added, however, that he would do his duty as a Senator and as a citizen when war was declared. Then he asked why we were declaring war, replying, "All because we want to preserve the commercial right of American citizens to deliver munitions of war to belligerent nations." "I feel that we are committing a sin against humanity and against our countrymen. I would like to say to this war god, You shall not coin into gold the life blood of my children. . . I feel that we are about to put the dollar sign upon the American flag." [16]

Senator John Sharp Williams entertained the galleries by replying, after a fashion, to La Follette. Reed of Missouri stated that the speech of Senator Norris might not be treason, but that it certainly grazed the edge of treason.

Borah had the highest regard for Norris and La Follette. Their speeches on this particular occasion brought from him no word of ridicule, no word of censure. Their courage was the sort of thing he loved to see. Probably he reflected that with such souls the country is safe, whether they are for or against war.

With mixed feelings, the Senator from Idaho arose to speak on the war resolution. He spoke briefly. "I do not find it

[16] *Ibid.*, April 4, 1917, p. 212.

possible on my part to vote against it," [17] he said. He seemed to wish that he could stand with La Follette, Norris, Gronna, and Vardaman ; but he could not. His vote for the war was consistent with his position during the period of neutrality, consistent with his views that American rights, whatever they may be, must be protected.

Where the law is concerned, Borah has always insisted that the people should have the benefit of it. He is for peace and humanity. But the law must be enforced until it is changed, and he does not think that neutrality laws should be changed in war time. Yet he voted for the war with extreme reluctance, and of all the votes he has cast in the United States Senate, he would like most of all to go back and change that vote.

In recent years Senator Borah has been quite willing to see our neutrality laws changed so as to prohibit American citizens from engaging in some of the practices which helped draw us into the world war. The neutrality legislation of August, 1935, comprehensive if temporary, won his general approval. The Senator would go further in some particulars than the statute goes. Thus, while the statute provides that "no citizen of the United States shall travel on any vessel of any belligerent nation except at his own risk, unless in accordance with such rules and regulations as the President shall prescribe," the Senator would prohibit such travel altogether, except perhaps travel which may be necessary in withdrawal from a war zone. His point is that "it is not alone the citizen who is involved, but the entire nation" — that the nation can not rid itself of the responsibility by simply leaving the citizen to exercise his own judgment.[18]

When the Administration neutrality bill was pending in January, 1936, the Senator seemed to believe that the Government should embargo arms, ammunition, and implements of war, and should prohibit all operations above normal trade with belligerents. He was unwilling, however, to leave to the President the discretion of modifying restrictions for the purpose of terminating or localizing a war. "I want to be neutral," he said, but "I do not think you can be neutral and

[17] *Ibid.*, April 4, 1917, p. 252.
[18] *Ibid.*, August 21, 1935, p. 13956.

engage in stopping war at the same time. Let us be neutral and keep out of war. If the war goes on, we can not help that." [19]

On that April 4, 1917, when Borah cast his vote for war, he made this statement : "I join no crusade ; I seek or accept no alliances ; I obligate this government to no other power. I make war alone for my countrymen and their rights, for my country and its honor." Here he declared himself in advance against any league of nations, against any foreign political commitment on the part of the United States, thus announcing a course to which he was to adhere with rigid consistency.

By inheritance, by instinct, by environment, by education, and by profession Borah is an individualist. By the same token he has always stood for national individualism. Political isolation, and political isolation only, will, in his opinion, give us peace and the opportunity to work out our own democratic destiny.

10 New York *Times,* January 23, 1936.

CHAPTER XII

A CONCEPTION OF AMERICANISM

As WE were putting our war machine in motion, Borah voted against conscription, and he is still glad he did. Before the vote on it had been taken in the Senate, a constituent wrote "our most beloved Senator" that it would kill patriotism. Former Governor Gooding also wrote him opposing conscription. Borah replied : "I am exceedingly glad to hear you say that conscription is a mistake. They are overriding and brow beating and insulting everybody who is opposed to conscription. If they continue to conduct this war along the lines and according to the program outlined, La Follette will yet prove to have been the biggest man of the occasion."

Senator Borah was opposed to conscription because it left out the spirit, the heart, and the soul which are essential for an army. "I oppose conscription . . . because it does not provide the best army, and I oppose it because it is fundamentally at war with the essential principles of free institutions." Conscription shows a lack of faith in the people's patriotism. It is based on the theory that there is a powerful element of "slackerism" in the country, and it is the basis of militarism. These were his views.[1] While not at present actively opposed to compulsory military training in high schools and colleges, if the matter were left to him he would strike out its compulsory phase.

In the spring of 1917 there was some gossip to the effect that the Senator would himself enlist for military service in Roosevelt's proposed expeditionary force. The Washington *Star* (May 4) strongly advised the Senator that he should stay where he was, that Senator Baker of Oregon had made this mistake in enlisting in the Civil War, and that in his untimely death the country had lost a very valuable statesman. It is doubtful, however, if Borah considered the question of enlistment very seriously.

Within a few weeks after the declaration of war, Borah was concerning himself with the problem of forcing wealth to pay

[1] *Record,* April 28, 1917, pp. 1442–1447.

for it. President Brannon of the University of Idaho wrote that this should be done, and the Senator stated that he was "thoroughly in favor of making the wealth of this country meet this war by direct taxation in so far as it is possible to do so. I would much prefer to conscript the idle wealth of the country than to conscript the idle boys. I greatly fear, however, that I shall not have the same support in conscripting the wealth that I might have in conscripting the boys." In August it was announced that Borah was the leader of a group of senators who would tax war profits 80 per cent. He was very definitely of that group which made war on the war profiteers.

In the summer of 1917, the Non-Partisan League, of which we shall hear more later, held an anti-profiteering meeting in St. Paul. Senators Borah, La Follette, and Gronna (N. D.), and Ray McKaig, a Non-Partisan League organizer in North Dakota, were present. Borah spoke not only against profiteering but also against the espionage laws, saying that if the Administration could not trust the American people, the time would come when the people would not trust the Administration. Business interests were denouncing Non-Partisan leaders and their friends, particularly La Follette and Gronna, as disloyal and as traitors.

After the meeting McKaig called on Senator Gronna at his hotel and found Senator Borah with him. McKaig started to speak of the difficulty the farmers were experiencing in presenting their case in the face of newspaper opposition. Senator Gronna interrupted to say that only yesterday he had seen his son march off to war, yet the papers were calling him traitor. He continued on this theme and then suddenly cried, "I can't stand it," and broke down and wept like a child. Borah put his arms around the North Dakota Senator and wept also. McKaig describes the scene as unforgettable.

Borah continued his campaign against profiteering. On May 31, 1918, he introduced a resolution calling for the Treasury Department to give the facts in its possession relative to profits and profiteering.[2] He said in explanation of his resolution : "There is one portion of the President's great message upon taxation, delivered a day or two ago, to which

[2] *Record,* May 31, 1918, p. 7231.

it seems to me sufficient attention has not been given in public discussion, and this is the part which reads as follows: 'There is abundant fuel for the light in the records of the Treasury with regards to profits of every sort. The profiteering that can not be got at by the restraints of conscience and love of country can be got at by taxation.'

"I am . . . in hearty accord with the expression of the President with reference to the method of reaching profiteering," continued the Senator. He added that if a private citizen had said what the President had said, "it would likely have started him upon the way to the penitentiary.

"A few days ago a noted woman in this country [Rose Pastor Stokes] with whose methods as to government most of us disagree, but with whose humanitarian objects and purposes many of us agree, was convicted in an American court. Here is the statement upon which that conviction was founded, or at least one of the counts of the indictment: 'No government which is for the profiteers can also be for the people.' Nothing is truer than that statement."

It can not be said that Senator Borah and his associates were able to prevent profiteering, but the Senator never lost interest in the cause. Here is a letter written to a friend back home in February, 1919: "I am satisfied that the real facts concerning Mr. Hoover's [Food] Administration will come out in time. Indeed, they are coming out pretty fast now. There is no possible doubt that the five great packers dominated the department so far as their interests were concerned."

Borah agreed with the President on other matters than that of taxing the profiteers. He supported the President on the Overman bill which gave the Chief Executive wide powers over the administrative agencies. When this bill had been passed, Senator Overman wrote the Idaho Senator that "Your valuable suggestions and aid in the committee and able speech for the bill on the floor of the Senate, and the part you took in the debate materially aided in convincing Republicans and Democrats of the necessity for such legislation. No Senator has done more to aid in the passage of important war legislation than you, notwithstanding the great opposition at times to many of these measures. I will say to you that I know the President appreciates your help in this great measure."

At about the same time, another Democratic Senator, John Sharp Williams, stated on the floor of the Senate: "Every patriotic American loves to listen to the voice of the Senator from Idaho whenever he talks in this chamber. I wish that every Democrat and every Republican in this chamber, including myself, were a mere duplication of the Senator from Idaho, who has kept his head level, himself in poise, his soul in loyalty, and his interests undisturbed by war passions." [8]

Some months prior to the passage of the Overman Act, there was introduced a bill which was designed to put the conduct of the war in the hands of a commission. The Senator from Idaho immediately announced his opposition to this measure. Democratic Senators close to the President asked Borah to speak in certain large cities against the measure. He did so. When he returned he received a very gracious letter from the President. It reads: "May I not express to you my warm appreciation of the whole spirit and purpose of your speech to the Far Western Travelers' Association? It is indeed heartening to see such a spirit manifested by the thoughtful men upon whom the whole country must depend for guidance."

When the President called for a Democratic Congress in 1918, under the plea that the Republicans in Congress had "sought to take the choice of policy and the conduct of the war out of my hands and put it under instrumentalities of their own choosing," he was obviously not thinking of Borah.

On July 26, 1917, Borah made one of his great Senate addresses of the war period. He felt that the American people did not yet know what they were fighting for and that they could not be expected to support the war enthusiastically until they knew. He said that he had voted for war not because of sympathy for France or for democracy in the abstract, but because American rights had been trampled upon. He concluded: This is "an American war, to be carried on, prolonged, or ended according to our interests."

The speech was almost universally praised, although the *Citizen* of Brooklyn said that there was some fault found with

[8] *Record,* April 24, 1918, p. 5567.

Borah "for disavowing any regard for the general cause of liberty as one of the motives of this country for going to war." [4] The *Christian Science Monitor* held that it was time the American people were being told that they were fighting for themselves — that fighting for humanity was not concrete enough for an objective. Colonel George Harvey wired: "That was a glorious speech, and made in the nick of time."

Former Governor Edward C. Stokes of New Jersey wrote that he agreed with the Senator entirely in his statement that the masses did not yet realize that this was an American war. They were, he said, simply yielding loyal but not cheerful obedience. The Governor, who had been making some war speeches, had found it "very difficult to stir up any enthusiasm . . . except among the college boys."

Some months later (March 18, 1918) the Senator made another war speech in the Senate. It was as much praised as the first. He showed the War as a conflict of life and death between countries with free institutions on the one hand and countries which emphasized the monstrous, tyrannous State on the other. "Shall men, shall the people be governed by some remorseless and soulless entity called the State or shall the instrumentalities of government yield alone and at all times to the wants and necessities, the hopes and aspirations of the masses?" This speech was reprinted and widely distributed in England.

Down in New Orleans Frank was proud, very proud, of his brother Will's war record as a statesman. He had written the Senator in the first period of the war to suggest that since the results of the war would be a benefit to coming generations it should be financed by borrowing for a period of perhaps a hundred years. Later, he wrote that, as usual, he was coming around to see it Will's way. He stated further that for years he had thought his brother was a fool to give up a lucrative law practice for a seat in the Senate, but that he had changed his mind on that also. Being a statesman, he said, was worth the price paid.

LATE in 1916 Mr. Borah had thought he might retire at the end of his second term, and on April 24, 1917, he addressed a

[4] Brooklyn *Citizen*, July 28, 1917.

communication to the people of Idaho announcing his intention but withholding his reasons for his decision. Gossip was rife. The guess furthest from the real reason was that of the Washington *Post* [5] to the effect that Borah might be dreading the ordeal of direct election. Perhaps this was intended as a joke. It was in any event, considering that Borah had advocated direct election since he had entered public life.

There is no doubt that the Senator was worried about his financial future. He was fifty-four years of age with a salary of $7500 a year. If he should retire from public life, accept an offer he had from a law firm in New York, he could easily multiply that by ten. If he waited for six or twelve more years the procession might pass him by and the voters themselves might prove ungrateful. He thought that he owed it to Mrs. Borah and himself to retire. But this was not the controlling reason. The Senator has never cared for money. He had given up money before and was to give it up again. His real reason for his announcement was that he could not support two war measures which Republicans and Democrats alike thought he should support : the conscription bill and the espionage bill.

Published opinion was unanimous against the Senator's announced purpose. From everywhere letters came asking him to reconsider. Newspaper editorials were of the same import. Even the Old Guard Republicans in Idaho, when they spoke out loud, had to say with as much sweetness as possible that Borah should not retire. These demonstrations and the discovery that he could, after all, support the greater number of President Wilson's essential war measures caused him to decide to be a candidate again. He continued to serve his country for $7500 a year, refused to take $10,000, when the salary was raised to that amount in 1925, until after the people had reëlected him in 1930. He now has very little income besides his income as Senator, probably much less than he had at the time of his first election in 1907.

The campaign of 1918 in Idaho was a very bitter one. The Non-Partisan League, another farm revolt organization, had spread across the country from Minnesota and North Dakota to the western boundary of Idaho. It arose largely out of

[5] Washington *Post,* April 29, 1917.

the fact that the farmer had not received his share of the general prosperity which came to his country shortly after the outbreak of the war in Europe. After America entered the war the League still held to its objective of looking after the farmers' economic interests, but, in addition, its membership favored very high taxes on war profits and opposed conscription and the espionage laws, all of which made the League an object of suspicion and hatred. In North Dakota the League captured the Republican party in the primaries. In Montana and Idaho it took possession of the Democratic party.

In its Idaho state convention the League deplored the low state to which the Idaho delegation in Congress had fallen, but noted "one splendid exception to this regrettable situation, and this is the record and attitude of Idaho's Senior Senator, Hon. William E. Borah. In his great fight against the greed of the profiteers in general and the power trust in particular, Senator Borah has shown that he stands first of all for the people. . . His courage and patriotism and splendid ability make Senator Borah by far the most commanding figure at this time in the Senate of the United States, and assures Idaho the honor and admiration of the nation. For these reasons we tender our unsolicited and frank expression of appreciation." [6]

Borah was pleased to have this endorsement. Other Republicans would also have been glad to get it. For example, there was former Governor Gooding, now a candidate for the Senate to fill the vacancy caused by the death of Senator Brady. The League officials actually produced a letter from Gooding in which he had asked them for an endorsement. The League did not endorse Gooding and he declared that the letter was forged, although a great many Idahoans were not convinced that it was a forgery. Gooding's campaign was devoted almost entirely to denunciations of the League and its leaders.

Theodore Roosevelt wanted to endorse the Republican ticket in Idaho because he thought well of Gooding for his vigorous action as Governor at the time of the assassination of former Governor Steunenberg and because he shared the popular suspicion and distrust of the Non-Partisan League.

[6] Wood River *Weekly Times,* July 10, 1918.

There was, of course, this complication : to endorse Gooding and denounce the League would mean a thrust at Borah, who was endorsed by the League. Borah smoothed the way for them. He wrote a friend that it would be perfectly satisfactory for Roosevelt to endorse Gooding and leave him out, that, for himself, he doubted the wisdom and expediency of these outside, purely personal, endorsements.

Mr. Borah was urged by many of the Republican leaders to repudiate the League's support. Although some of his personal friends advised him to accept this course, most of them kept silent or advised against it. A few quotations from the Senator's reply to one of these "request for repudiation" letters will give his position. This letter was written to Edwin T. Barber of Shoshone.

"Well, Barber, I have known the farmers of my State for a long time. This is not the first time they have endorsed me. I have always enjoyed their support almost regardless of party. Many of those whose support I have always had and been glad to have have now organized themselves into this League and through this League they have endorsed me again. I am now asked to repudiate the endorsement of this League composed entirely of those same farmers because it is said they are seditious and traitors. It is further said that unless I do so promptly I will be defeated. I refuse to do so, not because I have no evidence of their disloyalty but because I have the most conclusive proof of their loyalty. No man can tell me that the farmers or any considerable portion of them in my State are disloyal. Their sons are in the army and many of them did not wait to be called but volunteered. They have not only furnished their boys to fight our country's battles but these same men have done everything within their power to increase the food supply to feed the army. I observe also in the last liberty drive that they were among the first to go over the top. . .

"If it be said, as you claim, that there are individuals in the League who are disloyal my answer is that I will join with you or anyone else to denounce any individual who is disloyal whether he is in the League or in any of the other parties. If individuals are disloyal I see no possible reason why they should not be sent to prison. Certainly they ought to be.

Our laws are sufficiently broad and drastic to cover all sedition and all disloyalty. . .

"So far as the economic principles of the League are concerned, your letter does not call upon me to discuss them, but permit me to say that if that issue should become material the best way to settle such matters is to discuss candidly and tolerantly those issues and public judgment will ultimately determine which are wise and which are unwise. Whether those policies are wise or unwise they have a right to present them and to have them discussed. A man who will not listen to his antagonist present his case is afraid of his own case. If these matters and all other matters can be thoroughly discussed and everybody hear I will trust the people of the State as a whole to ultimately separate the wheat from the chaff. . .

"Will you let me add another paragraph to this letter already too long? But I like to look ahead, to think of the time when the bitterness, the suspicions and the intolerance of war have been put behind us and we settle down to resuscitate and build up our State. We will all still be in the State and all a part of its citizenship except those who have given their lives for their country. These farmers will still be a part of us. I do not suppose any loyal man ever forgave another for charging him with disloyalty. Vengeance for such a charge is the kind of vengeance, I take it, which the Bible attributes to divine power — it never dies. . .

"Loyalty and disloyalty with me are individual matters. I have never felt that it was safe to denounce and indict groups or great bodies of people for disloyalty or sedition. And I feel doubly sure of the injustice of such a course when it has reference to the people of my State or any portion of them."

The Senator not only had the endorsement of the League in this campaign, but he had also the tacit support of the Democratic Administration in Washington. Democratic Senators close to the President, men like Overman and Williams and Nugent, Borah's Democratic colleagues, assured Borah that he could have a letter from the President if he needed it in his campaign for reëlection. Because the Senator felt that he could manage without the letter, he never asked for it. Former Senator Dubois (Democrat after 1900) was quite openly for Borah, although, of course, he favored Senator John Nugent against Gooding for the short term. Dubois was busy and happy, planning, scheming, conferring, and writing many "Dear Billie" and "Dear Jonnie" letters. The Idaho Republican Senator did not reply to these communications, but, then, they hardly called for replies. They were in the nature of letters of information. Borah certainly did not repudiate the support of Dubois nor the less open support of Nugent.

On the other side, some of the regular Republicans were quietly working for Gooding and Moore, the latter being Borah's Democratic opponent. Around Orofino, a few days before the election, this dodger was being circulated : "Vote for U. S. Senators, for the long term, Frank L. Moore of Moscow, Idaho, and the vigorous solon of the Palouse valley, for the short term, Frank R. Gooding of Gooding, Idaho, the vehement shepherd of the Snake River Hills." It is not possible to say which group first started the bipartisan tactics, nor does it matter. Between Borah and Gooding there was never any friendship or coöperation except when Borah helped Gooding win the governorship in 1904.

The election figures stood : Borah, 63,587 ; Moore, 31,018 ; Nugent, 48,467 ; Gooding, 47,497. Of Borah's 63,000 votes the *Statesman* estimated that he received 43,000 of the 46,000 Republican votes, the 14,000 Non-Partisan votes, and 6000 of the 36,000 regular Democratic votes. It might be said that the astute Dubois made a good trade by supporting a certain winner on the Republican ticket in order to bring victory to a marginal candidate on the Democratic ticket.

One of the first acts of Senator Borah following his election to the Senate for the third term was to move that some of the repressive measures of the war be repealed. Behind this action we see one of the cardinal tenets of Borah's social philosophy. Against the Government's fear of disloyalty and radicalism which had led it to restrict the freedom of speech and of the press during the War, he placed these words from Milton : "Though all the winds of doctrine were let loose to play upon the earth, so truth be in the field we do injuriously, by licensing and prohibiting, to misdoubt her strength. Let her and falsehood grapple ; whoever knew truth put to the worse in a free and open encounter."

He was one of six senators who had voted against the original espionage bill in 1917. He considered that it was not only bad policy, indicating distrust of the people, but that it was also in violation of the Constitution, which guaranteed freedom of speech and of the press in war as well as in peace. The provisions for press censorship he thought particularly objectionable. He was quite willing to see the press held responsible for abuses, but he abhorred censorship. The Senator took the position which sincere free-press advocates in England and the United States had taken for one hundred and fifty years. Referring to the espionage measure in a letter to his friend E. A. Burrell, he said : "a more autocratic, more Prussian measure could not be found in Germany. It has all the ear marks of a dictatorship. It suppresses free speech and does it all in the name of war and patriotism."

In July, 1917, he wrote Mr. Hearst a letter, congratulating him upon his fight for civil rights in war time. In August he wrote John D. Works of California, ironically trusting that "this letter will find you still at large. If you are sojourning in some convenient jail I trust it will be a source of consolation to you."

In the spring of 1918 Senator Chamberlain introduced a bill designed to make the entire United States a zone of enemy military operations and to bring to trial by court martial any person who interfered with the operations of our military forces. Senator Borah, of course, objected to any such measure, writing a Federal Judge that he had "an utter horror of court martial tribunals. I always shudder when I see them trying even a member of the Army or Navy." But this measure was blocked by the intervention of the President, who stated, much to the gratification of the Senator from Idaho, that he was "wholly and unalterably opposed to such legislation."

But the original espionage bill was amended by the enactment of the so-called sedition bill, which carried, among other drastic provisions, one which authorized the Postmaster-General to close the mails to persons whom he might consider seditious. A strong minority of the Senators voted against this measure. Borah said he did not believe the President would sign it, but in this he was disappointed.

Despite the Senator's opposition to the repressive war measures, he took a rather practical view of the situation. He knew that if the Government itself did not enact stringent legislation the local "patriots," acting under no authority, would take vigorous measures to stamp out every conceivable form of disloyalty. His files contained many letters from persons who were being persecuted by local guardians of the Republic. People who could not buy liberty bonds, who stated that conscription was a poor way to raise an army, who preached in the German language, wrote, sometimes in anguish, of the strong-arm methods used against them in their communities. Although the Senator could not bring himself to support the severe restrictions Congress placed upon freedom of expression, his opposition to them was tempered with the realization that such legislation might give local vigilantes less excuse for roughness.

About a month after the Armistice was signed the Senator said: "I am in favor of wiping from the statute books every arbitrary measure and every imperious precedent of the war. I not only want to see them off the statute books, but I want to see them forgotten as precedents and eliminated from our political system." [7]

Nor was this speech the end of the matter with the Senator. He continued to advocate the repeal of repressive measures and to guard against the enactment of new ones. Borah's civil rights bill (S.5039) was introduced in the 3rd session of the 66th Congress and again in the next session. Designed to protect persons in the exercise of privileges and immunities guaranteed by the Constitution, it was the reverse of a repressive measure. A high officer of the American Defense Society wrote the Secretary of the American Federation of Labor that the Borah bill was "exactly the sort of bill that the communists, the I. W. W.'s, the anarchists and reds generally . . . would like to see passed." He took the Secretary further into his confidence and said that "from authentic sources we

[7] Dallas *Morning News,* December 17, 1918.

learned that a determined effort is being made by the communists to obtain from the Senate Committee on Labor the adoption of the Interchurch report on the steel strike as an official document." Senator Borah characterized this gentleman as an "undesirable citizen."

During these months immediately following the World War two letters came to the Senator's desk from two great newspaper men in New York. Borah had written Frank I. Cobb of the New York *World* to congratulate him on his editorials on individual liberty. Cobb returned the compliment, saying that the fight for liberty was the most important since the Civil War and that his difference with the Senator on the League of Nations did not in any way prevent him from appreciating the Senator's efforts for individual rights.

Frank A. Munsey of the New York *Herald* also congratulated the Senator on his great fight in the campaign of 1920, and then came to the point in this fashion : "Few, very few, had so much to give. God endowed you with great gifts. . . My radicalism, if I may call it so, is tempered with poise. I wish for your sake, yours were so tempered. . . These are observations of one who feels a warm interest in you." Borah's reply was most significant : "My radicalism consists in the attack, principally, upon those who use the Constitution of the United States when it protects them and trample upon it when it comes in their way."

In a noteworthy tribute to Senator La Follette, Sr., in June, 1926, Borah gave a broader characterization of radicalism : "The most familiar and the most universally accepted criticism of Senator La Follette was that he was a radical. 'Radical' is the full anathema which vested wrong hurls at those who would right wrongs. 'Radical' measures the highest intellectual effort of entrenched stupidity. . ." [8]

The Senator also viewed with disgust the deportation hysteria following the War. He made a vigorous speech against it in December, 1919. A New York lawyer wrote him that he had "uttered the first words of sanity that have come from any public man" on that subject. But another New Yorker, a member of the Union Club, wrote that the communists, the I. W. W.'s, and their kind were entitled to no

[8] *Record,* June 20, 1926, p. 11649.

consideration whatever and should be deported. The Senator replied: "I am opposed to deportation as a matter of policy, first, because it will prove wholly ineffective, secondly because it is a cowardly way to meet this great question. . . Why should we deport people into Russia and then go to the great expense of sending troops over there to shoot them?" (American troops had been sent to Russia, although we were not at war with that country.)

Soon after the War the Senator began to take an interest in the release of political prisoners. In 1919, Norman Thomas and others had written him in the interest of conscientious objectors and their treatment in prison. The Senator checked up on some cases and paid visits to General Crowder and other officials. When Eugene V. Debs was freed in 1921, the adjutant of a Legion post in Idaho asked the Senator's opinion of this act of clemency. The Senator answered at length.

"I would not myself have granted the pardon of Debs upon the principle and for the reasons given out by the pardoning power. There was nothing in Debs' individual case which in my judgment entitled him to particular consideration. If anyone was to be punished under the Espionage law for political opinions and expressions, I could not see why Debs should not be so punished. But I was in favor at the close of the war, and am now in favor, of a general amnesty for all political prisoners; that is, all individuals who are in prison by reason of their words or views or opinions or expressions concerning the war, or political matters, during the war. I would have granted and given a general amnesty to all such individuals. I am so utterly opposed to imprisoning or punishing men for criticism of government, or governmental action, touching in matters in either peace or war that I should have favored a general amnesty along the lines here indicated. Such policy has been pursued in every other country engaged in war. This great Republic, grounded in the principles of freedom of expression and a free press, ought not to lag behind.

"I opposed to the utmost of my ability and voted against all provisions of the Espionage law providing punishment for expressions or opinions either by speech or in writing. I thought then, and I think now, that such provisions were contrary to the letter of the Constitution, and I know they were contrary to the spirit of our institutions and at war with the whole theory of free government. I believe at all times in freedom of speech, in a free press, in the right of peaceable assemblage, just as they are provided for in the Constitution and just as they must exist, or we shall have no free government at all. In my judgment the manner in which the Espionage law was enforced in this country was a blot upon our institutions, a challenge to the very principles which we were supposed to be fighting for, and if carried on and continued, would utterly destroy the whole theory of a free government.

"I realize of course that there are some inconveniences and some evils which come from a free speech and a free press, but as Thomas Jefferson most wisely said : 'The evils which come from a free press and free speech are infinitely less than the evils which flow from an attempt to control or censure them.' One of the greatest Americans once said : 'Absolute freedom of speech is the test of fidelity in a free government.' That is my theory. No government, no class of men, and no views are so sacred that they ought not to be subject to criticism and subject to the fullest discussion, and no war was ever fought sufficiently sacred to justify punishing men for expressing a difference of opinion about it. Chatham denounced and Edmund Burke criticized, though both were Englishmen, the war of England against the American colonies. Webster and Lincoln criticized and denounced the Mexican war. I hold so long as men do not advise or urge the immediate commission of crime or the violation of law, they have a right to express their most pronounced opinions upon any subject which is before the people. If the American soldiers did not fight for this principle, then I misunderstand what the war was about. . ."

On June 6, 1922, Borah wrote the President on behalf of the political prisoners. "I should not trespass upon your busy hours nor seem to intrude upon your duties as an Executive except for the urgent and often repeated requests of those most vitally concerned, to wit, the families of those now in prison." He went on to say that he had spent some time investigating the facts relative to these prisoners; that if the President were familiar with these facts, he believed he would pardon the offenders; that clemency had already been extended to such prisoners in other countries; and that "some of the sentences imposed were absurdly cruel and unusual and could only have been imposed under the spirit and strain of war." Attorney S. O. Levinson of Chicago, at the beginning of a long friendship with the Senator, wrote his approval of the course taken and remarked that a miracle had happened — the *Tribune* of that city had showed some disposition to favor the release of the political offenders.

The Senator was now in earnest. He introduced and put through a Senate resolution calling upon the Attorney-General to report on the status of war prosecutions under the espionage act. He moved on June 30 for a discussion of a resolution granting a general amnesty to political prisoners. On October 2, he was in Chicago for the greatest meeting held there since the war. With Jane Addams, Raymond Robins, and other liberals on the platform, he spoke to a cosmopolitan audience of 5000 on the subject of recognizing Russia and releasing the war prisoners. Of the latter he said: "Instead of persecuting men with ideas to explain we should hire halls for them. . .

"The seventy-five political prisoners now in jail have been confined for four long years merely because they expressed an opinion. . .

"The real test of free government is free speech. You can chain up all of the liberties of a free government except free speech, and free speech will quickly unchain them all. . .

"The Constitution has left Congress with no power to abridge free speech, much less deny it. Yet there has sprung up a vicious doctrine that when war comes Congress can violate the Constitution. . .

"Congress did this in the espionage law and officials did it in preventing free speech. This doctrine is treasonable and diabolical and leads to anarchy and despotism. . ."

But there were other gatherings in Chicago. At a banquet at the Hamilton Club the Secretary of the American Sentinels grabbed a plate from the board and smashed it to a thousand pieces on the floor, shouting, "My compliments to Senator

Borah." Dr. George T. Harding, brother of the President, was at the same banquet table. He expressed himself as believing that there was special need for saving young men "when others were extending the hand of fellowship to conscientious objectors." [9]

In December, 1922, Borah wrote Attorney-General Daugherty on behalf of the political prisoners, and prepared an article for Norman Hapgood in *Hearst's International* on "Intolerance." "The article," said Hapgood, "is magnificent. Your voice rings strong and true. The country owes you much." During this period he wrote several other articles and made a number of addresses on this same subject. In his Lincoln Day address at Grace Methodist Church in New York in 1923, he emphasized that tolerance was an outstanding virtue of that richly gifted man who, "at the end of a fierce Civil War, when the whole political life of the nation had been poisoned with the searching passions of a long internecine struggle," had a heart "still free from malice" and a mind "unclouded by sectional bitterness."

He kept his interest in the amnesty movement throughout 1923. He had considerable correspondence with the Civil Liberties Union, which was urging the cause of the prisoners, and the Senator, who was planning more speeches on the subject and could not afford to make mistakes of fact, asked the Union to send him specific information.

On March 11, the Senator had another great meeting in New York. In the audience there were a great many radicals, to whom the Senator made it plain that although he stood for the constitutional right of all to free speech, he did not share their views on other questions. The speech was similar to his Chicago address of a few months before, but he elaborated his arguments somewhat. Toward the end he stated his idea of Americanism. "Americanism is liberty. And what is liberty? It is not a mere right to be free from chains, it is not a mere right to be outside the prison walls — liberty is also the right to express yourself, to entertain your views, to defend your policies, to treat yourself and your neighbors as free and independent agents under a great representative Republic."

[9] *Statesman,* October 15, 1922.

Senators Ladd, Norris, and David I. Walsh wired the meeting that they joined Borah in his plea for the release of political prisoners. They were supported by Senator Pepper, who had made a study of the cases of the political prisoners and had been advocating their release for some months. The fight went on until their release was finally effected.

The Senator's interest in the political prisoners gives us a very fair indication of his conception of civil rights, a conception which is sometimes a stranger to those in power. On September 4, 1923, he began a short note of congratulation to Norman Hapgood on an article he had written. But the Senator could not stop with that. He went on to say: "One of the most ironical, though tragic, features of the whole Walpurgis night is to hear the owl-like discussions of these automatons of power to the effect that all these disturbances, all this restlessness, all this inability to settle down, are due to free speech, to agitators, to too much personal freedom, and so the iron hand must be invoked and force must be employed. Men must be lashed into submission, thoughts, ideas, must be jailed. The prisons must be filled with men who object to oppression."

The ousting of the Socialist members from the New York assembly (1920), the Daugherty Injunction, in so far as it limited free speech and the right of assembly (1922), the demand of the officers of a Legion post in Aberdeen, Washington, that a local minister cease using German in his sermons, and the kidnapping of Kate Richards O'Hare at Twin Falls, Idaho, where she was scheduled to make a speech — all these roused the wrath of Mr. Borah.

Writing in *Liberty,* December 26, 1925, he told of having received many letters which urged him to propose legislation against those who questioned the teachings of Christianity. To one such letter he replied: "No more fatuous chimera ever infected the brain of man than that you can control opinion by law or direct beliefs by statute, and no more pernicious sentiment ever tormented the human heart than the barbarous desire to do so. . . I do not speak personally, and therefore I trust not offensively, when I say that whether in religion or politics, touching things divine or things earthly, I look upon those who would deny others the right to urge and argue their propositions, however irksome or pernicious they may seem, as intellectual and moral cowards. . . A religion or a government which cannot survive under the principle [of free speech and free press] established in that great instrument [the Constitution], be assured, cannot long be preserved by a denial of that principle." He continued by stating that those who seem to have the greatest fears of fascism and the greatest horrors of communism would themselves lay the very corner-stone of those systems in the United States by denying, just as fascism and communism deny, freedom of expression. Drive men with their noisy oratory from the forum and you drive them to the cellar to continue in whispers. In conclusion, he quoted with approval, "Better an uproar than a whisper."

The states' rights views of Senator Borah as set forth in Chapter X are the views which, more than any other he holds, meet with the approval of conservatives of the nation. Old-line Republicans and Democrats have them in mind when they say that Borah is "sound" on the Constitution. But he has other views on the Constitution and the American system which many, probably the majority, of these gentlemen hate and believe to be fraught with death. In their minds William E. Borah is all but an enemy of the Republic when he insists, as he invariably does, upon a strict observation of all of the personal-liberty provisions of the Fundamental Law of his country. Perhaps there are only a few people who are willing to "go all the way" on the Constitution which they profess to worship. Borah "goes all the way" — "too far," some would say. He is for the whole Constitution in peace ; he is for the whole Constitution in war, when we need it most. Americanism to him means civil, political, and even economic freedom.

CHAPTER XIII

THE MIRABEAU OF THE BATTALION OF DEATH

THE story of the League of Nations battle in the United States has been written by Senator Lodge, Professor D. F. Fleming, and others. The purpose of this chapter is to reveal Senator Borah's part in that fight rather than to write a summary of the historic struggle as a whole. With the emphasis on Borah some light may be thrown upon the League issue, but in trying to rewrite the whole story in one brief chapter neither history nor biography would be served.

The Senator is certain that the rejection of membership in the League of Nations by the United States was the most fundamental and satisfactory decision reached on foreign affairs by this Government since the promulgation of the Monroe Doctrine. Perhaps it is not possible to say who kept the United States out of the League of Nations, but there is no question that a large share of the praise or blame belongs to Borah. He was the original Irreconcilable. When other leaders were discussing the desirability of separating the Covenant of the League from the Treaty, or urging the necessity of "Americanizing" the Covenant, Borah was saying he would have none of it. Borah, more than any other man, stirred up anti-League sentiment among the people. He was the first to seek to counteract the influence of Wilson's speeches on the League. The success of his efforts showed Republican leaders that obstruction to the League might be politically expedient. Borah brought the lawyer's skill in exposing the flaws and jokers in a document, the orator's superb, exalted eloquence, and the patriot's sincere convictions to the side of the opposition. Impelled by little or no consideration for partisan advantage, he brought dignity and, at times, magnificence to an opposition which had little of the former and none of the latter.

Free at all times from a mean and petty spirit, generous to the sick man in the White House who had fathered the Covenant, Borah, of all the Irreconcilables, was the only one who held Wilson's respect. Indeed, in his bitter days of invalid retirement, the former President spoke of Borah with glowing affection. The Senator is proud of his part in keeping the United States out of the League ; he is equally proud of the fact that, while using all of his energy to wreck the President's most cherished plans, he retained the President's friendship.

On December 18, 1916, President Wilson addressed identical notes to all the nations at war requesting them to state definitely the terms on which they could make peace. Four days later Senator Hitchcock introduced a resolution (S.298) "That the Senate approved and strongly endorses the action taken by the President in sending the diplomatic notes. . ." The resolution was adopted in modified form on January 5, 1917.

In opposing the adoption of this resolution the Senator from Idaho fired his opening gun against any league of nations.[1] He called attention to these words in the President's note to the belligerents : "In the measures to be taken to secure the future peace of the world the people and Government of the United States are as vitally and as deeply interested as the Governments now at war. Their interest, moreover, in the means to be adopted to relieve the smaller and weaker peoples of the world of the perils of wrong and violence is as quick and ardent as that of any other people or government. They stand ready, and even eager, to coöperate in the accomplishment of these ends, when the war is over, with every influence and resource at their command."

The Senator said that such coöperation would mark a fundamental departure from the policy laid down by George Washington and would mean the scrapping of the Monroe Doctrine which was included in that policy. It would mean that we would join a league. The Senator referred to the League to Enforce Peace, now very active in all countries and headed in the United States by former President Taft. He read the purpose of that League which was to use economic and military sanctions against any nation which went to war without exhausting pacific means of settlement. He showed that President Wilson endorsed the principle of this League

[1] *Record,* January 5, 1917, pp. 892–896.

(Senator Lodge also supported it until February, 1917). To Borah such a plan was unthinkable. "We agree in advance," he said, "to authorize other nations to make war upon the United States if we refuse to submit some vital issue of ours to the decision of some European or Asiatic nations."

On December 21, 1916, two weeks before this formal speech against the Hitchcock resolution, Borah had said: "To want peace and to secure it are two different propositions. The one is a question of sentiment, the other requires a vast amount of judgment. I do not find fault with the President, but I want to be informed myself when I take part in the proceedings. . . We are likely to convince both sides in Europe that we simply want peace regardless of the worth of it, the reliability of it, or the honor of it. If such an opinion of our attitude — selfish, superficial, and indifferent of the future — obtains in Europe, we will have but little influence when the vital hour comes for action."

He said further that he was "an old-fashioned American"; that he would like to see the United States thoroughly prepared to protect its citizens so that it could devote its energies to working out our social and industrial problems; and that he would be glad to see the United States play the rôle of mediator in Europe when the time came, "but no alliances, no entanglements with Europe, and no European meddling in American affairs."

The Boston *Transcript* and a few other papers approved Borah's stand. William Jennings Bryan and Theodore Roosevelt did, the former adding, however, that the Senator ought to support the President's efforts to get the belligerents to state their aims because this could be done without supporting the League to Enforce Peace. Roosevelt ridiculed the whole League idea, saying it would not enforce peace but enforce delay. He stated that it was ridiculous of the League adherents to propose military action against any nation, right or wrong, which would not wait for arbitration. He said further that the whole idea was utterly silly and that no nation would accept it. There were many other letters and wires of commendation of the Senator's stand, an indication that popular support for such a position was stronger than his colleagues and the press realized.

The Buffalo *Express* carried this significant comment (December 26, 1916): "Senator Borah is the first of the prominent men at Washington to take direct issue with the President on what Mr. Wilson has begun to refer to as the abandonment of the policy of isolation." This early vigilance against any such charge was followed up by other Borah declarations on January 26, February 7, and April 4, 1917.

The nearest approach Mr. Borah ever made to endorsing Mr. Wilson's League was in an article he wrote for the New York *Times,* October 13, 1918. Several weeks before, the President had delivered a notable address in which he had said we could make peace only with the German people, not with the Hohenzollerns. The Senator gave this address his unqualified approval. Then he mentioned the proposed League. "But, after all, a league of nations – the haunting dream of noble minds – will still be a human institution. . . Metternich . . . found a league most convenient for his ambitious plans. . . After the league has been formed – if it is ever formed – nations will still be restless and men will still be ambitious."

WITH the war ended and Mr. Wilson in Europe, discussion of a League became rife. The original Irreconcilable introduced a resolution reaffirming his faith in the Monroe Doctrine as soon as the Sixty-fifth Congress convened for its third session (December 5, 1918). He followed this resolution up the next day with an anti-League speech.[2] The idea that a League should be set up which would deny to a nation its right to make its own righteous decision and enforce its own just judgments was abhorrent to him. Senator John Sharp Williams replied that the Senator from Idaho seemed content only with the law of the barbarians, the law of tooth and claw.

The Idahoan made another anti-League speech in the Senate on January 4, when only twelve Senators were in their places, and in various other ways manifested his purpose to fight to the limit against the League. February 15, he wrote the Chicago *Tribune,* one of the first powerful papers to oppose the League: "Your inspiring cartoon of the 12th tells

[2] *Record,* December 6, 1918, pp. 189 ff.

the whole story. It is a League to promote internationalism. The *Tribune* was never greater than in these days."

Of course, no one knew yet what the League was to be, but the Senator knew enough about what was being proposed to know that he would be unalterably opposed to the finished product. Consequently, when the Secretary to the President, at his request, invited the members of the Committee on Foreign Relations to meet the President at dinner to discuss the League, the Senator from Idaho sent his regrets.

His note reads: "I greatly appreciate your note honoring me with an invitation to meet the President February 26, to discuss the League of Nations – a matter of most vital concern to the whole country. Meetings at the White House, according to a long standing custom, are always regarded as strictly confidential upon the part of the guests. This meeting, I take it, would be regarded as especially confidential, otherwise the President would have spoken, according to his custom, to the open Senate. The differences between the President and myself on this question are fundamental. . .

"I feel, therefore, that I would not be fair to the President to accept his confidence or receive from him confidential information concerning this subject. Neither, in my view of the subject, could I accept information which I would not feel perfectly free to transmit to my colleagues or use in public debate. After much reflection I beg, therefore, to be excused from attending the meeting.

"In writing this note and in taking this course I mean no personal disrespect to or disregard of the President. I simply find myself in such disagreement with him, and feel so intensely concerning the matter, that I cannot do otherwise than candidly advise him of the fact."

This is the sort of thing on which the press fattens. A few papers praised Borah, a few more criticized him, but the greater number of them settled down to enjoy a joke. The Senator was asked why, in view of his reverence for the founders of the Republic and his insistence upon following all their policies and precedents, he had chosen to disregard a custom as old as the Republic that a White House invitation was a command.

The *News* of Newark (February 19) thought that "Senator

Borah might profitably employ the time he saves from the presidential dinner party by stuffing his ears with cotton, putting on blinders and taking a high resolve not to look at the public prints until after the crisis is passed."

The *Commercial Tribune* of the same date commented: " 'Who eats of the Arab's salt is safe from the Arab's sword' is tradition in tabloid. By the same token the Arab whose salt is eaten should have like immunity from the weapon of the eater. Evidently Senator Borah is of that mind."

A New Orleans paper recalled the story of General Glasscock who went to Congress from Georgia in the days of Henry Clay. "General, may I introduce you to Henry Clay?" asked a friend. "No, sir," replied the General, "I am his adversary and choose not to subject myself to his fascination."

The New York *Tribune* of February 21 printed what it conceived to be the Senator's favorite proverb: "Better a dinner of herbs where love is than a stalled ox and hatred therewith." The Indianapolis *Star* (February 19) made use of the word "ass," holding that the "Idaho blatherskite" was one, and of the word "brains," maintaining that he had none.

But these comments did not disturb Borah at all. He probably enjoyed them, although he did not write his appreciation to the editors of these papers the next day as he did to Mr. Hearst expressing admiration for his anti-League editorials. He suggested to the publisher that they meet to talk things over. The publisher replied that he would hold any day of the next week open for the Senator.

The Senator learned the details of the proposed League Covenant on February 15, and by February 21, the Senator had another speech against the League ready for delivery. This address, on "Americanism," was one of his great anti-League efforts.[3] He opened with the proposal that the question of American membership in the League, involving a change in our system of government, should be referred to the people, arguing that the Senators who would pass upon the treaty were only agents of the people and should not decide this issue until they had received authority from their principals.

"Mr. President, prior to the Administration of Washington,

[3] *Ibid.*, February 21, 1919, pp. 3911 ff.

America had been involved in every European war since colonization began. . . When Washington assumed the responsibilities as administrator of this Government, he immediately set about to change that condition of affairs." He followed this statement with numerous quotations from Washington's letters, quotations relative to American isolation. He went on to state that as Washington had established the policy of keeping out of European affairs, the Monroe Doctrine had established the policy of our keeping the European powers out of our affairs.

He said that Article X of the Covenant – "The high contracting parties shall undertake to respect and preserve as against external aggression the territorial integrity and existing political independence of all States members of the League" – would bring European and Asiatic intervention in the concerns of the Western Hemisphere and, worse, bring American intervention in the other continents, intervention that would mean helping Great Britain keep her hand on the throats of Irishmen, Indians, and Egyptians.

He said that the League Covenant had been written by Englishmen, principally by General Smuts, and that it was in the interest of England and not in the interest of the United States. "What has England given up in this League of Nations? What has she surrendered? Will some one advise me? Did she surrender the freedom of the seas? That was pushed aside at the first meetings of the conference as not subject to its jurisdiction. Has she surrendered her claim for the largest navy? What has she surrendered?

"On the other hand, we have surrendered the traditional foreign policy of this country, which has been established for one hundred years; and we have gone behind these powers and placed at their disposal our finances, our man power, and our full capacity to guarantee the integrity of their possessions all over the globe. Is it an even balance, is it an equitable, is it an honest arrangement between these great powers and the United States?

"I come now to another feature, which to me is even more interesting, more menacing, than those over which we have passed. Conceal it as you may, disguise it as some will attempt to do, this is the first step in internationalism and the first distinct effort to sterilize nationalism." Then he pointed to the internationalism of communism, and "wondered": "Are we, indeed, yielding our Americanism before the on-rushing tide of revolutionary internationalism?" This is one of the few times the Senator ever made use of the communist scare-crow.

His conclusion was: "Let us range ourselves along with Washington and Jefferson and Jackson and Lincoln and Roosevelt. Let us be true to ourselves; and, whatever the obligations of the future, we can not then be false to others."

The Senator received such an ovation that the business of the Senate was suspended for the time being. The congratulations showered upon him were unusual, if not record breaking. All of the Republicans shook his hand and praised him, although not many of them were ready to endorse his extreme position. Twelve or fifteen Democrats joined the procession around to Borah's desk.

Just what was the position of the Republican Senate leaders on the League at this time? Senator Knox had introduced a resolution (S.361) on December 3, 1918, which included among its "whereases" the statement that the Peace Conference should be concerned only with accomplishing the aims of the war: "That for the safeguarding of those aims the first essential is a definite understanding that the same necessity arising in the future, there shall be the same complete accord and coöperation with our chief cobelligerents for the defense of civilization." There was the further clause that "any project for any general league of nations" should be postponed for future discussion with all the great powers, victors and vanquished.

A few weeks later he explained his resolution.[4] "The object of my resolution is not to condemn in advance any league of nations – and least of all the existing entente, or a permanent understanding of all the English-speaking peoples – of a kind that might in time commend itself to the considered judgment of the American people. The object of my resolution is simply to postpone the larger and very disputable question of some comprehensive league of nations. . ."

The speech of Senator Lodge on December 21 dealt with

[4] *Ibid.*, December 18, 1918, p. 602.

the entire question of the treaty. He was concerned about the right of the Senate to advise with the President on the conduct of foreign affairs, on territorial adjustments, and so forth. He touched upon the league proposal only to raise some questions and to advise caution. He stated that "The attempt to attach provisions for an effective league of nations to the treaty of peace now making with Germany would be to launch the nations who have been fighting Germany on a sea of boundless discussion." [5] George Wharton Pepper, not yet a Senator but very active against the League, wrote Knox in April, 1919, that Lodge was unduly cautious on the League issue and that he was not coöperating with Pepper's organization against the League. As late as June 10, the nature of Senator Knox's opposition was expressed in a resolution (which failed to pass) that the treaty and the League Covenant be separated. With Knox the League was not yet "the evil thing with the holy name." In other words, in these early months when Borah was making frontal attacks on the League, Lodge and Knox were proposing only that the Covenant be separated from the treaty or that certain reservations be attached when the Senate should give its consent to ratification.

February 20, 1919, the *News Courier* of Charleston, South Carolina, presented a very penetrating editorial on Borah, Knox, and Lodge. Referring to the Idahoan's declination to attend the White House dinner because, as he put it, nothing could induce him to support the League, the editorial states: "From the moment when the League of Nations began to shape up as an issue, Senator Borah began to lay his course in a direction that seemed certain to bring him to where he now stands. His opposition to the President's policies attracted less attention than the opposition of Senators Lodge and Knox, but the line taken by the two latter was evidently a blind alley which could lead them nowhere while Mr. Borah's course, wrong-headed and mistaken though it has been, was at least consistent and led on toward a definite and clearly discernible goal. The difference between them may be indicated broadly by saying that the opposition of Messrs. Lodge and Knox was based on the idea that Mr. Wilson's

[5] *Ibid.*, December 21, 1918, p. 728.

policies were . . . a menace to the good relations now prevailing between America and the great peoples with whom she has been associated during the war; whereas Mr. Borah's opposition is based on the precisely opposite contention that Mr. Wilson's policies imply practically an alliance with the Entente nations. . ."

As the Republican Senators gathered around Borah to congratulate him on his "Americanism" speech of February 21 they said, "That was great; that was fine; we agree with you; but we have got to have some sort of league; everybody is for it." The "Lone Lion" smiled and said, "Well, I'm not."

About this time it was announced that the Idaho Senator was to visit various cities and speak against the League. The New York *Post* did not question Borah's ability or honesty but raised the question of his judgment "to suppose that in this matter the people are burning to rise and follow him. He is a ready and forceful speaker. But his plan to tour the country in opposition to the League of Nations strikes us as a case of a man taking himself with too portentous a gravity. The party effects of his course are already worrying Republican leaders." [6]

Certainly the last sentence of this editorial was absolutely true, although a few second-rate men like Senator Miles Poindexter showed signs of agreeing with Borah. About the first of March Borah told Senator Lodge that he had an invitation to speak in Boston. The Sage of Nahant threw up his hands: "Why, you must not do that. Wilson was just in Boston and he was given a great ovation. The people up there are all for the League. If you go they will pack your audience with pro-League people and heckle you. The results will be terrible." Borah laughed, and prepared to go.

Senator Lodge prepared his resolution "that it is the sense of the Senate that while it is their sincere desire that the nations of the world unite to promote peace and general disarmament the constitution of the league of nations in the form now proposed . . . should not be acceptable to the United States." This he attempted to introduce on March 4, but there was objection. Nevertheless, he submitted the

[6] New York *Post*, February 22, 1919.

names of thirty-seven Republican Senators who would vote against the Covenant as it now stood. Congress then adjourned.[7]

Senators Borah, James A. Reed (an Irreconcilable of the Democratic ranks), and C. S. Thomas went to New York and held a rousing anti-League meeting. Borah and Thomas went on to Boston where they were met by Beveridge. His Excellency Calvin Coolidge, the Governor, refused to attend the meeting and preside. Beveridge and Thomas spoke but Borah was the chief attraction. The meeting was a remarkable success, with hundreds outside hoping that Borah would say a few words to them when he came out. He did so, and while he was speaking a young man who had seemed to be thinking very hard suddenly exclaimed, "This is no League of Nations ; it is the sale of our country." The interjection took the crowd's fancy in a remarkable way and the gathering finally dispersed with anti-League feelings running strong.

On his way back to Washington the Senator spoke at Troy, Rochester, and Albany, New York, letting it be known in no uncertain terms that if he had his way the League of Nations would be "Twenty Thousand Leagues Under the Sea."

When he came back to Washington a number of Republican Senators were beginning to see the League question as a good political issue. Senator Lodge admitted that he had been mistaken, that he had had no idea sentiment against the League was so strong or could be made so strong. Senator Warren G. Harding said : "Bill, I'd like to get in the fight against this League of Nations, but the people of my state are all for it I'm afraid. Couldn't you go to Ohio and make a few speeches against it ; sound them out, you know? I'll arrange the meetings for you, but no one need know that I did it." The Idaho Senator had only contempt for this brand of "statesmanship," but it gave him an opportunity he wanted, so he went to Cleveland and several other places.

When he reached his hotel in Cleveland, newspaper men began coming in to chat. They "kidded" him, saying that there was no anti-League sentiment in Cleveland, no newspaper support for such sentiment, and that his meeting would be attended only by the survivors of Washington's army. But

[7] *Record,* March 4, 1919, p. 4974.

the Armory with a seating capacity of 7000 was overflowing. The Senator was in his best form and the crowd was with him. With the same success, he went on through Ohio, then to Colorado and to other states of the Middle West.

The Hearst papers, the Boston *Transcript,* the Chicago *Tribune,* and a few smaller papers supported Borah, but for the most part the papers either opposed him or advised more caution. But wherever Borah went he made news for all of the papers. Many Republican papers were making every effort to prevent the League from becoming a party issue. Papers favorable to the League took up Borah's objection that it was contrary to Washington's policy. The Philadelphia *Public Ledger* asked this question of Borah, "the ancestral worshipper" : "Is it to be supposed that the man who doffed a British uniform to lead a revolutionary army against British rule would hesitate timidly on the brink of a new departure because there was no tradition to support it?" [8] For good measure the *Ledger* called Borah a "political antiquarian and a pottering troglodyte."

As for England having six votes to our one in the proposed Assembly of the League, it was suggested that several of the members of the British Commonwealth of Nations were more American than British. It was further suggested that if the British Dominions could outvote us they could also outvote other nations. As for Siam having one vote and the United States having just one vote, it was hinted strongly in reply to the Senator that it might be a good idea to reduce Idaho's vote in the United States Senate. To the Senator's assertion that the League would abolish the Monroe Doctrine the papers answered that the leading historians of the country stated that such was not a fact. "Mr. Borah sets up a straw man and knocks him down with gusto" ; "he offers nothing constructive ; his substitute for the League is the status quo" are typical of press comments. The Des Moines *Register* had this to say : "Senator Borah is not an unthinking man. But he voices the sentiments of the unthinking." [9] But the Senator always had great enthusiastic crowds at his meetings, and his mail was filled to overflowing with encouraging letters.

[8] Philadelphia *Public Ledger,* February 24, 1919.
[9] Des Moines *Register,* February 25, 1919.

The Editor of the Salmon *Herald* (Idaho) wrote that he had "just read with ravenous interest your wonderful speech on Americanism" (the speech of February 21). A lawyer in Butte, Montana, wrote that he had no doubt that the people could be set right on the League question. All that was necessary was to unravel it and uncover it, he said. Beveridge wrote early in the spring that we would hear of reservations soon now, but that they would not save us, and encouraged the Senator to stand firm. He said that he had been worried about the position a certain great lawyer, who was very pro-British, would take on the League. Recently, however, he had heard from him to the effect that he was not only against the League himself but that lawyers as a class were turning against it fast.

Senator Borah's hatred of the League increased as the weeks passed. The amendment to the Covenant providing that the Monroe Doctrine was not to be interfered with did not appease him. The only difference between the Covenant with the amendment and without it "is the difference between putting an epitaph upon a friend's tombstone and leaving it blank."

His patience with the Republican leaders for fearing to take hold of the League issue was soon exhausted. He wrote a letter (May 7) to his friend James T. Williams, editor of the *Transcript*. After stating his opinion of the League he asked: "Can a partisan under such circumstances ask what about 1920? Can a political party under such circumstances stand aside – can it jayhawk between the lines and still expect to hold the confidence and respect of a vigorous and brave people? Can it decline to have opinions? Can a Republican go feeling and smelling around as the white-livered satellite of base expediency? It would be a thousand times better to stand forth even if defeated with certainty.

"If the Republican party could, even through defeat, save the sacred traditions of America, preserve American institutions and maintain unimpaired the independence and untrammeled sovereignty of the Republic, it would render a service second not even to its heroic service under the leadership of the blessed martyr.

"But suppose it should be said to such men as myself

that the party might be in favor of the proposition. Very well, let it say so. Let it surrender its place if it wants to as the defender of American institutions and American ideals. And let those who would abhor such hideous cowardice fumigate themselves and get out. Even this would be more honorable than to go skulking through such a fight without views or convictions or even an attitude. . . I despise a coward and I hate a traitor." Williams then wrote an editorial — "The Bravery that is Borah."

Borah received several hundred letters a day expressing appreciation of his letter to the *Transcript*. A week later he wrote Williams: "You will read this morning Senator Knox's brief but excellent statement" [that the League would be detrimental to the interests of the United States]. "The true line of battle is now being recognized. Those who are not for America are against her, and we are all learning very rapidly that you cannot amend a pact with treason and make it respectable. When this treacherous and treasonable scheme is dead and buried and in hell exceptional credit will be due to you." Every day the League pained the Senator more. It rose monstrous before his eyes, the sum of all villainy.

Senator Borah found a man after his own heart in the League fight, Senator Hiram Johnson, who on June 2 denounced the League as a gigantic war trust. Borah endorsed him wholeheartedly and unreservedly for the presidency because of his stand on the League, his demand for the withdrawal of American troops from Russia, his pronouncement for free speech, and his ideas on social reform.

A few days later the Senator received a letter which Chairman Will Hays was sending to all prominent Republicans. The letter asked for coöperation with the national committee. The "Little American" displayed remarkable restraint in answering it. He said only that Hays could expect no cooperation from him since Hays had said that the League was not a party issue but an American issue. He concluded with the statement that he was doing everything in his power to make it a party issue.

News came to Senator Borah early in June that there were copies of the peace treaty in New York. The treaty had not been signed. Furthermore, Mr. Wilson had agreed with his associates in Paris that the full text of the treaty should not be published until the treaty was signed. But Borah thought that if "Wall Street" had a copy, regardless of how Wall Street happened to get hold of it, there was no reason why the Senate should not have a copy. A representative of the Chicago *Tribune* procured a copy from New York, delivered it to Borah, who read it into the *Record*. This was an unprecedented proceeding – entering a treaty in the *Record* before it had been submitted by the President. Borah and Lodge were praised, defended, blamed, and ridiculed. "Sage-brush diplomacy" or not, the country had the treaty as a public document.

THE Treaty of Versailles, carrying the Covenant of the League of Nations, was officially presented to the Senate by President Wilson on July 10. The Committee on Foreign Relations held hearings for about two months, and Senator Borah, a member of that Committee, gathered information about the treaty not only from those who testified before the Committee but from every other available source. A great many of the provisions of the treaty, as well as the manner of its negotiation, were entirely unsatisfactory to Mr. Borah.

While he was full of indignation over the iniquities of this instrument, he received a letter from Doctor Frederick Lynch, editor of the *Christian Work,* relative to the threatened massacre of Armenians by the Turks. The Doctor had said : "It is simply a question whether the United States shall agree to act with England and France and the other nations which stand for righteousness and civilization to protect the weak nations and the innocent peoples of the world," etc.

"Really, Reverend Lynch," wrote the Senator, "in this enlightened day and age of the world a general statement like that is not sufficient. Your general statement is contrary to the actual facts. . . To begin with, you are perfectly familiar with the fact that this scheme which you advocate includes Japan, the most militaristic and despotic nation now in existence. You are also perfectly familiar with the fact that Japan is now engaged in literally destroying the Koreans as a distinct people. They are being shot down, decimated, their women outraged, their children disembowled, their aged and infirm massacred for no other reason than that the Koreans still love their country and aspire to independence. . .

"Secondly, you are perfectly aware that, in violation of every rule of morality and international honor, Japan has succeeded in having written into this treaty a clause which will transfer to her the domination and control of nearly forty million more people [Shantung] whom she will deal with in the same way that she is dealing with the Koreans. . .

"If you and those in your honored calling, and who stand for the Christian religion, teach such doctrines as that, and are willing to connive at such *criminal outrages,* and to compromise with such *immoral practices,* what in the name of Justice and Freedom is to become of the human race?

" 'Be not deceived! God is not mocked; for whatsoever a man soweth, that shall he also reap.'

"England standing for the protection of weak nations! Do you know that the people of Egypt are now in a state of incipient revolution and are being held in subjection by military force, that they asked for a hearing, simply a hearing, before this conference which created the League of Nations, and that they were denied even a *hearing?*

"Do you know that India is saturated with discontent and revolution, that they asked for a hearing and were denied a hearing?

"Do you know that Ireland has been struggling for her independence for seven hundred years, that her people are now being held down at the *point of the bayonet,* that the right of trial by jury and the writ of habeas corpus are being denied them, that men and women are being thrown into prison under conditions such as you would not permit your dog to suffer over night? . . .

"Do you know that the Koreans, in a last desperate effort to get their cause before the world, stole like hunted fugitives to Versailles supposing there before the moral leaders of the world and the movers of a New Era they would be heard? Nay, not so! Their despotic ruler, Japan, sat at that conference and forbade their appearance. . .

"With these people you ask me to form a permanent combination and bring this Republic down to that low level of debauchery and shame!"

The Senator's interest in downtrodden peoples has ever been one of his salient characteristics. His critics have humorously stated that the Senator himself behaves as an oppressed race, a subject nation.

With the Senator the Treaty of Versailles was one of the most iniquitous of all treaties and its League of Nations was simply a scheme for perpetuating those iniquities. Writing to his friend, Williams of the *Transcript,* in 1921, he said: "I am told that Viviani is an agnostic, a disbeliever in the existence of a God. I should think it would be quite natural for anyone who disbelieves in a God to thoroughly believe in the Versailles Treaty."

As the Committee hearings on the treaty were getting under way in July, 1919, Williams wrote Senator Borah that the uprising in New England was indescribable. "Feeling which you stirred in February is now aflame. . . You and Senator Johnson can save the day if there are thirty other patriots in the Senate."

It seems that as early as December, 1918, before anyone had more than a general idea of what the Covenant would contain, Colonel Theodore Roosevelt, Senator Lodge, and other Republican strategists had agreed on a way to handle the League question. The Republican majority in the Senate was to offer so many amendments and reservations to whatever plan the President might bring back from Paris that he would feel forced to reject it as approved by the Senate.[10] On the other hand, if the President should accept the Covenant with the accompanying amendments and reservations, the Republicans could then claim the credit for having Americanized the Covenant presented to them by an internationalist President. In either case, there was political capital for the Republican party in this procedure. Such leaders feared to oppose the League directly because public opinion seemed to favor a League and because, with a few mild reservations, a number of Republican Senators favored it.

[10] D. F. Fleming, *The United States and the League of Nations,* pp. 72 ff.

The Foreign Relations Committee made its majority report (signed by Lodge, Borah, and seven other Republicans) on September 10. It recommended adoption of the Treaty subject to forty-five amendments and four reservations. The next day the Democratic minority of the Committee recommended adoption without change. On September 15, Senator Porter J. McCumber (Republican), decidedly friendly to the League plan, recommended adoption subject to six reservations. The fight went on in the Senate while the President was appealing to the country for the League and it continued after the President had returned to the White House, a very sick man.

The Senators aligned themselves in three groups: Administration Democrats, temporarily led by Hitchcock, who would consent to the Treaty as written; Irreconcilables (about ten), led by Borah, Johnson, and James A. Reed, for whom no amendments or reservations could make the treaty satisfactory; and "Reservationists." There were several classes of reservationists. Those who insisted upon "fundamental" reservations were led by Senator Lodge, Chairman of the Committee on Foreign Relations. Milder reservationists, composed of Republicans and Democrats, had for their chief spokesmen Senators Kellogg, McCumber, and Thomas Walsh.

Borah went to the Middle West again, speaking against the League, attempting to counteract the influence of the President's speeches in that section. It was suggested to Borah by James M. Beck that the Senator was the ideal man to follow the President — that the Senator by his direct realism could soon drive Mr. Wilson with his "unctuous generalities" off the stump.

Williams, of the *Transcript,* asked Borah to give him his speeches in advance, but the Senator replied that he was not preparing anything in advance. He said he expected to speak, as he found it always necessary to do before popular audiences, "almost entirely from notes, and very meagre notes at that."

There was almost a riot in Chicago on September 10 for seats to hear Borah, Johnson, and McCormick against the League. Then Borah and Johnson went into Iowa and Nebraska. At Fort Dodge, at Omaha, and at other points the story was the same. "Frequently men jumped up hurling their hats in the air and shouting after the speaker had made some particularly fiery denunciation of the League pact." [11]

When Borah returned to Washington he received a letter from a member of the Iowa legislature telling him that he and Johnson had made a profound impression on the people of that state, the Des Moines papers to the contrary notwithstanding. "The people are with Borah, Kenyon, and Johnson. I hear it on every hand. . . Around the fireside at home Father used to say: 'Keep your eye on Billy, he will some day take his place among the great men of the Nation.' "

The Idaho *Statesman,* of Borah's home town, was not prepared to commit itself on the League in February, 1919.[12] It regretted that it was coming to be a party question. In the fall, the paper was beginning to show definite signs of hostility to the League, but not enough for Borah. "Now, Cal," the Senator wrote the Editor, "I wish you would hit this treacherous League a little harder. . . It is a contemptible, cowardly betrayal of the most fundamental principles of the Republic. Strike hard and strike often. What a pitiable figure the ex-President [Taft] is," explaining how treason is not treason.

The Governor of Idaho wrote the Senator that he had been with President Wilson and heard him speak for the League. The Governor said he was for Borah on the League question and that Idaho lawyers generally took his position. A warm friend of the Senator, a lawyer, wrote that the people had supported the League at first, but that now they were all for strong reservations or were thoroughly opposed to it.

The debates in the Senate went on. October 29, a vote was taken on the amendments to the Covenant offered by the Republican majority of the Foreign Relations Committee. The amendments were defeated, the mild reservationists voting against them with the Administration Democrats.

The Committee, assisted by suggestions from other Senators, particularly Kellogg, then prepared fourteen reservations. These were discussed until November 19. It was in the closing debate on ratification with these reservations that

[11] Des Moines *Register,* September 14, 1919.
[12] *Statesman,* February 23, 1919.

Senator Borah made what is commonly regarded as one of the Senate's oratorical masterpieces. He used neither manuscript nor notes, but he was full of the subject which had been uppermost in his mind for a year. Earnest as he was in opposing a treaty he felt would soon be ratified, his speech contained not the slightest trace of disrespect for the President. It is unnecessary to quote it at length. It can be found in a volume of Borah's speeches entitled *American Problems.*

The reservations had not met his objections to the League. He stated that the reservations meant nothing; that reservations or no reservations, our delegates in the League would feel morally bound to go along with the delegates of other countries; that other countries did not object to our reservations because they would interpret them.

As for a nation being protected because the Council of the League would act by unanimous consent, he asked: "Has not every division and dismemberment taken place by unanimous consent for the last three hundred years? Did not Prussia and Austria and Russia by unanimous consent divide Poland? Did not the United States and Great Britain and Japan and Italy and France divide China, and give Shantung to Japan?"

The commanding reason for his objection to the League was that it took us away from a policy followed for one hundred and fifty years, the policy of the Fathers. "I can not get my consent to exchange the doctrine of George Washington for the doctrine of Frederick the Great translated into mendacious phrases of peace. . . I know well the answer to my contention. It has been piped about of late from a thousand sources — venal sources, disloyal sources, sinister sources . . . the puny demagogue, the barren editor, the sterile professor now vie with each other in apologizing for the temporary and commonplace expedients which the Father of our Country felt constrained to adopt in building a Republic!"

American democracy would be ruined by association with autocratic powers, he said. "We may become one of the four dictators of the world, but we shall no longer be master of our own spirit." Democracy is not a mere form of government. "It is a moral entity, a spiritual force as well.

And these are things which live only and alone in the atmosphere of liberty."

Suppose the country, with no leader now like Washington, joins the League. "What no leader can or will do experience, bitter experience, and the people of this country in whose keeping, after all, thank God, is the Republic, will ultimately do. If we abandon his [Washington's] leadership and teachings, we will go back. We will return to his policy. Americanism shall not, can not die. We may go back in sackcloth and ashes, but we will return to the faith of the fathers."

In the middle of his speech came that part which is most frequently quoted, the part on the "Little Americans." Men were awed. They heard a voice filling the Chamber yet it seemed strangely far away. "Sir, since the debate opened months ago those of us who have stood against this proposition have been taunted many times with being little Americans. Leave us the word American, keep that in your presumptuous impeachment, and no taunt can disturb us, no jibe discompose our purposes. Call us little Americans if you will, but leave us the consolation and the pride which the term American, however modified, still imparts. Take away that term and though you should coin in telling phrase your highest eulogy we would hurl it back as common slander. We have been ridiculed because, forsooth, of our limited vision. Possibly that charge may be true. Who is there here that can judge the future? Time, and time alone, unerring and remorseless, will give us each our proper place in the affections of our countrymen and in the esteem and commendation of those who are to come after us. We neither fear nor court her favor. But if our vision has been circumscribed it has at all times within its compass been clear and steady. We have sought nothing save the tranquillity of our own people and the honor and independence of our own Republic. No foreign flattery, no possible world glory and power have disturbed our poise. . . If we have erred we have erred out of too much love for those things which from childhood you and we together were taught to revere — yes, to defend even at the cost of limb and life. If we have erred it is because we have placed too high an estimate upon the wisdom of Wash-

Courtesy of the New York Herald-Tribune

ington and Jefferson, too exalted an opinion upon the patriotism of the sainted Lincoln. And blame us not therefore if we have, in our limited vision, seemed sometimes bitter and at all times uncompromising, for the things for which we have spoken, feebly spoken, the things which we have endeavored to defend have been the things for which your fathers and our fathers were willing to die."

At this point Senator Lodge was in tears. "When I find

myself in tears," he said later, "I know I am listening to a great speech." Vice-President Marshall scribbled Borah a note: "May a mummy say that you almost galvanized him to life?" From the gallery came a note: "The Battalion of Death of the press gallery salutes the Mirabeau of the New Freedom."

A few days later a letter came from former Senator Beveridge, himself a great orator. "I have just read your closing speech on the treaty. Even if I were not in agreement with you I nevertheless would write you of my admiration of this superb utterance. This is one of the best things you ever did — one of the best anybody ever did. It is clear, simple, convincing, exalted. I do not at this moment recall a speech that more perfectly satisfies my conception of the standard of taste and genuine eloquence. Nobody can answer it — nobody will try to answer it."

The treaty with the reservations was voted down. The President had written Senator Hitchcock that he sincerely hoped that the friends and supporters of the treaty would vote against the resolution of ratification. The right wing composed of Administration Democrats who wanted the treaty without reservations and the left wing of Irreconcilables who did not want the treaty at all therefore closed in on the reservationists and crushed them, 55 to 39. Some citizens bemoaned "the greatest tragedy since the crucifixion of the Saviour of Mankind"; many deplored the "low political intrigue" of Senators; many others celebrated the survival of the Republic.

But the story was not ended. Compromise might yet pull the treaty through. Although Senator Lodge is supposed to have been pleased with the defeat of the treaty with the reservations which he as Chairman of the committee had reported, this was no proof that milder reservations, resulting in the ratification of the treaty, might not be adopted. If Mr. Lodge was pleased it was perhaps not so much because the treaty had been temporarily defeated, but because the President had been snubbed. Politically the situation was promising: the Republican senators had been ready to give the people the League and they would have given it to them but for the obstinacy of Mr. Wilson. Here Senator Lodge would have been glad to let the matter rest.

There was some difficulty, however, in the way of closing the door to further consideration of the treaty. The public demand for compromise was so great that Senator Lodge felt compelled to go into conference with the Democrats and the reservationist Republicans. The Irreconcilable Republicans had never been sure that Lodge would insist upon the fourteen reservations as the absolute minima of concession on the treaty and the suggestion that any conference looking to a modification of those reservations might be held caused them the gravest apprehensions. Late in December, Senator Johnson wrote from California to Senator Borah urging him to "see that Lodge does not yield or recede from the just American attitude he has assumed."

The bi-partisan conference got under way in January. Senator McNary, a mild Reservationist, says that Senator Lodge, "in the best of good faith," tried to bring the Reservationists into general accord. Lodge was quoted, on the 21st, as saying that he felt progress had been made. The next day and the next, reports indicated that the conferees would probably reach an agreement on reservations milder than the fourteen which had been rejected in the Senate on November 19. These reports thoroughly aroused the Irreconcilables. There were threats of revolt from Lodge's leadership.

On January 23, a Friday afternoon, Borah answered a telephone call. The man calling would not give his name, but he volunteered the information that Senator Lodge was in conference with Senator Simmons and other Democrats and reservationists; that they seemed nearly to have reached an agreement on Article X; and that Lodge was to declare for the treaty on that basis. The Senator was almost beside himself, but he retained possession of his fighting faculties.

He called Senators Knox, Johnson, Moses, and as many other "Bitter-enders" as he could reach on Friday afternoon. They had a meeting in which they decided to call the Chairman of the Foreign Relations Committee out of the bi-partisan conference and ask for an explanation. Senator Moses was elected to go to the meeting and ask for Senator Lodge. He knocked, asked for the Massachusetts Senator, and presently he appeared, looking rather foolish.

Back at the Irreconcilable meeting Borah was telling Sen-

Photo Keystone

SENATORS BORAH, LODGE, AND SMOOT

1920

ator Knox that he would have to talk to the Republican leader when he appeared. But the Senator from Pennsylvania, because of unpleasant personal relationships between himself and Lodge, begged the Idaho Lion to do the honors.

By this time Senator Moses had arrived with Senator Lodge, now somewhat irritated. The Idaho Senator looked at his chief and said : "Well, you are the Republican leader in the Senate and we are your colleagues in this League fight and we think we ought to know what is going on in that meeting you are attending."

The Republican leader became angry, but replied without too much display of temper that he frequently met with other members of the Senate, Republicans and Democrats, and that it seemed to him to be a perfectly proper procedure. He said that he could not express his pleasure at being called upon in this summary manner to give an account of himself and that he felt disposed to refuse to make explanations. He suggested that the Republicans could get another leader if they distrusted him.

The Idaho Senator was enraged. He did not control his feelings as well as Mr. Lodge. "I won't give you a chance to resign," he said. "I am going into the Senate Chamber Monday morning and say that the Republicans must have a new leader, and I will tell why one is needed."

Senator Lodge, now considerably agitated, trembled from head to foot. Then the Irreconcilables relaxed their severity somewhat and Senator Lodge regained his composure. They discussed the situation at some length, and finally Senator Lodge asked Senator Moses to conduct him back to the conference room. Lodge informed his conferees, who had been awaiting his return with some impatience, that he could not go on — that the agreement was off.

To push the advantage of the Irreconcilables a little further, Borah then wrote Lodge this letter : "For nearly nine months under great disadvantage and against the most powerful organization of sinister interests this country has ever known we fought to carry out your program of reservations which you and your friends contended would Americanize the treaty. Not one of these reservations was written by the so-called Irreconcilables. They were all the handiwork of the friends of the League." He stated further that any compromise on the reservations would be either a betrayal or a piece of hypocrisy for political purposes. "Candor compels me therefore to advise you that if this is the program of our party in the Senate I can no longer respect or coöperate with the party organization in the Senate. . . I propose to appeal from the organization to the voters."

Whether Senator Lodge was at heart an Irreconcilable or a Reservationist may be a matter of dispute, but it is difficult for one to resist believing that pressure from his mild Reservationist colleagues and the public forced him into the bi-partisan conference, and that the dire threats of the Irreconcilables prevented him from making any concessions in that conference. It seems that Lodge yielded to the political forces which he feared most. He must have been convinced that the Irreconcilables would bolt his leadership ; he probably felt reasonably certain that the Reservationists would not. After the ultimatum to Lodge on January 23, the Irreconcilables had no more difficulty with him. Three days later he advised the Democrats that any further conferences with them would have to be on the basis of their acceptance of the original reservations on Article X and the Monroe Doctrine. This ended any chance of a bi-partisan agreement on the reservations.

With only a few changes in the original reservations, the treaty was put to a final vote on March 19, 1920. The alignment was practically what it had been on November 19, Reservationists on one side and Wilson Democrats and Irreconcilables on the other. The vote was 49 for the treaty and 35 against it. A shift of seven votes would have ratified the treaty. Had the President allowed his followers to accept the reservations, these votes would have been forthcoming. Thus the Irreconcilables and President Wilson defeated the League !

In January, 1920, Senator Borah had written letters to various non-senatorial candidates for the presidency, asking them to declare themselves on the League. No candidate to whom he wrote had satisfied him. Senator Harding, to whom he did not write, had written to Fred Mandile in Massachusetts

Courtesy of Berryman and the Washington Star

on February 5, 1920, as follows : "I do not think it is necessary or becoming for this great Republic to hold aloof from the activities of the world or to refuse to contribute its full part to the advancement of the world's civilization." He said, however, that this should be done in the American way. Harding had voted for the League with the reservations on November 19, 1919. Senator Johnson was the only candidate who satisfied Borah, and he had declared for the Californian some months before he quizzed the other candidates.

Both Governor Lowden and General Wood incurred the Senator's extreme displeasure in their lavish expenditure of money in the presidential primaries. During the spring and early summer of 1920 Mr. Borah's time was fairly equally divided among three activities : insistence that the Republican platform declare against the League ; aid to Senator Johnson in the primaries ; and exposure of large campaign expenditures by Lowden and Wood, particularly the latter. Good Republican organization men and the press of the same class condemned Borah on all three counts.

Courtesy of the New York Herald-Tribune

In the Michigan presidential primaries Borah and Johnson talked chiefly about the evils of campaign expenditures, capitalizing on the Newberry senatorial election in that State two years before when so much money had been spent that it had now become a national scandal. "Nothing quite so adroit as the Johnson-Borah appeal to virtue has been seen in Michigan in this campaign, and in fact in very few campaigns," commented the Detroit *Saturday Night*. They marched up and down Michigan "with a flaming sword of

Courtesy of the Portland Oregonian

purity and a megaphone full of three-star righteousness." [13]

At the Auditorium Hotel in Chicago on the night of June 11 Borah spoke before an audience of 3000. "Suppose I go into that convention tomorrow and ask from the rostrum for Mr. Wood's representative to stand up and tell us what that nomination has cost. Suppose I should ask the other gentlemen to stand up and ask how much they have bid against Wood for the primary." He explained that Rome was in precisely that situation before its end. He would support any Republican who was clean, but none who was not.

Mayor Thompson had previously stated on the floor of the convention that he would not knowingly make himself a

[13] Detroit *Saturday Night*, April 10, 1920.

party "to placing the Republican nomination for President on the auction block." Mr. Hearst had talked with Borah at the Auditorium Hotel and it was gossiped that he had urged Borah and his Johnson crowd to bolt if Lowden or Wood should be nominated. Losing Illinois through Thompson's opposition and having Borah and Johnson raise the "boodle cry" in every state in the Union certainly must have been a possibility which caused the regulars to have cold chills. In any event, Wood and Lowden were dropped and Senator Harding got the nomination.

But interested as Borah was in having a "clean" candidate, he was still more interested in having an "American" plank in the party platform on the League, a no-League plank. Lodge satisfied the Irreconcilables at Chicago — he was against the League, even with the fourteen reservations. But his former Senate colleague, Winthrop Murray Crane, came to Chicago with a plank pledging the Republican party to ratify the treaty immediately. To be sure, there were some reservations, but as compared with the original fourteen reservations they were mild, so mild that only the Wilson Democrats would object. Borah was on the committee on resolutions. At the Blackstone Hotel he sat in a meeting with Crane, Colonel George Harvey, Senators Brandegee, Wadsworth, Watson and a few others. Crane believed that the party had to declare for the League in order to hold states like Massachusetts in the Republican column. Some others agreed with him. Borah said to Crane : "You are not advocating this League because the people want it, but because the bankers who are outside waiting to see you when you come out of this meeting want it." Crane, a quiet worker, a good "fixer," but almost never aggressive, now grew both angry and aggressive. There was a row with Borah and Brandegee on one side and Crane on the other, and George Harvey and Wadsworth acting somewhat as mediators.

Borah said he would leave the convention if the plank was put in the platform. Although not worried about that possibility, Crane showed concern when Brandegee said he would not run for the Senate in Connecticut if it went in. At this juncture Ogden Mills presented Mr. Root's compromise plank. The Crane League plank was then abandoned.

Courtesy of the Boston Post

The party declared, not for *the* League, but for a league — "for agreement among the nations to preserve the peace of the world." It believed that such an international organization should "secure instant and general international conference whenever peace shall be threatened by international action." But all of this was to be done without sacrificing traditional American policy.

The Senator from Idaho spoke in many states during the campaign. He denounced the Treaty of Versailles and its League. He hated the treaty because of the injustice it did to smaller nations and weaker peoples. He mortally feared and hated the League because it was designed to preserve iniquities of the Versailles Treaty, because it sacrificed American sovereignty, and because by going into it we would sacrifice the principles of Washington. But let it be emphasized here that the Senator did not simply say that League membership would be bad because it was contrary to Washington's teaching. He added, not always, to be sure, that he favored Washington's policy not solely because it had been his, but because it was the best policy for us now. The magic of the name Washington was such that he did not feel the necessity of explaining in every speech why his policy was best for us now. He had great meetings everywhere, even in Crane's and Lodge's Massachusetts.

When Harding wobbled on the League issue, Borah told the Republicans at campaign headquarters to schedule him for no more speeches. When Harding stiffened his resistance with the declaration that, "It is not interpretation, but rejection that I am seeking," Borah praised Harding and stayed with him until the end of the campaign.

IT was Senator Borah's most ardent nationalism that made the League his supreme abomination. His nationalism was — and is — as flaming as that which history tells us fired the patriots at Valley Forge. What is the explanation of it? A few suggestions may be hazarded. First of all he has always had deep reverence for great men. Naturally his reverence for the men who launched this Republic would have first place in his heart.

Besides, Borah is a lawyer. Talk of international organization, with the nations assuming broad and undefined obligations, with international law far from satisfactory in its development, has never appealed to many lawyers, at least not to many west of the Mississippi. Almost to a man, leading lawyers and judges in Idaho backed Borah in his opposition to the League. Some still shout their defiance at the League in saying they stood right with Borah on that; others smile a kindly smile of forgiveness for Borah's many transgressions, as they see them, when they say he was absolutely "four square" on the League.

One other suggestion for Borah's nationalism is offered. He touched upon it in his "Little American" speech. It is his

2340 S STREET N W

WOODROW WILSON
WASHINGTON D C

16th February 1922

My dear Senator Borah:

I had the pleasure of reading in this morning's paper the message you sent to the Woodrow Wilson Foundation in New York, in declining their invitation to dinner; and I take the liberty of writing to express my admiration of the qualities of heart and breadth of mind of which that message gives such interesting evidence.

Allow me to subscribe myself, with sincere respect;

Your friend,

Woodrow Wilson

Honorable William E. Borah,

Washington, D. C.

belief in American democracy, American freedom. This democracy is peculiar to ourselves and we must work it out alone. Going into an international combination might level it down, contaminate it, besmirch it. His nationalism is built upon his belief in the sufficiency of American democracy.

Two sentences of caution on Borah's nationalism must be set down. His nationalism is not big navy, big army, "the white man's burden" sort of nationalism — not jingoism. Furthermore, it includes, as the last chapter attempted to show, the essentials of liberty that many jingoes would deny their fellow-citizens.

THUS Mr. Wilson's program was defeated by an avalanche of nationalism in 1920, an avalanche which Mr. Borah helped to start. But Wilson did not go down to ignominy, certainly not in Borah's eyes. He retained his great respect for the man. Writing William Allen White late in 1921, he said: "I think it is fine that you are going to write the life of Wilson for the Modern Statesmen Series. You know how much I have differed with Wilson in some matters, nevertheless, I hold a wholly different view of Wilson from that held by those who find nothing great in him. He will have a tremendous place in history." It may have been about this time that Wilson on one of his drives around Washington saw Borah and remarked to a companion: "There is one Irreconcilable I can respect." Why? Because Wilson believed that Borah was absolutely sincere in his opposition to the League and was not more interested in party advantage than he was in the honor of his country and the peace of the world.

In February, 1922, the Woodrow Wilson Foundation in New York invited Senator Borah to attend a dinner. The Senator wrote a gracious letter of thanks. He explained that his duties in Washington prevented his attending, and he added that they were all working for the same things, even though along different lines.

On the next day Mr. Wilson, still having the reputation of being a good hater, wrote Senator Borah a letter which is reproduced on the previous page.

Two lines from Sir Walter Scott are not inappropriate —

"And the stern joy which warriors feel
In foemen worthy of their steel."

CHAPTER XIV

SWORDS AND PLOUGHSHARES

THE Republican marginal success of the congressional elections of 1918 was the precursor of the Old Guard's triumph in both executive and legislative branches of the government in 1920. Borah and the old progressives of the Taft days were delighted to have a Republican victory, but they deplored the fact that their party's leadership was the same which it had known ten years before.

In February, 1919, just before the Senate was reorganized under Republican leadership, Borah was reported to be remaining adamant to the overtures of the Penrose following and to have declared that if the Pennsylvania Senator was made chairman of the Finance Committee he would "put a chair in the middle of the aisle and sit there." But the League of Nations issue soon came to be uppermost in Borah's mind and he was satisfied with an arrangement which placed Johnson on the Foreign Relations Committee and gave Penrose the coveted chairmanship.

The great Republican victory of 1920 was taken by the leaders of the party as a mandate to return to "normalcy." This meant to them, among other things, that the government should "get out of business," assume a less censorious attitude toward business, and raise the tariff. It meant, also, that the party leaders should ignore such men as Borah, Johnson, and La Follette. Indeed, such a respectable paper as the Philadelphia *Public Ledger,* in its issue of December 4, 1920, was so unkind as to suggest that the party could now go on about its affairs in the Senate and put these three Senators "on the skids." It prophesied that Borah would "begin to roar as gently as a suckling dove" when he found that the party leaders were going to ignore him.

But the Senator from Idaho had no idea of being ignored. He planned to champion or oppose issues as they arose, regardless of consequences. Not only that, he intended to raise issues whenever he pleased. He was to continue to be his own judge of what constituted good Republicanism and good Americanism. It has been stated that Borah is the Republican opposition. This is not true. He has never consistently opposed an administration. He is simply for what he believes to be right and against what he considers wrong regardless of the character of the administration. Borah has always been a free lance on the *issues*. Confusion about Borah's position, let us repeat, arises chiefly over the fact that we expect a man to be loyal to a party leader or to a party program. Borah is not.

Talking with a member of the House from Idaho in 1923, President Harding said that he had tried in every way to get Borah to "come along," that he had always liked him as a colleague in the Senate and still liked him, but that he was not going to bother with him any more. Borah, he said, just goes his own way in spite of everything. "Precisely," the Senator from Idaho would say.

If the filling of the all-important post of Secretary of State in 1921 indicated the extent of the influence of the anti-League crowd, it was practically nil. Borah and his friends wanted Senator Knox for that portfolio, for then there would be no compromises with the League supporters. In December, a friend in Chicago, Attorney S. O. Levinson, wrote to Borah asking him to block the appointment of Mr. Hughes, who, he had heard, was to get the place. The Senator wired that he had talked with Knox and they had agreed there was nothing to the rumor. Two days later Levinson wrote that the *Tribune* was now saying that Hughes would be appointed. Late in January, Borah wrote Levinson that he had done all he could for Knox but that he understood the position would be tendered to Mr. Hughes.

But in other matters, even before Harding was inaugurated, the Senator from Idaho showed that he still had power. Out of office for eight years, returned by an unprecedented majority, the Republicans thought they should take over the reins of office in a blaze of glory, that is, have a very pretentious and expensive inaugural. Borah blew a big blast against that and the idea was killed.

Not so long after the Harding Administration was launched, Congress started to play politics with the soldiers' bonus question. Their plan was to pay the soldiers something the next year and then something about every six months until the total of several hundred dollars was paid. Said the Senator: "If the Republican party is courageous and honorable it will send this bill back to committee, and do one of two things — tell the country and the soldiers that the bonus cannot be paid in cash or face the prospect of doing it. This bill undertakes to promise four billions in cash to the soldiers and to promise to the taxpayers that it will not cost them anything. . . The scheme is unjust to the soldiers, the taxpayers and discreditable to the Senate." [1] Upon the President's suggestion the bonus question was put aside for a season.

The Treaty of Versailles not having been ratified, it was necessary for the Harding Administration to make a treaty of peace with Germany. A new treaty was prepared and presented to the Senate for its approval. This claimed for the United States the rights and privileges granted it under the Treaty of Versailles. All of the old Irreconcilables except James A. Reed and Borah were content to vote for the new treaty. With each month that elapsed after the Versailles Treaty was negotiated, in the eyes of the Idaho Senator, it fell lower into the realm of iniquities. He would not criticize the individuals who under the influence of war passion dictated that treaty, but now they had had three years in which to reflect. "We see now not alone the punishment it would visit upon the Central Powers, but we see the cruel and destructive punishment it has visited and is to visit upon millions, many of whom fought by our side in the war. We know it has reduced to subjection and delivered over to exploitation subject and friendly peoples; that it has given in exchange for promises of independence and freedom dependence and spoliation. . . It hangs like a storm cloud upon the horizon. It is the incarnation of force. It recognizes neither mercy nor repentance, and discriminates not at all between the guilty and the innocent, friend or foe. . . We know that Europe can not recover so long as this treaty exists; that economic breakdown in Europe, if not the world, awaits its execution. . . All this we know, and knowing it

[1] *Commercial Appeal* (Memphis), June 27, 1921.

we not only invite the lashings of retribution, but we surrender every tenet of the American faith when we touch the cruel and maledict thing. . .

"Let us have an American policy. Or, if the word 'American' be considered by some as provincial or distasteful — a term of incivility — then let us have a humane policy, a Christian policy, a policy based upon justice, resting upon reason, guided by conscience, and made dominant by the mobilized moral forces of the world." He praised Wilson for having carried this code with him to Europe, and regretted that it was sacrificed.[2] Already some observers were beginning to say that Borah was now the successor to Wilson as a moral leader ; nor did Borah resent the suggestion.

The Senator could not agree with his party on the Fordney-McCumber tariff. He wanted to get what tariff advantages he could for the farmers, stock men, and beet-sugar men, but he was unwilling to pay the price — to vote for exorbitant rates to protect eastern manufacturers in order to get the votes of Eastern Senators for moderate duties to protect the people of the West.

But the Senator would not vote for what he regarded as excessive duties even on products which competed with those of the Westerners. Here is an interesting letter he wrote (August, 1922) to Mark Austin of Utah, a close friend : "Nothing hurts me more than to find myself in disagreement with you and Hart and I can say frankly and most sincerely that my difficulty over the wool schedule arose entirely out of my personal friendship for some of those interested. I never would have gone as high as 28 cents if it had not been for that. . . I resolved every doubt in favor of the higher rate. . . I know something about how the 33 cents was arranged for, a system which I cannot endorse in legislation. I would rather quit the job and end the whole business.

"There is another side to this thing. As I said to you before, Austin, it takes votes to keep a party in power in this country. While others have been more successful in dealing with machine organizations than I have been, I have had some success in reading in advance public opinion." Then he

[2] *Record,* September 26, 1921.

says the party is going to fair badly at the hands of the voters if it does not cut down the proposed tariff increases. "Both, therefore, as a matter of principle and as a matter of expediency, it seems to me that 28 cents was as high as we could possibly go. Now, Mark, let's wait ninety days and see if I am not correct in my construction of the situation." Within ninety days the grand Republican majority in Congress had been reduced to an ordinary majority ; moreover, some members of this majority belonged to the Farm bloc and were in no mood to coöperate with the old high tariff Republicans.

The Harding Administration wanted to turn over to private concerns the vessels acquired by the Government during the war. The terms on which the vessels were to be surrendered were very generous and, in addition, the Government was to grant a subsidy so that they could be operated on a comfortable margin. Borah was one of the leaders in the successful fight against this proposition. He argued that it was wrong in principle to take money from A and give it to B ; that subsidies resulted in inefficiency, incompetence, and corruption ; that, politically, this subsidy would mean the installation of an immense lobby in Washington to preserve and to increase the grant. The anti subsidy people won a fairly easy victory.

The Administration thought the high taxes imposed on incomes and excess profits during the War should be materially reduced. The Mellon Bill was proposed, providing for the reduction of the highest surtaxes from 65 to 25 per cent. One of the leaders in the fight to retain the higher taxes was Senator Borah. The surtax levy on the highest incomes was lowered to 50 per cent, not to half that rate, as proposed by Mr. Mellon.

About the time the big coal strike started in the spring of 1922, Borah became chairman of the Committee on Education and Labor. "If the coal industry is not reorganized in the interest of the public," he said, "it will be up to the public to try the experiment of public ownership. I do not underestimate the task which the public will assume when it undertakes this. . . There is no possible explanation nor justification for the price of coal at the present time other than that of waste, bad management, and unconscionable profits."[3] He introduced a bill calling for a commission to look into the coal situation. It was referred to the committee of which he was chairman, but the four other Republicans on the committee would not consider the bill and refused to report it. They suggested to their chairman that he see the President and get his approval for the bill. The Senator went to see the President but got nowhere. Some time later the President appeared before a joint session of Congress and urged the passage of just such legislation as Borah had proposed. Borah's committee then reported his bill favorably, and Congress authorized the Interstate Commerce Commission to control coal shipments during the emergency and to force down unjust prices. Congress provided also for a coal director and created a commission to investigate the coal industry.

During the Harding years the Senator from Idaho opposed the confirmation of Taft as Chief Justice because he had dedicated his whole life to politics. He also opposed the settlement with Colombia, dear to the Harding Administration, and he put through the Senate, over the objection of Mr. Harding and the Senate Republican leader, Mr. Lodge, a bill to exempt American vessels from the payment of Panama Canal tolls.

BUT the great achievement of Borah (whom all good Republicans were supposed to ignore after it was perfectly clear that the election of 1920 was over) during this period was to force the Harding Administration to call the Disarmament Conference. Let it be said here that Borah has never opposed international conferences ; he believes in them. He opposes only political alliances and entanglements. In his efforts for disarmament the Irreconcilable of the League-fight days not only won a single-handed victory over the Administration, but he became the darling of millions whom he had thwarted on the League issue. On the other hand, he earned the quiet resentment of the jingoes whom he had so pleased in opposing the League. Here is some more of Borah's inconsistency ! It amounts to this : at one time he pleased one

[3] Baltimore *Sun*, April 3, 1922.

group and offended the other ; at another time he merely reversed the process.

Borah was for naval preparedness in 1916. He did not believe in a large army for two reasons : first, because he feared that large armies and democratic government were incompatible and, second, because he was of the opinion that our defense depended primarily upon the Navy. In the spring of 1916 he opposed the making of any substantial appropriations for a Volunteer Army and the National Guard. "It would be better defense," he said, "if we should take the amount which we are putting into the Volunteer Army and the tremendous amount which we are putting into the National Guards [about $100,000,000 per annum for the two organizations] and attach that amount to any naval program which would come to the Senate." He thought that this additional amount for the Navy would give us "a most complete and efficient naval protection for the Pacific Coast where, my friends, we will need it first if there is any real menace nestling anywhere against this government." [4] It seems obvious that the "menace" referred to was Japan.

Borah supported the three-year naval building program which Congress adopted in 1916. It called for an expenditure of nearly $600,000,000 and was designed to give us a naval strength approximating that of Great Britain in 1914. The Senator said in speaking for the measure : "This is a program which I presume no one wants, but it is a program which some of us believe to be necessary. . . The Premier of Japan a short time ago said that the only way that diplomacy could become effective was where it was backed up by sufficient force. When he thus spoke he was not, I take it, making a threat but uttering a most practical precept of international action. . .

"I perfectly agree with those who reject the theory that any particular nation is planning an attack upon the United States. But I reject the other theory . . . that because there is no specific purpose to that end anywhere observable . . . there is no danger and hence no necessity for preparing to meet danger." Then he quoted Washington on preparedness.

Near the end of this rather brief address, he came to a signifi-

[4] *Record,* April 13, 1916, p. 6028.

cant consideration, a consideration of foreign commerce. He said that our commerce should grow or we would lose in the world struggle. "If we are going to play that part which we should play and which we are entitled to play, shall we hope to do so without the ability and the means to protect our own and without that preparation which shall insure respect to the flag and a due regard for our rights?" [5] Of course, this was "big navy" talk, which Borah abandoned completely after the World War.

In 1921, the Senator was interested in a reduction of armaments for reasons of economy and the maintenance of peace. Always interested in keeping the cost of government down, and never content with the gesture of economy which is often expressed in reducing appropriations for a few small bureaus whose friends have little political power, Borah went boldly to the heart of the problem with the declaration that no substantial economy could be achieved if reductions were not made in those services which cost the most, namely, the fighting services. He wanted to see the standing army reduced from 175,000 to 100,000. He considered that we had no need of 13,000 army officers. The program of naval construction which Secretary Daniels (and later Secretary Denby) proposed he rejected as unnecessary and entirely too costly.[6] "Borah opens war on naval measure," read a headline. "We predict that the Navy, having the most big guns, will win," commented the Portland *Oregonian*. But the Navy did not win a complete victory. The Senator's batteries were probably the most effective oral implements used in destroying about $100,000,000 worth of hoped-for naval armaments in the Congressional debates of 1921.

Important as the purpose of economy was in the Senator's mind, his chief reason for proposing disarmament was his desire to preserve peace. Why should the three great naval powers be building ships except for use against each other? Why should not the United States, Great Britain and Japan say, "Let us enter into an agreement to stop naval competition?" For the time being, Great Britain with her large navy had already practically stopped naval construction, but there was

[5] *Ibid.*, July 17, 1916, p. 11171.
[6] *Ibid.*, February 17, 1921, p. 3316.

almost feverish activity for naval armaments in the United States and Japan. A Senator from California had said that Japan was a menace. "I do not regard Japan as a menace in any such sense as used," said the Senator from Idaho. "I realize, of course, the difficulties between these two great nations [the United States and Japan], or rather differences of view between the nations as to vital questions, might lead to a situation where one would be a menace to the other . . . but those difficulties are not insurmountable. They can be settled without war, in my judgment, by bringing Japan and the United States into a conference upon naval competition. . .

"As far as immigration is concerned, or the race question, or the land question, they are questions that ought to yield to a conference, and until they are brought into conference I do not think we ought to assume that they are not to be settled except in the processes of war." He said that the real menace between Japan and the United States lay in the legislators of each country saying that the other is a menace, and that a large navy must be constructed for protection.

He concluded that "war with Japan could easily come within the next quarter of a century should we get into a great naval competition, accompanied by threats and denunciations; that is, indeed, the path of war." [7] (Yet the Senator voted for the Japanese exclusion bill in 1924, a measure which severely strained the relations of the two countries. The Senator's reason for this vote was that the domestic situation on the Pacific Coast was such that the defeat of this measure would have brought violent racial conflicts in that area.)

The bases, then, of Borah's resolution for a disarmament conference were the economic burden, the futility, and the menace of competition in naval armaments. He first introduced his resolution on December 14, 1920. It requested the President to call Great Britain and Japan to confer with the United States for the purpose of reaching an understanding respecting a 50 per cent reduction in their naval building programs within the next five years. The resolution was referred to the Committee on Foreign Relations.

The Committee reported the bill favorably on January 19,

[7] *Ibid.*, March 1, 1921, p. 4169.

1921, and on February 15, Mr. Borah offered his resolution as an amendment to the naval appropriation bill. Two weeks later Senator Edge proposed that the resolution be attached to the naval bill, and the motion passed the Senate unanimously. This particular naval bill, however, failed to become a law, due largely to Borah's fight against the excessive appropriation for battleships.

Josephus Daniels, Secretary of the Navy in Wilson's Cabinet, General Pershing, and General Bliss came out for Borah's proposal. Elihu Root wrote a letter urging delay until Harding should be inaugurated. Borah said that delay was peculiarly adapted to killing disarmament. Newspapers called attention to the timeliness of Borah's resolution, mentioning the staggering burden of armaments in an impoverished world. The press reaction was generally favorable. Frederic William Wile of the *Public Ledger* wisely observed that Borah's fight for naval retrenchment and the disarmament resolution was revealing him in the rôle he would play for the next four years, that of a free lance, a "splendid isolationist." He said Mr. Borah will proceed along constructive lines, persistently and unterrified, looking for nothing in 1924 except reëlection to the Senate.[8]

When the new Congress convened in special session after Harding's inauguration, Borah reintroduced his resolution (April 13). He again offered it as an amendment to the naval appropriation bill on May 4, showing that tenacity which "is by no means the least of his qualifications." Something had to be done now, so Senators Hale and Poindexter went to see President Harding and talked about the resolution. The President was opposed to the movement. "I gathered from what was said there," observed Senator Hale, cautiously, "that the President thought it was not necessary for Congress to go ahead in this way with a resolution asking for disarmament." [9] Even before this statement was made on the floor of the Senate, Harding's objection to the resolution was in all of the papers. The President was beginning to feel that he would have a lot of trouble with the Senator who had "helped him in" on the League of Nations issue.

[8] Philadelphia *Public Ledger,* February 13, 1921.
[9] *Record,* May 13, 1921, p. 1418.

On May 26 the Senate adopted Borah's resolution as an amendment to the navy bill by a vote of 74 to 0; not that all the Senators approved it — far from it — but opponents took this method to get rid of Borah's troublesome insistence, in full confidence that the House would defeat the plan. "The newspapers of the country, with almost one voice," said the Washington *Star* the next day, "acclaim Senator Borah's resolution as a mandate from the people to the President to take the first step toward checking the naval race which many feel is leading the nation to another war." But a few papers stated that Borah had won only a paper victory and that we should go ahead with our armaments.

After the bill went to the House, a substitute was offered for the Borah amendment, a substitute which seems to have been drawn up at the White House during a conference between the President and some members of the House. This substitute was simply a generalization to the effect that in the matter of disarmament full faith was to be given to the President to proceed in his own way. But this substitute was defeated in the House. An agreement was then reached in conference between the Senate and the House that the House would vote separately on the Borah amendment. The President then sent the following message to the House: "I am vastly more concerned with the favorable attitude of the Congress on this question than I am as to the form of expressing that attitude. . . I think it has been pretty well understood that the Administrative branch of the government has already been seeking information with regard to the attitude of foreign nations on the general subject of disarmament." The same day (June 29, 1921) the House passed the Borah resolution 330 to 4. Borah was then willing to vote for the navy bill, something over $100,000,000 having been lopped off.

Mark Sullivan observed that this triumph of Borah was "a pure case of leadership based on responsiveness to public feeling." The *Public Ledger,* which had suggested a few months before that Borah be "put on the skids," but which recently had been pioneering with Borah for disarmament, regarded the passage of the resolution as an "indisputable triumph" for the Senator. "It is notorious that his zeal," that paper continued, "evoked mixed emotions in Administration quarters. At one time – and only a few weeks ago – President Harding took public occasion to say he did not relish the idea of 'having the Executive hand forced by Congress' in the realm of disarmament." [10]

In the same issue of the *Ledger* was printed a letter from Senator Borah. "Today's vote in the House is fine," he wrote, "but those who are deeply interested in the cause of disarmament must understand that this is but a step. . . Disarmament can not be accomplished unless the masses keep their shoulders to the wheel every hour of the contest. . . I do not believe we can for a moment afford to turn this matter over to the diplomats and go about our business in the belief it will be worked out. Nothing would please the militarists of this and of other countries more than to have public sentiment die down. . ."

On July 7, he wrote for the *Evening Sun* on two things that would bring about war between the United States and Japan : "First, secrecy on the part of the respective governments . . . with an occasional intimation by parties in power that the situation is very serious – too serious and too dangerous for the people to know the facts. Secondly, a naval race between the two peoples, with an occasional announcement to the effect that we must have the greatest navy in the world in order to protect ourselves from a subtle enemy. The close observer has not failed to note that it is being quietly put out by those who are opposed to disarmament that Japan's attitude toward questions in the Pacific makes it impossible for us to consider disarmament, and then in order to avoid being more explicit, the people are informed that the facts cannot be divulged. . ." A few days later he wrote to the *Public Ledger* and to the New York *World* urging these papers to keep up their good fight for disarmament and to insist upon publicity in the forthcoming conference.

The State Department announced on July 10, that Great Britain, France, Italy, and Japan had been approached on the subject of a disarmament conference. On August 11, the formal invitations were sent out. Senator Borah continued

[10] *Public Ledger*, June 30, 1921.

Courtesy of the New York Herald-Tribune

to congratulate the *Ledger*, the *World*, and other papers for their support of his conference proposal and urged them to continue in the faith. The Editors continued to write Borah for letters and articles on the subject of disarmament. In one letter Frank I. Cobb, of the *World*, said that he had just seen Mr. Wilson and that he had "the highest respect for your intellectual honesty." Borah's old allies in the League fight, the *Tribune* and the *Transcript*, were not being heard from.

It would seem that Senator Borah might have been chosen as one of the American delegates to the conference, but he was not asked. The reasons are fairly obvious. First, he made it perfectly clear from the beginning that he actually believed that naval construction should be reduced by 50 per cent. In a speech at Asbury Park on August 30, he said: "The most hoary-headed lie which ever tormented the human race is the old wornout lie – proved false a thousand times – that great armies and great navies are assurances of peace. It ought no longer to vex the ears of the people or disgrace the lips of leaders. Armies and navies are incitements to war; are in fact, if we judge the future by the past, assurances of war. As General Smuts, the finest mind and the best heart in Europe, at least uncovered by the great war, has nobly said: 'If the instrument is ready for use the occasion will arise and men will arise and use it.'"

The Senator gave the second reason for his not being asked to serve as a delegate. It was that he was considered unable to work in double harness. When his brother Frank asked him if the President had requested him to serve, he said: "Not loud enough for me to hear it, although I wasn't expecting to hear anything of that kind and I might have overlooked it. I rather suspect he will not repeat it, however, if he has." He explained that he had no resentment whatever over not being asked.

Armistice Day, 1921, was the day before the Conference convened. The delegates had arrived in Washington and they attended the burial of the Unknown Soldier. They heard Rosa Ponselle sing, as few had heard her sing before, "I Know That My Redeemer Liveth." They heard President Harding in closing the ceremony repeat the Lord's Prayer in fitting intonations. They read in the papers the next morning that people in distant cities had fallen on their knees as they heard the prayer. The Conference opened under favorable auspices.

The history of the Conference has been written repeatedly. It will not be rewritten here. But it must be recorded that Senator Borah was displeased when President Harding suggested that the Conference might serve as a precedent for an association of nations. The Senator was pleased with what it did in the matter of limiting the construction of capital ships, very impatient with it for not dealing with sub-

Courtesy of the St. Louis Times

marines. The Senator was not fooled by the fact that the plenary sessions of the Conference were open, or by the fact that the committees gave out long communiques at the end of each of their sessions. He felt almost certain, and experienced correspondents agreed with him, that the Conference was reaching important decisions on delicate matters *via* private conversations between individuals. He denounced this secrecy.

The Conference did not confine itself solely to the question of disarmament. One other important question it had to deal with was the Anglo-Japanese Alliance. The United States could not help wondering against whom this alliance was. The Four Power Pact was substituted for this alliance.

The United States, Great Britain, France, and Japan undertook to insure the peace of the Pacific. This sounded like another association of nations to Borah, as it did to many others, and he denounced it. He considered it just a part of the old alliance system which had tortured Europe for three hundred years. "If I were a League man," he wrote Norman Davis, "I would fight this thing as persistently as I am, because it is the system which makes it impossible for a League of Nations to exist." But the treaties were ratified after Senator Lodge, a delegate to the Conference, spent some anxious days trying to explain them to the Senate.

From William Allen White came this letter: "My dear Bill: I don't blame you for feeling sore, and then on the other hand I would feel sore if the Washington Conference and the treaties had not been forthcoming and gone through.

"I never knew the machinery of it, but you may remember that during 1920 thirty-one of us pro-League Republicans got out a circular saying to vote for Harding and get the League of Nations; that's what it amounted to in polite, diplomatic, and political language. I was solicited to sign by Hoover, and I understood in a general way at the time that Root and Hughes were sympathetically backing the movement. Someone went to Harding. I don't know who it was. They got a promise out of him to stand by a league of nations [this was just after Borah had forced Harding to speak out against the League] which so far as I was concerned was as good as The League of Nations. The difference between an article and a particle is not visible to the naked eye in politics. Later I understood from Hoover that the old man was performing, and he certainly has performed. What he has done to you fellows is a plenty, and if it had been done to me I would have been equally ripsnorting."

Senator Borah has never lost his interest in disarmament. It was Borah who brought to the attention of the Senate in 1929 the activities of Mr. Shearer in attempting to prevent an agreement at the Geneva Conference in 1927. Two days later President Hoover denounced big-navy propagandists. President Hoover wanted Borah to attend the London Conference in 1930, but the Senator thought he could serve the cause better by not going. Again the President wanted him to go, as head of the delegation this time, to the World Disarmament Conference in Geneva in 1932. The President wrote: "It seems to me the situation is one which even more urgently requires your leadership than ever before." But the Senator, after some reflection, concluded that he was not the man for the place.

At the time the Senator declined the second opportunity to attend a disarmament conference, he said: "If the big-navy group wants to carry its fight for excessive naval expansion to the people, let it do so. The President can risk such a fight with composure. The country will be with him." Back in 1928 he regarded the sudden spurt to build American cruisers as sheer madness and the charge that pacifists were preventing the country from having "adequate defense" as tommyrot.

Late in 1931 he spoke over the radio to a peace delegates' meeting in Paris. He mentioned the pledge to disarm which is in the Versailles Treaty and he spoke of its violation. He spoke of the great burden of armaments. The militarists broke up the meeting. In 1932, he was saying that Germany was right in seeking equality of armaments, but that Germany should insist that other nations reduce to her level, not that she should build up to their level. The next year he praised President Franklin Roosevelt for bringing disarmament back to the center of the stage.

Interested as the Senator has always been in curtailing fighting equipment, convinced as he has always been in the futility of force, he soon came to see that all disarmament conferences were really armament conferences. As early as May, 1922, he was getting disgusted with the dawdling of the experts and diplomats in the matter. "Within the last few days," he wrote, "there have been representatives of seven nations here conferring upon deadly gases, and so on. I sometimes wish to the Lord that they would blow up." "Insincerity in disarmament has been reduced to a science," he said in 1929.

Reflection upon the reasons for the failure of disarmament conferences led the Senator to think that failure to reach an agreement respecting the "freedom of the seas" might be the prime obstacle. This idea he developed in 1929. Nations were building ships in order to protect, as neutrals, their rights of commerce when other powers might be at war. He argued that Mr. Wilson had been absolutely right in stipulating as one of his Fourteen Points that the seas should be free. England and France had refused to discuss this question at the Peace Conference and it had not been discussed openly at any of the disarmament conferences. What is needed, wrote the Senator in the Washington *Herald* (July 7), is an "international agreement, accepted by all the maritime powers for the protection of sea-borne trade in time of war as well as in time of peace." This, he said, "would remove the dominating obstacle to a reasonable understanding between all maritime nations. It is the only way, it seems to me, that you can eliminate competitive building in naval armaments. It would create an atmosphere of trust and confidence instead of suspicion and fear." Wilson was not the first nor will Borah be the last to tackle the problem of the freedom of the seas. Sometime, perhaps, an agreement on the subject may be reached, but even then it is doubtful if the atmosphere will be saturated with international trust and confidence, since rigorous restriction on neutral commerce may mean life to a belligerent nation.

As long ago as July, 1921, Senator Borah said that there should be no reduction of the Allies' war debts to the United States except as a reduction of armaments was brought about by the European powers. The London *Nation* said it was by no means easy to refute the Senator's argument. The Senator made a similar declaration from time to time and there was a great deal of favorable press comment on his statement. In August, 1922, Mr. Bryan wrote that he approved of Borah's position, except that he did not go far enough. Why not, suggested Bryan, put the proposition affirmatively? That is, offer cancelation to the Europeans if they will disarm. Another statement which Bryan made, and one which will not cause anyone to discount his foresight, was this: "I think the debt is *worthless* and will never be paid. If we can use a *worthless* debt to buy a *priceless* peace" what a bargain it will be! In reply to the Commoner's suggestion that he state the matter affirmatively the

Senator said that he was not in position to make the proposal, that it was up to the Executive department.

The truth is that Borah was not ready to go as far as Bryan was at that time. Beveridge was worried for fear Borah was weakening in his insistence upon payment and he wrote him a letter saying that he had heard that Walter Lippmann had persuaded him to change his mind. Borah replied that he had not changed his position; that he was not willing to offer cancelation for disarmament; but that if the time ever came for cancelation he would certainly be against it if it was not accompanied by disarmament.

Writing for the London *Daily News,* January 10, 1923, the Senator ventured "to believe that we will not curtail or adjust debts in order to keep vast armies. We will not support vast schemes of exploitation. . ." Then came the French occupation of the Ruhr, which the Senator characterized as being in violation of the Treaty of Versailles and as ruthless militarism, as a proof of the folly it would be for the United States to reduce debts without requiring disarmament.

This act on the part of France caused the Senator to take a very strong stand against debt cancelation. He pointed out that the nation which raised the greatest complaint about the debts, accused us of being "Shylock," insisted with the other debtor nations that America, to the hurt of her own taxpayers, forgive the debts, gave the greatest demonstration of militarism. He was particularly insistent that this nation, France, certainly the most prosperous of all our former allies, should pay.

His argument for payment as it stood about 1925 is here summarized. First, the United States has already canceled a large part of the debt. Second, France has a contract with the United States to make payment. Third, the American public men are the agents of the people and they have no right to cancel more of the contract until the American people say they may do so. Fourth, if France does not pay, the American taxpayers simply carry the debt. Fifth, the French taxpayers in terms of dollars pay only about half as much tax per capita as the American taxpayers. Sixth, France is able to borrow billions from American banks at rates of interest much higher than the American Government charges France on the war debt. (Bankers consider these loans good investments.) Seventh, France is prosperous. Eighth, she has a standing army of 700,000, is building more airplanes than any two other powers combined, has 200,000, soldiers fighting the Riffs, threatens Syria, and opposes disarmament. Of course, admitted the Senator, a man may not be able to pay his laundry bill if he spends all of his money on yachts. Ninth, France has acquired a great deal of valuable territory as a result of the war. Tenth, America's debt to France has long since been paid in full.[11]

It was pointed out to the Senator that he was in error on the last point to the extent that gifts on which no payment was ever expected, demanded, or offered were made by France to America, as follows: through Beaumarchais 1,000,000 livres were advanced in 1776; through Franklin 2,000,000 in 1777, and 6,000,000 in 1781; and in 1782, interest of approximately 2,000,000 was remitted on the loan of 1778.[12]

The Senator did not allow the French "to evoke the memory of their wounds." He thought that Russia had an equal right to make a claim on that basis. Nor did the Senator give any particular attention to the difficulty of paying a foreign debt when the tariff laws of the creditor country were such as to prevent large importation of goods from the debtor country.

The Senator did not hate France, but he lost his patience with those Frenchmen who pleaded that all should be forgiven and whose statements indicated that they had little intention of paying the debt whether it was forgiven or not.

With another group of people he had even less patience. These were the men and women who sailed from New York or Boston each year for France and who told the French people, often French government officials, that America would of course cancel the debt in time and that they need not pay any attention to Senator Borah, the Chicago *Tribune,* or Mr. Hearst. In 1922, President MacCracken of Vassar College, while in Switzerland, wrote the Senator about

[11] *Record,* January 22, 1925, p. 2279; and Washington *Star,* April 26, 1925.
[12] J. H. Latané, *A History of American Foreign Policy* (revised by D. W. Wainhouse), p. 65.

conditions in Europe, stating that it was idle to hope that the United States could avoid coöperating with European nations considering that the half of our debt was there. The Senator agreed that the United States should help, even assume leadership, "but that leadership will be destroyed and undermined just in proportion as we tie up with Europe so long as Europe persists in armaments and in her imperialistic policies. . . What Europe needs now . . . is not coddling, not sentimental sympathy, but she needs to be told the actual truth that she is persisting in her own suicide. . ."

If Borah did not hate the French, the French certainly did hate him. They hated him because he told them just what their difficulty was as he saw it. He spoke plainly, just as if he was speaking to newspaper men in his office. He did not soften his criticism because he happened to be Chairman of the Senate Committee on Foreign Relations. This the French could not understand. As a matter of fact, he thought that the French were a great people, that the only trouble with them was that they had not pondered sufficiently that verse of Scripture which reads "They that take the sword shall perish by the sword" and had pondered too much four words in the Lord's Prayer — "forgive us our debts. . ." But he did not give as much space as he might have to the French qualities he admired.

The French thought he hated them as a people. They called him everything uncomplimentary and opprobrious from "vile" to "pig." One of their cartoons represented the tri-color being pulled to pieces by a very vicious animal designated as "Dog Borah."

Here is a gem from a French publication of 1925: "Washington, eight o'clock in the morning, Rock Creek Park. The dew is dropping from the trees. A rider comes along looking even less important than Sancho on his donkey. His collar is badly fixed, his tie is in disorder, the white shirt tail shows from underneath his badly buttoned waistcoat and the trousers which he is wearing without suspenders. Hop! hop! Senator William Edgar Borah pepped up with bacon and eggs, two cups of tea and three Bible verses is taking the daily promenade prescribed for him by his doctor. Hop! Hop! He wears no hat, his hair is disheveled, his forehead wrinkled by anger, misanthropy and ambition. Hop! He mumbles: 'France has not paid!' 'Yas!' answers from under his tail the little pony of the Far West. . .

"His muscles and his ideas are stiff. Through his mother he has Irish blood corpuscles in his veins, the paternal corpuscles originating in Germany have hardly been diluted by some hundred years of Kentucky. Through his mother he therefore resembles Lloyd-George which is only half reassuring. He is like all Celts a gloomy, melancholic, erratic lunatic. . .

"He has a nickname of 'Irreconcilable.' This means that since the day when he left Tom's Prairie School Mr. Borah has kept half a dozen small ideas all closely connected. In his case there is a mixture, a real cocktail of childishness and intellectual sclerosis. . .

"Mr. Borah's ideas do not date from Tom's School, they date from the time of Uncle Tom's Cabin. The respect which is paid him by the American citizens somewhat resembles the veneration with which the memory of Washington is surrounded. There is something of a mummy and of an obelisk about him."

The argument about war debts and reparations continued. The world-wide depression came and even some of the rank and file began to realize the truth of what many economists had been saying, namely, that the war debts would not be paid. In mid-summer 1931, Senator Borah approved the Hoover moratorium, a plan whereby Germany was to pay no reparations for one year and the Allied debtors were to pay no war debts for an equal period.

The Senator was now ready to agree to cancelation of the war debts if the Allies would cancel their claims for further reparations from Germany, reduce armaments, revise the Treaty of Versailles, and open their markets to American goods. He was now putting his emphasis on the opening of markets for American goods. In a speech of April 19, 1932, as the Lausanne Conference to consider adjusting the reparations was about to convene, he dwelt at length upon European armaments and tariff walls. The London *Spectator* of May 7 agreed that there was a merit in the Senator's contention, although it noted that the United States headed the list in expenditures for armaments. If the cancelation of intergovernmental debts, it continued, "is part of a new attitude of the world to its problems ; if there is hope of closing the reparation controversy ever ; if the Disarmament Conference now sitting at Geneva is really to do the job it was meant to do and get armaments actually and visibly reduced ; if the paralysis that has fallen on international trade is to be ended by some concerted effort that will get the wheels of industry moving once more ; then America may convince herself that the cancelation or drastic reduction of debt is no mere thankless piece of enforced charity, but a stroke of sound business. . ."

On July 9 the nations' delegates at Lausanne signed the "lasting settlement" which removed about nine-tenths of Germany's obligation in reparations. A few weeks later (July 24) Senator Borah made a very enlightened radio speech on the whole subject of debt cancelation. "Will reduction or cancelation bring to the people of the United States an equal or greater benefit than the amount which they may collect from the debts ? Will such a course open foreign markets for the products of the farm and the factory, cause the price level to rise, put an end to unemployment and thaw out the frozen credits of the banks ?"

His conclusion was that cancelation, combined with the revision of the Versailles Treaty, disarmament, and a reopening of the channels of commerce, would give the American people far more than they could possibly lose by writing off the war debts.

He believed that a world economic conference should be held. Indeed, he had suggested an economic conference from time to time since 1922. Other anti-League Senators were horrified at his suggestion, but Borah told them that they were still suffering from the shell shock they had received in the League fight. As for himself, he had opposed the League only because he considered it a political alliance, not because American participants in its deliberations might be associated with foreigners and have to hear them speak in "unknown tongues" of the world's social and economic problems.

"The voice of statesmanship, of true patriotism, of enlightened self-interest made itself heard" in this appeal, said the Philadelphia *Record*.[13] "Senator Borah sees what other leaders are too blind to recognize : an interdependent world linking wheat fields of Kansas with the factories of Lancashire, the tractor workers of Detroit with the oil wells of Rumania, the money magnates of Wall Street with the tin miners of Bolivia." The *Record* was of the opinion that the Senator's speech would cause a sensation abroad.

The German Foreign Office expressed its gratification and noted the great moral effect of the message. *Il Giornale d'Italia* greeted his suggestions "with heartiest sympathy on account of their worth and their affinity with Mussolini's principles in this matter." This inspired article also approved linking cancelation with disarmament.

Le Temps said that the chief significance of the speech was that it indicated the existence of an effort on the American side of the Atlantic to meet the political and economic necessities of the present hour and testified to the fact that the American people would come to see that debt cancelation would be to their interest. London papers hailed "Borah's conversion" and welcomed his suggestion for an economic conference.

Hitler's Germany has "revised" the Treaty of Versailles, economic conferences have been held with no appreciable achievements to record, the intergovernmental debts are in default, armaments have taken a jump upward, and the Senator has proposed that private loans to Europe be prohibited by law. The goal to be achieved is worthy, but so far many of the efforts made to reach it have been futile.

The pessimism with which this chapter seems about to end may be relieved somewhat by a summary of a warm personal note which Prime Minister MacDonald, a friend of ten years' standing, wrote his "Dear Borah" when he read the reports of his speech on July 25, 1932. He supposed that it was the most irregular thing in the world for him to write to Borah on a matter so highly official as the communication which appeared in the London newspapers on the morning after the Senator's speech. But his old friendship was warmed by what

[13] Philadelphia *Record,* July 25, 1932.

he had read. He knew that Borah would be the last to believe that anything done at Lausanne was of the nature of a move against America, whose position in all this trouble about Debts and Reparations the Prime Minister not only understood, but sympathized with to the very utmost. But he had no intention of saying a word to influence Borah one way or another. He just felt, whilst reading the papers, that he would like to shake Borah's hand and say "bully."

CHAPTER XV

CONSCIENCE AND COURAGE

THE Harding Administration fell far below "normalcy" in some of its personnel. Senator Borah considers it the worst administration the country has ever had; in it America scratched the bottom. Before going into Idaho for Borah's big fight for reëlection in 1924, it is desirable to follow his career as "a conscience" in this and the Coolidge administrations. His conscience has ever been his treasure, his guide. In following it he has preserved his self-respect.

The Republican congressional victory in 1918 had brought to the United States Senate Truman H. Newberry of Michigan, on whose election something like $200,000 had been spent. People who believed in democratic government generally agreed that this sum was entirely too much to spend. The amount was dozens of times in excess of what the law allowed a candidate to spend in a campaign, but since Newberry had expended this money chiefly in the primary election, and since the Supreme Court of the United States held that a primary election was not an election, Newberry was not sent to prison.

Good people believed that he should not be sent to the Senate. Newberry was seated, however, because he met all of the qualifications imposed by the Constitution for membership. But in view of the money scandal, the Senate reserved, for later consideration, the question of Newberry's fitness for his seat. If Mr. Ford, his opponent, had been given the place which Newberry occupied temporarily, there would have been an equal number of Republicans and Democrats in the Chamber. The Democratic Vice-President would have broken the tie, thus placing the Senate organization in Democratic hands until the end of Wilson's Administration.

After the Harding election, the Senate, despite the President's disapproval, considered the matter of unseating Newberry. Borah early came out against "Newberryism." A. H. Vandenberg, later Senator from Michigan, wrote Borah that he was opposed to Newberry's methods in the primary, but after Newberry had been nominated, he was for him in preference to Ford. He said that he agreed entirely with Borah that Newberry should now be unseated.

A correspondent in Michigan wrote the Senator of his astonishment that Borah was trying to unseat Newberry, who was not only a Republican but one who had helped in the League fight. Borah replied: "If Mr. Newberry's vote had been decisive, we would today be a member of the Versailles Treaty, an instrument which is plunging Europe down to economic hell. And, we would also be a member of the League of Nations with a few ineffective reservations — reservations which Viscount Grey declared publicly would be ineffective once the United States was in the League. . . But, I recognize the right of Mr. Newberry to have cast his vote just as he did cast it. . ." He then explained that he was for unseating him because he had been the beneficiary of a "corrupt graft election."

In January, 1922, Senator Poindexter wrote an open letter in defense of Newberry's title to his seat. It was widely printed in the State of Washington, and an officer of a farm organization wrote Borah asking for suggestions as to how the Poindexter letter could be answered. The Senator from Washington had written: "Senator Newberry was not in Michigan during either the primary or the final campaign." Borah said this point could be answered by the statement that "he received almost daily, reports by letter, by wire and by telephone from his own selected agents who were carrying on the campaign in Michigan." Against Poindexter's statement that it was not charged that Newberry himself expended any money, Borah suggested the answer that the larger portion of money which was expended was checked out of the account of Newberry's brother. But when his brother's account got low, funds were checked out of Senator Newberry's account into his brother's account. To Poindexter's statement that the Supreme Court of the United States had vindicated Newberry, Borah explained that the correct answer was that the Court had done nothing of the kind — that the Court had simply held that the law under which Newberry was convicted was void and had not gone into the guilty action of Newberry.

A speech which Borah delivered in the Senate against Newberry's retention of his seat was sent to farm and fruit growers' organizations in Washington State.[1] About 30,000 copies were distributed from Puyallup.

The regular Republicans, under the influence of the Administration, had enough votes to prevent the exclusion of Newberry, but the resolution under which he was allowed to retain his seat read as follows: "That the expenditure of such excessive sums in behalf of a candidate, either with or without his knowledge or consent, being contrary to sound public policy, harmful to the honor and dignity of the Senate, and dangerous to the perpetuity of a free government, such excessive expenditures are hereby severely condemned and disapproved." Senator Norris, another leader in the fight against Newberry, said this means, "We will seat you this time, but . . . we will never again seat anyone under such circumstances."

Senator Borah in a letter gave this meaning to the resolution: "Newberry is told in so many words that his conduct was disreputable such as to imperil the very life of the Republic, but nevertheless he shall retain the fruits of his efforts. If any man had told me that such a resolution could have passed the Senate . . . I would have denounced him as a slanderer of the institutions of my country." In another letter he wrote: "I will venture to say that you couldn't put that kind of a resolution through a board of councilmen in any city in the United States."

Senators who were voting that Newberry should retain his seat were warned that the time would soon come when they would have some difficulty in retaining their own. Those who gave the warning were good prophets, for a number of Senators tainted with "Newberryism" lost their seats the following November. Among them was Miles Poindexter, whose letter in defense of Newberry Borah had helped the Washington farmers to answer and in whose state tens of thousands of Borah's speeches against Newberry had been distributed. After this election, observing that the Senate now had a sufficient majority to oust him, Newberry resigned.

[1] *Record,* January 10, 1922.

Although chronologically it will carry us ahead of our story, logic compels us to consider at this point the cases of other "Senators-suspect," the Smith-Vare cases which grew out of the elections of 1926. In these cases Senator Borah expounded his conception of the duties and powers of the Senate to deal with such men.[2] Both men were unquestionably elected by a large majority in their respective states. Before they presented themselves to take the oath as Senators it was generally known that they had expended in the primary elections large sums of money, much larger sums than Newberry was charged with expending. Resolutions were introduced in the Senate denying Smith and Vare their seats, and these resolutions were subsequently passed by large majorities.

Although Senator Borah was filled with nausea at the idea of these men becoming permanent members of the Senate, he was opposed to the resolutions. He thought they should be seated, given an opportunity as Senators to explain and justify their conduct in the primaries, and then unseated if their elections were tainted with corruption. In a letter to the Editor of the New York *World* he summarized his position on the whole matter.

"*First,* That the primary is a part of the 'election,' as that term is used in the Constitution." He believed the Court had erred on this point in the Newberry case.

"*Second,* If there was corrupt use of money in the primary, that fact should render null and void the election.

"*Third,* That the Senate, in passing upon the 'qualifications' of a Senator, is not confined to the question of age, residence and citizenship [the three qualifications imposed by the Constitution], but may include any disqualifications which in the judgment and conscience of the Senate render the party unfit to be a member.

"*Fourth,* That when a state sends a man to the Senate with credentials valid upon their face, that party is entitled to take the oath. In other words, the state is entitled under such circumstances to be heard and to be heard upon the Floor of the Senate with its full constitutional representation and through the individual whom it has chosen to repre-

[2] *Ibid.,* December 7, 1927.

sent it and to be heard upon an equality with those challenging the judgment of the state.

"Fifth, That after the Senator-elect has taken his oath and is permitted to occupy his seat as a Senator, the charges are referred to proper committee and, upon the report of the committee, the Senate takes up the matter for final action and disposition.

"Sixth, That if the facts show there was corrupt use of money in the 'election' (including the primary), or if the facts disclose a condition which in the judgment of the Senate unfits the Senator-elect to become a Senator, he should be excluded.

"Seventh, That all this may be done by a majority vote — that all these proceedings are under Article I, Sec. V, Clause 1 [Each House shall be the judge of the elections, returns and qualifications of its own members] — and not under Article I, Sec. I, Clause 2 [Each House may with the concurrence of two thirds expel a member].

"Eighth, That this being in fact a contest between the Senate upon the one hand the state and the voters upon the other, the proceedings should be had with the utmost regard for the rights of all parties to be heard and as nearly as possible upon a basis of equality.

"Ninth, The power of the Senate under Article I, Sec. V, Clause 1 has practically no limitation, save the judgment and the conscience of the Senate. Therefore, any disposition to act arbitrarily or without due regard to the rights of all would not be justified."

But the Senate did not accept Borah's argument, although he showed that, except during Reconstruction times, Senators-elect with credentials regular on their face, had always been seated. On one extreme there were Senators who favored seating Smith and Vare because they believed that they had all the qualifications required by the Constitution — age, residence, and citizenship — and that the Senate had no right to impose additional qualifications as Borah asserted it had under Article I, Sec. V, Clause 1. On the other side were many senators who, with all deference to Borah as a constitutional lawyer, believed that his argument was a quibble. What difference does it make, they asked, whether a man is refused a seat or given his seat and then unseated? This view prevailed and Smith and Vare were not permitted to take their seats.

We go back now to the Harding Administration, to the scandals which arose in it and which became notorious soon after President Coolidge took the Chief Magistracy in 1923. Senator Borah was not aware that the Secretary of the Interior was turning over valuable oil lands for illegal considerations until the storm broke, for he wrote William Allen White in April, 1922, in response to a question, that Secretary of the Interior Fall was "open, candid, and courageous. The charges made insinuate he has sinister motives with reference to certain matters. But I have never found anything upon which to base such a conclusion."

Because Secretary of the Navy Denby had been connected, perhaps innocently, with the oil scandals, the Senate called upon the President in February, 1924, by a vote of 47 to 34, to remove Mr. Denby from office. Before the vote was taken, the President happened to have as dinner guests Silas H. Strawn, former Senator Pomerene, and Senators Brandegee and Borah. Mr. Coolidge made a remark to Mr. Strawn relative to the debate on the resolution now pending in the Senate which led Borah to conclude that the President would feel obligated to remove Denby if the resolution passed.

As the guests were leaving, Borah said to Brandegee, "Did you hear what the President said to Strawn?" The Senator from Connecticut said that he had, and he asked the Senator from Idaho what he thought of it.

Borah said, "Well, if he removes Denby on that resolution I 'quit.' "

"Why don't you go back and tell the President that?" Brandegee asked. So Borah and Brandegee went back, and they told the President that the Senate had no power to force his hand in any such manner. At the conclusion of the conversation, the President said: "Borah, you have studied all these things, I wish you would dictate a message you would send to the Senate if you were President and such a resolution should be presented to you."

Mr. Borah took this simply for a compliment and forgot

all about it until the next day when the President's Secretary, Mr. Slemp, called him over the telephone and asked if he had dictated that message. The Senator then prepared it, and read it to Senator Brandegee over the telephone. Senator Brandegee suggested a slight alteration. A day or so later, the resolution having passed, the Senate received a strong message from the President, citing Madison and Cleveland on the executive power to the effect that the dismissal of an officer was exclusively an executive function. It was, of course, Borah's message. The President had added a statement of his own that no Democrat or Republican would escape just punishment through Executive protection.

Let it be clearly understood that Senator Borah was not holding any brief for Denby. It was simply a constitutional question with him, a question of Senate encroachment upon the Executive.

More interesting than the part the Senator played in maintaining the Executive power in the Denby affair is the part he played in the earlier efforts to force Daugherty out of the Cabinet. When the Ohio politician's name was presented for the post of Attorney-General in March, 1921, the Senator had some misgivings. He discussed the question with several colleagues who said that there were no specific facts which would disqualify Daugherty and that he should be confirmed. "I permitted the matter to go by," wrote the Senator in 1925. "I felt then and I have felt a thousand times afterwards I did not do my duty."

In August, 1923, when Coolidge took the oath of office, Borah made a statement in Spokane, Washington, to the effect that the new President should be given every chance to make good and that he was the logical candidate for 1924. When the Senator called on the President in Washington for the first time, he could see at once that he appreciated the statement, although he gave no oral expression of appreciation. At the beginning of this conference the President told Borah to make any suggestions he liked. At the end of the conference he repeated this invitation. Whereupon Borah made a suggestion. It was, "Get rid of Daugherty." This was before any scandals had become public and the President was astounded. The Senator went on to explain that trouble for the Administration was coming and coming fast and when it arrived Daugherty would be the heaviest load the Administration would be carrying.

Mr. Coolidge was impressed, but he said he just could not relieve Daugherty. To remove the strongest political supporter and the warmest personal friend of Harding would be taken as a repudiation of the Harding Administration, or as the meanest sort of personal spite. It would be very strongly resented.

Then on January 29, 1924, Senator Wheeler introduced his resolution calling upon the President to ask Daugherty to resign for his failure to prosecute certain forms of corruption. Mr. Coolidge sent for Mr. Borah at his apartments. Borah wanted to know if the matter was social, ordinary business, or urgent business. The reply was that it was business and urgent. So Borah hurried to the White House.

He had been there just a few minutes when Daugherty was announced. The Senator knew at once from the expression on the President's face that he had arranged to bring him and the Attorney-General together. The Senator was slightly irritated at this but said nothing. The Attorney-General was somewhat sarcastic. He said: "Well, don't let my presence embarrass you." The Idahoan scorned the idea of being embarrassed. Daugherty wanted Borah to tell him why he should resign; Coolidge apparently had the same thought. "I know there are some who want me to resign," said Daugherty. "There is Pepper who wants me to resign because I would not recommend one of his men for judge. Then there are others whose desires I have thwarted who want me to resign." To Borah he said: "I don't know why you want me to resign. I have never had to turn you down. You have never asked me for anything."

Borah told the Attorney-General that he would not tell him why he should resign, that matter being one the President could more appropriately explain to him. Nevertheless, Borah and Daugherty talked an hour about the situation created by the Wheeler resolution. The President never once opened his mouth. But when Daugherty left, the President said: "Senator, I reckon you are right."

The next day Senators Fess and Willis (Ohio) were called

to the White House. They advised the President that the removal of Daugherty was unthinkable – it would split Ohio in half and give it to the Democrats in the next election. The President "reckoned" that Fess and Willis might be right also. Consequently, he delayed requesting Daugherty's resignation until it was almost too late.

The oil scandals, the scandals in the Veterans' Bureau and in the Attorney-General's office which had been unearthed largely by Democrats playing a very proper rôle as an Opposition party, found no defender in Borah. Nor did he criticize the Democrats, even by implication, for what they had uncovered. On Sunday, April 6, speaking before the College Men's Law Enforcement League at Calvary Baptist Church (Harding's Church) in Washington, he replied to those Republicans who had sought to minimize the scandals, to hush them up, and to prove that the Democrats who had exposed them were not above reproach. He said that the government should be purged of "the slinking, secret, sordid enemy which has been at work in our midst." He praised the Democrats for having exposed it. "That may disqualify Senator Borah as the keynote orator of the Cleveland convention," commented the New York *World*. "But it qualifies him highly as the keynote orator of that great central mass of the American people who, regardless of party, are looking for somebody to rise above the tortuous pretext and lame apology and express the anger of honest men at the sordid betrayal of a nation's interests."

The President, of course, was thoroughly honest inside, but he could not bring himself to speak out against corruption in his household. Republican leaders for the most part, whether honest inside or not, followed the President's example of keeping fairly quiet about misfeasance and malfeasance in high places. If the results of the election in 1924 were any indication, the American people were quite willing to have the matter hushed up. But we reserve the election campaign of 1924 until some other manifestations of conscience have been considered.

Shortly after Coolidge was inaugurated in 1925 he desired to appoint Mr. Charles B. Warren Attorney-General. Warren's business affiliations were such that a number of Senators thought he should not be confirmed, particularly when they reflected upon their negligence in not making an attempt to block the confirmation of Daugherty. Such an attempt was a bold undertaking. Borah wrote a political confidant in Idaho that he had tried it only once or twice and that he had concluded that a nominee would be confirmed by the Senate "even if he was in the penitentiary at the time." But James Reed, Thomas Walsh, Borah, and some others started out to see what they could do to block the Warren confirmation.

As the contest drew near to its close, the President realized that he had a fight on his hands, and in the morning of the day when the Senate voted on Warren, he sent for Senator Borah. "I very much want Warren in my Cabinet," he said. "Can't you help me?" The Senator replied: "I am very sorry, Mr. President, because I think the President ought to be able to pick the men for his Cabinet. I am sorry also for personal reasons. But I must vote against your man." All the President said in response was: "Well, in cases like this there is nothing to do but for a man to vote according to his conscience." The Senator appreciated this deeply, for no other President had ever let him off so easily, so understandingly. In truth, Borah and Coolidge understood each other perfectly, and admired each other as do understanding men who sometimes differ.

Out of respect for President Coolidge Borah had hoped to avoid taking the floor against Warren, but Walsh told him that his position was being misunderstood and that he would have to speak. Borah was in his office when he had this conversation with Walsh and he told the Montanan he would be in the Chamber in a few minutes and would speak. He soon put in his appearance, making what he and others regard as one of his best arguments. It was extemporaneous in the sense that the Senator had not prepared a speech for the occasion, but as far as the subject was concerned, the Senator had studied it for years. Like practically all of Borah's speeches, it was short, requiring only about twenty minutes for delivery.

The keynote of this speech of March 16, 1925, was that in the matter of these appointments the Senate as well as the

Courtesy of the New York Herald-Tribune

President had an obligation to perform under the Constitution. The President nominates and the Senate confirms. "The argument has been advanced here and elsewhere that the Senate ought to yield entirely to the judgment of the President. Such is not the Constitution. Such is not the obligation we have assumed." The Democrats and "radical" Republicans prevented by a narrow margin the confirmation of Warren.

Borah received a number of letters of complaint, communications charging him with disloyalty to the President. To some he replied that they were much more worried about his disloyalty to the President than was the President himself.

In 1928, we find another manifestation of conscience. It became known early in the spring of that year that $260,000 of "oil" money had come into the possession of the Republican party. Borah wrote a letter (March 5) to the chairman of the national committee. It reads, in part, as follows: "The investigation of the oil scandal now has disclosed beyond peradventure that the Republican party received large sums of money, or securities, from Mr. Sinclair which the Republican party cannot in honor and decency keep. . . No political party is responsible, as a party, for the wrongful transaction of individual members who in secret betray it. But when the transaction becomes known to the party, it must necessarily become responsible if it fails to repudiate the transaction and return the fruits thereof. I feel that this money should be returned to the source from which it came. . . I venture the opinion that there are plenty of Republicans who will be glad to contribute from one dollar up to any reasonable sum to clear their party of this humiliating stigma, and that all you have to do is to indicate that course. . ."

The chairman's reply was that the money had been collected before he became chairman and that judgment should be suspended for a time. The Springfield *Republican* characterized this reply as "callous and shifty," revealing a politician with a conscience unequal to a moral emergency.[3] "Excellent advice is that of Senator Borah. It cannot be followed too soon." A few other Republican papers endorsed Borah's stand, but for the most part they suggested the difficulties in the way of such procedure or ridiculed the idea.

Borah proceeded to look for the Republican conscience through an attempt to collect the money. During the first few days of the "conscience Fund" drive there was some promise of success, but contributions soon dwindled. The country was prosperous, well satisfied with Republican rule.

[3] Springfield *Republican*, March 13, 1928.

Courtesy of Spencer and the Omaha World-Herald

Why should it bother about a little indecency here and there? The papers began carrying brief items under such captions as "Brother Borah's Conscience Fund Drive Not Over the Top." They asked how he was going to make Mr. Sinclair take the money back, if the drive should prove successful, and made other good-natured taunts characteristic of those who are not too moral but who feel that they are moral enough, at least sufficiently moral that the Lord has blessed them with abundance of worldly goods.

The Senator gave up his quest for funds and returned the money he had collected. Perhaps this is one of his enterprises on which he did not "go through." On the other hand, it might be said that he did go through – that he searched for the Republican conscience until he found that there was none!

In concluding the references to conscience at this point there is no intention to infer that these represent all of Borah's efforts to keep his party pure. These are simply some of the outstanding examples of that endeavor. Nor does the working of the Senator's conscience limit itself to his and his party's actions. All of the activities of the United States are morally weighed by him. He has been appropriately called "The Conscience of the Republic." Of this we shall learn more later.

WE return now and pick up the political thread in the first year of the Coolidge Administration. Who was supporting the President, the regulars or Borah? That depends upon what issues one has in mind. If the Warren affair was the issue, then, of course, the Old Guard supported the President and Borah did not. If the Marines in Nicaragua, or "bolshevism" in Mexico, or American membership in the World Court are taken as issues, the same general answer may be given. But what was Coolidge's big issue, the issue which perhaps 90 per cent of the newspapers and the people, regardless of party, thought of in connection with Coolidge? Was it not economy? Who does not recall his emphasis on that issue! Who does not recall the harmless, friendly gibes at it, gibes which, like those at the old Ford car, helped endear it to the public! "Coolidge is riding an electric horse to cut down the White House oat bill," was one of them.

On this issue of economy Senator Borah supported the President 100 per cent. Long before Coolidge was President, perhaps even while he was Mayor of Northampton, Borah was talking about the necessity for economy in the Federal service. His argument for the Federal income tax in 1909 was not simply that the Government should have more money to spend, but also that taxes might be more equitably levied and that the people might be made more conscious of the cost of government. Before the World War he often complained of bureaucracy and the waste of public funds and he fought the "pork barrel." His very first speeches following the Armistice were for retrenchment in expenditures.

While Coolidge was Vice-President, Borah continued to

hammer at waste and extravagance. "The beginning of each fiscal year," he said in 1922, "is the open season for party hypocrisy in the matter of governmental expenditures. In this midsummer season each year the party which happens to be in power makes a report. . . The country is thereby advised how expenditures have been cut and taxes are being lowered. It has become so ludicrous a performance that like the Roman oracles they do not look at each other while the deliverance is being made." He went on to show how the cost of government, national, state, and local, had increased ; how taxes, especially the farmers' taxes, had been increased. He kept this up. Speaking at a number of points in Idaho in the fall of that year, he divided his time fairly evenly between the rising cost of government and the need of his state for a thoroughgoing direct primary law.

In Manchester, New Hampshire (Colonel Knox's town), he spoke, May 24, 1923, on the need for governmental economy. "Heavy taxes destroy initiative, discourage frugality, and deprive families of those things, education and comforts, which make for good citizenship. It keeps thousands of children out of school. It keeps happiness and contentment out of millions of homes. I find no language adequate to condemn the waste of public money. . .

"We passed a budget law, you will recall. Great things were expected of it. Great hopes were entertained. Much was made of it politically. . . But one day the budget law came in conflict with the 'pork barrel.' After the most thorough investigation by the Budget Committee, it allowed $37,000,000 for rivers and harbors. In my opinion, this would have taken care of all the legitimate enterprises. But, without ceremony and with a manifestation of great impatience, the Congress raised that amount to $59,000,000. And so disappeared the Budget System, except as a political shibboleth. . ."

On November 15, 1923, he was saying : "The plain, immediate, imperative duty of Congress is to relieve the taxpayers of this country of a part of the great burden they are now carrying." When the oil scandals were beginning to be revealed, he stated, February 14, 1924 : "It is only a step from official extravagance to official corruption. They are whelps from the same kennel." On April 22 there was another speech on the tax burden and the waste of public funds.

How would he save money? By reducing armaments, through educating the people to elect Congressmen who would have moral scruples enough to eschew the "pork barrel," by reducing offices by about one-third, and by resisting the appeals of able-bodied veterans for special financial favors.

And this brings us to the question of the soldiers' bonus. From the beginning until 1935 he was opposed to this measure. He spoke against it in 1921 and helped defeat it. The issue came up in the next session and he made a speech against it (February 13, 1922). The Pocatello Post No. 4 of the American Legion sent him the following wire on April 3:

YOUR ABSURDLY FALLACIOUS SPEECH OPPOSING BONUS UNANIMOUSLY CONDEMNED BY POCATELLO AMERICAN LEGION. YOU OPPOSED THE WAR. YOU OPPOSED FOREIGN LOANS. YOU OPPOSED SENDING TROOPS. YOU OPPOSED ESPIONAGE LAW. YOU APPARENTLY ARE OPPOSED TO EVERYTHING BUT BORAH. WE CAN HIRE AN OBSTRUCTIONIST FOR LESS MONEY. THE NATION NEEDS CONSTRUCTIVE WORK AND FEWER SPEECHES.

The Senator replied the next day: "I have just received your telegram condemning my opposition to the cash-bonus bill. The language of your telegram is such that I realize it is useless to reply and that anything I may say will receive but little consideration. . .

"If I wanted to stay here at the price of my convictions, this would have been one of the first purchases for political power which I should have contracted — this would have been one of the first compromises I should have made. It would have been most agreeable personally and it would have been advantageous, doubtless, politically. It is your privilege to condemn my course. But I beg you to know that it was taken with as much personal regret, yes, with more personal regret, than any position I have taken in the Senate. I felt I could not do otherwise and discharge my obligation to the people as a whole and to the country.

"I observe in your telegram the threat which you impliedly make as to future political punishment. It was wholly unnecessary for you to make this threat. It reflected no credit upon you and it has had no effect whatever upon me. When you come to that fight in which you propose to inflict punishment, you will doubtless be able to say many things in the way of censure upon my public service. But one thing neither you nor anyone else will be able to say, and that is that I ever sought to purchase political power by drafts upon the public Treasury, or that I chose to buy a continuation in office by putting $4,000,000,000 upon the bended backs of the American taxpayers. I haven't much respect for the man who buys office, even though he pays for it with his own money. But the most slimy creature which disgraces American politics is the man who buys office by paying for it with appropriations out of the public Treasury and charges his venal political obligations to the taxpayers. . ."

Replying to a friend in Boise who wrote to congratulate him on his letter to the Legion, he said: "Their telegram and my letter to them were made public at their own instance — not mine." But the Legion post did the Senator a great favor. Practically every newspaper in the country carried the Senator's letter or parts of it. Editorials were written under such titles as: "A MAN-SIZE SENATOR," "A STATESMAN UNAFRAID," "A REAL MAN," "SENATOR BORAH'S DEFIANCE," "SENATOR BORAH'S WAY." The Baltimore *Sun* editorial was entitled just plain "BORAH," who "stands out in the public life of the capital as commandingly and as suggestively as the Washington monument," who unites "to brains and convictions 100 per cent honesty and courage."

The Senator received many letters from veterans, especially from disabled veterans whose needs he always considered, commending his course. The whole affair was a great triumph for Borah.

The Congress passed the bonus bill that year for the first time. President Harding vetoed it. The veto was overridden in the House but not in the Senate. Mark Sullivan (September 22, 1922) gave Borah the credit for holding the lines in the Senate. "The soldiers' bonus is a settled issue," Sullivan guessed badly, "not only for the present session of Congress but forever. It will never again come so near to winning in any future Congress as it did in this. . . Whether you like or do not like this final outcome of the bonus give the principal credit for it to Senator William E. Borah of Idaho. It was largely his aggressive energy that built up a following in the Senate from almost nothing and it was chiefly the outspoken courage of his speeches and writings that crystallized enough feeling throughout the country to bring about the present result."

In 1924, after the bonus bill had been passed, the Senator received a letter which he enjoyed. It is pasted in one of his scrap books just below a veterans' cartoon captioned, "Support your friends — Defeat your enemies." Here is the letter: "Why in hell are you always against the world war veterans? 6 years don't last forever? You must be a hell of a Senator? Why are you against the adjusted compensation bill? always against the veterans, Cause? You are a hell of a patriot? You never did mention the Sinclair oil grafter? you dont forget to make speeches in the U.S. Senate against world war veterans? I believe Sir the war veterans all of them in Idaho are having your record against them all right.

"Sir. Kindly pay attention to my letter?"

The depression beginning in 1929 finally brought the Senator around to the point where he was willing to pay the veterans cash for the certificates on which money is not due until 1945. He came to this view, he said, because he thought the country needed a larger volume of currency, because Congress has long since agreed to pay the veterans, and because many veterans were still in great need in 1935.[4]

THE Republican reverses in the congressional elections of 1922 sobered the powers that be in Washington, Borah wrote. "If I may be permitted to say so, I am more respectable with the 'regulars' here than I have been for a long time." But if Borah was respectable with the regulars, the regulars were just barely respectable enough for him. He said the Republicans had to change their program or there would be a third party. During 1923 he had considerable correspondence with J. A. H. Hopkins, chairman of "The Committee of Forty-Eight functioning as The Liberal Party." This Committee wanted to draft Borah for their presidential candidate,

[4] *Record*, May 23, 1935.

but he gave them little encouragement. There was talk of Borah for the Republican nomination in 1924 which no one took very seriously. Then Coolidge took the oath of office and Borah was much better satisfied than he had been since 1920.

Some effort was made to put Borah down as a running mate for Coolidge. The idea was distasteful to Borah. "I have no desire to sit mute and be a figure head for four long years," he wrote a judge in North Dakota; "in fact, I would die of nervous prostrations, and secondly, I have no desire to become President by accident." Holding the view that he had no more chance for a Republican nomination for the Presidency than he would have had he been born in Russia, he remained firm in his determination not to accept a nomination for the Vice-Presidency as the time for the 1924 convention approached. He declared in a letter to a former United States Senator in Idaho: "I have always felt that one of the saddest things in the world was for a person to attempt suicide and not succeed but to maim himself for life. Politically, I think that is just what that would be."

It was thought for some time that Borah would be the keynote speaker at the Cleveland convention, but when on April 6 he came out with such ringing declarations against corruption in the Republican Administration and praised the Democrats for exposing it, the idea evaporated. The Baltimore *Sun* congratulated Borah, as follows: "It is not likely that Mr. C. Bascom Slemp [the President's political Secretary] will be eager to share his quilt with one so painfully outspoken on matters of that kind. One cannot help but believe that Senator Borah deliberately set about to discourage any attempt to make him a voice for the Coolidge campaign and thus hobble his spirit of freedom. As a roaring lion seeking whomsoever he may devour the gentleman from Idaho is a national asset. As a domesticated animal wearing a Coolidge collar and a Slemp license tag he would be a total loss." [5] The Senator did not even attend the convention.

But Coolidge still hoped to get Borah as a running mate. While the convention was in session he instituted a hunt for him one morning and finally located him in Rock Creek Park.

[5] Baltimore *Evening Sun,* April 7, 1924.

It was another urgent business call from the White House. When Borah arrived, the President told him that he wished very much he would take a place on the ticket. "Which place, Mr. President?" asked the Senator, impishly. The President did not enjoy the joke.

There is a story that Old Guardsmen at the convention conceived a deep plot to ensnare Borah. The plan was to offer him the nomination for Vice President, get his acceptance, then have the convention fail to nominate him. This failure to get the nomination after having expressed an interest in it would discredit Borah in Idaho and might even cause him to lose his seat in the Senate. About 1:30 A. M. of June 12, Borah received a call from Cleveland to the effect that he could have the nomination, and he was urged to accept. He positively refused, thus spoiling the plot, if there was one.

The Senator was taking no chances with the convention. On June 12 he wired Beveridge at Cleveland:

> I PHONED YOU LAST NIGHT TO WITHDRAW MY NAME IN CASE IT IS PRESENTED. PLEASE BE SURE TO DO SO. BUT IF THEY SHOULD NOMINATE ME ANYWAY, THEN I AUTHORIZE YOU TO READ THE FOLLOWING TELEGRAM TO THE CONVENTION. . . "I GREATLY APPRECIATE YOUR MANIFESTATION OF CONFIDENCE BUT I MUST BE PERMITTED TO SERVE IN THE WAY IN WHICH I CAN SERVE BEST I THEREFORE MOST RESPECTFULLY BUT POSITIVELY DECLINE THE NOMINATION FOR THE VICE PRESIDENCY. THIS IS FINAL. I THANK YOU."

The managing editor of *Labor Age* wired Borah congratulations on his "fine refusal to betray La Follette and the Progressives." Although the Senator did not consider for a moment going off with the Progressives, he was distinctly sympathetic and friendly with the La Follette-Wheeler crowd, the Progressives of 1924. He had written to a young man in Oregon some months before the campaign started: "You say you hate to see me line up with such radicals as La Follette. Now, I have a great admiration for La Follette. I think he is a sincere and patriotic man. . . I take some pride in the fact, Ralph, that every measure with which I have been particularly identified, with the possible exception of one, will be cited in the next campaign as a reason why the Republican party ought to stay in power." Then this significant comment: "I may be a little irregular at the start, but I am quite regular on the finish." The reader might understand the Senator to have meant that he was in the habit of making trouble for Republican administrations between elections but was given to supporting the party ticket at election time.

But he did not mean that. He explained what he meant in a speech in Idaho in 1922. The explanation was that he often started on an issue alone or with a few other irregulars as supporters and that frequently the party came to see it their way, thus making them regular. He said that he was irregular on the League at first, but regular at the close of the fight; irregular on disarmament for the first few months of his agitation, but soon the Administration took over his idea, stamping him with regularity. In fact, the Administration soon forgot that the idea had originated with Borah. He mentioned a number of State issues he had championed as irregular which in due course were given the brand of regularity by other Republican leaders.[6]

The big issue the Progressives submitted to the American people was that of the power of the courts to nullify an act of Congress. They would by constitutional amendment deprive the courts of such power. Borah could not endorse their stand on this question, although he did deplore five-four decisions and had introduced a bill in 1923 which would require seven judges of the Supreme Court to concur before an act of Congress could be declared unconstitutional, except in cases of ambassadors, public ministers and consuls, and those in which states were parties. Daniel Webster, Martin Van Buren, Henry Clay, and other statesmen-lawyers had approved a similar measure, but this was quite different from the La Follette proposal that the Court should be denied the power altogether. The editor of the Wall Street *Journal* wrote (February 6) that he approved Borah's bill and hoped he would not be embarrassed. Discussing the bill in a letter to the editor of the *Spokesman-Review* (October 29), the Senator said: "I am perfectly aware that some of the ablest lawyers in the country think it unconstitutional, but if it is, the Court will undoubtedly say so." Later, Borah came to the con-

[6] *Capital News*, October 10, 1922.

clusion that such legislation would be unwise. He still deplores five-four decisions, but sees no feasible method for their prevention.

When the campaign of 1924 had taken shape and it had become apparent that the Republican tactics against La Follette were to denounce him as a radical, even as a traitor, Borah was disgusted. He stayed with Coolidge, however, because he thoroughly believed in the personal integrity of the President, approved his economy program, and was convinced of the futility of the third-party movement.

But the Senator had no enthusiasm for the Republican Administration as a whole and he would not take the stump for Coolidge. In fact, the Republican managers and some friends of the Senator were having the "jitters," especially after the Idaho Progressives endorsed Borah for the Senate, until he made one speech in Idaho (October 7) in which he said Coolidge was making progress in the direction of economy. "To my mind it made one of the great issues of the twentieth century. It presented a problem in government that no other President – and I do not wish to speak disparagingly of the great men who have gone before – had the courage to raise and stand upon." Some of the papers credited Borah with saying that "President Coolidge is the greatest man in political history." This version came to the La Follette headquarters and the manager wired Borah asking if he had made such a statement. Borah wired (October 11) that he had not, that he had praised Coolidge only in the matter of economy.

This was about all Borah would say for Coolidge in the campaign. Colonel Raymond Robins and Attorney S. O. Levinson, now mightily interested in the outlawry of war and in Borah's political future, were very much disappointed. "I am very sorry you and the Colonel seem to be disappointed or dissatisfied with my work or attitude in this campaign," the Senator wrote Mr. Levinson. "I think if you were more familiar with the situation with which I have to deal, particularly in my own State, you would not feel as you do. . . I have managed not to say anything I didn't believe and not to refrain from saying anything I did believe, so that I will have no retreating to do in the future."

Mr. Levinson then wrote him a very friendly letter, telling him how hard he had worked to build him up politically with men of consequence. He said a few good speeches for Coolidge would make him the leader in the campaign instead of Hughes, who was now the leader. He suggested that this course would make Borah *the* leader in 1928. But Borah's silence on Coolidge continued to be rivaled only by the President's reputation for silence.

How did Borah get along in his own campaign for reëlection in 1924? The answer to this question takes us back to 1920. Idaho Republican leaders interpreted the Republican landslide of that year, as did the national organization, to mean a return to high tariffs, less government in business, and the like. Borah could not go all the way with them on the tariff, he insisted "too much" upon economy, he wanted to liberate the political prisoners, and, horror of horrors, he advocated the recognition of Soviet Russia.

Republican business men in Idaho were not satisfied with Borah. One of their representatives, then in Washington, went to the Senator and told him frankly that business men did not like to see him so friendly with men like Senators Johnson, Norris, and La Follette. He said they wished Borah would take a definite stand on the issues. In return, the Senator asked the man to name an issue on which he had not taken a stand. When he could not name one, he said, "But you always take the wrong side." The Senator replied, "I instinctively take the humanitarian side."

But the supreme offense of Borah in the eyes of the regulars was his insistence that Idaho Republicans enact a new primary-election law. The original primary law of 1909 had been repealed in 1919. It is said that Governor Davis had promised Senator Borah that he would veto the repeal, but "the heat was turned on" and he signed the bill.

The regulars told Borah that he would be renominated for the Senate in 1924 whether they had the convention or primary system. They could not understand why Borah held out for the primary system when his job did not depend upon it.

Borah was much interested in the primary bill which was

in the 1921 legislature. This bill was defeated, apparently because the lower house would not give in to the Senate on a plan to improve and grant a franchise on the St. Maries River.

The state convention of 1922 came out frankly against the primary system. Borah was furious. He went all over Idaho in the campaign of that year denouncing this betrayal of the people and calling upon the Republican candidate for governor to repudiate the platform. In his opening address at Meridian, he said: "If I were in C. C. Moore's place I would kick that platform into the dust heap. . . I don't care two cents about a platform. Nobody knows tonight what the platform was upon which Harding was elected. Who pays any attention to the platform in the Congress of the United States? All this is rot about meeting and writing a platform. It is forgotten before you get home. . .

"My critics in this State say I am interested in this primary because that is the only way I can get reëlected. I consider that a great compliment. . . But I realize that the course which I am pursuing in this State is just as hazardous to me as anybody else. I realize perfectly that it is incurring a position which will be arrayed against me for all time to come. I don't care two cents about it. If they will lift the burden off the people of this State, if they will reform the fiscal policy of this State, if they will give the people of this State what they want, they can take the Senatorship of the United States, if they can get it, and give it to anybody else they want to, but so far as I am concerned, the next two years belong to me. Nobody but God Almighty can take them away from me, and during that period I am going to say precisely what I think and advocate the policies in which I believe, regardless of the political consequences to me or to the Republican party. . ." [7]

But Charlie Moore would not repudiate the Republican platform, and he was elected governor. A number of the candidates for the legislature said they would vote for a primary law if elected, and from the results of the election it seemed that there were good prospects for the enactment of such a law. Borah was in constant communication with

[7] *Ibid.*

members of the legislature and other leaders in the State during the 1923 session. "I had a long talk yesterday with Solon B. Clark, the Democratic Senator-elect from Mackay," he wrote a friendly editor. "You will find him a man well worthy of getting in touch with." He wrote to J. A. H. Hopkins of the Committee of Forty-eight, asking him to bring influence to bear upon progressives in the legislature. Hopkins did so. A primary bill was passed but vetoed by the Governor who, according to the *Statesman,* would have been unfit to be governor had he bowed "to insult and temporized with Borah." [8]

Of course, the Republican organization in Idaho, even under the convention system, did not expect to defeat Borah for reëlection to the Senate in 1924. Some had a forlorn hope that he might be left out, but what the wiser heads expected to do was to make Borah come with some humility to the convention for the nomination, to make Borah prove that he was a Republican before they would give it to him.

Borah was so low in the estimation of organization men in Idaho during this fight for the direct primary that they thought it quite proper to commit burglary at his Boise office and get possession of his mailing list. At least this is the information which one organization man, at one time a state officer, was willing to impart.

When Borah spoke in Lewiston, not a single member of the County Committee would attend his meeting. But he had a packed house nevertheless, and former Senator Heitfelt (Democrat) paid him courtesies. A leading Democrat from Moscow called for him to take him to his appointment in that town.

When President Harding came to Pocatello in 1923, Governor Moore, in introducing him, said that the people of Idaho did not endorse Borah, certainly not his position on Russia. A little later Borah spoke on the recognition of Russia in Pocatello. When he had finished, a lawyer came forward and said: "My God, Senator, I am glad you did not try to convince us of anything worse." A few years later, the Senator helped Moore to get a place in the Land Office.

During 1923 John Hart of Rigby, for years one of the

[8] *Statesman,* October 18, 1922.

Senator's best friends and most trusted political advisers, was writing in detail of political events in Idaho, explaining how each key man felt about practically everything. "A certain man is hurt about your reference to a hand-picked convention ; you had better write him a nice note. So-and-So likes you, although he is against you on the primary. You ought to let him hear from you. Old Mr. A. is alarmed at your position on Russia. There was an important meeting of a few carefully selected Republican leaders at Pocatello last week. They tried to get me to desert you on the primary issue. You might write to X and say you heard there was a meeting and ask how it came out." This was the sort of information and advice Hart gave.

It was stated a moment ago that the organization had no great hope of defeating Borah for the nomination in the convention. But there were other methods of dealing with the situation. A man who is still very active in Idaho politics and whose name must be withheld, tells this story. Some Republican leaders came to a leader of the Progressives of the La Follette class, now getting well organized in Idaho, and said : "If you will pick a good man as your candidate for the Senate, we will help you elect him. We will try to prevent the nomination of Borah in our convention, but if we are unsuccessful, we will help you elect your man in November." The Progressive took counsel with his committee. The committee refused to enter into any such agreement, declaring that Borah was the logical candidate of the Progressives for the Senate.

Ray McKaig, a Progressive organizer, went all over Idaho lining up the Progressives for Borah. He has given an interesting account of his experience in one rough, anti-Prohibition community. Some of the toughest looking characters there viewed Ray with suspicion and asked him rather pointedly just what his business was. He explained that he was organizing for Borah. "Aw, that's awright," the men laughed. "If you're for Borah you're welcome about these parts anytime."

The Republicans toyed with the idea of finding a good Republican to run against Borah. Stanley A. Easton, a leading business man of the State, was often mentioned as the proper man, but nothing came of it. Late in February John Hart wrote Borah that the party fight against him was just about over, that only a very few snipers were left to carry it on.

Yet the state convention held in March for the purpose of choosing delegates to the national convention was completely in the hands of Borah's party enemies. Without ceremony they removed Hart from his post as national committeeman, a place he had held for twelve years. The convention could have repudiated Borah but dared not do so for fear it would weaken the state ticket in the coming campaign.

Senator Borah would not attend the state nominating convention which was held in August. He wrote Hart: "I am satisfied that my presence there would mean necessarily a fight over the platform. If I thought I could win out, I should not hesitate to go. But knowing that the convention is largely dominated by those opposed to some of the most vital things, I could not hope to do other than simply make trouble."

The Progressives, the successors of the Non-Partisans of 1918, had already met and nominated Borah. The Republican convention realized that it would disrupt the party not to follow suit. So Borah entered the campaign with two nominations, just as he had in 1918.

In his main speech of the campaign, the one in which he pronounced for Coolidge, he expressed his great appreciation for the Progressive nomination, and added: "They knew at the time they endorsed me, that I was a Republican and that I expected to remain such." To the Republicans he said: "I am not unmindful of the fact that there are those in this State who think I am not a good party man. I presume that arises from the fact that there have been times that I have voted and expressed my views out of harmony with what appeared to be the policies of the party. It would be insincere on my part to apologize for the past and it would be misleading and deceiving you if I were to say that you might expect anything different in the future." [9]

With the endorsement of two political parties, by both their national and state organizations, of Labor and of the Anti-Saloon League, and with the New York *World,* which was

[9] *Capital News,* October 8, 1924.

supporting the Democratic candidate for President, appealing editorially to the people of Idaho to "Reëlect Borah Triumphantly," the Senator, out of the State for some time during the campaign, busied himself on his own behalf.[10] He made particular use of letters and some friendly newspapers. "Enclosed find copies of two letters," he wrote a gentleman in Moscow. "I wish you would select some real active, well acquainted Progressive, if you can, and give these letters to him and have him go over the county to leading Progressives and show the letters to them. I will be glad to take care of the expense." And again he wrote to the same man: "Enclosed find an editorial from the New York *World* [the one mentioned above]. If you can get the *Mirror* to reproduce this in good fashion it would be vastly helpful." The President of the *Capital News* had written Borah earlier in the year that he would "make any sacrifice" in his behalf. As the campaign neared its end, the Senator wrote him: "I may want to use the columns of the *Capital News* considerably in the next eight or ten days. I wish you would have a talk with the boys and tell them to make the best use possible of anything I send them."

It is appropriate here to summarize Borah's method of campaigning. *First,* is the personal appeal to the voters, which is no appeal at all in the ordinary sense of the word, but is rather a report to the voters on the state of the Union and his stewardship. Speeches are made throughout the State whenever the Senator has opportunity to make them and one can not determine from them whether or not the Senator is in a campaign for reëlection. *Second,* he coöperates with a few key men of unquestioned loyalty, some regular Republicans, some, perhaps a greater number, "radical" Republicans, and two or three Democrats. The Senator scorns an organization. His little circle of personal backers has no organization. Borah deals with them individually. *Third,* he makes good use of newspapers. He has always had some valuable newspaper support. The support has varied at times, but in general he has been able to count on the *Capital News,* the Pocatello *Tribune,* and the Wallace *Miner,* to

[10] New York *World,* October 23, 1924.

mention only some of the larger papers. The Lewiston *Tribune* (Democratic) has invariably dealt fairly with the Senator, at times praised him highly.

In this particular campaign Borah had his greatest fight since the pre-convention campaign for the nomination in 1906. When the votes were counted in 1924, Borah was found to have won over his Democratic opponent by 4 to 1. Borah's vote was 99,846. The Republican candidate for governor had the next highest number of votes — 65,508.

The Senator had a small sum of money for use in this campaign which was contributed by a friend interested in the outlawry of war, a plan in which Borah was by this time also greatly interested. The Senator spent $992.47 of his own money, returning, according to the Newark *Evening News,* the $2500 the national committee had sent him. The *News* jestingly remarked that the Senator was establishing a very bad precedent and that he ought to be stopped. "Yet at the thought recollection intrudes with a fable attributed to a more or less nebulous writer named Aesop. 'But who,' asked the oldest mouse, 'will bell the cat?' "[11]

[11] Newark *Evening News,* December 4, 1924.

CHAPTER XVI

THE CHAIRMAN OF THE COMMITTEE ON FOREIGN RELATIONS

WITH the passing of Senator Lodge, the Senator from Idaho became Chairman of the Senate Committee on Foreign Relations in December, 1924. It is difficult to imagine two statesmen more unlike than Lodge and his successor. They approached each other only in their interest in political history and government. Even here, however, Lodge's interest had been somewhat academic whereas Borah's chief interest was in bringing the experiences of the past to help solve the problems of the present and future. Lodge was the man of letters; Borah was the intellectual force in current affairs.

Robert M. Washburn, who enjoyed the confidence of both Lodge and Borah, contrasts the two in a delightful manner.[1] Lodge, he says, was always physically fit, but he did not impress one with the fact as the Idahoan did. Borah, although not heavy, suggested the heavyweight because of his virility. Borah had speed, like that of another son of the Middle West who had gone to Idaho and then to the nation's Capital — Walter Johnson. Lodge offset this advantage with a certain skill, emulating the great Christy Mathewson, who in his years of waning strength relied more and more upon the "fade-away" ball. Resorting to sea terms, the writer says that Borah suggested more the power of a battleship, Lodge the "versatility, skill and effect of the submarine."

Lodge was adorned with a hirsute curl, a badge of the Beaconese of Boston. Borah had a mane, as characteristic of his West as the curl was of Boston. Borah retained his black slouch hat, often worked in his shirt sleeves. Lodge was seldom seen without a "boiled" shirt. Washburn added that Lodge's clothes were made for him; Borah's were simply bought by him. In later years, however, the Idahoan has been no stranger to tailors.

Mr. Lodge never thought of money because he had never

[1] Washburn's Weekly, in the Boston *Transcript*, May 8, 1933.

been without it. Mr. Borah has seldom thought of it because he has never had much and has had little desire for it. "What would I do with money?" he asked Washburn.

Men listened to the Senator from Massachusetts, hoping to follow him, because he was the party leader. Men listen to Borah because he is Borah; in fact, they cripple each other to get seats to hear him, even in Lodge's Boston, but they hope he will not persuade them to follow him.

The Scholar of Nahant was as convinced of the righteousness of the Republican party as any member of a junior league who has never read a book on politics or economics. Borah troubles the leaders, who pretend to ignore him as they scout around to find out where he stands. Lodge believed Republicans were above attack. The righteous Senator from Idaho has at times believed they were beneath attack.

Washburn makes one other strong point that should never be overlooked. There were always able men in Massachusetts ready to step into Lodge's place, but Borah was the first "eight-cylindered" man to come out of Idaho. This gave the Idahoan a great advantage in independence. He could romp and play and still hold his seat.

Of course, Washburn did not pretend to exhaust the contrasts. Others come easily to mind. Lodge was of the old school, Borah primarily of the new, notwithstanding his reverence for the Fathers. Lodge stood for secrecy in international matters until public opinion forced a concession. Borah was a leader in that public opinion which forced the concession. "You might just as well argue in favor of a secret declaration of war as to argue in favor of secret consideration of a treaty which may result in war," Borah declared. Lodge was something of an imperialist and voted for the naval increases following the war; Borah could not tolerate imperialism and feared that big navies would bring the opposite of the peace their advocates maintained they were intended to preserve. Lodge was an old-time Republican on the tariff; Borah voted against the Fordney-McCumber bill. And, to mention one other point, Lodge never shared Borah's almost Pentecostal faith in the people.

Not all of the students of international law and diplomacy were perturbed when Borah succeeded Lodge as Chairman of the Foreign Relations Committee. While perhaps a majority of such people had taken a stand against Borah on the League issue, this issue was practically dead now. At about this time Borah wrote a critic in Idaho that if the Democratic leaders could get the League from around the party's neck without anyone's seeing how it was done, they would be the happiest mortals alive. The World Court and the war debts were now the live issues, and in a general sense the groups which opposed Borah on the League were now ready to oppose him on these matters. Yet for the most part they appreciated his efforts for disarmament and endorsed his position against any high-handed conduct on the part of the United States in the Caribbean area. Let it be recorded also that there were some scholars in the country who opposed as much as Borah did foreign political entanglements of any kind. They viewed his accession to the chairmanship with great satisfaction. One distinguished professor of international law wrote him that he expected now for the first time in a decade to see the United States with a foreign policy independent of that of Great Britain. As a whole, the country was pleased to have Mr. Borah take the last step up the ladder to the chairmanship. It was everywhere conceded that if the seniority rule gave him the post he was no less entitled to it on the basis of ability.

Soon after Senator Borah became Chairman of the Committee, Mr. Hughes announced his resignation as Secretary of State. Even while Lodge was Chairman, Borah had made plenty of trouble for Mr. Hughes. It cannot be said that Mr. Hughes resigned because of the change in the Senate Committee, but there were those who strongly suspected this to be the case. The New York *World* was decidedly of this opinion.[2] In place of the covert obstruction of Lodge and Brandegee, the *World* saw a new obstruction to Mr. Hughes, "the open obstruction, idealistic and generous, of Borah." The *World* continued: "The conflict between Hughes and Lodge was a conflict between good and evil, between an honorable policy and a most selfish one. But the conflict between Hughes and Borah promised to be the conflict of two good men who misunderstand each other and won't travel the

2 New York *World*, January 14, 1925.

same road to the same goal. There is no joy in such a battle except for Satan."

Certainly it is true that the two men presented another contrast of personalities. Mr. Hughes suggested something of Mr. Wilson's righteousness — Mr. Borah something of Colonel Roosevelt's square deal. We do not press the analogy, but one writer said that in a revolution Wilson might conduct a terror, while the Colonel would be almost certain to have no more executions than were necessary for a good show. Frank Simonds observed that Borah had a passion for humanity, Hughes a passion for principle. The luckless traveler beaten by robbers and left for dead would have received the same treatment if Borah instead of the Good Samaritan had happened along, says Simonds. Mr. Hughes can not bear to see anyone in error ; Mr. Borah can not endure seeing one in pain. Borah would relieve the pain ; Hughes might be strongly of the opinion that the pain was due to error.[3]

A great many people who observe the processes of government want a Foreign Relations Committee Chairman who will let the Secretary of State direct our foreign policy and who will support that policy in the Senate. This, they say, is the only way in which the country can be assured of a definite foreign policy. A man like Borah, in their opinion, should never be Chairman of the Senate Committee. Such a man should be Secretary of State and thus assume executive responsibility for an executive function. As Chairman of the Senate Committee he can not direct foreign policy, except on an occasional issue. During the greater part of the time he is embarrassing the Secretary of State or actually obstructing his program. This is the argument and there is some merit in it, but it would be necessary to amend our Constitution to prevent a Chairman like Borah from doing the thing he did as Chairman. Borah is opposed to such an amendment. He conceives of "prevention" as a very proper function of the Chairman — not the sole function by any means, but an essential one. He considers also that the Chairman has a perfect right to advocate such things as disarmament conferences and the recognition of Russia, despite the disapproval of a State Department. In other words, he regards the Senate as

[3] *New Republic,* February 6, 1924.

a coördinate — not a subordinate — body in the conduct of foreign relations.

Now that Borah was one of the senior Republicans of the Senate and without any question its most commanding figure, why did he not take the leadership of that body? It is reported that Harding, in 1921, made some unsuccessful overtures to win him over as an Administration spokesman. Back in 1922 his friend John Hart had written from Idaho suggesting that he "step to the front with a view of taking the leadership. . . We all know that you have the ability, and that you have the courage, and while we all respect Senators Lodge and McCumber yet they are handicapped on account of their age and do not have the 'pep' that one who holds the responsibility of leadership should have." The Senator replied that he could not assume leadership because he could not sponsor policies which he did not approve and which the regular Republicans wanted put into force. That is Borah's reason — he would not and could not lead in putting a party program through the Senate. As leader in the Senate he would have fought with the same deadly weapons and with the same expert marksmanship any party measure he opposed. He could and did serve as a valiant champion for certain administrative policies, but he knew and all others who understood him knew that he would be about the last Republican in the Senate to entrust with a program. For other reasons Borah was unfit for leadership. He hated and still hates routine; he wanted to be free to work with the matters which interested him most and to ignore those which did not interest him. Borah was unsuited for leadership because he blazed too many trails; only the advanced guard accompanies a trail-blazer. Besides, leaders must to some extent work through caucuses and conferences. Borah despises them, particularly the party conference in which attempts are made to whip men into line for this or that measure or program.

He could not follow any better than he could lead, and for the same reasons. Each issue, each measure, he must judge on its own merits, weigh it in his own mind and conscience, regardless of what the attitude of the party or party leaders might be. How can we have party government on any such basis? How could we have a Borah on any other basis?

As Chairman of the Foreign Relations Committee Borah settled down to do the things he loved to do : study a problem thoroughly, prepare an address on it, deliver that address at the psychological moment in the Senate and defend his position against arguments from all quarters of the Chamber.

Many people think that the Chairman should have done one thing he has never done. They think he should have gone abroad. Chester Rowell commented upon American travel abroad in 1931 and noted that only forty-nine persons from Idaho had made application for passports. "These, of course, did not include Idaho's most famous citizen." [4] But Rowell was less critical of Borah for not having been abroad than he was of the Senate for making such a man Chairman of its Committee on Foreign Relations. He went on to say what many others had said, namely, that Borah could know nothing of foreign countries, their peoples, their language, their literature, their history, their traditions, their prejudices, their economic and political problems. He even said that the Senator was not interested in the people of other countries.

Borah has always realized that he could learn a great deal by foreign travel. But the kind of traveling the Senator wanted to do he considered practically impossible for the Chairman of the Foreign Relations Committee. He wanted to go into a country and mingle with its people as he mingled with the people in the small communities in Idaho. To do this would take a great deal of time, time he did not have to spare. Then, he was worried about another thing. If he went abroad, three-fourths of his precious time would be taken up by more or less official entertainment, which he detested even at home.

A very warm friend of the Senator's in Idaho, a friend with a trace of mysticism, gives another reason for the Senator's failure to go abroad. It is that his great friend once consulted a fortune-teller who interfered with our foreign relations to the extent that she told the future Chairman of that Senate Committee to beware of the water, that he would die at sea or on the water somewhere. Perhaps this would not influence the Senator, thinks his devoted friend, but for the fact that

[4] San Francisco *Chronicle*, March 7, 1932.

practically everything else the seer foretold has come to pass. The friend noted, not without satisfaction, that when he finally persuaded the Senator to get in a boat with him on one occasion, he was visibly afraid on the water and showed unmistakable signs of relief when they came back to land.

Borah was the most widely read and quoted American in Europe. Many Frenchmen and some Englishmen looked upon him as their greatest hater in America. Yet they all wanted to see the "ogre." Germans threw beer mugs at each other in arguments over the meaning of his words. The Poles knew what Borah thought about the Polish Corridor question and some may have craved an opportunity to assassinate him. Peoples in the smaller oppressed countries, particularly Hungary, loved him passionately. Russians would have given him a parade at the Red Square. Mussolini probably wanted to hear at first-hand how he ruled the United States without curbing free speech and muzzling the press! Prime Ministers and great newspaper publishers begged Borah to come to Europe, to come and make speeches if he would, but in any event to come. Borah was pleased with their invitations.

Despite the boresome rounds of entertainment ahead (and the dread warnings of the seer) three times he made his plans to go to Europe. Three times he canceled his reservations. Each time some urgent domestic situation deprived him of his trip. In 1922 he could not go because he had to go back to Idaho and denounce the Republican organization of that State for repudiating the primary-elections system.

A man usually does the thing he wants to do most. Borah wanted to go to Europe but he was more interested in domestic affairs; therefore, he stayed at home. Besides, Borah may have had the feeling that he would lessen the weight of his pronouncements in Europe if he permitted its people to see him in the flesh. He may have felt that he was the American Mr. Shaw to the English. He may have noticed how much more eager the Americans were to have Mr. Shaw visit them because he said he would never come to America. Incidentally, Mr. Shaw once wrote on a postal card, Borah "is the only American whose brains seem properly baked; the others are either crumbs or gruel." Perhaps the Idaho Senator felt that a trip abroad might impair his "circulation" over there. He was reaching Europeans almost daily from his forum in the Senate and through prepared statements for the press. That was what he wanted.

There is no disposition to minimize the value of travel abroad for a member of the Foreign Relations Committee of the United States Senate. Yet it has often been observed that information picked up by travel, even extensive travel with long stop-overs, is quite likely to be superficial. A few good books and articles on a country may give one a much better key to it than would a visit. Both reading and travel are supplementary. But assuming that one can not do both, which is the better for a grasp of the fundamentals? There are those who join Borah in recommending the books, the articles, the newspapers.

Borah did read on foreign countries and foreign affairs. He did more – he studied. Often someone would write him recommending a certain book. "Thank you, I read it last week," he was likely to reply. Then he would add, "Have you read so and so? If not I think you will find it worth your while."

But reading matter available to the general public was not the only source of information for the Chairman who had never been abroad. Newspaper correspondents in Europe wrote him. They dropped in to see him when they came to Washington. Some American diplomats wrote him. A few foreign officials corresponded with him. Purely personal letters occasionally passed between Borah and the Prime Minister of Great Britain when MacDonald held that post. Once Borah wired the President of Mexico for information. He got it, and brought some praise and much criticism upon himself for not having gone through the State Department with his request.

Perhaps the man who was of the greatest assistance to the Senator in interpreting foreign events was George A. Schreiner, an Associated Press representative in Europe since before the World War. Naturally Schreiner was something of a linguist and often gave the Senator a translation of some significant document or a digest of a new book which was not published in English.

Among those with whom the Senator consulted on Foreign Affairs, we mention only Walter Lippmann, Herbert Bayard Swope, Raymond Robins, Salmon O. Levinson, Bernard M. Baruch, Claude G. Bowers, Frank I. Cobb, Edwin Borchard, David Jayne Hill, James Brown Scott, George Grafton Wilson, Oswald Garrison Villard. These are perhaps a fair sample. The "provincial" Chairman was always very grateful for suggestions from such men. Sometimes he followed their suggestions. Every once in a while he would write to some individual or to several at the same time seeking light on a particular situation.

Being the best-known American to those in foreign lands, the Senator often received letters from Americans who happened to be abroad: business men, students, and travelers. Much of the inside information he had on Nicaragua came from an American physician residing there. Private citizens of foreign countries wrote the Senator letters, sometimes very illuminating ones. All letters from abroad which raised an intelligent question or threw light upon a situation he answered, often at length.

Thus the Senator was most decidedly interested in foreign peoples and countries and took pains to be advised of their problems by every means save travel. Mr. Schreiner says he has never seen a man so adept at sifting the wheat from the chaff, so detached, so persistent in following the main trail, never becoming confused, to use the terminology of the hunt, by the rabbit trails through which a wise fox may run to throw his pursuers off his own.

Studying foreign relations as he did and having no particular limits in mind for the activities of the Chairman of the Committee, the Senator was usually ahead of the State Department. He had been ahead of the State Department on disarmament several years before he became Chairman. In like manner he was ahead on the matter of the recognition of Russia and on the war debts. He pushed the State Department into the scheme to outlaw war. In general he made life at the State Department a bit uncomfortable, although he and Mr. Kellogg, having been Senate Colleagues, understood each other fairly well.

As Chairman, the Senator still believed in open diplomacy

and in sheer frankness. He did not understand the meaning of a "delicate question." He thought any question was brought nearer to solution by open discussion between honest men. He did exactly what he wanted to do, and he said exactly what he wanted to say, both for domestic and foreign consumption. He often spoke aloud in the Senate the sentiments that other men held but conveyed to each other only in whispers in the drawing-room. We have already noted something of his frankness in speaking of the French debt situation. He was equally clear and frank in his denunciation of European armaments, his condemnation of the Treaty of Versailles, and his pronouncement that America would never join the League. When Laval visited the United States in 1931, the flock of French correspondents who accompanied him came trooping to Borah's office. The Chairman was more cautious than usual. He opened the interview with, "Shall I speak frankly, gentlemen?" Of course the gentlemen of the press wanted just that. The Senator proceeded to tell them what was the matter with Europe. A few hours later, both in America and abroad, the Hoover-Laval conference was only secondary news. Laval was irritated and said he had come to see the President, not Borah. There is reason to believe he regretted having made this statement. At any rate, he did have considerable conversation with Borah at Secretary Stimson's dinner. The Senator still spoke frankly about what Europe should do and in particular about what America was not going to do. The Premier thanked him cordially, confessed to having been misinformed.

MENTION has been made of the fact that Borah reached the whole world through his speeches and his newspaper interviews. It is quite in order then to give some attention to his technique in these two closely related particulars.

The Senator is proud of his speeches. There is nothing of the swagger in his pride, nothing of the "Well, how did you like that?" or "Didn't I put it over that time?" in his attitude. But when intelligently complimented on a good address, he shows all of the pleasure of a modest boy who feels that he has justly and honestly won a declamation contest. He is obviously and frankly pleased when he has made a success of a speech. There is no other activity by which he sets as much store. His career, he thinks, can be read in his speeches and he is willing to let posterity judge him by his public utterances.

How does he prepare his speeches? He studies a question carefully. He does not delegate any study. The nearest he ever comes to delegating a piece of research is in directing one of the boys in his office (usually some law or graduate student in one of the Washington universities) to find a speech or an article by a certain man on such and such a subject. The Senator studies not only the points he expects to develop but the points the other side would emphasize as well. He prepares not only to speak but to defend his position when attacked. His study may extend over several days or several weeks.

When does he speak? He may have all the material assembled and remain perfectly silent. He will not speak unless he considers the time is ripe. Experienced observers have remarked over and over again that he has an uncanny sense of timeliness. He knows when the public is ready to hear him. He knows when a speech will get proper publicity and when it will not. Earnest men have written him begging him to speak on a subject dear to them and to him, but he has refused to speak, saying nothing would be gained by a speech just now. It has been said that when Borah speaks on a subject, it becomes an issue because Borah is such a remarkable speaker. This is not the whole truth. The subject becomes an issue not simply through the Senator's sheer forensic power, great as that is, but because he has made the speech at the right time.

In his younger days he often wrote his speeches out in full. He seldom does this any more except for some of his radio addresses. Whether speaking in the Senate or before some gathering in a city auditorium, all he will have with him are a few very fragmentary notes, some newspaper and magazine clippings, and perhaps a book or two. When he was scheduled to speak at a big dinner in New York in 1920, Colonel Harvey, who was to preside, asked him to send his manuscript. The Senator replied that there would be no manuscript; he would speak from notes he would prepare while on the train from Washington. Once after a radio speech Mr. S. O. Levinson wrote him that he certainly could make his "tongue speak in unison with the heartbeats of humanity" and asked for a copy of the speech. The Senator replied that he had not written it. But the radio people had taken down his address and furnished Levinson with two copies, one of which he sent to the Senator with his compliments.

Perhaps the boldest thing the Senator ever did in the way of not preparing a set address occurred when he met Doctor Nicholas Murray Butler in the great Prohibition debate in Boston in 1927. A number of newspaper men were on the train which carried Borah to Boston. One of them asked the idle question: "Well, have you got your speech ready?" Receiving a nod which he took for an affirmative reply, he asked the Senator what he was going to say. It developed that the Senator had made no preparation for the debate. With some concern the man asked him what he expected to do. "Why, I'll wait and hear what Butler has to say and then reply to him," answered the Senator with a confident smile. Borah won the decision, maintaining the dry side, in Boston. Of course Borah had, in a broad sense, been preparing for this debate for years.

This incident illustrates a point about Borah's preparation for a speech. It does not include the arrangement of adjectives, the careful tintings for oratorical effect, nor does it include the arrangement of material except in its main outline. He studies the subject and leaves the details of arrangement to chance, that is, to the circumstances which surround the delivery of the speech. He thus speaks directly to his audience as every powerful speaker does. A microphone placed too high annoys him dreadfully because it prevents him from looking directly at his audience.

But this explanation of Borah's preparation for his speeches is still incomplete. He is steeped in the masterpieces of English and American statesmen from the ascendancy of representative government to the present time. He has read them all, over and over. He reads them for their subject matter, for their method, for their literary quality, and for the pleasure and recreation they give him. He has analyzed them carefully. He has drawn a conclusion regarding the strength and weakness of each man as a speaker, of each address as a speech. To a man calling on him in 1934, he remarked: "I have just been rereading Webster's reply to Hayne. While it was a great effort, it seems to me that Webster put himself too much on the defensive; that he lacked aggressiveness, was too negative." The Senator knows the where, when, who, and why of the greatest debates in the English-speaking world. For example, he has decided conclusions concerning the relative merits of the arguments of Pitt, Burke, and Fox in their historic debate, in 1791, on the question of British intervention in the French Revolution.

He has studied the art of debate and oratory from the great masters, not from the little handbooks which have been prepared by professors of "elocution." But he follows no master. He quotes the masters some, but not a great deal considering his familiarity with them. He has assimilated them and from that assimilation has evolved a style entirely his own. It is clear, simple, direct. The words are remarkably well chosen. There are few superfluous phrases.

But his speeches have character as well as style. They have an unmistakable sincerity and fervor, a strong ethical or spiritual note. There are appeals to sentiment but none to prejudice, unless the invocation of the Fathers may be said to be an appeal to prejudice against political commitments with other countries. Above all, his speeches are free from personalities — not that he always avoids making an opponent feel uncomfortable, but he does it with logic and irony.

The Senator's own recipe for a speech is: know your subject, believe in your subject, have the courage to say what you think. He emphasizes the theme, sincerity, and courage. He does not ignore other things, but he feels that these follow naturally if the three main principles are adhered to.

Borah suggests Bryan in his sincerity, in his fervor, in his courage as a speaker. Neither ever bellowed or roared. But Bryan had the better voice, although Borah's voice is excellent. Bryan studied the technique of speaking more as a college student of speech would study it. He excelled Borah in enunciation and gestures. Borah leaves Bryan far behind in theme, in the logical and compelling presentation of his subject. Borah piles sentence upon sentence (a little less rapidly at seventy than he did at fifty), each sentence crystal clear, each a complete thought in itself, the omission of which would seriously mar the argument.

Thomas R. Marshall, who as Vice-President listened to Senate speeches for eight years, wrote of Borah in his *Recollections*: "I have many times heard fall from his lips specimens of oratory which, if they had been uttered by Cicero, or Webster, or Burke, would have become the common heritage of the school boys of today for declamation purposes. . . From my standpoint he has the one fault of genius – now and then he permits his enthusiasm to overshadow his logical powers; but these instances are so rare as hardly to be worth mentioning." [5]

During the greater part of his career as Senator, the press galleries and the public galleries have been quickly filled when he arose. And what is much more significant, his colleagues have filled their seats. "When he speaks," wrote "Bob" Washburn, "the Senate doors open inward only. Then a dropped pin in the Chamber makes a noise like a bursting shell in No Man's Land. Then ninety-five Senators sit in silence – because they like a good show and not because they prepare to follow. Then there is a hush, and moths rest on the gavel of the presiding officer." [6]

In debate in the Senate one of Borah's chief weapons has always been the question. Even the great Root was sometimes floored by the interrogations of the young Senator from Idaho. When Borah's friend Brandegee was maintaining that a certain amount of secrecy was necessary in discussing "delicate questions" in foreign relations, Borah interrupted to ask what these "delicate questions" were. Are they not, he asked, likely to be questions of doubtful righteousness?

In the debate on the Warren confirmation in March, 1925, James Reed, Thomas Walsh, and Borah carried the honors. The methods of the three men were very effectively compared by William Hard.[7] Reed was described as a fighter who could and would use a club, bite, kick, choke, or gouge

[5] From "Recollections," by Thomas R. Marshall, Copyright 1925, used by special permission of the publishers, The Bobbs-Merrill Company.

[6] Washburn's Weekly, in the *Transcript*, March 9, 1925.

[7] Washington *Times*, March 21, 1925.

out eyes, but whose chief weapon was the sword. Walsh was described as a fighter also, but a more subtle, even a more dangerous foe. Walsh used the net. He beguiled his opponent into getting into the exact position he wanted him ; then he threw his net over him. There was no escaping from Walsh. Borah, no less a fighter, but less obviously a fighter than the other two, was the most deadly of the three. He used both the net and the sword. He was less vicious with the sword than Reed, showed more mercy with his net than Walsh. Skilled in the art of debate by study and practice, he scorned any movement which did not carry with it precision, grace. He did not charge and slash with his sword ; but he waited until he was charged, whereupon he dispatched his adversary neatly. He did not throw his net over his opponent ; he simply spread it and allowed his opponent to step into it, whereupon he pulled the string.

It is frequently observed that speeches and debates do not change votes in legislative bodies. But men like these do change votes. There is not the slightest doubt that they defeated the Warren confirmation. Mark Sullivan has given Borah the credit for defeating the soldiers' bonus in 1922. Borah won quite a little following in the Senate against the confirmation of Mr. Hughes as Chief Justice. When Borah was closing his speech for the gold bill in January, 1934, the Democratic leaders passed the word around — "now is the time to vote." Mention of this date suggests another fact. It is that Borah's power as a Senate orator has not waned particularly with the passing of the years or the influx of Democratic majorities. His speech of May 17, 1934, opposing the delegation of powers to the President in the matter of reciprocal tariffs, takes its place by the side of his best addresses on constitutional questions. "When he had finished," commented George Rothwell Brown of the Universal Service, "he had made history."

ONE of the most common remarks about Senator Borah is that he knows how to handle the press. Colleagues, even those with a background in journalism, sometimes wonder how he does it. A few have been so unkind as to imply that Borah courts the newspaper correspondents.

Why does Borah get so much publicity, so much favorable publicity, even in papers which oppose him? This question has already been answered in part. In the discussion of Borah's speeches the statement was made that he never spoke unless he had something to say; that there was never any mistaking his meaning; that he was sincere and courageous in his utterances; that he made his speeches at the appropriate time; and that he often presented a new issue. Obviously speeches of this kind have great news value. Another reason is that Borah often represented a minority, sometimes a minority of one. A good, vigorous minority speech has more value to the press than a stodgy one by a majority leader. A conservative leader seldom appeals to the imagination; never invites conflict. The independent wins the public's admiration by his originality and daring.

As for Borah and the newspaper correspondents, they have always been friends. The Senate press gallery has almost from the first year of Borah's senatorship respected him more than any other Senator, save perhaps Senator Norris. Borah respects the newspaper men. He has never publicly critized them, nor has he ever belabored them as a class in private. The same is true for the newspapers. He has never referred to the press as "corrupt," "kept," "venal," "sordid," or "sinister." Belief in the function of the press, although admitting abuses, is a part of the Senator's faith in American democratic institutions.

At the time of the League fight some reporters discovered that Borah was the man to talk to. He would tell what he knew and ask the reporters to tell what they knew, all in the strictest confidence. The relationship was wholly informal and mutually profitable. It developed into an established custom.

When the Senate is not in session, each afternoon at three o'clock the Senator has "a session" for correspondents in his office. A word about this office will give some indication of the working habits of the Senator and of the nature of the conference. It is a large office, with "a cavernous, rugged atmosphere." There are large chairs, a massive desk, a lounge, and many shelves of books. There are books, folders, manuscripts, and memoranda piled high on the lounge, on

SENATOR BORAH'S PRESS CONFERENCE

some of the chairs, and around the Senator's chair. His desk is covered with books and papers also. In front of him there is a clear space on which he does his writing. An office manager or an efficiency expert simply could not tolerate the manner in which the Senator keeps his office! "It's strange how things disappear around this office," remarked the Senator one day when he was somewhat irritated at not being able to find a manuscript.

The reporters find places and the informal conference begins. Any reporter may ask any question he desires; he may make any observation he pleases. The Senator answers questions and asks questions. Issues are raised and debated at this unusual gathering. The Senator is frankness personified in these conferences; some have said that he is frank to the point of indiscretion. But "indiscretions" are strictly confidential, and no confidence has ever been violated. The reporters and the Senator meet simply as man to man. There is nothing like it in Washington. It is an opportunity which young reporters, in particular, covet. The Senator feels that the give and take of the conferences is hardly less valuable to him than it is to the "boys." They like Borah because he is intelligent and makes news for them. That is another reason why he has a good press.[8]

He would have a still better press if some editors and publishers did not tell their Washington correspondents to "let up" on Borah. It is reported that a Republican publisher in Idaho so advised his correspondent at one time. A New England writer, a warm admirer of the Senator, sent him a copy of an article he had written on him. He hoped the Senator would not mind the "smear" he gave him in one place, explaining that there was nothing personal about it, that he did it in order to satisfy his censor.

Much of the Senator's correspondence is with editors and special writers. He numbers Colonel Knox, Hapgood, Lippmann, Bowers, Kent, Sullivan, and many other editors and writers among his friends. They write their congratulations, suggestions, warnings, and often inclose editorials. He is perhaps quicker to congratulate an editor upon some policy

[8] The Brooklyn *Eagle,* January 7, 1923, *The Christian Science Monitor,* November 10, 1926.

than the average editor is to pay him a compliment. Many a letter has gone out of the Senator's office to some leading editor inviting him to drop in when in Washington. Editors often ask Borah for articles. He complies when he has the time and the interest. He has written articles on practically every major subject on which he has spoken in the Senate. Norman Hapgood and many other writers think the Senator could have made a great success as a journalist had he chosen that profession. His writings are clear, vigorous, to the point, and read very much like his speeches.

THE Senator knows a great deal more than "what he reads in the papers." But he does read the papers. He reads with some care the editorials in the New York *Times,* the New York *American,* the Baltimore *Sun,* and the Chicago *Tribune.* In its day the New York *World* was one of his favorites. He reads a number of papers from his own State and often writes to their editors. In the days when the Lewiston *Tribune* was edited by that doughty champion of states' rights, A. H. Alford, its editorials often caused the Senator to be proud of the fact that it was published in Idaho.

The Senator has never subscribed to many magazines. His method is to look them over at the news stands and buy those which contain articles he wants to read. The *Atlantic Monthly,* the *New Republic,* the *Nation,* and *Harper's* are among his favorites.

Pasted in a scrap book for the year 1907 are magazine and newspaper articles covering such public questions as the direct primary, employers' liability, the currency, the Negro and the Republican party, the public domain, forestry in the United States and abroad, stock gambling, socialism in England, peonage in the South, J. P. Morgan, Labor, corporations, the guaranty of bank deposits, the right of employment, and prohibition. These clippings represented the wide range of his interest. They were by no means the only source of his information. From his first term in the Senate until now he has delved into heavy documents, American and foreign, and mastered them if they threw light upon the issues before the Senate.

But Borah has never been satisfied with current literature,

documents, and statistics. For pleasure, inspiration, and enlightenment he has read the great political philosophers. Burke, Bentham, and Mill are his English favorites; Hamilton, Jefferson, Madison, Marshall, Calhoun, Kent, and Cooley are his favorites among the American authorities. Senator Lodge's *George Washington* he rates as a great masterpiece. Those who have only a general knowledge of Borah's technique in speaking are familiar with his method of quoting from the great statesmen and philosophers. Any suspicion that they are used as a display of learning is soon vanquished when one recognizes that they usually have a very direct and often practical bearing upon the subject at hand. The observation has frequently been made that few men in public life succeed as well as the Senator in bringing so much of their general reading to bear upon the issues of the day.

General literature has always occupied a great deal of Borah's recreation time. He never tires of the Bible, Shakespeare, Milton, and Emerson. Paul's speech before Agrippa he lists as one of the greatest recorded oratorical achievements. Over and over he speaks of the inspiration he has drawn from Emerson's essay on Self-Reliance. He enjoys Hawthorne for his style. He likes Eliot, Balzac, and Dickens, but Dickens the least of the three. Contemporary novels interest him little; some of them he detests; a few he has broken over his knee and tossed into the waste basket. His reactions to contemporary novels are about the same as those of parents of the middle class whose children are adolescent.

He keeps up particularly well with everything that is published on biography and history. He also reads a great deal in economics. He often stops at book stores and looks over the newer publications. He knows the writers. When Professor A. B. Hart identified himself before stating his business with the Senator, the Senator laughed and explained that for years he had read everything he had written. When Will Durant followed the Hart procedure in a letter, the Senator replied: "Well, now, really, Mr. Durant."

Of Glenn Frank's *Thunder and Dawn* he wrote: "As is my custom I began reading it from the 'end' and read 'Treason of Statesmanship' first. I was so deeply interested I began as normal people do and read it through from the beginning."

Lloyd Paul Stryker's *Life of Andrew Johnson* won his praise as the best biography since Beveridge's *Marshall. The Tragic Era* by Bowers he could hardly put down until he had finished it. "The depth and variety of meanness, the resourcefulness of low intrigue, the narrow, bitter, selfish instincts of 'great leaders,' are painted with rare judgment and a master hand. But also the courage, even the political martyrdom of a small group of noble men who saved this government . . . are presented with no less genius." Borah was equally enthusiastic over Bowers' *Party Battles of the Jackson Period,* and it was at his suggestion that Bowers undertook to write *Hamilton and Jefferson.*

The Senator has never written a book, although he has often been asked to do so. In 1922 he might have written one entitled *Disarm* had he had the time. In later years he has frequently been asked by publishers to write his memoirs, though no one has succeeded in getting him interested. But he has been assembling material for years on agitators. He has no definite plan for a book, but he thinks he might write it some time. His idea is that young men with no means, no organization, no powerful friends, can start on a public career by agitating or advocating some noble cause. His book, if it is ever published, will review the career of some of the world's great agitators. What the Senator thinks of agitators is set forth in a few words in a tribute to Senator La Follette, on June 18, 1925:

With "ability of rare order . . . untiring in industry . . . unrelenting in purpose . . . as incorruptible as he was fearless . . . I suppose he will take his place in history, in the view of some, as an agitator, and in these days we are not favorable to agitators. But, as such he will have the company of the noblest spirits of history. Agitation has its place and an indispensable place in the life of free government, and if a man is devoted to his country, as I believe La Follette always to have been, his service is often the highest type of statesmanship."

After reviewing La Follette's achievements, he continued: "Generally denounced and often for a time baffled, nevertheless there is the record of things done, and now accepted.

'There is often a great sense of loneliness in the discharge of high public duties.'

"The old Bishop, in Hugo's great novel, said to the hunted galley slave: 'This door does not ask a man who enters whether he has a name, but if he has a sorrow.' This was the guiding principle in the life of Bob La Follette. Human suffering, human misery, oppression, injustice, could at all times and under all circumstances enlist the uncompromising support of this gladiator. . . He preferred 'to go to the house of mourning rather than to the house of feasting.' "

FROM first to last Senator Borah has refused to waste his time. He has not spent much of it relaxing in the company of his colleagues. He has spent practically none of it in Washington society, although he has friends in Washington with whom he visits. At his office he is one of the most difficult of all public men to see. Newspaper men may see him; people from Idaho may see him; friends from the little town in which he was born and from the little town in which he first practised law may see him; but others must make a strong case with his secretary. Once a man just had to see the Senator. "He is riding in the park," said his secretary, "and he will probably go direct to the Chamber from home." The gentleman stationed himself at the Senator's private door in the corridor and waited. When the great man appeared, he grabbed him and got an appointment for three o'clock. The secretary did not see the Senator in his office that morning and, characteristically, he neglected to tell her about the three o'clock appointment. At five minutes of three the man reappeared in the secretary's office. "I have not seen the Senator since you were here this morning," she explained. "Well, I have," replied the man in triumph. "I met him *riding his horse down the corridor* just after I had talked to you."

Obviously, his office staff must try to protect him from letters also. He receives hundreds every day. Those which raise a problem, offer an intelligent suggestion, make a worthy plea, or fall within this general classification, he sees and answers. Crank mail, hobby mail, and mail which clearly comes from a propaganda machine, he ignores. It does not even go to his desk. One young man was very much offended because a letter he had written criticizing the Senator for his newspaper interview at the time of Premier Laval's visit was not placed on the Senator's desk. He did what such a person is likely to do — he wrote his local newspaper a letter about it. Other newspapers took it up with some merriment, but few failed to commend the Senator's secretary.

THE question of how the Senator keeps fit is no doubt one that a great many people would like to have answered. He has kept fit primarily through temperate habits — no alcohol, no tobacco, not even any coffee. Unlike many teetotalers, he is very temperate in his eating. "Well, just what does he eat?" ask some people. They must fortify themselves and ask the Senator. Candidly, he thinks it is none of their business. Furthermore, he thinks interest in him should be confined to his position on public questions. That one should ask him what he eats for breakfast instead of what should be done to rehabilitate China irritates him. He is not interested in the sauerkraut-juice vote, the butter-milk vote, the pancake vote, or the "spizirinktum" vote.

The Senator has always taken a little exercise, but not much. For a time he belonged to the Senate exercise club, but for the most part he has taken his little exercise at home. There is one exercise that the Senator has always enjoyed which dates from his youth on the farm. That exercise is riding. One of the many little slanders this rather good horseman and horse lover has endured with complacency is that he rode only because his doctor has positively ordered it. After an illness a few years ago, he was very much concerned about when he would be able to ride again. Keeping a horse in Washington and buying books have been his two extravagances.

For some years he had a beautiful horse, the thoroughbred "Jester." He and Jester became fast friends through their early-morning jaunts in Rock Creek Park. Jester was a bit temperamental and resented not being noticed during the ride. One day when the Senator was thinking about some problem of state, Jester called his attention to this neglect by shying at a squirrel. For this, Jester received a few sharp cuts with the whip. After the ride the Senator offered Jester, according to custom, a lump of sugar. Jester now cut the Senator with his whip — he refused the proffered sugar. Back at his office his alert and accusing conscience prevented the United States Senator-at-large from concentrating on his work. All day long the picture of his horse refusing his sugar was before him. Late in the afternoon he went to the stable, petted Jester, begged his forgiveness and knew that he had received it when the thoroughbred accepted two lumps of sugar. In time Jester was retired, but among his master's treasures in his bedroom is a head of Jester, done by an artist.

After Jester had been sent to the pastures to spend the remainder of his days in ease, a man in Virginia presented the Senator with a new mount. They had hoped to name him Idaho, but the papers announced somewhat prematurely that his name was "Al Smith" (this was in 1927). The Senator then compromised with the name "Governor."

"The Lone Rider of Idaho" did not always ride alone, but usually he did. He did it because he liked to ride alone, because he rode early in the morning, and because he rode in all kinds of weather (canceling his ride only when it was too slick for the horse to keep his feet). The outfit the Senator wore when riding in the rain resembled very much a policeman's costume for such occasions. One nasty, rainy day a lady hailed him with: "Officer, can you direct me to the Zoo?" The Senator reigned in his horse in some surprise and gave the directions. The lady was not quite sure she had spoken to an officer after all, and by way of apology — if one were needed — she said: "I take it that you are a guide." Whereupon, the Senator increased her confusion by remarking: "Many people don't think so, Madam."

About 1930 incessant activity had brought Borah to a run-down physical condition. A little rest improved him, but it finally became necessary for him to undergo a major operation in 1933. He maintains that following recovery from the operation he felt better than he had for fifteen years. But having had to stop riding for some time, he did not return to it, offering as a reason that it was a bit of luxury he could ill afford. Nowadays he walks a great deal, often in the evening with his neighbor, Joseph Tumulty.

Other forms of exercise and recreation which have mildly interested the Senator from time to time are camping, fishing, and visiting parks. His interest in fishing may be expressed in the language of an old doctor who, when asked to go on a fishing trip, replied : "Oh, yes, I'd love to go with you boys but for the fact that in a crowd there is always some damn fool who will want to fish." What Borah wants is the recreation of solitude with the opportunity to read history and biography, not the exercise and annoyance of fishing and hunting. When he goes to the mountains he takes two suitcases, a small one for his clothes and a large one full of books.

The Senator delights in relaxation in the sunshine. Often before making a speech he may be seen sitting on a bench by the fountain across from the Senate Office Building. Frequently he finds a secluded spot in Rock Creek Park to read his Sunday papers. Up in his end of town he may be seen not infrequently sitting on a bench taking the air and talking to children, a form of diversion which he particularly enjoys. He takes pleasure in conversing with older men he chances to meet as he strolls or sits in the Park. He shuns those who would impress him with their knowledge or importance, but he delights in those who talk with him somewhat as the ranchers of Idaho do – about their personal problems, their children, and so forth. He became particularly fond of one group of elderly men whom he often relaxed with in this way. One was leaving town on a certain day. The Senator was at particular pains to be at the regular meeting place the day before he left to wish him a pleasant visit with his children. A few days later he was asking other members of the group if any of them had heard from Mr. So-in-So.

From the personal side this is the Senator at his best, the Senator in conversation with plain, honest folk. Here he lacks only one thing, a talent which President Arthur had in such a marked degree – that is, the capacity of making an individual feel at once that he is in the presence of a friend. The Senator waits for the other man to begin to make a case for himself before he smiles a most pleasant smile and puts him at his ease. An alert but rather nervous young man called on the Senator as he was sitting in his yard in Boise to see if he could get an appointment for a conference. It took him a few seconds to explain this, during which time the Senator regarded him in a manner as friendly, but no more friendly, than Mt. Borah. But the instant the boy had completed his preliminary statement, the "Mountain" smiled and asked in a voice as benign as that of "De Lawd" in *Green Pastures*: "What do you want to see me about, son?"

In conversation the Senator is a delight, whether he is discussing with Idaho girls the burden the tariff imposes upon cosmetics; or is in animated conversation on logging with two lumber jacks who have boldly walked into the home of the President of the State University and asked for their hero because their Ford did not bring them to Moscow in time to hear an address by their "Bill" Borah; or is examining the silver question with a Senate colleague. He has no small talk, but he has a decided sense of humor and relates little humorous incidents connected with great events in a particularly entertaining manner. His steel-blue eyes are intense, piercing, but kindly. His square head, firm mouth, and fighting jaws denote will. His face is rugged, his complexion ruddy. His features are very mobile and give range for every emotion. As he talks one is impressed with his kindliness, his modesty, and his intellectual power which is entirely free from arrogance. His contempt is not for smaller minds but for the selfish, the dishonest, the low, and the base minds. Unlike many good talkers, he is a good listener. He asks questions.

Few brilliant men have less conceit or less arrogance or more consideration or more human sympathy than the Senator from Idaho. No representative of the people has ever had more respect for or more genuine interest in the people he represented. No champion of democracy has ever been more democratic in his personal relationships.

CHAPTER XVII

ANTI-IMPERIALIST

SENATOR BORAH'S opposition to the Wilson policy of recognition in Mexico and his criticism of the President for his failure to take a firmer stand in protecting Americans in Mexico were given brief mention in Chapter X. The relations of the United States and its neighbor to the south became somewhat less acute after 1917, but Borah retained an interest in the Mexican problem.

M. E. May, former Governor of Washington, wrote the Senator in 1921 that he was sending him G. A. Chamberlain's *Is Mexico Worth Saving?* The Senator's letter of thanks contained a statement not infrequently found — he had already read the book ; Chamberlain had sent him a copy. In fact, Chamberlain had done much more. He had urged Borah to study Mexico, mentioning specific books and documents he should examine. He had suggested to him that he could work out a solution for the Mexican problem and get credit for a constructive job while other men were picking things to pieces.

Following the promulgation by the Mexican Government of its land and petroleum laws in December, 1925, there was a strong movement on Washington by American business interests in Mexico which claimed that these laws confiscated their property in the subsoil. The relations between the two Governments again became strained. The Chairman of the Foreign Relations Committee announced that Mexico had a perfect right to regulate her own internal affairs and that as long as no international law was violated our citizens with interests in Mexico had no just cause of complaint.[1] When, after about a year, there was some indication that the United States might withdraw recognition because of the actions of the Mexican Government, Borah declared that this would solve no problem and stated that there was no

1 *Record,* March 9, 1926, p. 5265.

reason why the points at issue should not be ironed out on a friendly basis.[2]

It was about this time that certain types of American business men were learning that the way to destroy the influence of critics who suggested that they were not acting in the public interest was to "pin a red tag" on them. This sure-fire ammunition was now brought into use against Mexico. High officials of our Government were persuaded to use it and one of them declared that there was a "Bolshevik hegemony in Mexico." The finding of this mare's nest caused many people to recall in derision the old line — "An' the Gobble-uns 'll git you ef you don't watch out!"

The peak of the Mexican crisis was reached about Christmas of 1926. On January 5, 1927, Borah again raised his voice for a gentlemanly adjustment with Mexico, stating that English oil interests seemed to have been able to make a satisfactory arrangement. In the same address he denied that the Monroe Doctrine had any point in the case, a very definite indication that he considered the Doctrine less inclusive, still less a cloak for imperialism, than he had in 1916. In 1929 he wrote Professor James W. Garner that the original declaration of Monroe was "essentially a protection of the Central American countries. As it has been construed it is a menace to them."

Borah came forward soon with the proposal that the dispute over the land titles be submitted to arbitration.[3] He coöperated with Robinson and other Democratic Senators, and the arbitration resolution was put through the Senate on January 25 by a unanimous vote. The President was not particularly impressed by this opinion of the Senate. William Allen White wrote Borah to keep after Coolidge for arbitration. He was surrounded by Wall Street oil men, White pointed out, and would be hard and mean and uncompromising with Mexico if the Senate did not stay on guard.

Borah was in frequent communication with Professors S. G. Inman and C. W. Hackett and other authorities on Mexico and the Mexican controversy. The Senator pre-

[2] New York *Times,* November 25, 1926.
[3] *Record,* January 13, 1927.

ferred the counsel of the professors to that of the American citizens who held property in Mexico. Letters from the latter group ran usually as follows: "The 'natural rights' of Americans are being confiscated in Mexico. Now that you stand so high with the Mexican Government for your proposal of arbitration, you ought to influence that Government to give back to us our rights to the subsoil [oil]."

Senator Borah continued in the belief that there was not "a single issue involved between the United States and Mexico, or any Central American countries, but may be adjusted upon peace lines and in perfect harmony with the dignity and rights of the United States. We have formed a habit of rushing Marines hither and thither in Central America and of imperiously dictating to those people. . . Mexico is asking to change fundamentally some of her land laws and it is claimed this change has the effect of confiscating some property belonging to Americans. This is a question which should be arbitrated. The people of the United States do not believe in war to settle land titles."[4]

Not being satisfied with the information which the American oil companies and the State Department were giving out and being particularly irked at the frequent request that the information given be kept secret, Senator Borah cabled President Calles, asking him specifically how many oil companies had accepted and how many had not accepted the new Mexican petroleum law and requesting the names of companies. The President cabled back that 380 companies had accepted and only 22 had not accepted, the former holding nearly 29,000,000 acres and the latter less than 2,000,000. Among companies not accepting the new law were those in which Doheny, Sinclair, and Mellon had interests.

Borah was roundly criticized by a great many men in high places and by practically all the papers which had been with him in his fight against the League of Nations and the World Court for not going through the State Department for his information. Some stated that he had violated the law against private individuals negotiating with a foreign government. Borah characterized this criticism as an "expression of agony which comes from a fear of the facts." And

[4] Statement of January 15, 1927.

Borah got the information which the country very much needed. It seemed now that with such a large majority of the companies complying with the Mexican law there was no particularly good reason why the twenty-two hold-outs should not comply also ; their claim of wholesale confiscation must be something of an exaggeration.

In a speech at New Haven on March 20, 1927, Borah made a strong defense of Mexico. He reviewed her history, quoting Professor Hackett and others on the unhappy experiences of that country with exploiters. He argued with great force that that Republic had a perfect right to work out her own problems in her own way as long as she did not violate international law. Mexico, he said, is doing her best to see that justice is done all around. He declared that Mexico, in view of internal conditions, was doing remarkably well at protecting foreign interests. Like so many of his speeches, this one, in addition to reviewing the history and law involved in the question, carried a decidedly ethical tone. His "God has made us neighbors ; let justice make us friends," was headlined in thousands of newspapers. Although the conditions in Mexico at this time were not exactly similar to those which obtained eleven years before, this speech may still be said to show a breadth of knowledge of and tolerance for Mexico which was largely absent in his speech on January 12, 1916, in which he advocated vigorous action against our neighbor.

With the strong support Borah was getting in the country for *his* Mexican policy, it became necessary for the President to take notice. Colonel Raymond Robins is the authority for this story. One morning Coolidge asked Borah to breakfast. "Well," said the Chief Executive, "Ambassador Sheffield is coming home from Mexico and, confidentially, he is not going back. Who should succeed him ?" Borah said he would do some hard thinking. Borah asked Robins who the man should be. Robins said he would think hard, too. A friend of Dwight Morrow, the Colonel asked him who should go to Mexico. Morrow acted very strangely when asked the question and the Colonel asked what the trouble was. "Why," said Morrow, "the President has asked me to fill the place and I would accept if I thought I could get confirmation in the Senate, but I am sure Borah will not let a Morgan partner have the place." The Colonel said: "I agree with you. I don't believe he will."

After dinner the future Ambassador and the Colonel went into the study. Robins made some comment to the effect that real financiers were coming to the conclusion that nothing could be gained by trying to force a people; the only gains came through mutual advantage. Morrow said, "I can show you what I think," and pulled out several pages of an address he had made before the New York Chamber of Commerce or some such organization. The Colonel says it reflected his own sentiments exactly. Mr. Morrow was very much surprised when his guest, whom he had supposed was ready to settle down for a comfortable chat, said: "I have got to go, and let me take this with me?" "That is the only copy I have, and what is your hurry?" asked Morrow. "I am sorry this is your only copy, but it is not doing any good where it is and I have use for it, therefore I take it and go. I've got to catch a train."

He was in Washington the next morning and at the Borahs' for breakfast. He asked the Senator the state of public affairs. The Senator said that the Mexican situation looked bad again and that the Yankee in the White House wanted to appoint a Morgan partner as Ambassador to that country. "Can you beat it?" he asked. Presently the Colonel, without mentioning any name, handed Morrow's speech to the Senator. As he read it his face lighted up in agreement. "That is pretty good coming from a banker," commented Robins. "I agree with him entirely," affirmed the Senator. "Well, that is Morrow's speech," added Robins. "I'll vote for his confirmation," concluded Borah, in the well-founded belief that here was the right man for the difficult Mexican post.

The success of Ambassador Morrow in straightening out the Mexican tangle is a matter of common knowledge. It may not be a matter of common knowledge that Morrow preferred Mexico City to Paris or London. When he and Robins were discussing the matter in New York, Robins had asked why he was willing to go to Mexico when the President should offer him one of the most attractive posts. Morrow's reply was that if he received one of those places the country would be serving him, but that by going to Mexico he would be serving his country. The Senator was so satisfied with the Ambassador's stewardship that he wanted Hoover to make him Secretary of State.

Two events of December, 1927, one throwing light on the character of a government and the other on the character of certain men, are worthy of being recorded. In this month the Supreme Court of Mexico declared unconstitutional parts of the law against which Americans had been protesting. In a statement for the Chicago *Tribune* (January 1, 1928) Senator Borah cited this as an evidence of the good faith of Mexico. He stated further that the fact that an unconstitutional act had been passed by the Mexican Congress was no evidence of bad faith any more than the occasional confiscatory acts of our own Congress and state legislatures were evidences of bad faith. The Senator had never defended the Mexican law against which Americans complained; but he had said from the first that he thought Mexico was acting in good faith and that the differences between the two countries were essentially of a justiciable character.

The other event was the wild charge that Senators Borah, Norris, La Follette and one or two others had been offered bribes by Mexican authorities. It seems that Mr. Hearst had paid $15,000 for documents supposed to substantiate the charge. Nevertheless, the integrity of the Senators listed as possible bribe-takers was such that the story was discredited at once. When the Senate Committee investigating the charge called the name of Borah and mentioned $500,000 which might have come his way, the Senator smiled and the committee room was filled with a roar of laughter.

In the earlier stages of Mexican revolution (about 1915) Borah had said that, much as he deplored the religious persecutions in Mexico, we had no right to complain on that ground. He was still of this opinion in 1929. But when the new anti-religious crusade of 1934 and 1935 was launched, he could not remain silent. He introduced a resolution charging that "American citizens of the Christian faiths have been outraged" and declaring that "such anti-religious activity in Mexico is contrary to the traditions of freedom of conscience and liberty of religious worship, which are the cherished attributes of all civilized governments." He wanted the Senate to "protest" and "strongly condemn" and to authorize the Committee on Foreign Relations to hold hearings on the subject of religious persecution of Americans in Mexico.[5] He explained in a letter to a friend that "if this was a matter confined exclusively to Mexico — however much we might abhor it — there would be little we could do, but it is not confined to Mexico. There is ample evidence to show that American schools have been closed; American citizens have been killed and their property confiscated," etc. Of course, there were others in high places at Washington who did not accept the Senator's view. They held that as long as Mexicans and Americans in Mexico were treated alike in the matter of religious restriction our Government had no legal cause for complaint.

THE Nicaraguan Republic has ever found one of its staunchest friends in William E. Borah. He was the sole Republican voting (1911) against the Knox-Castrillo convention which failed of ratification by one vote. This convention would have enabled Nicaragua to secure a loan of $15,000,000 from American bankers on very favorable terms for the latter. Secretary Bryan later presented a pact with Nicaragua which would give the United States the canal rights and the privilege of intervention whenever the independence of Nicaragua and the life and property of American citizens should be in danger. Borah opposed this treaty because in his opinion the United States was not only purchasing canal rights but also making an arrangement whereby her citizens could exploit the little Republic.[6] The Latin American countries were alarmed at Borah's analysis of the situation. The Foreign Relations Committee of the Senate also showed some concern and returned the treaty to the Executive Department because of the intervention provision. In August, 1914, a new treaty, with the intervention scheme eliminated, was drafted and it was finally ratified. Borah opposed this treaty also, a "treaty with . . . a country unable to defend itself, which has officers that we put into power by virtue of a vessel of war sailing into

[5] *Record,* January 31, 1935, p. 1298.
[6] New York *Times,* July 22, 1913.

Courtesy of the Chicago Daily News

its port, a government which exists at this hour, by virtue and by virtue alone, of our Marines, who are camped in the capital of that little country." [7]

But despite the elimination of the threat of intervention from the language of the treaty that was adopted, intervention in Nicaragua went on without let or hindrance. Borah kept his eyes on that country. On December 8, 1922, the New York *Call* reported him as saying : "The people of Nicaragua today are being exploited in shameless fashion by American corporations protected by United States Marines." The forces are there "without the slightest sanction of either justice or international law." Writing for *Collier's* of January

[7] *Record,* January 13, 1915, p. 1500.

31, 1925, he tried to remove the thorns from the Monroe Doctrine. He said the Doctrine "does not give to us the right, or the color of right, to invade territory, to tear down governments and set up others. . . The Monroe Doctrine is not a stepmother's creed."

He spoke out again in his article "The fetish of Force," (*Forum*, August, 1925). He characterized as the most regrettable chapter in the history of our international affairs our dealings with the Central American countries since 1900. "We have been impatient. We have not been just at all times. . . We have swiftly and without sufficient cause appealed to force. . . Possessing great power, we have used it without adequate justification. The invasion of Nicaragua was unnecessary and therefore unmoral. . . Who can contemplate without sorrow and humiliation a great and powerful nation, inexhaustible in wealth and unmeasured in manpower, imperiously invading a perfectly helpless country, seizing and holding for years her capital, and while thus in control of her capital and directing her affairs, making a treaty with her. And why did we invade her territory and for what reason did we seize her capital? Let someone state. I have never seen a defense of the course that was worthy of a moment's consideration. I think our conduct toward Santo Domingo and Haiti equally indefensible. There was apparently, or on the surface at least, some justification in these instances which did not exist with reference to Nicaragua. . ."

The Washington Government hoped to withdraw the Marines after an election was held in Nicaragua in 1924. But the election left matters in a worse state. Pedro Diaz came to power with American sanction. When President Coolidge and Senator Borah conferred on the situation, the Senator vigorously opposed the President in his plan to aid Diaz, who had requested it. But the Coolidge policy prevailed, and Borah continued his attacks upon it. He declared that there was no need for the Marines in their only legitimate capacity, that of protecting American nationals, and that "The policy of the United States toward Central and South America should not rest solely on mahogany and oil or depend for its execution on warships and Marines." [8]

As Congress was about to adjourn the short session in 1927, Borah presented a resolution recommended by the Foreign Relations Committee 10 to 8. It provided for an investigation by that Committee of "conditions and policies bearing upon the relationship between the Central American countries, Mexico and the United States." Administrative disapproval smothered the resolution. A cartoonist made the suggestion that the Chairman might join the Marines and thus go to Nicaragua with the approval of the Administration. A columnist thought the Administration was very foolish to kill Borah's plan, for he could be much more of a menace to the Administration by remaining in Washington and meeting the gentlemen of the press every day than he could possibly be riding a pack mule in Nicaragua.

The Senator's opposition to Coolidge on Mexico, Nicaragua, the World Court, and Russia was occupying a great deal of newspaper space in the spring of 1927. It was about this time that one wag asked, "Who is the other Senator from Idaho?" and another responded with, "Why, er, isn't Borah both of them?" It was remarked also that the other Senator from Idaho ought to know how the King of Italy felt.

How did good regulars feel about Borah? How did those whose regularity was something less than a religion feel? Here is an illustration which answers both questions. The Senator had been invited to Utica just after he had spoken out against the Coolidge policy in Nicaragua. An old stalwart of that city wrote a public letter protesting against any dinner in honor of the man who would not support Coolidge. His letter made the Borah dinner a great success. The toastmaster tendered Borah "a whole-hearted, sincere and undismayed welcome." Instead of making the speech he had intended to make, Borah, entering into the spirit of the occasion, talked in an extremely informal and delightful way about his experiences in Washington, how often he opposed the President and how often he was with him. He said he would be on the firing line for the party in 1928 when some

[8] February 20, 1927.

of the "regulars" would be at home trying to figure what they could get out of the tariff.[9]

Developments in the Nicaraguan affair made it possible for Borah to get back on the firing line in 1928 as he had promised. Mr. Henry L. Stimson was sent to Nicaragua in April, 1927, and the agreement he negotiated, because of its provision for a fair election in Nicaragua, was satisfactory to the Senator except for the fact that it provided for American support for Diaz until the election could be held. But this arrangement he considered the best that could be made under the circumstances and he gave it his support. He therefore opposed the resolutions, introduced in the Senate in the early spring of 1928, calling for the immediate withdrawal of the Marines. He had not changed his views that a great wrong had been done by sending the Marines there in the first place, but he simply looked upon the Stimson agreement as the best solution of the problem.[10] For his support of the Administration in this matter he received a letter of congratulation and appreciation from Secretary Kellogg and not a few humorous comments from newspapers to the effect that they always knew when an election was in the offing by Borah's swing in the direction of regularity.

But events justified Borah in supporting the Administration. The election was held and President Moncada was inaugurated on January 1, 1929. Although there was some delay in getting the Marines out, they were finally withdrawn.

THE Platt Amendment, under which the United States undertook to preserve Cuban independence and guarantee a government adequate to the protection of life, liberty, and property, the Senator desired to see repealed. In a statement he submitted for *Collier's* on March 21, 1933, at the time of serious disorders in Cuba, he declared that he was unwilling to see the United States allow the outrages to continue in Cuba when we had the obligation under the Amendment to prevent them. At the same time he declared for the repeal of the Amendment so that the peculiar obligation would be removed. He thought the Amendment had a very bad in-

[9] March 29, 1927.
[10] *Record,* April 19, 1928.

fluence in Cuba in that it paralyzed any initiative Cubans might want to take against a despotic government for fear the United States would intervene to preserve that government. He favored repeal of the Platt Amendment, except for the obligation to preserve the independence of Cuba, which in any case we could preserve under the Monroe Doctrine.

In September, 1933, he opposed any intervention in Cuba and backed the new President Grau San Martin. Before that President passed from power he wrote the Senator a letter of appreciation. It reads, in part, as follows: "Permit me to tender to you my best thanks for your liberal and persistent efforts towards the downfall of the Machado tyranny and, very particularly, for your magnificent defense of students . . . when subject to military court martial. Later on your written statement following the massacre of the Valdes Daussa boys was the finishing touch to the tottering dictatorship. Your wonderful insight into our situation as evidenced by your recent remarks on intervention, has aroused our admiration and enhanced the enduring debt of gratitude which fills our hearts."

The Senator took a position decidedly friendly to the Haitians. In April, 1922, the McCormick Committee on American Occupation recommended that it be continued and reported that it had been beneficial to the Haitian people.[11] Borah said that he had never understood why we went in. "First it was said we went in to protect life and property. Yet property there was at least as safe as it is in New York City, and no American or foreigner had lost his life there." [12]

As the United States was planning to evacuate Haiti in 1930, the Senator declared: "Over twelve years ago we dissolved their Assembly by force of arms and since that time they have not been permitted in any substantial way to have anything to do with their Government. They are completely disfranchised. The United States Government ought to be ashamed to stand before the world at this time with all our professions of peace and against military power in the attitude of keeping a military heel upon a helpless people." [13]

[11] Senate Report No. 794, 67th Cong. 2nd ses.
[12] New York *Times,* May 2, 1922.
[13] *Ibid.,* January 9, 1930.

The Senator has never been one of those who have justified American intervention in Central America on the grounds that it has been "so good" for the peoples who objected to it. With the exception of his position on Panama questions and with the possible exception of his attitude toward Mexico during the Wilson Administration, he has been unfailing in his manifestations of friendship for the other Republics of the Western Hemisphere. In looking for a friend north of the Rio Grande to match Borah, Latin American peoples turn back to Monroe, Clay, and Lincoln, but none of these statesmen had to manifest friendship in the face of the fierce conservative opposition which Borah often encountered.

BORAH was immediately and thoroughly aroused when he learned that the Peace Conference of 1919 had handed over to Japan Germany's rights in China's Shantung. Over and over again in his denunciations of the Versailles Treaty he singled out this particular iniquity. He criticized Wilson for yielding to the demands of Japan, although he was generous enough to say that he knew the President hated the deed as much as he did and yielded only because he thought it was necessary to do so in order to get his League of Nations. He was immensely pleased at the "reaffirmation of good policies" shown by Japan's agreement at the Washington Conference to return Shantung to China.

Borah came out in 1925 for the abolition of extraterritorial rights in China. According to Raymond Clapper he was the only Senator who favored such a move at that time.[14] His correspondence files of this period are full of letters on the subject of extraterritoriality from professors, newspaper men, ministers, and the public generally. Many letters came from China, including one from the Minister of Foreign Affairs of the Nationalist Government. The Senator himself wrote a great many letters on the subject. He wrote the Baltimore *Sun* a long one relative to an article by a professor who was fearful of what would happen to the whites in China once extraterritoriality was abolished. The Senator said the reasons given by the professor for retaining the privilege in China were the same as those given for retaining it in Turkey

[14] *Nation*, April 13, 1927.

a few years before. He explained further that no one was seriously advocating that the privilege should be abolished overnight but that the idea was for the great powers to co-operate in abolishing it as soon as possible.

Of course there was a "red" scare to help prevent this particular type of liberation in China. A Congressman, much concerned about the Bolsheviks, wrote the Senator. Borah replied : "It seems to me that we are overworking these days the 'red' proposition. Whenever a people becomes dissatisfied with oppressive measures and rebel, they are called 'reds'. . . I was interested some time ago in counting up the number of places and instances where powerful governments were asserting that the 'reds' were in control and making trouble. There were thirteen different places in thirteen different countries. And it developed in every instance that the people who were making the trouble were the people who were being oppressed and exploited. I haven't any doubt at all but that Russia is playing as strong a hand as she can in China. So are Great Britain and Japan, and so are other nations.

"The 'reds' are not the authors of the child labor rules of China. The 'reds' are not maintaining the old and worn out treaties. The 'reds' are not in control of forty of her different cities and ports ; and the 'reds' are not maintaining the unjust and unfair customs laws."

Early in May, 1927, the President had said in New York that American friendship for China was proverbial, and that the American Government was now most sympathetic with the Chinese in their attempt to realize a republican form of government. He explained that American ships were in Chinese waters at that time for the sole purpose of protecting citizens as the Chinese would protect them if they had a stable government. He emphasized that the American policy in China was the opposite of that of aggression.

In a speech at Cleveland, on May 9, the Senator quoted the President's words with warm approval. Continuing, he read from another official source that force was the only argument that the Chinese understood or respected. The Senator denounced this doctrine of force "in all its cruel and bloody detail. It means the right of foreign powers to exploit the natural resources of China. . . It means that we will exercise our influence, through force, to destroy the nationalistic movement of 400,000,000 people. . .

". . . If force is used in China it will not be because China does not understand anything but force. It will be because those who use force do not understand anything else. If force is used in China, it will not be because of a lack of moral perception upon the part of China, but the lack of moral conception upon the part of those who use it."

When Japan resorted to force in Manchuria in 1931, Senator Borah declared at the dedication of the William E. Borah Outlawry of War Foundation at the University of Idaho (September 24) that "even though Japan's reasons were ten times as truthful as it can be assumed they are, there is no justification for force in Manchuria." He opposed the suggested economic boycott on Japan because he regarded it as a poor method of influencing Japanese action and as one likely to lead to retaliation and the use of armed force. The only hope the Senator could see for settlement was through an international conference with the Japanese authorities.[15] He expected little from the League of Nations and his interpretation of his own Kellogg Pact was that it gave no basis for action against Japan.[16]

In his efforts for the Chinese the Senator made himself the best known American in China, particularly in 1927. The North China *Star* in this year stated that any educated Chinese, young or old, when asked to name a character in American history, invariably answered "Lin-Kun," and when asked to name the greatest living American statesman, nine out of ten of them replied "Bor-Ah."

THE United States acquired the Philippines as Borah was entering public life. His interest in those days was almost entirely in domestic questions and the only attention he seems to have given the Philippine issue was in his reference to Carl Schurz, whom he denounced; included in his list of denunciations was the fact that Schurz was an anti-imperialist. But Borah's hostility to Schurz probably cooled his own

[15] New York *Times,* October 15, 1931.
[16] *Record,* January 7, 1929, p. 1281.

feeling against imperialism. At any rate, soon after he became Senator he declared for Philippine independence at the earliest possible date.[17]

When the Jones Act, fixing no definite date for independence, was before Congress in 1916, Borah favored an amendment which would get the United States out of the Philippines in a near and definite future. He said that such a move would be for the material advantage of the United States and that, "if we were to leave the Filipino people within the next two or three or four years they would be benefited by our presence there just as much as if we should stay there for fifteen or twenty years, and then leave them . . . for no people in the history of the world have ever acquired anything like a capacity for self-government within less than centuries."[18] He was opposed to the Jones Act as passed, because in acknowledging capacity for self-government it failed to fix any time when independence should be granted. The Senator was of the opinion that the American people would be opposed to freeing the Philippines for a long time to come and that the Act held out a false hope to the Islands.

Borah continued his interest in freedom for the Philippines, declaring in 1922 that he had always thought that when we took them we repealed the Declaration of Independence. But as late as 1930 he wrote: "In my opinion, we are further away from independence than we were ten years ago, and we are closer to independence now than we will ever be again."

What the love of liberty for other peoples could not do, the growing belief that imperialism was not economically profitable and the complaints of farmers and labor about Philippine competition following the decline of 1929 could do. The Hawes-Cutting Act, granting independence after some ten years, was passed in 1932. Borah opposed this bill because it delayed independence too long, provided for an American naval base, and committed the United States to a treaty arrangement for the preservation of Philippine neutrality. Yet when President Hoover vetoed the bill, the Senator decided that he would help override the veto. He changed his view, he said, because the passage of the bill had revealed a great

[17] *Ibid.*, June 15, 1909, p. 3237.
[18] *Ibid.*, January 24, 1916, p. 1439.

divergence of opinion among responsible people and he despaired of ever seeing passed a bill which would be satisfactory to all parties.[19] This bill was rejected by the Philippine Legislature. In March, 1934, the Roosevelt Administration put through a modified bill which was acceptable to the Senator and to the Filipinos. "The Sugar Lobby Frees the Philippines," stated one publication. The Dean of the Senate wrote the editor that he was in error, for many of the sugar people were opposed to independence. Some beet-sugar men in Idaho wrote the Senator protesting against it, and Senator Smoot, almost an apostle of sugar, had voted against independence in 1932. Borah explained that the most persistent lobbies were against this fulfillment of the obligation of the American Government to the Philippines. He mentioned those representing the Navy, investors, and imperialists in general.

MENTION was made earlier in this chapter of the Senator's references to China in his speech at Cleveland on May 9, 1927. He spoke not only of China but also of Mexico, Nicaragua, Russia, war debts, and peace. The address reveals not only the opinions of the Chairman of the Foreign Relations Committee on these subjects but also his ideas of the proper technique of conducting foreign affairs. From a reasonably full knowledge of the subjects on which he spoke he reported frankly, informally, and even entertainingly on the foreign situation as he saw it. He said that the people should know what was going on in our foreign relations ; that a knowledge of them would prevent war ; and that the people would not stand for conditions which brought on war if they knew about them. But the most remarkable aspect of his address was the concluding sentence in which he asked for questions from his audience. Just when had a man in his position, to whose words the world listened, given a public audience such an opportunity and exposed himself to such risks ? The questions came and the Senator answered one after the other to the edification and delight of the crowd.

It cannot be measured with any degree of accuracy, but there is reason to believe that such public addresses by the

[19] *Ibid.*, January 17, 1933, p. 1916.

Senator did help to shape our foreign policy, particularly during the Coolidge Administration. People crowded to hear him. They listened in over the radio. They read his speeches in the papers. It can hardly be doubted that Borah built up a public opinion which forced the Administration to tone down its policy in Mexico and Nicaragua. At any rate, this is his conception of the proper way to conduct foreign relations : tell the people what is going on and they will force their governments to follow honorable courses. His faith in the people of foreign countries is hardly less than his faith in the American people. If he suspects foreign countries, it is because he suspects their rulers.

In this chapter we have seen something of the Senator's interest in and sympathy for the peoples of smaller, or weaker, or undeveloped countries. Concerned about these peoples, he is even more concerned that his own country in her relations with them should scorn force and deal justly and with forbearance. Most fittingly, a writer once sent the Senator a book inscribed, "To the Conscience of the Republic."

CHAPTER XVIII

BORAH-RUSSIAN RELATIONS

NO OTHER position Borah has ever taken has brought him such general condemnation from his countrymen as his advocacy of the recognition of Soviet Russia. On no other position was he so constantly misunderstood and deliberately misrepresented. Since his stand on Russian recognition typified him in the popular and righteous mind at his worst, it naturally reveals him at the very peak of political courage. So bitter were statesmen, clergymen, editors, and the great majority of the public against Borah for championing this cause that few of them seemed to appreciate the sheer courage, even audacity, the Senator was displaying.

On July 26, 1917, Borah criticized the Allies and the United States for their lack of response to the proposal of the Kerensky government in Russia for peace without annexations or indemnities.[1] About the time the Bolsheviks were coming into control, he was saying that America should send a commission to Russia to aid her in the solution of her problems. When the red revolution was accomplished, he continued in the view that the United States should lend a hand to the Russian people. The last word is the one he emphasized. As for Lenin and Trotsky, he said : "I think they are disloyal to everyone on earth except themselves." But he dissociated them "from the great body and mass of the Russian people." [2] The people, he said, "are the supreme concern and entitled to the sympathy, the counsel and confidence of free peoples everywhere" and "entitled especially to the help and guidance, the unselfish and beneficent leadership, of this Republic." [3]

With statesmen all around him having the jitters, with the Department of Justice on its "red hunts," and with newspapers screaming Bolshevism, sometimes at Borah, the Senator declared that the Russian people had a right to set up a socialistic system if they wanted one, although it was abhorrent to

1 *Record,* July 26, 1917, p. 5497.
2 *Ibid.,* January 9, 1919, p. 1167.
3 *Ibid.,* July 13, 1918, p. 9054.

him. Abhorrent to him also was the fact that American troops were in Russia for the purpose of interfering with the domestic affairs of that country. The grim conviction of the great majority of Americans that the reds should be exterminated wherever found lest America awake one morning and find the red flag flying from the Capitol the Senator considered absurd and childish. His own Americanism was such that he knew that no Soviet theories could contaminate it; his faith in the Americanism of his fellow-countrymen was such that he was confident that no amount of Soviet propaganda could wean them from it. Here was a patriot so American, so full of confidence in his country and in the judgment and good sense of its people, that he was regarded by 100-percent Americans as un-American on the Russian question!

Early in 1920 Borah argued that it was high time normal trade relations were being reëstablished with Russia; he insisted that the treatment Russia had received since the revolution was contrary to all sound theories of commerce. To those who feared the resumption of commerce would encourage communism, he replied that, on the contrary, it would reveal the inadequacies of the system. He added that if the Russians were determined to adhere to their system in any case, nothing would be achieved by non-intercourse except ill will and suffering. The suggestion that trade be resumed struck a responsive chord with a number of business men, some of whom had been writing to Borah advocating that step for several months. Even in 1920 Borah was saying that Russia should and would soon be recognized. In the political clamor of the time this passed without much notice, but former Governor E. C. Stokes of New Jersey wrote the Senator that he was showing his usual good judgment. In December, 1921, he stated that the government of the Soviets was without any doubt the *de facto* government of Russia and as such should be recognized.

Paving the way for a formal resolution for the recognition of the Soviets, the Senator, on May 4, 1922, demanded that diplomatic immunity be withdrawn from Boris Bakhmeteff, the so-called Russian Ambassador in Washington. He was really an ambassador from the tombs, a ghost of the Kerensky government now dead and buried for nearly five years. Concerning the "ambassador" the Baltimore *Sun* asked : "What is Bakhmeteff to us and what are we to him, diplomatically? Does he represent a State Department policy, or merely a State Department courtesy? Mr. Borah must be answered because he is asking what the country wants to know."[4] Of course the asking of this question revealed the absurdity of Bakhmeteff's position. He was edged out of the diplomatic circle in Washington and took refuge in Paris.

On May 15, 1922, Borah introduced his formal resolution for the recognition of Russia. It was tabled. There we may leave it while we ascertain the sources of the Senator's information on Russia.

He read widely in books, papers and documents, English and American. In 1921, he wrote to John Spargo stating that he was reading all he wrote on Russia and asking him to come to Washington to spend several days with him. Bishop Luther B. Wilson, of the Board of Foreign Missions of the Methodist Church, who spoke rather favorably on Russia in Washington in December, 1922, engaged Borah's interest. He wrote the Bishop asking for more information. The Bishop answered that the Soviet Government was as firmly established as any government in Europe ; that the people were not particularly enthusiastic about it, but they expected nothing better if it should be overthrown ; that the Government did not maintain itself by terror alone ; that the key to the European situation was the recovery of Russia and Germany ; and that the latter country was fast going to chaos under the Versailles Treaty. It was really a letter very remarkable for its insight and the Senator accepted it as authoritative.

One of the Senator's leading and constant advisers on Russia was Colonel Raymond Robins, who of all the "wise men among the Allies" had made the right guess about Russia. Robins sent to Borah the man who, as the Colonel generously put it, had enabled him to make that guess – Mr. Alexander Gumberg, Secretary to the Colonel while he was in Russia. Among the other men with whom he advised we find Norman Thomas, Norman Hapgood, Scott Nearing, James G. McDonald, Felix Frankfurter, John Haynes Holmes, Jerome

[4] Baltimore *Sun*, May 10, 1922.

Davis, Samuel Gompers, James P. Goodrich (who after a visit to Russia became convinced that the Soviet system would stand), Sherwood Eddy, and Walter Duranty.

Beginning in 1922 and running through 1925, Borah put on an intensive campaign, in the Senate and out, for the recognition of Russia. After 1925 he relaxed his efforts only slightly.

What were his reasons for advocating recognition? One of the first he mentioned (but not one that he stressed greatly) was that the Soviet Government was less tyrannical with and more advantageous to the Russian people than the former absolute monarchy. *Second* (and this reason he stressed), "George Washington and his Cabinet in which were Alexander Hamilton, Thomas Jefferson and others was probably the greatest Cabinet ever formed under the American flag and yet they granted recognition to France when that country was in a similar plight to Russia of today. They did not approve of the means being used in the revolution but they decided for recognition of that country." [5] Then he went on to show that the invariable American practice for more than a century after that was to recognize any government which actually held authority in a country, without regard to what our officials might think of the political theory upon which that government was founded.

Third, we owe it to the Russian people. "I care nothing for theories or doctrines over there: I see only 170,000,000 Russian people, a great people, ultimately to be a powerful people, struggling in almost blinded madness to be free of the inhumanities and cruelties of the past. It is with those people as a people that we should sympathize, and of them as a people we should think when forming our policies and mapping out our program. To say that the people do not want the present government of Russia is not borne out by the facts." [6]

Fourth, "Until we have established trade with Russia we cannot have that prosperity which our friends tell us of [merely] by passing high tariff laws."

Fifth, Russia and Germany are dangerous to the peace of

[5] *Capital News,* October 6, 1922.
[6] *Record,* May 31, 1922, p. 7909.

Europe and they are dangerous to that peace (1922) because the alliances and combinations against them are forcing them into each other's arms.

Sixth, The Russians can be trusted. "Sixteen governments have concluded treaties of trade with Russia and have granted her recognition. If property is not safe in Russia, why is it that these countries who have concluded treaties with Russia are trading with her, yes, and seeking still greater trade with her?"

Seventh, "Is it not time to take some risk in favor of peace? Suppose we do not recognize the government of Russia until it breaks down. What will step in but greater chaos, bloodshed, famine and disease? If we become instrumental in this downfall by refusing recognition it will be almost as serious as a declaration of war." [7]

To the argument that recognition would let loose in the United States the Bolsheviki, who, with their propaganda of unrest, would lead to the overthrow of the Government of the United States, he replied that those who advanced the argument slandered American institutions and Americans. Was not our system strong enough to risk a comparison with that of Russia? Were the American people such fools that they could not see that while communism in Russia might be an improvement over the regime of the Tsar that was no argument for the adoption of communism by the United States? He admitted that the Russian idea might make some progress in the United States if those charged with the responsibility for the conduct of affairs did not give more attention to the crying needs of the hour, for "Bolshevism is a disease of unrest and discontent." But "if you take off the burden under which the people of the United States are struggling today with their high taxes, Bolsheviki may overrun the United States preaching their doctrines of discontent without fear of harm being done. A contented, prosperous people have no time and will not listen to Bolshevism. Lift the burden from the shoulders of the American people, bring back peace through the world and Bolshevism will disappear from the world like mist before the morning sun." [8]

[7] *Capital News,* October 6, 1922.
[8] *Ibid.*

When it was argued that we should not recognize Russia because its government was anti-religious, the Senator stated his regret that there was any religious persecution. He said that there was much less persecution, however, than was commonly reported because a great deal of the so-called religious persecution was nothing more than the ordinary operation of the laws against political obstructionists and traitors. Furthermore, he argued the right of Russia to do as she would about religion, that being fundamentally a domestic question.

But the Russian dictators are just plain murderers and assassins, it was said. How could the Senator recognize them? "We recognized the old Tsar government for nearly a hundred and fifty years. We didn't approve of it, and there never was a more cruel, bloody or more unconscionable government. . . We recognized Turkey, but we have not approved of the bloody history of Turkey for the last five hundred years." [9] Then he would state his deep regret that there had been so much violence in the revolution, but would add that the Russians were simply following the method they had learned under the Tsars and that he did not see how they could have had a successful revolution otherwise.

A million times it was said that no government should be recognized which had repudiated debts, regardless of the circumstances under which they might have been contracted. History records other cases of repudiation, the Senator answered, and a man "so far removed from realities" as William Jennings Bryan was writing Borah in 1922 that the European nations would not pay their war debts to the United States.

"Senator Borah," one can imagine a sweet lady saying to him after he had finished an address, "why are you a Bolshevik?" At least, one can hardly avoid the conclusion that many people considered Borah a Bolshevik. He explained in every speech, certainly in every speech outside of the Senate, that he held no brief for communism. He was only saying that Russia had a right to have that sort of system if she wanted it and that it was sound statesmanship, good business, and high morals for the United States to recognize that government. But millions of people, it seemed, were never able to understand why a man would advocate recognition without endors-

[9] The Cleveland *Press*, May 10, 1927.

ing communism. Some newspaper editors could not understand it. A great many others pretended not to understand it. To admit an understanding of Borah's position would leave less ground on which to oppose him because, as he so clearly showed, American history was on his side.

In December, 1923, Soviet Commissar of Foreign Affairs, George Chicherin, asked Secretary Hughes to discuss problems standing in the way of recognition. Mr. Hughes wrote (December 18) a rather severe note in reply. He said that if Russia wanted to restore confiscated property, assume the debts she had repudiated, and cease her efforts to undermine the American Government, she could do so. He ignored the counter-claims the Soviet Government had against the United States for our intervention during the revolution.

Borah wrote to Colonel Robins at once. "I feel, as I am sure you do, that the reply of Hughes was exceedingly unfortunate. . . I take it from the remarks of Senator Lodge and Senator Lenroot that their contention will be that the Soviet Government is responsible for the actions of the Third Internationale. I would be glad to have you write me, Colonel, your views upon this situation. . . I would like to have you give me also your views and your information with reference to the Soviet Government, being responsible for any propaganda in this country during the last three years." The Colonel wrote in some detail, even indicating the correct pronunciation of a certain Russian name.

In his reply to Hughes and Senators who defended the Secretary's position, Borah stated that the evidence upon which Mr. Hughes built his argument about Russian propaganda in the United States was three years old. His own investigation, he said, failed to reveal any current instances of such propaganda. He had thought for some time that Russia would be willing to make a reasonable financial settlement. Early in 1924, a subcommittee headed by Borah held hearings on his resolution for recognition, and at the conclusion of the hearings he again declared : "We cannot have peace, disarmament or normal conditions until the Russian problem is settled." [10]

Among business men who had their eyes open to realities

[10] New York *Times*, April 3, 1925.

and among liberals, Borah found acceptance of his proposition that Russia be recognized, but he knew that the country as a whole was overwhelmingly against him. He did not mind this. In fact, he often told his audience that he knew 99 of every 100 of them disagreed with him, but that made the discussion more fun. After a good speech there was evidence that the percentage in opposition had been reduced somewhat and Borah was satisfied. Occasionally a paper of some consequence would come to his aid. When he was heckled in his address before the Association of Stock Exchange Firms in New York in the spring of 1927, the *Journal of Commerce* strongly supported Borah with this observation: "It is not easy to understand why such notions continue to be cherished by otherwise intelligent Americans who presumably know that all the leading industrial nations of Europe have yielded to the compulsion of facts and acknowledged the Soviet Union to be a Government in law and in fact as well as in name." [11]

When we had signed the Pact renouncing war with fifty-odd nations including Russia, Borah hoped this would pass as a recognition of Russia on our part; but the State Department made it clear that while we might sign a treaty on which we could recognize the official signature of a Russian plenipotentiary we still were not recognizing the Russian Government! Writing to Lippmann of the *World* in praise of an enlightened editorial of July 25, 1929 on Russia and China, Borah suggested that the *World* might now come out for the recognition of Russia. "What an incongruous, indeed, what an absurd, position we are in. Russia has signed the Peace Pact. We have put it forth to the world as the solution of peace," and yet we are not on speaking terms with one of the signatory powers. Lippmann replied that the *World* was absolutely with Borah on Russia and was only waiting for an opportune moment to launch the campaign. Borah suggested that a good time to begin would be upon the return of the delegation of American business men then in Russia.

The name of Borah was a familiar one in Russia from the time he began his agitation for recognition. His pronouncements were eagerly scanned by Soviet officials and highly publicized. He was looked upon as the one great and power-

[11] *The Journal of Commerce,* May 2, 1927.

ful friend of the Soviets in America and treated accordingly. So potent was his name in Russia that a personal appeal from him could almost invariably produce results. When the American aviators Eilson and Borland had a misadventure in Siberia, Borah cabled Litvinoff who instituted search for the lost men. A month later he was writing to Amtorg in New York, stating that American Jews wished to help their brothers in Russia with a gift of seventy-five carloads of flour for Passover and expressing the great hope that the head of Amtorg and the Russian government would give permission for this transaction. If priests and rabbis were persecuted in Russia, an appeal to Litvinoff *via* Borah was sufficient to effect cessation if the persecution had no other than an anti-religious basis.

Not so long after Borah started his advocacy of recognition, it occurred to some American who wanted to see Russia that a letter from Senator Borah would be just the thing to carry along. The magic power of these letters over Russian officials was soon noised around and the call upon the Senator for letters became very common. Doctor William L. Burdick, of the University of Kansas, tells a rather typical story of the value of one of the Borah letters. His passport had been viséd at the Russian Embassy in Vienna, and he supposed everything requisite for admission to Sovietland was accomplished. But when he reached the border, his passport was taken up and he was told that it was not good. "Why is it not good? What is the fault with it?" asked the Doctor. "I am not telling you why," the officer replied grimly. "I say it is not good." The official was importuned further but without avail. Finally, the Doctor said: "Very well, I will then turn back across the line into Poland again." "You will not return," said the officer. "You will stay here until we can make inquiries." The Doctor was by this time somewhat frightened, and even if the matter should finally be adjusted satisfactorily, he did not relish the idea of a sojourn in the abominable little town of Negorolye.

Then he had an idea. "Did you ever hear of Senator Borah of the United States?" he asked the officer. "Yes, I've heard of Borah." "Can you read English?" continued the Doctor. "I can read English a little, but the head officer can read it very well." The officer was immediately furnished with the Borah letter which he carried to the head officer. Soon the chief of this port of entry appeared, greeted the Doctor pleasantly, and said: "Your passport is quite all right. The officer made a mistake. You will please take your train for Moscow." The Doctor tried to find out what had caused all the trouble but the officers would only repeat: "It is all right; quite all right; all right; just a mistake."

"Tell Senator Borah we want the United States to recognize us," the Russian called to the Doctor as his train was leaving for Moscow.

Some of the suspicions of the Russians concerning the low moral tone of capitalist countries were confirmed by the bearers of one of the Senator's letters. Several college boys went all over Russia borrowing money on nothing more than the Senator's signature to a note stating that they were students and citizens of the United States and that he hoped the Russians would be good to them! If the Soviets were given cause to withhold their confidence in American students, the Senator left them no reason to doubt his personal integrity. He straightened up the matter as best he could.

Borah's interest in recognition never flagged. There was seldom a month in which he did not have a further comment or address to deliver on the subject. In 1929 he attacked the crass materialism and hypocrisy which had marked the interests of governments and individuals in the Russian problem since the revolution. Reviewing for the New York *American* (March 31) Mr. Churchill's *The Aftermath*, the Senator wrote of the Allies' intervention in Russia as follows: "This conflict in Russia was a contest between two Russian forces. On one side were the representatives of the old regime; on the other side the Soviets. Therefore according to the interventionists' theory shoot and murder the Soviets on sight. And finally, parley! For what purpose a parley?

". . . The parley was to enable them to take a look at Russian oil, examine the possibilities of increasing trade, not justice but profits, not humanity but financial gain. This, according to the story brought the parley and this, in my judgment, is true."

About the same time, in a letter to the Idaho Falls Chamber

of Commerce, he expressed himself concerning more recent European and American interests in Russia. "These leaders have put aside their great horror of Bolshevism long enough," he said, "to lay the basis of their monopoly to secure vast oil concessions from Russia and thereby stay the possibility of cheap oil reaching the European markets.

"It was only a few months ago that Sir Henri Deterding was in a fearful state of benevolent anxiety for fear people would go to Russia and make contracts with those 'treacherous repudiators' and thereby suffer great loss. Mr. Hughes, when Secretary of State, warned all men to stay away from these people, who were irresponsible and with whom it was dangerous to do business. But even he, it appears, could not persuade the Standard Oil Company — for I am sure he must have exerted his reasoning powers in that direction — to hold back from this great peril."

Progress in winning converts to the idea of fellowship with Russia continued to be slow. The rank and file of middle-class Americans continued to suspect Borah of having unholy designs. His good friend Rockwell wrote from Idaho that he had talked with a man who had a sort of Doctor Crane book which he circulated privately and which had in it such stuff as, "unless a man has felt a lump in his throat — unless moisture has filled his eyes when he has looked upon Old Glory," etc. Now, this man, said "Rock," finally broke out with: "Borah is a traitorous —— ; the greatest menace we have in America." A very responsible man wrote the Senator, asking how on earth he could support recognition when he had before him daily the awful facts about Russia printed in the New York *Times* and the Chicago *Tribune*. The Senator's very courteous reply to this letter included a paragraph on newspapers and the news. A few former officers of the A.E.F. wrote Borah that they were through with him, and many D.A.R. chapters, including the "Bitterroot" Chapter of Montana, added their protests against the idea of recognition.

When our country was well into the economic depression in December, 1930, Borah predicted that we would soon be on the dole. But one action which should be taken to avoid the dole was that of stimulating trade with Russia. "It was only a short time ago when one of our distinguished American statesmen declared that Russia was an economic vacuum. . . Nevertheless, the foreign trade of Russia last year was something like $890,000,000. . . This economic vacuum is now buying something like $150,000,000" worth of goods from the United States. He would offer every facility for increasing this trade instead of putting obstacles in the way of it, as it seemed to him the Treasury Department was doing.[12]

He pressed again for the recognition of Russia in a speech in the Senate on March 3, 1931. His main points were that the Soviet Government would not collapse; that the United States was losing money by refusing to take notice of it; that communism was no threat to America; that if we failed it would be due to the defects in our own system, not to propaganda from Russia.

The crisis in Russo-Japanese relations in 1932, arising out of Japanese aggressions in Manchuria, advanced the cause of recognition in the United States Senate. For some years there had been a few other liberal Senators who favored it, but now there were signs of support from quarters which had looked, with Mr. Winston Churchill, upon the Russian experiment as so much "baboonery." To be sure, this new interest grew out of the possibility of munitions trade, but the Senator was willing to welcome recruits whatever their motives for enlistment.[13]

But the interest of President-elect Roosevelt in Russia was the first strong encouragement the Senator had received in his campaign for recognition. Borah thought that the time had come at last. During the "interregnum" following Roosevelt's election, there was some talk of sending a commission to Russia for a little investigation preparatory to recognition. The original champion of recognition was opposed to this. He explained in a letter to Jerome Davis that it would simply give the reactionaries time to organize against recognition, and that it would be viewed with disfavor by the Soviets, conveying, as it would, the idea of distrust. He said the thing to do was to appoint an ambassador to Russia on March 5. If this were done, he thought discussion would die down in twenty-four hours, and other matters could then be adjusted.

12 Washington *News* (UP), December 12, 1930.
13 New York *Times*, April 23, 1932.

When President Roosevelt, shortly after his inauguration, included Russia among the Governments to which he sent his disarmament note, the Senator was highly pleased. "We are dealing with Russia direct, and this is the important fact," he said. "We are no longer proceeding upon the theory that Russia does not exist." [14]

When the President in October invited Russia to send an emissary to confer on recognition Borah stated (October 21) that bringing about amity at this time with Russia "would be nothing less than a stroke of genius," and that "it would be in accord with the President's initiative and courage, more than once disclosed in great emergencies."

On November 11, Maxim Litvinoff wrote the Senator this letter : "I have learned with deep regret that your engagements do not permit you to be in Washington during my brief visit. My own schedule has permitted me to see virtually no one outside of the official conversations, but I had looked forward to a quiet talk with you.

"You, I believe, were the first American in high position to realize the full implications of amicable relations between your country and mine. The present occasion is in large measure the result of your vision and your persistent efforts. I therefore feel that you yourself have contributed a chapter in American-Soviet relations which will be remembered gratefully in both countries. . ."

With recognition accorded, Borah wired the President : CONGRATULATIONS. IT WAS THE FINE BIG COURAGEOUS THING TO DO. The Senator and Litvinoff exchanged wires of congratulations and felicitations.

Colonel Hugh L. Cooper and others in charge of the big farewell dinner for Litvinoff in New York had planned to have Borah deliver the address of the occasion, but a severe cold contracted in Boise kept the Senator in bed after his return to Washington. As it was, the Senator's wire was one of the big events of the evening : PROFOUND GRATIFICATION. . . ESTRANGEMENT IS AT AN END. FRIENDSHIP TRADE AND COMMERCE ARE TO TERMINATE SIXTEEN STRANGELY WASTED YEARS. . . THESE TWO GREAT PEOPLES ARE ENTITLED TO LIVE IN FRIENDSHIP. . .

[14] *Ibid.*, May 17, 1933.

Borah's preference as Ambassador to Soviet Russia was Colonel Raymond Robins, although he did not make any recommendation to the President. Jerome Davis, another man mentioned for the place, would have been quite satisfactory to the Senator. For some strange reason he seems to have had no acquaintance with Mr. William C. Bullitt, who received the appointment.

Admitting that not all of the advantages he expected to flow from recognition have materialized, the Senator, nevertheless, does not for one moment regret his leadership in the long fight. If nothing had resulted from recognition except that two great powers now speak to each other he would consider his efforts well spent.

The advocacy of recognition revealed certain qualities in Borah which we might do well to summarize. *First,* it was a courageous fight. If a man had wanted to be nominated for the presidency, he could not have taken a course which would have carried him further from the realization of that ambition.

Second, he advocated recognition not only because Washington and Jefferson had recognized revolutionary France but also because he thought America had been wise in following the policy of recognizing any governments which actually held the power. Any other policy of recognition amounts to intervention.

Third, his nationalism was back of his efforts. The United States would certainly claim the right to set up any kind of government she desired and would properly insist upon recognition. Russia should be accorded the right we claim for ourselves. Borah is such a *consistent* nationalist that he believes in nationalism for other peoples. Nationalists are often strongly flavored with imperialism. That is, they think nationalism is a very fine thing for their own country and for a few other countries whose standards of government are similar to those of their own ; but otherwise they prefer the lyrics of the White Man's Burden or the religion of Nordic superiority. Borah believed in political freedom for all nationalities.

Fourth, he was never prejudiced against the Soviets because of their form of government. He viewed this as something entirely distinct from the problem of recognition. If he had less horror of communism than many others, it was because he had more faith in human nature. He sincerely believed that communism was a disease, a neurosis due to centuries of oppression and economic misery and that the Russian people would be cured of their "baboonery" if they were treated by other peoples as human beings.

Fifth, he had no fear of Russian propaganda in the United States. He believed congressional committees looking behind telegraph poles and poking behind billboards for communists were the height of the ridiculous. He had too much faith in the good sense of the American people to think they might be misled by a few agitators. The menace in America, he thought, was not in Soviet propaganda but in America's failure to solve her own problems.

Sixth, he displayed a grasp of realities : there was Soviet Russia ; it seemed likely to stay for some time ; its trade was of value ; the friendship of its people was worth having. Every citizen of the United States knew it existed and practically very other government in the world had recognized it, but the United States was in the position of that Russian professor in the story who wrote a book entitled *The Elephant, Does He Exist ?*

CHAPTER XIX

"WE HAVE SCOTCHED THE SNAKE"

SENATOR BORAH considered the movement to make the United States a member of the Permanent Court of International Justice (otherwise known as the World Court) as another scheme for getting the United States into the League of Nations. His fight against the Court he regarded as a continuation of his fight against the League. The Court issue, he thought, brought up the old question of political entanglement with foreign powers — hence the title of this chapter.

At the outset it must be stated that the Senator was not opposed to *a* world court. His peace plan, including his idea of a court, will be the subject of the next chapter, but as reference will be made to it from time to time in the present chapter, it is desirable to state the plan in its barest outline. Borah favored a world court entirely divorced from any political ties or obligations, a purely judicial court, which would have compulsory jurisdiction in all international cases. It would operate under a code of international law which would include among its provisions one making war a crime and individuals who bring on war international criminals. The judgments of the court would be enforced by the decent respect of mankind for the opinions of an international judicial tribunal.

Article 14 of the Covenant of the League of Nations provides that a World Court shall be established which "shall be competent to hear and determine any dispute of an international character which the parties thereto submit to it. The Court may also give an advisory opinion upon any dispute or question referred to it by the Council or by the Assembly."

The problem of how the judges for the Court should be selected, the problem over which framers of plans for other international courts had often racked their brains without success, was solved by this committee, at the suggestion of Mr. Root and Lord Phillimore, by the provision that each nation should be entitled to nominate four candidates and that the Council and the Assembly, each voting separately, should elect the judges from this list of nominees. Thus all nations had equal voice in making nominations, all had equal voice in voting in the Assembly, the great powers being given an advantage only in the Council, where they could control a majority of the votes.

It is generally conceded that this Court is more in the nature of a judicial body than any of its predecessors, the arbitral tribunals, had been. The courts of arbitration had been constituted for each case as it arose, the parties to the dispute choosing the judges. The World Court was given permanent judges who should hear all cases referred to it. Furthermore, there was more certainty as to the law to be applied in the new Court. Article 38 of the Court Statute reads as follows : "The Court shall apply : international conventions . . . establishing rules expressly recognized by the contesting states ; international custom, as evidence of a general practice accepted as law ; the general principles of law recognized by civilized nations ; . . . judicial decisions and the teachings of the most highly qualified publicists of the various nations, as subsidiary means for the determination of rules of law."

Considering the long devotion of the United States, as indicated both by theory and practice, to the judicial settlement of disputes between nations, it was expected that the United States would become a member of this World Court. After some fifteen years of discussion she is still not a member. The explanation of this is found in part in Borah's opposition to American membership.

Ten days after Borah introduced in the Senate his resolution calling for the outlawry of war and his international court, President Harding sent (February 24, 1923) a message to the Senate asking advice and consent to American adherence to the World Court Protocol. He suggested certain mild reservations which would render the United States "wholly free from any legal relation to the League." The President's message was accompanied by a letter from Secretary Hughes who strongly endorsed the Court and laid down four harmless reservations designed to free the United States from any possible entanglement with the League.

The Foreign Relations Committee was still the Committee which had ruined Wilson's League idea and it looked with suspicion upon any proposal which tended in that direction. But Borah announced his willingness to support the World Court proposal if the Court was to be governed by law and was to function essentially as the Supreme Court of the United States functioned.[1] The Supreme Court of this country has, of course, compulsory jurisdiction in cases between the states and it does not have, in the opinion of many authorities including Borah, any sanctions for enforcing its judgments in such cases other than the feeling by the states that they are morally bound to carry them out. Our Supreme Court is relatively free from ordinary political influence and entirely free from the obligation to give an "advisory opinion" upon the request of the President or Congress.

It did not take Borah long to decide that the World Court met none of these tests. He quickly concluded that none of the great powers, including the United States, were willing to trust themselves to the Court to the extent of giving it compulsory jurisdiction in their disputes, a jurisdiction they could give the Court by signing the "optional clause." With equal celerity he was able to conclude that, despite the assertions of the President and the Secretary of State, the Court was tied up with the League, a political body, and that the Court had force, all the force of the League, for its sanctions.

On April 11, 1923, Borah gave out this statement: "I am of the opinion when President Harding gets further along in the discussion of the League Court that he will conclude that he is in error when he contends that this Court does not take us into the League. . . There may, or may not, be sound reasons for going into the League, but no one can sustain the contention that by going into this Court we do not go into the League. The members of the Court are elected by the League. The vacancies in the Court are filled by the League. The Court has no existence, and can have no existence, except upon the initiative of the League. . .

"The Court is paid by the League. The League calls upon it for counsel and advice and the Court is bound to give that counsel and advice. When it comes to the League the Court is not a court at all, but simply an adviser and counsellor. Suppose that the League asks the Court for counsel upon a

[1] New York *Times*, February 26, 1923.

vital matter and we, as members of the Court, join in giving that counsel and advice and the League acts upon it, are we not bound by the action of the League and morally bound to carry out the program of the League?

". . . We would be members of the League for the purpose of the election [of Judges] and in that election almost every conceivable question of international concern will be involved. . ."

As President Harding got "further along in his discussion of the League Court," he did (June 21) exactly what Borah predicted he would do and what Borah and a few others forced him to do — he declared for complete divorcement of the Court from the League. This, he explained, could be done by empowering the Court itself to fill any vacancy arising from the death of a member or retirement for whatever cause, without interposition from any other body. Borah expressed his satisfaction with the progress the President was making in finding the light.

In opposing the League of Nations a few years earlier the Senator had been frank in stating his opposition to any kind of league whatsoever. He had admitted that certain types of leagues might be much less objectionable than others, but he had strongly advised all those opposing the Wilson plan to stick to that and not be drawn into a discussion of various forms of leagues; otherwise their attack would lose most of its force. The Senator, however, believed in an international tribunal so sincerely that he presented over and over his own plan in opposing American membership in the World Court. Lest we lose sight of it, his plan is repeated: codify international law; as part of that code make war a crime; set up your court with compulsory jurisdiction; and let the opinion of enlightened peoples enforce its decisions.

"You do believe in a world court, so why will you not compromise and take the one you can get in the place of the one you want but can't get?" he was often asked. In one such letter a minister suggested that the Framers of the Constitution had been willing to compromise. "You say that I ought to compromise," replied the Senator. "I am perfectly willing to compromise, so long as I do not . . . sacrifice what I believe to be fundamental principles essential to the cause of peace." The Senator knew the Fathers had a reply ready for the statement that they had compromised at the Philadelphia Convention. He quoted Washington who said : "If to please the people we offer what we ourselves disapprove, how can we afterwards defend our work ?" In referring to this minister's letter he remarked to a friend that the minister would doubtless be unwilling to compromise on "light wines and beer."

But Borah was willing to take less than his own plan for a court. He wrote a friend on June 11, 1924, that he would support adherence to the World Court if it could be completely divorced from political control. His opinion was that even when it was freed of all political connection with the League it would still be relatively ineffective as an instrument of peace, but that in time, when international law was codified and when all the powers were members and were accepting compulsory jurisdiction, it might be made effective.

At the time (December, 1924) Borah became Chairman of the Committee on Foreign Relations, practically nothing had been done with the World Court proposal, despite the fact that it had been before the Committee for nearly two years. President Coolidge had favored American adherence, with the Hughes reservations, in his first message to Congress and now, following his election, he repeated the endorsement, adding, however, a reservation to the effect that the United States should not be bound by any advisory opinion of the Court upon any question which the United States had not voluntarily submitted. Borah stated, on December 6, that he was quite willing, even anxious, to bring the matter before the Senate. He said, however, that the appropriation bills and agricultural legislation should have right of way, and there was a strong implication in his statement that these matters would consume nearly all of the short session. He stated further that it would take some time to work out a plan which would divorce the Court from the League. The Court proposal was not reached in this session. There was a great deal of comment, much of it indignant, at the manner in which a few Senators could obstruct the known will of the vast majority of the American people.

In the special session of the Senate called immediately after the inauguration of Coolidge, Senator Swanson (March 5) introduced a resolution for American adherence subject to the four simple conditions originally proposed by Secretary Hughes and the later additional one suggested by President Coolidge. By a vote of 77 to 2 the Senate agreed to consider the Swanson resolution on December 17, 1925.

Borah considered the suggested reservations wholly inadequate. The judges would still be elected by the League and the Court would still be an adviser to the League. He continued to say that international law must be codified before a court could function properly. In an address before the American Society of International Law, Mr. Hughes, no longer Secretary of State but still actively interested in the World Court, said that those who oppose adherence to the Court until such time as we have precise international law "have objections of that academic character which put hurdles in the way of Progress." This was understood to be a reference to the Senator from Idaho. Mr. Hughes continued: "I should say that the work of such a Court would be the best assurance that we should have that development." [2]

During the summer and fall of 1925, Borah continued, in various public addresses, to state his objections to the World Court and to explain to his audiences his ideal of an international court of justice. His leading addresses were in Boston and Chicago.[3] The Chicago *Evening Post* examined his speech in that city in a critical but not hostile spirit.[4] It expressed absolute accord with the Senator in his plan to promote peace but could not associate itself with him in his seeming desire to await the arrival of the perfect. "Civilization did not evolve that way. It did not sit in darkness waiting for Edison to create light from electricity. It groped its way with candles and oil lamps and, for a long time, did it better with gas, until the incandescent film emerged from the Wizard's laboratory."

The *Post* did not deny for one moment that the Senator was correct in his contention that the League created the Court. But it criticized him for not telling his audience that a very

[2] April 23, 1925.

[3] Before the Unitarian Laymen's League, Boston, May 11, 1925, and before the Woman's Roosevelt Republican Club, Chicago, October 20, 1925.

[4] Chicago *Evening Post,* October 22, 1925.

similar plan for a court had been approved in all essentials at The Hague in 1907 and that it failed of adoption only because there was no agreement upon the method of electing judges. To the Senator's objection to the League function of fixing the judges' salaries, the *Post* argued that they had to be fixed by some authority and observed that a political body (Congress) fixes the salaries of our Federal judges without noticeably undermining the independence of the courts.

In all his speeches against the Court the Senator dwelt at some length upon the fact that the League was authorized to ask the Court for advisory opinions. The *Post* was of the opinion that "he conveyed the impression that this was an unheard of thing in the function of courts; but he must know that the Supreme Court of Massachusetts, under the Constitution of the State, exercises this function for the legislature of Massachusetts; and no ill has resulted to either court or legislature so far as we have heard." This journal might have mentioned five or six other states which followed the same practice and might even have noted that so strong a constitutionalist as Mr. James M. Beck had recommended that the Supreme Court be empowered to give advisory opinions on the constitutionality of proposed legislation.[5]

The *Post* criticized the Senator for not stating that in one instance – the Eastern Carelian case – the Court declined to give an advisory opinion. The paper quoted Judge John Bassett Moore, "whom the Senator quoted more than once when it suited him," on the Carelian case, as follows: "What was done in this case plainly shows that the Court was acting as an independent judicial body; but when I say this, I do not want the inference to be drawn that the Court understood itself to be resisting any pressure whatsoever in the matter. There was none."

In a letter to a judge in Idaho the Senator had written: "I am frank to say that I have never known nor ever heard of such sordid, corrupt, and thoroughly financed propaganda as is going on in regard to the World Court. They think they see, and they do see, an opportunity to put us into the League of Nations." In his Chicago speech he made a similar assertion regarding propaganda and charged that the friends of the

[5] *Time,* December 29, 1924, p. 4.

Court were suppressing certain facts. The *Post* admitted that the charge might be true. "The Senator's manner of argument is an example of how it can be done."

The *Post's* editorial concluded: "Senator Borah does not persuade us that we should decline to subscribe to the Court Protocol. . . He holds before our eyes the vision of an ideal court, but he does not tell us how we are to get it, how it is to be established, how its judges are to be named, who is to pay them. He takes us back to the situation which baffled the wise men at The Hague in 1907, and proposes no solution for the problem which they failed to solve. We are as eager to realize the ideal as he. We believe it will be realized more surely and more speedily by accepting the Court as it is, and introducing as opportunity serves these modern improvements which, with the Senator, we regard as much to be desired."

One is bound to admit that a number of the *Post's* criticisms of Borah's presentation of the case against the Court were well founded. But who, in opposing a policy in a public address in a great auditorium, is going to bring out points in favor of the other side? It is simply not done, and it is not done for the very plain reason that the argument is lost before a popular audience if too much is admitted. Borah was out to defeat American adherence to the World Court. He believed that was the first thing to be accomplished in getting his own peace plan adopted, a plan, let it again be recalled, which he had presented to the Senate before President Harding proposed that America become a member of the World Court. In fights in which honest and patriotic men are on either side (and there are few issues on which the sheep are all on one side and the goats on the other) each side is quite likely, and not without some basis, to charge the other with not telling the whole story, or with misrepresenting the case.

With the Court issue coming before the Senate in December, 1925, a group of thirty-eight famous men wrote Borah on November 30 that he should not try to block consideration of the Court Protocol since at least two-thirds of the Senators and a large majority of the people favored it. The Senator replied that they were League people and that he could not accept them as advisers. He promised, however, that his ef-

Courtesy of the Philadelphia Record

forts against the Court would be only in the direction of separating it wholly from the League. Whiting observed in his column in the Boston *Herald* that the thirty-eight distinguished men had said the same thing about public approval of the Court that had been said about public approval of the League in 1919. He raised the interesting question : Can Borah win a sufficient number of Senators away from the Court to defeat it ? He was waiting eagerly to see how much opposition Borah could develop.

The Senator's files were filled with protests and entreaties over his position on the Court. Occasionally he received a communication commending his position, but the bulk of his mail was in commendation of the Court. *Unity* of December 14 carried these significant lines : "The Churches, the colleges, women's clubs, public mass meetings, etc., are being mightily stirred by vague appeals to peace idealism to support the Court. Against this flood of noble but ignorant fervor stands Senator Borah . . . equipped with his superb ability as a lawyer, orator and creative statesman, convinced of the ineffectiveness of the existing Court to accomplish any works of peace, stirred by the vision of the opportunity now before America to use her present strategic influence to lead the world to a peace that shall endure. Senator Borah has the facts, the prophetic vision to understand these facts, the intellectual power to interpret them, the political position to use them. In spite of all signs to the contrary, the campaign for the Court is doomed to failure unless conducted on very different lines from those forecasted at this hour."

The day after the Court question was opened for discussion in the Senate, Mr. Borah spoke in opposition to American adherence, basing his objections, in this particular speech, entirely upon the relationship the Court bore to the League of Nations. He did this with considerable skill, proving the connection of the Court with the League from the writings of friends of both. He quoted Judges de Bustamente and Loder, Sir Eric Drummond, Sir Robert Horn, M. Leon Bourgeois, Mr. Root, former Governor Sweet, and many others.[6]

In a later speech on January 22, 1926, he explained in some detail his other chief objection to the Court, the objection to the Court's sanctions of force. He opened by paying a strong tribute to Wilson, who was opposed to the European idea of preserving peace by force and who fought valiantly but vainly for his principle against the old-school diplomats of Europe. He quoted from continental authorities to prove that the old law of force against which Wilson had protested was still the law of European powers; that these nations insisted the League should be a League with force behind it, force which should be used against a nation which did not observe its decrees; and that the sanctions of the Court were the same as the sanctions of the League, that is, that the judgments of the Court might be enforced in extreme cases by armies and

[6] *Record,* December 18, 1925.

navies. This was abhorrent to Borah. The United States Supreme Court had no such sanctions in enforcing its judgments in cases between the states, a designed omission on the part of the framers of the Constitution the wisdom of which the years have attested over and over. The states, with the approval or demand of the people, have simply accepted these judgments. If the idea of force behind the decree of the Supreme Court is intolerable to the states of the Union, how much more intolerable is the idea that force should be used in carrying out the judgments of an international tribunal against sovereign nations of the world? Madison said that force against a state of the Union would amount to a declaration of war. Would not force against an independent nation most certainly constitute a declaration of war? Force is incompatible with peace and justice between the nations. Behind the sanction of force, for whatever purpose it may be used, is the specter of war. Let the Court have no other sanction than that of the "force" of enlightened public opinion throughout the civilized world. This was the tenor of his argument.

Borah had no hope of preventing the Senate from giving its consent to the ratification of the Protocol, but he wished to put himself on record against a political court and a court which had the sanctions of armed force. He offered reservations to ensure these points, the one providing that no advisory opinions be given by the Court, without the consent of the United States on questions in which the United States has an interest, being adopted by the Senate as a fifth reservation. There are those who claim that had the Senate left the matter open to debate, Borah would have won enough support to defeat the proposal. The later history of the Court issue in the United States gives considerable ground for this opinion. But cloture was invoked and the Senate voted (January 27, 1926) 76 to 17 for membership in the World Court subject to five reservations.

Relative to Borah's part in the World Court debate, the British "Round Table," in an article, "Senator Borah and Freedom of the Seas," makes this statement: "It was painfully clear that Senator Borah, who led the opposition, had read the Statute of the Court and was familiar with its decisions. He knew so much more about the subject than the supporters of the Court that he reduced them to confusion." [7]

But ratification did not end the campaign as far as Borah and a few others were concerned. Two days after the Protocol was accepted, the Idahoan wrote a friend in Boise: "It seems to me that a fair construction of the resolution with the reservations as passed would leave no doubt as to the fact that the proponents of the Court wholly abandoned their first position. . . As the thing is now, the Court, as a Court, is utterly worthless. The most objection I have to it is that while they were willing to destroy the Court [presumably the reference is to the reservation that the Court shall give no advisory opinions in cases in which the United States has or claims an interest without the consent of the United States] they were not willing to separate the institution, whatever it may be called, from the League.

"Of course, as Austin Chamberlain said this morning in his interview from London, it is only the first step. They have determined, Charley, to put this country into Europe. . . Hundreds of thousands, and even millions, of dollars will be expended for that purpose. A more wicked, corrupt, deceitful propaganda was never carried on than was carried on for this Court and will be renewed tenfold to get us formally and technically into the League.

"I hope my friends at home will understand that I must give every ounce of energy and ability I have to this cause from now on. . .

"I received the telegram from the group to which you refer but, of course, I paid no attention to it. I know the Leaguist whenever I see him or hear from him."

Times had been only tolerable, politically speaking, with the former Mayor William Hale Thompson for the past three years. He was now grooming Colonel Frank L. Smith as a senatorial candidate in the hope of displacing McKinley and incidentally he was warming himself up for the next mayoralty race in Chicago. Since McKinley was a World Court man, it seemed to the Thompson-Crow-Barrett organization that nothing could serve their cause better than a good anti-

[7] *Round Table,* March, 1929.

Court speech by Borah under their auspices. Still full of wrath for the Senate for putting on cloture in the World Court debate, Borah was pleased to accept the invitation to celebrate the birthday of the father of his country by delivering an address in Chicago. Thompson had the Congressional salute of seventeen guns fired for Borah; he put him in a parade which was estimated to have been thirty-five miles in length; he reserved for him the presidential suite at the Sherman, where Frank L. Smith called to see him; and he had a great banquet served, at which the Senator, already somewhat irritated by the pretentiousness of his quarters, passed up the banquet fare for a little chicken salad. The speech was all the Thompson crowd had hoped for. At the auditorium the Senator and Thompson were given ovation after ovation. On all sides the affair was pronounced a great success. McKinley was badly scared.

The Senator denies that he went to Illinois and later to Wisconsin for the specific purpose of defeating McKinley and Lenroot, and it may have been true, as the New York *Times* put it, that these two Senators were already dead and could not be killed deader.[8] But if they were dead and buried, the Senator from Idaho may be said to have thrown a few more shovelfuls of dirt on their political graves. The *Times*, always supporting the League and the Court, also stated that, having slain a dead Senator, the opponents of the Court would then claim his destruction as a wonderful repudiation of the World Court. When Smith defeated McKinley, Borah declared (April 14): "It's a magnificent thing that the great State in which sleep the ashes of Abraham Lincoln leads out in the fight to be rid of foreign entanglements."

Secretary of State Kellogg sent (March 2, 1926) the Senate resolution to the Secretary General of the League and the signatories of the Court Protocol, requesting that he be informed in writing whether they would accept the American reservations. The Council of the League decided to call a conference of the signatory powers for the purpose of considering the reservations. The United States was invited to attend this conference, but declined to do so, the Secretary of State writing that the reservations were "plain and unequivo-

[8] New York *Times*, February 26, 1926.

cal" and that they must be accepted by the forty-eight signatories before the United States could become a member of the Court.

The conference of signatory powers had no particular difficulty in approving four of the American reservations and the first part of the fifth, but the second part of the fifth reservation caused trouble. It read : "Nor shall it [the Court] without the consent of the United States, entertain any request for an advisory opinion touching any dispute or question in which the United States has or claims an interest." The conference could not believe that it meant exactly what it said, for this would give the American Government the power to prevent the Court from giving any advisory opinion. The Conference wanted a supplementary and clarifying agreement on this provision, but President Coolidge, perhaps sensing that reaction had set in against the Court, insisted that no further negotiation was necessary, that the meaning of the reservation was perfectly clear — as clear as he thought his later announcement, "I do not choose to run," should have been to the American people.

Here the question of American adherence to the Court rested for some time, giving Borah an opportunity to press his own peace plan, which was put through in 1928, in a greatly modified form as the Pact for the Renunciation or Outlawry of War.

With this Peace Pact signed and ratified by practically all nations and with a committee of jurists examining the Statute of the World Court for the purpose of proposing necessary amendments thereto, the time seemed propitious to Secretary Kellogg in February, 1929, to reopen the question of American membership in the Court. The "Root Plan" was the result of this overture. Under this Plan a way was provided by which the United States would be advised of a request upon the Court for an advisory opinion and the manner defined in which the United States should state its approval or objection to the giving of such opinion. Its most significant provision was that the United States might withdraw from the Court if the League, after consideration, decided that the United States did not actually have an interest in a case in which it had objected to an advisory opinion.

Senator Borah could not accept the Root Plan. "An examination of the present formula," he wrote, "will disclose that reservation five has been wholly emasculated. Sir Cecil Hurst eliminated the provisions of the original Root formula which preserved reservation five. As the matter now stands, the advisory jurisdiction is admitted, it stands unimpaired, and the League may call for the exercise of this jurisdiction upon any subject or dispute which may arise or any controversy. The sole remedy we have left is to finally get out of the Court. In other words, we are to burn down the house in order to make sure our escape, and even then we may get badly hurt. After we get out of the Court, the Court goes forward and renders its opinion upon the particular subject matter which caused our departure." [9]

In the fall of 1929 Attorney S. O. Levinson, who had worked with Borah so long on the plan for the outlawry of war and who had agreed with Borah in his reasons for opposing the Court in 1926, wrote Borah that, with the ratification of the Outlawry Pact and with the presentation of the Root formula for American membership in the Court, he assumed the Senator was now ready to support American membership. He took the precaution, however, of stating that he had never undertaken to present Borah's views on a subject unless he heard them from his own lips. C. C. Morrison, editor of the *Christian Century,* also a valiant worker with Borah for outlawry of war, wrote Borah about the same time Levinson did. He said it was reported in the Chicago *Tribune* that the Senator would lead the opposition in the renewed fight for the ratification of the World Court Protocols. He expressed his indignation that a writer should take the liberty of making such a statement, since he (Morrison) knew that the Senator could now support American membership in the Court! These letters are interesting because they reveal that the Senator's friends and co-workers could not predict his position on the question as presented in 1929. Borah restated his objections, as indicated above, to the Root formula in his kindly letters to these friends and he explained that the friends of peace should be content to go slowly.

President Hoover and Secretary of State Stimson recom-

[9] New York *Sun,* April 12, 1929.

mended the ratification of the protocols, but the Senate took no action upon them during the Hoover Administration. Popular interest in the Court died down. Borah's hostility to it mounted, however, when he heard of the Court's opinion on the proposed Austro-German Customs Union in September, 1931. This was an advisory opinion in which the Court held, eight to seven, that the proposed customs union would be in violation of the Financial Protocol of 1922, which obliged Austria to "abstain from any negotiations or form any economic or financial engagement calculated directly or indirectly to compromise [its] independence." There was a great deal of comment to the effect that the former Allies had managed to get the Court to pass upon a political question and in a manner favorable to those opposed to the economic recovery of the Central Powers. The Senator felt sure that this was the case. When the opinion was announced, the Senator said he was not ready to make any statement until he had read the entire opinion. "I want to see," he wrote the New York *Sun,* "by what miserable sophistry they justify such an opinion."

The country as a whole continued its disinterest in the Court, although there were a number of organizations which sought constantly to have it brought up for consideration in the Senate. In January, 1935, the Court issue was probably the deadest political issue in the land. President Roosevelt suggested that the Senate proceed to give its consent to the ratification of the Court Protocols which had been awaiting its action for nearly six years. It was very generally assumed that only Senators Borah and Hiram Johnson and a few other bitter-enders not so well known would vote in opposition. Then Mr. Hearst got into action through his string of papers and in particular through John A. Kennedy, his number-one Washington representative on this issue, and James T. Williams, Jr., chief editorial writer for Hearst papers. Father Charles E. Coughlin concluded an anti-Court radio address by reciting the 83d Psalm, which, with his interpolations, reads in part as follows: "O God . . . thy enemies have made a noise. . . They have said: Come and let us destroy them, so that they may not be a nation, and let the name of Israel (America) be remembered no more. For they have contrived with one consent: they have made a covenant (League of Nations) against thee."

The Father urged his countless hearers to wire their Senators to vote against the Court. They did. Telegrams were received in great batches at the Senate office building. Fifty extra telegraph clerks had to be hired. When the Senate had voted, it stood 52 for and 36 against ratification, seven votes short of the required two-thirds majority. Fifteen Senators wired their congratulations to Father Coughlin.

Senator Borah declared that this vote of rejection was the most important Senate action since the World War.[10] He denies that last-minute propaganda defeated the Court issue, maintaining that few, if any, Senators switched sides on account of it.

These things may safely be said of Borah's opposition to the World Court: *First,* he was absolutely sincere in his opposition.

Second, His opposition was primarily on the grounds that the Court was connected with the League, that it was subject to political control, and that it had the sanction of force.

Third, he was not opposed to an international court, to one which would be strictly judicial in character, which would have compulsory jurisdiction, and whose judgments would be enforced by the honor of nations and the conscience of their citizens. But since so many authorities think the Senator's court would be impossible of attainment, except by gradual progress, they consider that his position, in effect, amounted to opposition to any practicable international court.

Fourth, the stand the Senator took was thoroughly approved by jingoes, militarists, and seekers after war profits. With the idealism of the Senator they had nothing to do, with his proposed court they would certainly have nothing to do, but in playing such a large part in defeating these Court Protocols, weak and ineffective as the Court might be, he was absolutely their man.

[10] This story of the defeat of the World Court Protocols in 1935 is well told in *Time,* February 11, 1925.

CHAPTER XX

A VENTURE IN IDEALISM

"Let us proclaim absolute truths. Let us dishonor war." These words were spoken by Victor Hugo at the grave of Voltaire. They contain the germ of the principle which animated a little group of talented, industrious, unselfish, and determined idealists in their campaign to outlaw war.

In March 1918, in the days when the League to Enforce Peace was being so attractively presented by William H. Taft and so earnestly and eloquently discussed by Henry Cabot Lodge and when the proper organization and procedure of such a League were common topics of consideration in fashionable drawing-rooms, before bar associations, and at teachers' conventions, an attorney of Chicago, Mr. Salmon O. Levinson, wrote an article for the *New Republic,* entitled "The Legal Status of War." "War," declared Levinson, "comes under the sanction of international law." Any war, no matter how unjustifiable, is a "legal war." International law assumes that there must be wars and attempts to lay down rules for their conduct. The defect of this proposed League to Enforce Peace, stated Levinson, is that "it does not propose to declare war illegal ; it proposes simply to refine those regulations under which war is legal ; to increase the preliminary ceremonies which must be gone through in order that the benediction of legality may descend upon a war." Levinson suggested that instead of laws *of* war we should have laws *against* war ; war should be made illegal. "War, though made illegal, might still conceivably occur but it would be branded as a crime and the force of the world would be organized to deal with the criminal." Differences between nations must be settled by an international court, backed by force to execute its decrees. "In the course of time the very existence of a tribunal where all international wrongs may be redressed would render the great force behind it protective and merely potential, like the force now behind our national and state tribunals." These were the essential points in Levinson's article.

In discussing the proposed League of Nations Covenant in the spring of 1919, Senator Knox had asked the question: [1] "Do its provisions abolish war and make it hereafter impossible?" Then he cited a number of its provisions which recognized war and still other provisions which might even require war under certain circumstances. "Instead of abolishing war," he concluded, the Covenant "actually sanctions, breeds, and commands it." This Senator said he would go far and risk much to abolish war, and he gave Mr. Levinson invaluable aid on his project. But Senator Knox died before the question had been publicly presented.

Five other pioneers in the movement should be given special mention. They are Colonel Raymond Robins, Professor John Dewey, the Reverend John Haynes Holmes, Doctor Charles Clayton Morrison, editor of the *Christian Century*, and Professor James T. Shotwell. Robins, the advocate and orator for the Outlawry of War, traveled in thirty states. His part was significant for another reason – he had a tremendous influence with Senator Borah. Doctor Morrison added his voice and pen to the cause, sharing with Colonel Robins and the Reverend Holmes the credit for popularizing the movement with the church people and a large section of non-church people while Levinson was reaching key men.

Professor Dewey not only gave the weight of his name to the theory of outlawry, but he was also one of its most active supporters from its earliest stages. He added his voice to those of Levinson and Robins in urging Borah to give political leadership to the cause. Nor was Dewey any stranger to Borah. For a long time before this particular movement was initiated the Statesman had been reading the Philosopher with pleasure and profit.

Of the men not in public life who pushed the outlawry movement, no one except Mr. Levinson worked at it more persistently than Professor James T. Shotwell of Columbia University. He was later in coming to the idea than was Levinson and the plans of the two men as they were finally worked out differed, the lawyer opposing the use of force to make outlawry effective and the professor earnestly contending that this "sanction" was necessary. The two men seldom

[1] *Record*, March 1, 1919, p. 4690.

saw eye to eye. They were in accord at only one time and then for but a short period. They and their respective followers agreed in 1925 to join in supporting outlawry of war and the World Court. Two months later President Coolidge proposed American membership in the World Court but said nothing about outlawry of war. The Shotwell group, favoring the Court, with or without outlawry, withdrew from the agreement. Despite their incapacity to work together, both Shotwell and Levinson are entitled to credit for the Pact of Paris, which was the culmination of their somewhat divergent efforts.

Mr. Levinson had explained his idea to Senator Borah while Senator Knox was still alive, but he had relied primarily upon the Pennsylvania Senator to promote his plan at the Capitol. With the passing of Senator Knox, Levinson and Robins (an early "convert" to and ever after an indefatigable worker for the outlawry of war) came to Borah and urged him to champion the cause.

The Senator was greatly interested, but one point in the Levinson plan disturbed him. That was the provision that force should be used by the law-abiding nations against a nation which went to war. Borah refused to endorse the plan unless that feature could be eliminated. Robins agreed with Borah on this point, but Levinson "stuck by his guns" for some time. Robins and Levinson went to Doctor James Brown Scott, who took Robins' view that force should not be used. Levinson was still unconvinced and once he and Robins, in the figurative language of the latter, "almost came to blows" in a taxicab over their differences. Borah pulled down Farrand's Records of the Philadelphia Convention and turned to the debates relative to the use of force against a state of the American Union. The three, Borah, Levinson, and Robins, went through the arguments of Hamilton, Madison, and Ellsworth against any such sanction for the Federal authority. The wisdom of the Fathers brought the three idealists to agreement : the sanction of Outlawry would be the compelling power of public opinion.

Mr. Levinson wrote Senator Borah in December, 1921, warning him that Hughes and Coolidge would get us into the League if they dared and that Harding was only mildly opposing it. Now is the time to push outlawry, urged the Chicago attorney. The beauty of it is that there can be no compromise in it and everyone can understand it. Borah replied that as far as he could see he was in accord with their plan, but he did not now have time to give it the study he felt it needed. He did, however, on January 19, 1922, have Mr. Levinson's plan printed as a Senate Document (S.115).

In the spring of 1922 Colonel Robins went over the country announcing that Senator Borah would lead the movement for the outlawry of war. The Senator and Mr. Levinson were busy preparing the proposal for presentation in the form of a Senate resolution. "The only point of any consequence that has been raised against our outlawry plan," wrote Levinson to Borah (June 12), "relates to the power of the International Court in criminal cases. . . The question has been asked, as to how the International Court would handle an international lawbreaker or war criminal. It has been suggested that if the Court has the power to extradite and punish officials of a given country, as for example, the President of the United States, such power would be tantamount to a super-state. . .

". . . I still object as much as you do to any form of super-state, if it is humanly possible to avoid it and still get rid of war, and, of course, Knox entertained the same view. On careful analysis, I find the 'risk' to be not at all necessary." (Senator Knox had stated in March, 1919, that he would "risk" much to abolish war.)

Levinson then referred Borah to that provision of the Constitution which empowers Congress "to define and punish piracies and felonies committed on the high seas *and offenses against the law of nations.*"

"This power has been sparingly exercised," Levinson continued, "largely because we have had no real law of nations. . . What the world needs is International Law created 'for an assured and permanent state of peace.' Striving for such a state of peace, through the outlawry of war, we find already resident in Congress the power to handle war criminals. Perhaps the jurisdiction should be limited in each country to its own offenders. As outlawry is a people's movement, it should be their business to see to the punishment of their own international criminals. . .

"The responsibility for good faith should be with the people themselves as our whole proposition rests upon the major premise that 95 per cent of the civilized people of the world are against the bloody institution of war.

"What we are doing today in this country is not greatly different. We are prosecuting war profiteers; that is, war criminals. If there is a difference between this class of criminals and those that foment, promote, and initiate war, it can only be a difference in degree, not of kind. . .

"The foregoing argument is merely defensive and serves to relieve the timid mind of the fetish of inviolate sovereignty which traditionally holds so many minds in a vise. . .

"I have taken considerable pains with this matter, because . . . it is the only proposition that might conceivably be broached as a point of departure from your position on the League. . .

"Our program as distinguished from the League of Nations is not based upon preponderance of power or alliances, or any qualities of force. It is based upon the peaceful organization of the civilized nations under a reign of law, evidenced by a comprehensive code and administered by the greatest court which the world can produce. The concept of force behind the court, even if it exists, is entirely secondary. For example, our own national affairs are based upon law and not upon force, although in all except the jurisdiction over states, force is behind the courts. It is largely potential and protective. But, as I have said, the necessity for international force is altogether obviated in our program."

A few weeks later Borah wrote Levinson: "Hot as it was I spent a couple of hours last night working over and working on the resolution with reference to the outlawry of war. I have been working at it at different times for the last two or three weeks. The more I deal with the subject the more I am interested in the principle."

Then he came to the point of his letter: "We propose to make war a crime and then to provide punishment for it. Suppose we make war a crime and a nation like Germany, or Japan, begins war, how are you going to punish that nation except by war? You know Burke said you can't indict a whole nation. And if we resort to war to punish a nation which has gone to war, we are right back where we are now — settling war by war. Now the thing we must settle is: How we are going to give sanction to our international code when it has incorporated into it that war is a crime? You can't bring a nation into court, and besides, it might not pay any attention to your court, and likely wouldn't."

This was Borah's suggested solution: "Can we reach this proposition . . . by declaring war to be a crime and then punishing individuals who are responsible for the making of war, the declaring of war? We have made dueling a crime, but there we punish the individual. We have made piracy a crime, but there we punish the individual. Now, can we make war a crime, and in order to make punishment successful, confine it to the individuals who are responsible for beginning the war? If so, how would you express this in your resolution? And must we not express it in the resolution, or it will be immediately said that we do not get anywhere."

Levinson's reply, soon forthcoming, gave the Senator some material which helped him give affirmative answers to the questions he had raised. His suggestion was that each nation should obligate itself to punish its own war criminals.

But the most interesting parts of Levinson's letter treated of other points connected with outlawry. "I have been at infinite pains," he said, "not only to enlist the coöperation of pro-Leaguers, but to convince them that until the League abandons its basis of force and accepts the theory of Outlawry, they ought not to lend it further support. It would be false modesty not to say that I have met with large and unexpected success in this line."

Then this warm friend of the Senator became personal. "Great as your rising fame is there seems to be a general criticism that you are always in the opposition and that you have done nothing really constructive. To this I immediately retort that you are the single author of the Washington Conference with its attendant momentum for disarmament and peace. But somehow people usually follow the fortunes of men in [executive] power and office and have largely forgotten your contribution, because you, as well as Knox, were insufferably and inexcusably ignored.

"Therefore I do not want you to treat this Outlawry matter as my own resolution in any sense. I feel in my heart of hearts that this will furnish you a great constructive issue that will disarm such political enemies as you made in the League fight. . . An intimate friend of mine in Boston said to me the other day : 'If Borah presents this resolution, he will deliver a wholesome shock to the country because most people, including myself, have thought of him as opposed to any international peace project.' "

Levinson explained that he had made considerable progress with his idea abroad, especially in England, as well as in America. He mentioned letters of endorsement he had received from men of standing, including one from Judge John Bassett Moore.

"Suppose you present your Resolution and make your speech on the very day (July 29) of the International 'No More War' demonstration ?" suggested Levinson. "It is an impulsive idea, but impresses me strongly."

But Borah was not ready yet. He continued to work and rework his resolution. When he had completed it he sent copies to such men as Doctor James Brown Scott, director of the Division of International Law of the Carnegie Endowment for International Peace and Mark Sullivan, asking for their comments and criticisms.

On February 14, 1923, ten days before the Harding-Hughes proposal for adherence to the World Court was presented to the Senate, Borah introduced his resolution.[2] It is deemed advisable to reproduce it in full :

Whereas war is the greatest existing menace to society and has become so expensive and destructive that it not only causes the stupendous burdens of taxation now afflicting our people but threatens to engulf and destroy civilization ; and

Whereas civilization has been marked in its upward trend out of barbarism into its present condition by the development of law and courts to supplant methods of violence and force ; and

Whereas the genius of civilization has discovered but two meth-

[2] *Ibid.*, February 14, 1923, p. 3605.

ods of compelling the settlement of human disputes, namely, law and war, and therefore in any plan for the compulsory settlement of international controversies we must choose between war on the one hand and the process of law on the other ; and

Whereas war between nations has always been and still is a lawful institution ; so that any nations may, with or without cause, declare war against any other nation and be strictly within its legal rights ; and

Whereas revolutionary wars, or wars of liberation, are illegal and criminal, to-wit ; high treason, whereas under existing international law wars of aggression between nations are perfectly lawful ; and

Whereas the overwhelming moral sentiment of civilized people everywhere is against the cruel and destructive institution of war ; and

Whereas all alliances, leagues, or plans which rely upon force as the ultimate power for the enforcement of peace carry the seeds either of their own destruction or of military dominancy to the utter subversion of liberty and justice ; and

Whereas we must recognize the fact that resolutions, or treaties, outlawing certain methods of killing will not be effective so long as war itself remains lawful, and that in international relations we must have not rules and regulations of war but organic laws against war ; and

Whereas in our Constitutional Convention of 1787 it was successfully contended by Madison and Hamilton that the use of force when applied to people collectively — that is, to States or Nations, was unsound in principle and would be tantamount to a declaration of war ; and

Whereas we have in our Federal Supreme Court a practical and effective model for a real international court, as it has specific jurisdiction to hear and decide controversies between our sovereign States ; and

Whereas our Supreme Court has exercised this jurisdiction without resort to force for 135 years, during which time scores of controversies have been judicially and peaceably settled that otherwise might have led to war between the States, and thus furnishes a practical exemplar for the compulsory and pacific settlement of international controversies ; and

Whereas an international arrangement of such judicial character would not shackle the independence or impair the sovereignty of any nation : Now, therefore, be it

Resolved, That it is the view of the Senate of the United States that war should be outlawed as an institution or means for the settlement of international controversies by making it a public crime under the law of nations, and that every nation should be encouraged by solemn agreement or treaty to bind itself to indict and punish its own international war breeders or instigators and war profiteers under powers similar to those conferred upon our Congress under Article I, section 8, of our Federal Constitution, which clothes the Congress with the power "to define and punish offenses against the law of nations" ; and be it further

Resolved, That a code of international law of peace based upon equality and justice between nations, amplified and expanded and adapted and brought down to date, should be created and adopted ;

Second. That a judicial substitute for war should be created (or if existing in part, adapted and adjusted) in the form or nature of an international court, modeled on our Federal Supreme Court in its jurisdiction over controversies between our sovereign States, such court to possess affirmative jurisdiction to hear and decide all purely international controversies as defined by the code or arising under treaties, and to have the same power for the enforcement of its decrees as our Federal Supreme Court, namely, the respect of all enlightened nations for judgments resting upon open and fair investigations and impartial decisions and the compelling power of enlightened public opinion.

A reading of this resolution makes it perfectly clear that Borah was desirous of going much further for peace than the League and World Court people were willing to go, or thought it advisable to try to go. He would outlaw war, provide a code of international law of peace, establish an international court of compulsory jurisdiction to decide all international controversies, and give that court, not the sanctions of force for the execution of its judgments, but the sanctions of "all enlightened nations for judgments resting upon open and fair investigations and impartial decisions . . . and the compelling power of enlightened public opinion." But in the confusion which arose over Borah's opposition to the World Court the great body of American people were fairly sure that Borah was opposed to any kind of international court or to any agreement for peace.

Borah, Levinson, Robins, and Morrison continued to press the cause of outlawry. Borah did not serve the cause by speeches alone. He had his newspaper interviews and not infrequently articles appeared over his signature. He did not always go as fast as the others wanted him to go, but he was no less devoted to the cause. His political instinct sometimes told him to remain quiet when his co-workers thought he should be making a "ringing declaration."

On April 22, 1924, Colonel Robins wrote Borah asking him to speak out strongly and clarify the public mind on outlawry. "Many have asked why you did not support Johnson, and whether or not you have abandoned your position of 1920. Others inquire why you do not support the President. I am eager that you should in a great statement in the Senate, show your position as fundamentally constructive, thus differing from the hopeless isolation of these repudiated Senators on the one hand, and from the futilities of Hughes, Pepper and Coolidge on the other. . ." The Senator replied that he wanted to do just what the Colonel suggested, but that he could not find language to tell him "how nerve-wracking and harrowing are the multitude of things which demand one's time and attention here."

Colonel Robins was asked to campaign for Coolidge in 1924. He said : "Nothing doing unless he will come out for the outlawry of war." But Coolidge satisfied him on this point and, as the Colonel puts it, he "went to bat for him." When the President, in his Armistice Day address following his election, expressed an interest in outlawry, Borah wrote Mr. Levinson as follows : "I suppose that you and Colonel Robins . . . are walking around in the clouds. Well, you are both certainly entitled to tremendous credit. I feel that the glory is his and yours."

The World Court issue of necessity took the greater part of Borah's time during 1925 and the first part of 1926, but, as recorded in the last Chapter, he mentioned his peace plan in a number of his speeches against the World Court.

He reintroduced his Resolution for Outlawry on December 9, 1926. This was after the excitement about the World Court had died down and after the Conference of signatory powers had indicated that the fifth of the American reservations to the Court Protocol could not be accepted without further negotiation.

Levinson and Robins continued to write Borah many letters, often letters urging him to go forward on outlawry. In February, 1927, the Colonel wrote a warm, vigorous letter earnestly asking him to undertake in the form of a Senate speech a major offensive against war. Borah replied : "Intuitively I arrive at conclusions with reference to speaking on these subjects and intuitively I feel that this would not get across at this time."

On February 9, 1927, Mr. Levinson wrote Senator Borah: "As you know Raymond is most eager to have a powerful authentic statement from you before your Resolution again becomes functus on March 4. He is worth any twenty men for us." Mr. Levinson urged the Senator to have a conference with him and the Colonel. The Senator wired that this would have to be deferred until after March 4, as every minute was occupied. Mr. Levinson then expressed his great fear that Colonel Robins would break with Borah on this account, but the Colonel remained steadfast, conceding the Senator's right to follow his own convictions. However, Mr. Levinson did not abandon his efforts to get Borah to make a speech on outlawry. On February 12, he wired that a statement from him would help Colonel Robins answer the charge of church people that outlawry was a dead issue; that after all, outlawry was just a red herring which had been used against the League and Court. A few days later came another wire from Levinson calling the Senator's attention to a statement by Irving Fisher to the effect that outlawry was politically dead. But Borah, finding no suitable time during the short session, made no speech.

But on April 6, 1927, the movement received a new impetus from the other side of the Atlantic. Professor James T. Shotwell, in his volume on *War as an Instrument of National Policy,* makes the statement that M. Briand's announcement on that date, that France stood ready to subscribe with the United States to an agreement to outlaw war, opens a new chapter in the world's history.[3] In view of the record made for outlawry in the United States before 1927, a record to which Professor Shotwell contributed a part, one is tempted to suggest that the chapter opens in America with Levinson, Borah, and others rather than in France with Briand. But certainly M. Briand and the man who put the words into his mouth, Professor Shotwell, are entitled to full credit for opening a new chapter on the outlawry of war.

The polite offer of M. Briand did not attract any particular

[3] Page 41.

attention in America until President Nicholas Murray Butler, in a notable letter to the New York *Times* (April 25), called upon America to consider the French offer.

After the Butler letter, Sherwood Eddy wired Borah asking if something could not be done about Briand's outlawry suggestion. The Senator wrote Eddy (April 29): "His idea of Outlawry is so utterly different from your idea and my idea of Outlawry that I could not seriously and conscientiously take hold of the matter. However, if there is anything which you think I could do or should do, I wish you would write me fully."

Senator Borah made his first public statement on the Briand proposal in a letter to the League of Nations Non-Partisan Association on May 6. In this letter he expressed his desire that the French Prime Minister put his proposal in the form of a treaty. A few days later the Senator delivered an address in Cleveland, Ohio, on our foreign relations. In response to the question from his audience — "Will you please state your alternative to our membership in the League of Nations for the lessening of the chances of war and for better international coöperation?" — the Senator replied: "M. Briand . . . has proposed that the United States and France enter into a treaty outlawing war, putting the ban of criminality upon war as an institution for the settlement of international disputes. Three [four] years ago I introduced a resolution in the Senate . . . providing for the outlawing of war between all nations, and I would take M. Briand's proposal to outlaw war between France and the United States and extend it to all nations . . . I would adopt a code of international law. In that code of international law I would declare that war, as an institution for the settlement of international disputes, is a criminal institution, and I would hold responsible under international law any individual or any groups of individuals who would bring on . . . war as these groups of individuals did bring on the world war." [4]

About the middle of May Borah received a letter written in Paris on May 7 by a man who requested the Senator not to give his name. But he gave the Senator exact information.

[4] Cleveland *Press*, May 10, 1927.

He said that it had occurred to him that the Senator might be interested in the Paris origin of the outlawry idea. "It was not that of M. Briand, but of an American professor . . . Mr. Shotwell, of Columbia University, who had been lecturing in Berlin, happened to pass through Paris. He mobilized the American press correspondents here and requested them to insert the outlawry of war paragraph in the Prime Minister's requested and anticipated message. They did so, and M. Briand obligingly repeated it to them, word for word, Mr. Shotwell's draft. Mr. Shotwell returned to the United States and his chief, Doctor Butler, wrote the well-known letter to the *Times* regarding a treaty.

". . . The friends of peace in the United States accept the idea at its face value, it appears. Here it is a source of mystification or of amusement. . . When the proposal is not laughed at, it is considered as a belated bid for an alliance, for the idea of American duty to France will not down. . ."

Naturally this letter did not reassure Borah, revealing as it did the hand of the internationalists and the Paris attitude. But Mr. Levinson had gone to the French capital to explain, as the chief exponent of Outlawry, what the Americans meant by the term. Late in May Professors James T. Shotwell and J. P. Chamberlain, of Columbia University, drafted a comprehensive treaty for the renunciation of war, arbitration, and conciliation. This draft received wide publicity in the United States and abroad. Mr. Levinson, in Paris, at the suggestion of *Quai d'Orsay,* drafted a much simpler treaty which received much less publicity. This Levinson draft was the one Briand and Leger used as a basis for their own, even more simple draft. It was presented to the United States on June 20. Its two articles of eight lines condemn war as an instrument of national policy, in the name of the people of the two countries, and pledge their governments to settle all disputes by pacific means.

Senator Borah regretted that the proposed treaty did not outlaw war but simply contained an agreement not to go to war — an entirely different thing. He was disappointed that there was no call for the codification of international law. He thought for a time that the next step was for the United States and France to call an international conference for the dual purpose of outlawing war and codifying international law. These points he made in a letter to Mr. Levinson shortly after Briand had submitted the treaty. Later, he decided that the treaty could do no possible harm, committed us to no sort of entanglements, and might be the first step toward his plan of outlawry. He concluded to see what could be done.

One of the standard books on American Diplomacy comments upon the fact that for six months after the French had submitted their proposed treaty the State Department "kept its own counsel, and maintained an air of mystery about the very existence of the proposal." [5] The following paragraphs may hold some explanation of this situation.

Colonel Robins, lunching with the President early in the summer, remarked in characteristic fashion : "Mr. President, you have immortality lying all around you in this proposal to outlaw war and you are doing nothing about it."

The President : "Well, the people are not interested in that proposition ; they probably think it is impractical."

The Colonel : "They ought to be interested, and it is practical, and I understood you were for it when I was campaigning for you in 1924." He continued to discuss the matter with the President until he agreed to speak to Secretary of State Kellogg about it.

But Secretary Kellogg, according to authorities, knew nothing about outlawry. Furthermore, he was too busy with other things, too worried about problems in Mexico and Nicaragua and the disarmament conference at Geneva, to take on the additional burden of outlawry of war. However, in June, Borah persuaded him to give Levinson an interview. After that Borah instructed the Secretary in outlawry. The Senator reported to Levinson in the summer of 1927 that he had had a difficult time with Kellogg but that he had finally succeeded in "making a dent." But later in the summer Borah wrote Levinson that Kellogg would never take any action on the proposal.

The advocates of outlawry had a great deal of press support and they continued their campaign even though the

[5] J. H. Latané, *History of American Foreign Policy* (Revised by D. W. Wainhouse), p. 747.

State Department was saying practically nothing. Borah succeeded in having the National Grange (membership about 800,000) endorse outlawry in a resolution which he had written for the organization. In a wire to the Armistice Celebration held by International House at the Hotel Astor in New York, on November 10, 1927, he made this very significant statement: "M. Briand has suggested the first step. Let us suggest the second and include Great Britain, Germany, and Italy. That would furnish a real foundation for outlawing war."

Thus, both in his speech in Cleveland on May 9 and in his wire to New York on November 10, Borah suggested that the Briand treaty be made a multilateral pact renouncing war. So far as is known, the extension of the Briand idea to include other nations originated with Borah. Indeed, Borah's resolution of 1923 had called for a multilateral agreement.

Yet the Secretary of State remained silent on the proposal to outlaw war, except to say that it was not a simple matter and that he did not care to discuss it. President Coolidge, despite his moment of generosity with Colonel Robins in the summer, was (November 25) saying that there was no short cut to peace. At this juncture Doctor Butler again defended the Briand proposal.[6] There was evidence that the university president was in advance of the President of the United States in judging public opinion on this question.

On December 22, 1927, Secretary Kellogg appeared before the Senate Committee on Foreign Relations for the ostensible purpose of getting the committee's reaction to a new arbitration treaty with France, a treaty which was to take the place of one made in 1908. This meeting is admirably described by Pearson and Brown in *The American Diplomatic Game,* a volume which is accepted as authoritative on the negotiations to renounce war.[7] In the preamble of the new arbitration treaty was a sentence "condemning" but not "outlawing" war. It was inserted for the purpose of disposing of the whole question of outlawry. The American State De-

[6] Drew Pearson and Constantine Brown, *The American Diplomatic Game,* pp. 26–27.

[7] *Ibid.,* pp. 27–28.

partment did not want to be troubled further with this "fanciful scheme" and the French wanted to drop it since its American sponsors now wanted a multilateral treaty renouncing war.

When the Secretary had explained his treaty to the committee and the committee had indicated its assent, Chairman Borah said : "But, Mr. Secretary, all this does not dispose of the proposal to outlaw war." The Secretary was displeased to have the old subject arise to plague him so soon. He said that this country did not want any alliance with France.

Borah persisted, urging that the Government should make a counter-proposal to France that all nations should join in a pact to outlaw war. For one reason or another every member of the committee agreed that such a counter-proposal was in order. The Chairman then advised the Secretary of State that it was the sense of the committee that the Secretary proceed with the negotiations on that basis.

On December 28, 1927, M. Briand received an answer to his proposal of June 20. Secretary Kellogg stated that "the two Governments, instead of contenting themselves with a bilateral declaration . . . might make a more signal contribution to world peace by joining in an effort to obtain the adherence of all of the principal powers of the world to a declaration renouncing war as an instrument of national policy." He suggested further that all powers might then subscribe to the treaty.

This proposal of a multilateral agreement was what the French had feared they would receive for an answer. The French reply came on January 5, 1928. The significant feature of it was in the suggestion that "all wars of aggression" be substituted for "war as an instrument of national policy." Borah and all other friends of outlawry insisted that no such substitution be accepted. No nation ever wages a war of "aggression." In any case, there is great difficulty in defining "aggression." Soon after the State Department received the French note Borah wrote Doctor Morrison that matters were going along very satisfactorily at the Washington end of the line, but he added : "I have not much faith in the other end of the line. Never have had. I trust I am to be surprised, however."

On January 11, the Secretary of State wrote the French Government, asking directly why it had changed the formula and inquiring if this change implied a change of purpose. The disappointing French reply to this note came ten days later. It raised the question of the obligation of France as a member of the League of Nations, as a party to the Locarno treaties and similar treaties relating to peace and neutrality, and asked if she could renounce war without contravening those obligations. This was a poser for the State Department. Mr. Levinson was in California at the time but he hurried to Washington, preparing en route suggestions for a reply to Briand. He had a conference with Senator Borah and presented his draft. Drawing heavily upon Levinson's draft, Borah answered the latest French note in a letter to the New York *Times*. His main point was that France, in fact, could not agree, in harmony with her commitments to Belgium and the Little Entente, to a bilateral treaty with the United States, agreeing never to go to war with us. The reason was clear. For, suppose the United States got into war with Belgium, or Poland, or Czechoslovakia, France would be prevented from going to the aid of any one of the three nations because she had agreed never to go to war with the United States. On the other hand, in a multilateral treaty which would include all nations, a breach by one of them would release the others so that France could carry out her commitments. This letter, although it was not immediately apparent, really marked the turning point in the negotiations. It had a profound influence in Europe.

As the negotiations with France were proceeding, somewhat slowly, in February Borah introduced a resolution (S.157) calling for a recodification of the rules of maritime law in war time. Mr. Levinson wrote him that this was a great mistake. His opinion was that Borah was compromising outlawry. What was wanted, he said, was *outlawry,* pure and simple, and to propose that rules of war be considered was something of an admission that outlawry might not work. Borah's reply was a statement of that very possibility: that "all treaties may be broken. But unwearily we go forward in the hope that ultimately the human mind will be trained away from war."

In April, Doctor Morrison urged Borah to press his original resolution for outlawry (the Briand-Kellogg negotiations were not based on Borah's resolution) in view of the developments between Kellogg and Briand. Borah dissented from this view with the statement that what was coming out now was in the direction of outlawry and that it would be a mistake to urge the resolution at this time. About the same time the Senator wrote Mr. Levinson that he had just had a conference at the State Department. "I think the next move will be a very important one," he said. "I am of the opinion that we are reaching the place where foreign powers will have either to accept or reject our proposition substantially as made."

It should be explained here that negotiations between France and the United States had come to a halt on March 30, *Quai d'Orsay* having stated to the United States on that date that it could not proceed further with the plan as America conceived it and that further efforts on its behalf would have to be assumed by the American Government. On April 13, three days after Borah had had his very satisfactory conference with the Secretary and Under-Secretary of State, the Secretary of State dispatched identical notes to Great Britain, Germany, Italy, and Japan, reviewing the history of the negotiations with France and asking these powers to consider a general treaty renouncing war. From this time forth developments toward securing a multilateral treaty were rapid. Borah may have been of some direct help in lodging the American idea in the British mind by his purely personal letters to Lieutenant Commander J. M. Kenworthy, M.C., and Messrs. Wickam Steed, Lloyd George, and Ramsay MacDonald.

Mr. Hoover's acceptance speech did not carry a sufficiently strong pronouncement for outlawry to suit Mr. Levinson. He wired Borah: "Address disgustingly anemic on our subject especially in contrast with reiterated paramount need of preparedness. Is this all we are to expect?" Borah wired his friend: "Rome was not built in a day. Continue to pray incessantly."

Colonel Robins had an explanation for Hoover's lukewarm utterance on outlawry. It was stated in a letter to

Borah, as follows: "*First,* because he is a Quaker by inheritance and suspect by all the militarists and imperialists; *Second,* the Chicago *Tribune* and some of the lesser press in the Middle West are hard to hold in line on the 'dry' of our platform and candidate; and *Third,* he hates Kellogg so cordially that his gorge rises at the task of making that small imperialist in his dotage IMMORTAL."

Shortly after the Republican candidate had made his acceptance speech and the interesting correspondence concerning the same had been exchanged, the Pact of Paris, or the multilateral treaty renouncing war as an instrument of national policy, was signed at Paris (August 27). The evangelical Colonel Robins wired Borah the day before the Pact was signed that his outlawry associates would be thinking of him as the signatures were being affixed "with deep gratitude of your consummate statesmanship in negotiating this supreme achievement. History's verdict will vindicate your superb leadership."

To be sure, the treaty carried no provision for the punishment of war criminals, nor was there a provision for the codification of international law, nor a provision for the establishment of a world court of compulsory jurisdiction, all of which were called for in Borah's plan. But there were four points about the treaty which pleased Borah. *First,* it had been negotiated successfully because of the pressure of public opinion; *second,* it made a clear positive declaration against war; *third,* it depended for its enforcement upon "the compelling power of enlightened public opinion" and upon that alone; and, *fourth,* it left the United States the absolute right of self-defense, including the right to maintain the Monroe Doctrine, and no obligation to take any coercive action against nations which might violate the treaty. He was sure of all of this, but he received still more assurance from the venerable Mr. Root who, in response to Borah's request for comment, stated that he agreed with him entirely.

In the Senate Borah explained and defended his treaty as long as there were any questions concerning it or arguments against it. He successfully opposed any reservations or interpretations. He declared that the qualifying notes other nations had written about the treaty did not affect it in any way. Even Senators Moses and Reed (Mo.) finally gave way to Senator Borah. Every Senator except Blaine of Wisconsin voted for it (January 15, 1929), although many Senators felt that it was an idle gesture.

Some of the old anti-League crowd outside of the Senate were worried about Borah. They told him that they could not see how a man could be for that treaty and not be for the League. "Look out," they said, "they will have you mixing up in European affairs yet!" This concern was expressed not by Tom, Dick, and Harry, but by responsible men, including one very distinguished professor of international law. Borah laughed and stated that the League recognizes war and may commit its members to war, whereas the Pact carries no such obligation.

But in the Senator's mind it carried an obligation likely to be more fruitful in results, the obligation of peoples not to go to war against each other. He conceived of this Pact as having been literally made by the people. Events leading up to its ratification had given a demonstration of the "compelling power of public opinion." He looked to this same public opinion to keep governments from violating it. Yet he knew that governments would from time to time go to war, despite the treaty. He knew that, treaty or no treaty, people might lose their heads. What he had in mind was this: that the treaty was a part of the process of education against the institution of war and that in the progress of civilization, with all of its backslidings, sometime peoples would learn that there was no profit and no honor in war.

There is a great deal of Borah in his fight for this treaty — his belief in the power of a simple, honest declaration, his abhorrence of force for the "enforcement" of peace, his faith in the people, his love of humanity as shown by his effort to outlaw its worst enemy.

About the time the treaty was being signed Senator Borah wrote Mr. Levinson: "Your name will go down along the side of the Hebrew prophets." Quietly Mr. Levinson inquired among friends as to the most appropriate manner in which to give a very tangible demonstration of his estimation and appreciation of Borah's part in the movement. In 1929 it was announced that the Chicago attorney had established at the University of Idaho "The William Edgar Borah Foundation for the Outlawry of War."

Let this chapter be closed with two excerpts from Senator Borah's address at the inauguration of this Foundation, the first being a tribute to Mr. Levinson and the second the Senator's statement of the incompatibility of organizations of force and his program of peace.[8]

"A lawyer by profession, engaged in active practice, daily advising in large business affairs, he yet found time for the great cause which was nearest his heart. The time and study he gave to the subject were extraordinary. His enthusiasm drove him past all obstacles and his restless and well-trained mind seemed to find inspiration rather than discouragement in the many questions which the problem presented. He was the first within my knowledge to reach the daring conclusion that war, as an institution, could, and should, be outlawed, placed beyond the pale or recognition of international law. His conception of peace was to condemn and renounce the use of force in international relations. A peculiar and exceptional glory attaches to his name by reason of this fact. In this view he long stood alone. But he labored untiringly. He built argument after argument around his theme. He has lived to see the great principle for which he contended recognized throughout the world. I regard the Peace Pact as the embodiment of the principle for which he has so earnestly contended. It may be that this principle is in advance of the times. Time alone can tell. But permanent peace must rest at last upon this great foundation principle. I pay sincere tribute to his ability, his vision, his great moral courage. . .

"Much has been said, and will continue to be said, for the doctrine of force dies hard, about implementing the peace pact. It is said that we must put teeth into it — an apt word revealing again that theory of peace which is based upon tearing, maiming, destroying, murdering. Many have inquired of me: What is meant by implementing the peace pact? I will seek to make it plain. What they mean is to change the peace pact into a military pact. They would

[8] September 23, 1931.

transform it into another peace scheme based upon force, and force is another name for war. By putting teeth into it, they mean an agreement to employ armies and navies wherever the fertile mind of some ambitious schemer can find an aggressor. Implementing the pact, putting teeth into the pact, is to revert to the doctrine of force in all its hideous, hellish brutality. Force, as a factor in international controversies, has been tried out for three thousand years, and at this very hour it has brought the world near to a state of economic chaos and financial breakdown, it has filled the earth with the maimed and the insane, it has crowded the hospitals in three continents with youth of the land, it has wrecked and destroyed in a large measure the economic system until hungry men and women tramp the streets and the highways for work which they cannot find. I have no language to express my horror of this proposal to build peace treaties, or peace schemes, upon the doctrine of force. I never have, and never shall, support any scheme of peace based upon the use of force in international controversies. . .

"But you will say : War may come. So it may. But if it comes, let it come as an outlaw in violation of peace treaties and in violation of international law, and not under the sanction and by the authority and with the blessings of the advocates of peace. Let it come as the criminal comes, as the murderer comes, not with the approval of law and under some fantastic scheme by which you would differentiate between good and bad murder, between good and bad wars, but in violation of all law. I take the position that there is not an international controversy but may be peacefully adjusted if the will to settle it peaceably is at hand. And it will be at hand if the enlightened public opinion of the world so decrees. This is the doctrine and the belief of S. O. Levinson, inadequately interpreted by my poor self. This is the doctrine of this foundation. When it ceases to be the doctrine of this foundation, I trust someone will erase my name from the title. This is not said in jest. I shall leave this part of my address in the archives of the University."

CHAPTER XXI

THE HAMMER OF THOR

NO MAN did more than the Senator from Idaho to make Herbert Hoover President of the United States. Perhaps Borah thought Hoover was a progressive. William Allen White had Written Borah in 1922 that Hoover was greatly interested in the progressive program. Borah worked for Hoover before the convention as he had never worked for anyone except Roosevelt in 1912, and he campaigned for Hoover after his nomination as he had never campaigned for any other candidate. The Senator felt that the United States had had quite a sufficient number of graven images and near morons for President. He believed that Hoover would bring distinction to that office. Moreover, he thought Hoover was with him on the farm question and Prohibition, the two domestic issues in which the Senator had the most vital interest. Of course, the Senator knew that Hoover might flirt with the League of Nations and the World Court, but he felt fairly sure that as long as the United States Senate was at the other end of Pennsylvania Avenue this little diversion would do the country no harm.

Borah's chief service for Hoover was in making the Middle and Far West safe for him. The Senator convinced the great trans-Mississippi empire that Hoover was (1) sufficiently progressive, (2) a friend of the farmer, and (3) an ardent believer in the Eighteenth Amendment and its enforcement. Another significant contribution the Senator made to Hoover was in the South. Since his speech in the Senate (1908) on the disorder of the Negro soldiers at Brownsville, Texas, Borah had been looked upon by southerners as one of the few Republicans who understood and appreciated them. His support of the Prohibition Amendment and his opposition to the Woman Suffrage Amendment and the national anti-lynch bills had met with general favor. His friendship with such southern senators as Bacon, Bailey, Glass, and Williams had served to increase his popularity in Dixie. Consequently, southern audiences were willing and eager to hear Borah speak on Hoover, Prohibition, and Tammany corruption.

Before going into the campaign of 1928, it is desirable to bring the history of farm relief and Prohibition up to that date. Even while fighting the World Court, advocating the recognition of Russia, trying to get the Marines out of Nicaragua, championing justice for Mexico, calling for disarmament, insisting upon the payment of war debts, and appealing to the conscience of the world for the outlawry of war, Borah did not forget the farmer. His Perishable Agricultural Commodities bill was first introduced in December, 1927, and during the period preceding the election of Hoover he continued to press it. This measure was finally enacted into law in 1930 (Ch. VI).

But the farm bill which aroused the greatest interest in the two years preceding the Hoover-Smith campaign was the McNary-Haugen measure, designed for "securing equality for agriculture in the benefits of a protective tariff." This measure provided that a farm marketing board should buy enough of certain farm products to raise the domestic price of each product to a sum equal to the foreign price of this commodity plus the American tariff. The board was to sell this produce in the foreign market at the price prevailing in that market. Our domestic buyers, when purchasing one of the products covered by the McNary-Haugen measure, were to be required to deliver to the farmer "equalization certificates" purchased from the marketing board at a price fixed by the board. At stated times the farmer would turn in his certificates to the marketing board and receive from the board the money paid in for the certificates less his share of the loss the board had sustained in purchasing and marketing the exportable surplus of the commodity.

Waiving the question of constitutionality, Borah was opposed to this measure because it did not do enough for the farmer (April 10, 1928). He asserted that the farmers' taxes had increased from one-tenth of receipts in 1913 to one-third in 1921 and that they had mounted at somewhat the same rate from 1921 to 1926. He declared that farmers paid 16.6 per cent of their income in taxes in 1922 as compared with 11.9 per cent for other people. "If this is the true situation — and I have gathered these figures from sources which I think will not be questioned and from different sources, but they are all practically the same – upon what possible theory can we hope to establish the equality of the farmer with the other industries of the country when we propose to impose upon him a tax to take care of whatever remedial legislation he is to enjoy? Upon what theory can we ask the farmer to pay especially for remedial legislation, a thing which has never been imposed upon any other industry in the United States? Let us assume the tax is constitutional. Is it just, is it equitable, is it doing what you profess to do, giving the farmer an equal opportunity in the struggle for success? How many farms now ready to be sold for taxes will you save from the hammer if you continue this inequality?"

The Senator was in favor of eliminating the equalization fee and making an appropriation of $500,000,000 for carrying out the provisions of the act. This amount, he said, would not equal the amount of taxes the American farmer had paid into the Treasury in excess of the sum he would have paid were his taxes proportionate with those of other industries. But his colleagues were not ready to vote an appropriation which he considered necessary in order to give the farmer the sort of protection manufacturers were receiving through the protective tariff, a protection which cost them nothing aside from contributions to the Republican campaign fund. The bill passed with the equalization fee; President Coolidge and his advisers gave it a strong veto; and there the matter rested until the Republican convention met in Kansas City in June, 1928.

But the great domestic issue with Borah in the late Coolidge period was Prohibition enforcement. The proposed Prohibition referendums of 1926, particularly the New York proposal, made this a live question. Borah came out as the principal guardian of the Constitution, in the Senate and out, in the spring of 1926. Speaking before the Presbyterian General Assembly at Baltimore, May 30, he said: "I believe the liquor traffic to be a curse to the human family. Whether sold in the open saloon or the brothel, its natural haunts, or secretly purveyed in defiance of law, the wicked stuff works its demoralization and ruin to individuals, communities, and states. . . Misery and poverty and remorse mark its maledict course. . ."

Then he came to his main argument. "But even a greater question than the liquor question is the capacity of the American people for constitutional government. There is the provision of our Constitution ratified by every state in the Union, save two, plain and unmistakable. The question of the hour is : Shall we live up to and enforce that provision of the Constitution until in the orderly method pointed out by the Constitution we see fit to change it ? Can we enforce the law which we have deliberately made ? . . . I am infinitely more concerned about the willingness and ability of our people to meet that test than I am about the liquor traffic, brutal and ruthless as I know it to be. . . To disregard our Constitution, to evade it, to nullify it, while still refusing to change it, is to plant the seeds of destruction in the heart of the Nation — is to confess before the world that we have neither the moral courage nor the intellectual sturdiness for self-government. . .

"I would not myself interpose obstruction tactics in the way of the Nation again considering the wisdom or unwisdom of the Eighteenth Amendment. I am perfectly willing, if the votes are at hand and the procedure is in the orderly, constitutional way, that the matter should again be considered in the light of these years of experience. But as long as the Constitution stands we should not compromise or falter in its execution. . ."

The State of New York had submitted this question to a referendum : "Should the Congress of the United States modify the Federal act to enforce the Eighteenth Amendment to the Constitution of the United States so that the same shall not prohibit the manufacture, sale, transportation, or exportation of beverages which are not in fact intoxicating as determined in accordance with the laws of the respective states ?"

"If this scheme could be put into effect, forty-eight states would construe the Federal Constitution," declared the Senator, "and the Federal authorities would have to accept the forty-eight constructions. . . If this referendum interrogatory has any meaning at all, it is that every state shall determine for itself its own construction of and obligation to the Constitution of the United States, and that construction is to bind the Federal Government. That doctrine was shot to death at the battle of the Wilderness. . ."

The Senator went on to say that the candidates for office should declare themselves on this question ; that the people had every right to know how the candidates stood ; and that no candidate and no party had any claim to public confidence unless this issue was met. "We are advised by the newspapers that in one great state they are hunting for a candidate for governor who has no view on this liquor question and who has never expressed himself. They overlook one qualification. Their candidate should not only have no views on the subject, but he should be incapable of forming, or entertaining any views. He would be an ideal candidate in this spasm of referendums! . . ."

The Bridgeport *Post,* discussing this speech, said that Borah combined all the necessary qualities, including "narrowness, prejudice, bigotry and a perfect willingness to trample all over the right of any person who does not think exactly as he does," for a candidate for the presidency on the straight dry ticket.[1] But the Boston *Herald* considered Borah's utterance honest and fearless.[2] Furthermore, it asked why, if Borah was a candidate for President, he would be so foolish as to irritate the Germans on the Prohibition issue as he had just irritated the Italians in his opposition to the Italian debt settlement.

This speech and others like it made the front pages all over the country. Borah had forced the issue. There was just one way to get rid of Prohibition and that was by constitutional amendment. New York and other states with their referendum proposals were simply taking the place of South Carolina in her nullification efforts of a century ago. He placed the referendum supporters, including Senator Wadsworth, Nicholas Murray Butler, and Elihu Root, in an awkward position, and his denunciation of their scheme had much to do with the defeat of Wadsworth in New York in

1 Bridgeport *Post,* May 31, 1926.
2 Boston *Herald,* June 2, 1926.

the election of 1926. Writing to John Q. Tilson, October 7, 1926, Borah said he could not help the Republican party in New York. But "I would like to say here that if the Republican party were simply advocating in New York the resubmission of the Eighteenth Amendment, I would not hesitate a moment to go in to New York, so far as that issue is concerned, and support the candidate. I think it is a perfectly proper thing, if one so desires, to advocate a change in a law. . . But this is a wholly different proposition. It is not change, it is not modification, it is nothing less than nullification."

The Senator used the term "nullification" over and over in condemning the proposals to let the states determine what beverages were intoxicating under the Eighteenth Amendment. The champions of such procedure thought they had found a vulnerable spot in his armor. On March 17, 1914, in a notable Senate speech opposing the Woman Suffrage Amendment, Borah had said that the Fifteenth (Negro Suffrage) Amendment was a dead letter : that it was circumvented by the South with the consent of the Nation (Ch. X). Here, then, was nullification by the Senator's own admission, said the "referendumists." Why should the Senator raise such a loud cry about nullification, granting for the sake of the argument that nullification of the Eighteenth Amendment is proposed ? Was the Senator not inconsistent ?

The Senator had an answer. He did not take refuge in a statement expressing his scorn of consistency ; nor did he reply that one nullification justified another. He met the charge direct. He stated his case in a letter to Walter Lippmann (July 23, 1926). After Borah had made the statement about the Negro being denied his rights in the South under the Fifteenth Amendment, Senator Bacon, an able lawyer from Georgia, told him that he was mistaken, that an investigation would show the South was not violating that Amendment. The Idahoan then proceeded to examine the laws by which the Southern states prevented practically all Negroes from voting. He found that persons who could not read and write were not permitted to register ; that those who did not pay a poll tax were likewise kept off the list ; that persons convicted of crime, even very petty crime, were excluded ; and that there were many other restrictions designed to disqualify the unfit. But there was no provision in the laws of any state which singled out Negroes as a class and declared that they should not vote. He found that the laws did not prevent men from voting on account of race, color, or previous condition of servitude (the classes protected by the Amendment), but that men were prevented from voting because they were ignorant, propertyless, convicted of crime, and so forth. He concluded that Senator Bacon was right. Indeed, the Supreme Court of the United States had held that such laws did not violate the Fifteenth Amendment. Now, of course, these laws were designed to keep practically every Negro from voting, and they had that effect, but they were drafted in such a way as to meet the requirements of the Fifteenth Amendment.

Borah held not only that the suffrage laws of the Southern states were constitutional but also that they were wise, particularly those imposing an educational test. "These educational tests," he said in this letter to Lippmann, "are in my opinion an embodiment of the principles which Lincoln announced and are wise and just laws, not only from the standpoint of the entire South, but in the interest also of the Negro. It would have been better had a test of the Fifteenth Amendment been that of intelligence rather than that of color. But politics would not admit of so wise a course. Even the great Charles Sumner declared that to enfranchise this uneducated mass was foreign to his convictions and to his whole habit of thought but that he felt that politics required it."

Borah's argument in defense of the South is a perfectly good constitutional argument. There was one point, however, which was omitted – the administration of the suffrage laws in the South. Every honest southerner knows that the laws were not administered fairly, that white men were held to have the proper qualifications under the laws while Negroes with equally good or better qualifications were often excluded. Perhaps the "equal protection of the laws" clause of the Fourteenth Amendment was being violated if the Fifteenth Amendment was not. At any rate, the Supreme Court held in Yick Wo v. Hopkins, a case involving discrimination against Chinese in granting laundry permits, that "though the law itself be fair on its face and impartial in appearance, yet, if it is applied and administered by public authority with an evil eye and an unequal hand, so as practically to make unjust and illegal discriminations between persons in similar circumstances, material to their rights, the denial of equal justice is still within the prohibition of the Constitution." [3] But, of course, to anyone who made the charge that the suffrage laws were administered with an "evil eye" the Senator might have replied that the courts of the United States were open to those who had suffered from administrative discrimination.

Borah continued his speeches favoring Prohibition as a policy and hammering home the necessity of enforcing the law in order to maintain our free institutions. He went into the South and in a speech at Augusta, Georgia, on July 18, 1926, captivated the southerners with whom he had been popular from his first year in the Senate. In addition to his speeches, he gave interviews and wrote articles on the subject. He worried the Republican high command not a little. As he had embarrassed the leaders by insisting that the League of Nations be a party issue in 1920, he was now giving them headaches over his insistence that Prohibition be made the issue in 1928.

This proposal to make Prohibition a party question troubled some of the drys as well as the Republican leaders. The former opposed making it a party question because there were drys in both parties ; Borah replied that there were wets in both parties also. He said that unless the party, as a party, takes a position and puts its prestige behind enforcement, there will be no enforcement worthy of the name, merely skirmishing between the lines, always an anxious avoidance of giving offense to the drys on one hand and the wets on the other.[4] This "jayhawking" on an issue Borah could never endure.

He found in Doctor Nicholas Murray Butler a man he could respect. Both agreed, amid much "tut-tutting" of Republican and Prohibition politicians, that the Eighteenth Amendment should be the issue in 1928, Butler standing for

[3] 118 U. S. 356.
[4] *Christian Advocate,* July 14, 1927.

its repeal and Borah for its retention and enforcement. Robert M. Washburn, President of the Roosevelt Club of Boston, arranged for a debate on this very question between Borah and Butler under the auspices of the Club. This classic was staged on April 8, 1927.

Doctor Butler opened the debate by stating that a man prominent in Republican party management had asked him a a short while ago with some show of asperity : "Why do you insist upon stirring up the subject of Prohibition ? It is good for one more election." The Doctor explained that the Eighteenth Amendment was substantive legislation and had no place in the Constitution ; that attempts at its enforcement had led to the grossest violations of civil rights guaranteed by the Constitution ; that Prohibition and civil rights were in conflict. He amused his audience by quoting Senator Borah's reasons for opposing the Woman Suffrage Amendment and asking why they were not equally applicable to the Prohibition Amendment.

While Doctor Butler was speaking, Senator Borah outlined the proposition he was to undertake to support. He said that he believed Prohibition could be enforced, that it was entitled to a fair trial, for perhaps twenty-five years, before there should be talk of repeal. He asked what the advocates of repeal had to offer in place of the Eighteenth Amendment — government sale and distribution of liquor or the old saloon ? Either, he said, was unthinkable. To Doctor Butler's question, Why he opposed the Nineteenth Amendment on the ground of states' rights and favored the Eighteenth on the same ground, Borah replied that states which wanted Woman Suffrage could have it without the Amendment but that states which wanted Prohibition could not have it because the wet states shipped in liquor, despite the Kenyon Law which was designed to protect them (see also Ch. X). But what about the wet states ? Butler had asked. Have they no states' rights ? "Certainly they have," was Borah's reply. "But the wet states can ship wet into the dry states, but the dry states can not ship dry into the wet states." In closing, he quoted Washington on the duty of every individual to observe the Constitution and Lincoln on the duty to abide by all laws and on the evils of intemperance.

The nine judges gave Borah the decision six to three, but the Republican leaders scored both Borah and Butler at zero for debating a question on which Republicans differed. It is true that William M. Butler, Chairman of the Republican National Committee, cautiously appeared and shyly sat on the platform during the debate. But the good face he put on the situation only slightly obscured the curse put on the meeting by the resignation of Frank W. Stearns, intimate friend of Coolidge, from the Roosevelt Club for staging the debate. If raising this issue filled Republican leaders with dread, it pleased Attorney William Gibbs McAdoo, who wrote Borah that he was going to try to make his own party take the stand Borah advocated for the Republican party.

In the months that followed, Borah continued to insist upon a straight declaration in the Republican platform of 1928 for the retention of the Eighteenth Amendment. It seemed monstrously absurd to him that "everybody except the deaf and dumb and the candidates" would be discussing Prohibition in that year.

WHEN Coolidge announced in the summer of 1927 that he did not choose to run the next year, Borah accepted the President's statement as "unequivocal and sincere," thus paying him a compliment and at the same time giving him a little push in the direction of private life. The Senator received many letters urging him to run for President. The Progressive organizer and Grange leader in Idaho, Ray McKaig, was sounding out sentiment for Borah as early as January, 1926. In that month he conferred with Rudolph Spreckels and Franklin Hichborn in San Francisco and Lew Head, the Progressive leader in California, in Pasadena. McKaig's idea was to get Progressive support for Borah, which support he considered would strengthen him with the regular Republicans who would then nominate him. The Progressives would then support Borah on the Republican ticket. The Californians were impressed with McKaig's plan and Lew Head wrote Borah asking if McKaig was really speaking for him. Borah replied (January 11, 1926) : McKaig "has some idea about the future and has been conferring and communicating with a great many people apparently in regard to it.

The matter being so particularly personal, I have not, of course, encouraged him in this matter for the simple reason I have not felt that there was anything to be achieved along that line as he sees it. . . Naturally, I am not indifferent to the views expressed by my friends upon this matter but by reason of my doubt in regard to it, I have not encouraged it."

About the same time the Senator's old friend, Jim Hawley, now an octogenarian, wrote from Idaho that "Will" should be President, and that he and many other Democrats would vote for him. Borah responded warmly, but explained that the Republican leaders would never let him get the nomination. "A very prominent leader in business and finance in New York City said to me a few days ago : 'Personally, I would like to see you President, but the people with whom I associate and play the game think you are entirely too independent and they do not know where an administration of yours might lead.' That I think expresses it."

Borah had no hope of getting the nomination. From time to time he was mentioning Senator Norris as his candidate. But he was willing to allow his own name to be used for the purpose of winning the Progressives over to the Republican party and for the purpose of giving him sufficient influence in the Republican party to enable him to write several planks in the platform for 1928 and name the candidate. To the suggestion that his "very distinction" would keep him from being President as it had kept Webster, Clay, and others from the prize, the Senator replied that he would not ordinarily claim such relationship and "yet I feel probably I had better crawl in there as a matter of consolation. That is the most comforting escape suggested yet."

But McKaig continued his work and Borah encouraged him in it. The Senator hoped that the Western states as a unit would rally to him or some other liberal Republican, and expressed his belief that the West would have no influence at the convention, otherwise. Late in 1927 McKaig was urging Borah to announce his candidacy because he had carried him as far as possible until that announcement was forthcoming. He said that the wet Smith was sure to be nominated and that Borah was the man who could beat him on the Prohibition issue. "Announce your candidacy," he urged, "and turn loose that bunch of wild Grangers on the wet and dry fight. . . All the farm relief and every other economic question goes to the scrap heap at once. . . There is no harder working bunch of folks in the world than the law enforcing groups. . . They work for nothing and spend their time and money like water." Ray repeatedly urged Borah to come out before some others "run off with the whole works." But the Senator wrote McKaig only that he would have to have time to think over his suggestions. And that is as far as the matter ever progressed.

Lacking the interest, perhaps because he felt that the effort would be futile, to push his candidacy for the presidency, he retained his interest in the enforcement of the Eighteenth Amendment as the political season advanced. In fact, he considered it the most important issue before the country. He did what he had done in 1920 with the League of Nations question. He interrogated the candidates for the presidency. On February 9, 1928, he wrote a much publicized letter to Herbert Hoover. It reads:

"Your friends have placed you in line for the nomination for the Presidency. I venture in view of that fact to ask your views upon a matter in which there is a wide and deep interest throughout the country. I am sure you will be free to express yourself upon this important issue.

"First, Do you favor incorporating in the next national Republican platform a plank specifically referring to the Eighteenth Amendment to the Constitution and pledging the candidates and the party to a vigorous, faithful and effective enforcement of the Amendment and the laws enacted to carry into effect the constitutional Amendment?

"Second, What is your attitude and what would be your attitude toward the Amendment and its enforcement in case you are nominated and elected?

"Third, Dó you favor the enactment into law of the principle embodied in the New York referendum that the Congress should modify the Federal Act to enforce the Eighteenth Amendment so that the same shall not prohibit the manufacture, sale, transportation, importation or exportation of beverages which are not in fact intoxicating, as determined in accordance with the laws of the respective states? In

THE SECRETARY OF COMMERCE
WASHINGTON

February 23, 1928

The Honorable
William E. Borah
United States Senate

My dear Mr. Senator:

Upon my return to Washington I have taken up your letter.

I feel that the discussion of public questions by reply to questionnaires is likely to be unsatisfactory and ofttimes leads to confusion rather than clarity. Replies to the scores of such inquiries on many questions are impossible.

Out of my regard for your known sincerity and your interest in the essential question, I will, however, say again that I do not favor the repeal of the 18th Amendment. I stand, of course, for the efficient, vigorous and sincere enforcement of the laws enacted thereunder. Whoever is chosen President has under his oath the solemn duty to pursue this course.

Our country has deliberately undertaken a great social and economic experiment, noble in motive and far-reaching in purpose. It must be worked out constructively.

Yours faithfully

Herbert Hoover

HH:AGS

other words, do you favor a program of legislation which will enable every State to determine for itself the alcoholic content of beverages to be manufactured, sold and transported throughout the country.

"Fourth, Do you favor the repeal of the Eighteenth Amendment, or the repeal of the Volstead Act ?"

This letter by a Senator, urged by no organization, backed by no group, representing no party leaders, but expressing the desire of plain people who would not be satisfied with a meaningless declaration for "law enforcement," brought forth the historic "noble experiment" reply from Herbert Hoover.

As the day for the convention approached, Borah went back into American history and drew for the politicians a lesson from the futile efforts of Clay and Van Buren to keep the question of the annexation of Texas out of the campaign of 1844. He said that the general conclusion seemed to be that both parties should adopt a moderate plank on the Eighteenth Amendment. He made this idea ridiculous by suggesting a "moderate" enforcement of the Constitution, which would be like talking about a citizen of "moderate" loyalty, a public official of "moderate" honesty, a political party of "moderate" decency, a newspaper of "moderate" respectability, a woman of "moderate" virtue.

Before Borah left Washington for Kansas City, he was in daily conference with Hoover over the party platform and it was understood that they were in accord on all important matters of policy. The platform as adopted by the convention carried the Borah planks on Prohibition, outlawry of war, campaign funds, labor, and farm relief *via* the protective tariff. The farm board proposal was not Borah's.

As had often happened in the Senate, one of Borah's chief contributions in the convention was in what he was able to prevent. Many farm delegates wanted the platform to declare for the McNary-Haugen equalization-fee type of relief. There was danger of a revolt. Borah was pushed to the platform to close the debate on the farm-relief question. H. I. Phillips, writing in the Kansas City *Times,* and many other observers gave Borah full credit for putting out the fire.[5] Corn-belt speakers had threatened the G.O.P., said Phillips, with "everything from flat tires and fallen arches to collapse and extinction." The flames were getting out of control when Borah "galloped up the ladder and turned on the hose." He emphasized the fact that there was a farm problem and that the farmer should have relief. Then he showed that the equalization fee would not bring that relief. "There is no authority under the Constitution of the United States which permits a Congress to delegate to twelve men

[5] Kansas City *Times,* June 14, 1928.

the power to impose a tax or an equalization fee upon a citizen of the United States without his consent. It would not be a free government if it could be done. And if anybody should propose to amend the Constitution so as to give a Congress the authority to delegate that power to a bureau the farmer would be the first to fight such tyranny. It is unconstitutional, and the President of the United States found that out. Having reached this conclusion, he so declared, declared it long ago. . .

"But, my friends, suppose it is constitutional. . . I could never for myself get my consent to give to a bureau, a bureau the members of which the farmer can neither select, recall, or control, the power to levy a tax or a fee or a charge upon the American farmer to whatever extent in its judgment it thought proper to levy. This power as proposed is given so that the charge may be levied upon every farmer of the United States whether in his judgment he should be a member of or come under the control of the bureau or not. In other words, it is proposed to delegate a power which will deny the farmer the right to stay out of the scheme, which will deny the farmer the right to get out of it, and which will make him pay for his imprisonment while he is there. . ." The incipient revolt was squelched and nearly every delegate went home satisfied with the platform.

As for the nominations, there was no hitch in nominating Hoover, public opinion having demanded it. But there was some contest over the vice-presidency. The leaders talked of Dawes, Governor Fuller of Massachusetts, Senators Moses, and Curtis. All of the old animosities against Dawes were paraded at the second session of the leaders and he was dropped. The Sacco-Vanzetti affair put Fuller out. Channing Cox, former Governor of Massachusetts, was substituted for Fuller, and it was understood that he was to have the nomination. The morning after this arrangement had been made, Borah met Smoot in the lobby of his hotel and asked who got the vice-presidency. When Smoot mentioned Cox, Borah exploded and wanted to know if they had all gone crazy. "Why, what is the trouble?" asked Smoot.

"Trouble! None excepting that nobody outside of Massachusetts ever heard of Cox. This convention has got to nominate Curtis and is going to nominate him or I shall know the reason why. . . If anyone else is put up I shall go before the convention and present his name myself and make a fight for it and I think I can put him across."

"Oh, don't do that; just hold off and I'll see about it," Smoot said. A wire to Washington brought Hoover's approval and the thing was done.[6]

It is probable that Borah preferred Norris to Curtis but Norris had wired that he was no more interested in the vice-presidency in 1928 than Borah was in 1924. Borah was satisfied with Curtis on Prohibition and the farm question and he believed he would help hold the farmers of the Middle West in line for Hoover. Besides, the elevation of Curtis to the vice-presidency might make a place in the Senate for Borah's old friend at Emporia, Kansas, William Allen White. At any rate, Borah's speech nominating Curtis was the speech of a well-satisfied man.

Borah was more pleased with the Republican candidate for President than he had been with any candidate since Roosevelt ran in 1904. He approved of Hoover as a man and, in addition, Hoover had approved of the Borah planks in the platform. It was generally predicted that a new Borah had come to light, a constructive Borah, an affirmative Borah, a Borah who would support a Republican President. Some observers suggested caution about such a conclusion. They surmised that Borah was simply satisfied for the moment and that if Hoover should start to follow Bascom Slemp and Claudius Huston instead of Borah the public would hear a great deal from the old Borah. In fact, those who had studied Borah's career were pretty sure that the old Borah was the real Borah — that he would continue to follow issues rather than Presidents.

But there was no cloud on the horizon during the campaign. In the East, in the South, and in the Middle West Borah spoke not only for the Republican party but also for the candidate of that party, pronouncing his name over and over again, as he had pronounced no candidate's name for many a year. It was Borah, not Hoover, who answered

[6] New York *Sun*, June 16, 1928.

Smith, and perhaps Borah more than Hoover who carried the states directly west of the Great Lakes and the "backsliding" states of the South. Although Mr. Hughes came down from Mt. Olympus and pronounced judgment several times during the later days of the campaign, Borah was easily the leading Republican speaker. He satisfied in every way the ardent Colonel Robins who, following Hoover's acceptance speech, wrote Borah that he knew the Senator now felt "the call to throw the spear of Nestor, strike with the sword of Pericles, and wield the hammer of Thor, in this campaign."

Smith made his acceptance speech on August 22. The next day, in the Idaho *Statesman,* Borah gave him a drubbing for taking the Underwood tariff as the ideal in such legislation and stated that under that tariff the farm market for mutton, beef, pork, eggs, butter, etc., was practically ruined.

Immediately after the Smith speech, Mrs. Mabel Willebrant had wired Borah to make a smashing comment on it. She said that Smith's idea seemed to be to amend the Eighteenth Amendment in such a way that the states could establish the old South Carolina dispensary system, which system, she said, could be safely challenged. She urged Borah, as the national spokesman for the decent law enforcement forces, to speak while public attention was on the subject and expose Smith's political quackery. On August 24, Borah denounced the government liquor-store idea, quoting from Canadian papers stories to the effect that people were drinking more and that there was more bootlegging under the government control plan in certain provinces than there had been under the old system.[7]

Borah's first big speech of the campaign was in Detroit. H. M. Morden, in the *Border Cities Star,* says that he started to speak from a prepared address which abounded in splendid phrases, each of which meant something. But this required more from the audience than it was willing to give — some quiet reflection, the sort of coöperation the Senator was in the habit of getting from an Idaho audience. Actor and artist that he was, skilled at gauging an audience, he saw that

[7] *Statesman,* August 24, 1928.

MRS. BORAH

he was getting nowhere. He threw down his stack of notes and mentioned the name of Herbert Hoover. The audience broke loose and he met them on their own ground after that. He praised Hoover to the skies. He ridiculed Smith's acceptance speech and his Omaha speech. "He says that he will appoint a commission for farm relief as soon as he is elected president. How patient the farmers will have to be!" declared the Senator. "Seriously," he continued, "I have the greatest respect for Governor Smith." Even this drew gales of laughter from his audience. Morden was sure the campaigner's humor was spontaneous, for Mrs. Borah, who sat on the platform, laughed at all of his witty comments.[8]

In South Dakota, Borah was scheduled to speak at the State Fair. The arrangement was such that he had to speak in competition with all of the farmers' displays, including some very fine prize bulls. The Senator was angry and got temperamental on the train after they had started for Minneapolis, where Borah was to make his next speech. He said he was not going to speak at Minneapolis but was going on to Washington. Colonel Robins, who was in the private car with Borah, "kidded" him awhile, but the Senator soon went to bed. Robins saw to it that the car was switched off at Minneapolis. He says that Borah was a bit peeved the next morning to find that he was in Minneapolis but after some discussion he agreed to go on with the speech.

In this speech of October 3, he criticized Smith for saying he would leave the question of the St. Lawrence Waterway to Congress and said that since this was an engineering problem we had better have an engineer for President. He defended Hoover against Smith's charge of not having spoken out against the oil scandals when he was a member of Harding's Cabinet, and suggested that if the Governor was going to put the campaign on the basis of associations he would have to explain his association with Tammany Hall. Of Smith on farm relief, he said: "He has come and gone, he has spoken, he has delivered his message to the farmers of the West, and I will say tonight, not in severity but in charity, that there is not a man living who can tell what Governor Smith's position is upon the farm problem." Of Herbert

[8] *Border Cities Star,* September 20, 1928.

Hoover on the same, he said: "I doubt if there is a farmer within the sound of my voice tonight . . . who would doubt the ability of Mr. Hoover to solve this problem. Bear in mind that Mr. Hoover stated in his acceptance speech that it is the most imminent problem before the American people today. Bear in mind that he pledges himself to the solution of the problem. Then bear in mind that Herbert Hoover has never set himself to the solution of any kind of an economic problem that he has not made good." Then he defended the Republican candidate at some length against the charge that as Food Administrator he had been unfair to the farmers during and immediately after the war. And finally, "Now, if it is not too late, I am going to say a word or two about Prohibition. . . All these plans and schemes talked of in this campaign can accomplish but one thing, and that is the nullification, not the repeal of the Eighteenth Amendment. . ." [9]

The auditorium audience for this speech was estimated at about 12,000. The radio audience can only be guessed at, but judging by the number of requests which came to Republican headquarters for copies of this speech, it must have been very large. Hoover wired: "That was the greatest speech of this campaign." Colonel Robins, General Hugh S. Johnson, and many others who followed the campaign say that this speech turned the states in this section of the country from Smith to Hoover.

"I listened to your Minneapolis speech," wrote Ray McKaig from Boise after the campaign had closed. "There was —— and ——, both of a cynical slant on anything or anybody affecting progressive republicanism. As you got warmed up and were handing the opposition body blows that were landing with staggering force, these men got so excited that they could not sit still. Your voice sounded like you were in the next room with the door wide open." These men "were just like they were listening to you in a wildly enthusiastic audience. Finally, —— phoned to the Western Union and dictated a congratulatory telegram. Now my point is, I know these men very well and if you pulled them off their

[9] New York *Evening Post*, October 20, 1928. (This was the speech of October 3 and it was not published in full until October 20.)

feet a thousand miles away, what were you doing to other men listening in and whose enthusiasm is much easier aroused than theirs?

". . . That speech was a classic. There were sixty thousand copies . . . sent here to Idaho. . . If a Granger was in doubt we handed him one of your Minneapolis speeches and it did the work. For it read as it sounded over the air, and that is unusual for a political argument." As Ray saw it, this speech ended Smith's hold over the farmers and it was Borah's best effort in the campaign.

About the time of the Minneapolis speech, Borah received a letter from one of the leading newspaper men in Oregon. Make Hoover come out against power scandals in specific terms, with special reference to power companies' attempts to purchase seats in the Senate, to defeat investigation, and to get their propaganda into the public schools, he urged. Hoover will disappoint many people who have been instinctively for him if he does not rise above complacent party smugness, he continued. Smith's recent gains, he said, are due to the fact that he has been making those issues — "carrying the ball." Borah replied that he had talked with Hoover several times about those matters. "I do not know what his intentions are with reference to public expression. But I feel very sure in my own mind as to what his course will be when the responsibility is placed upon him. . . I am not in the least uneasy about what kind of administration he will give us. . ."

Late in October McKaig was worried about "that speech of Hoover branding the proponents of public ownership of water power as socialists. Can nothing be done?" he wired Borah. The reply: "Let us go through with the fight for in the sum total it will be infinitely better for us all."

The end Borah had been working for since 1926, the event he anticipated, the reassembling of the Progressives in the Republican fold, was coming to pass. Certainly Borah was responsible for winning McKaig, H. F. Samuels, and other Progressive leaders in Idaho for Hoover and keeping them in line for him. His influence was potent in accomplishing these ends with Progressives in other states as instanced by the correspondence with the Oregon Editor. To be sure, some of the old Progressives like Senator Norris went over to Smith.

Popular in the South from the day he entered the Senate because of his disposition to understand the problems of the South and because of his states' rights views, the Senator was given remarkable receptions by southern audiences before whom he devoted his time chiefly to Prohibition, immigration, and Tammany Hall. "Does Governor Smith stand for anything that North Carolina wants?" the Senator asked in Charlotte. "Do you want Tammany Hall moved from New York to Washington; the repeal of Prohibition and the letting down of the immigration bars?" The audience roared a "No" to each of these interrogations.[10] After speaking in Nashville, Tulsa, Chattanooga, Richmond and other southern cities, the Senator declared that Hoover would carry North Carolina, Tennessee, Kentucky, Florida, and probably Virginia and Texas. He did.

In 1935 a woman with some sense of humor wrote Borah from Texas asking him to come to that state to address a woman's-club convention. We will have about a thousand women in attendance, she said, five or six of whom are not typical. But come on anyhow, she urged; you owe us something for having come down here in 1928 and sold us a "marshmallow" for President and having had the South follow you as a Pied Piper.

But it may not have been the clanging of the "Hammer of Thor" nor yet the tuneful notes of the Pied Piper which did the most to turn the South to Hoover. There are those who believe that the greatest, if largely silent, force for Hoover in that area was the anti-Catholic sentiment.

Borah condemns religious prejudice in unmeasured terms. Scheduled to speak at a Methodist Conference in Peoria, Illinois, in September, 1928, he canceled his engagement when one minister stated before the Conference that the "candidacy of Alfred E. Smith should be denounced from every pulpit of the Methodist Church in America" and a bishop defended the activity of the Church in the Smith-Hoover campaign.[11]

[10] Associated Press dispatch, October 17, 1928.
[11] Louisville *Courier-Journal,* September 24, 1928.

An incident at Nashville, Tennessee, troubled the Senator not a little and he heard of it from time to time for months after it occurred. Senator Newell Sanders introduced Borah with a rather long speech in which he said that the South was Protestant and would have a Protestant President, or words to that effect. Borah's exact words in opening his remarks are in dispute, but he recalled about two months later that he said something like this: "I shall not likely do more than amplify some of the subjects covered by Mr. Sanders, such as immigration, Prohibition, and so forth." The Associated Press reported Borah to have said: "Senator Sanders has made my speech." Toward the middle of his speech the Senator avoided the mistake Blaine had made, stating that the religious question had nothing to do with the campaign, but this was lost in the publicity given the alleged opening sentence. Borah's slip was in not denouncing the religious issue at the very beginning of his speech. He can be forgiven, however, for in all probability he was thinking about what he was going to say and paying very little attention to what the long-winded Sanders was saying.

On October 20, Hoover wired Borah that he very much hoped he could come East for a speech in Baltimore and in cities of the northeast. The Senator went to Washington, had a conference with Hoover (October 26) in which, presumably, he pointed out the gravity of the situation caused by Norris' declaration for Smith and stressed the necessity of an announcement by the Republican candidate that a special session of Congress would be called to deal with farm relief if he were elected. A few days earlier Governor McCullem of Nebraska had urged Hoover to take this course in order to hold the West, and the Governor had left Mr. Hoover with the impression that the candidate would follow his advice. Later, it was reported from the Hoover headquarters that nothing had been decided regarding the special session. Emerging from his long conference with Hoover, Borah seemed determined to force the issue of the special session. The Senator did not say what Hoover thought of the idea, but he stated with some emphasis that he himself was "thoroughly in favor of an extra session" if the short session could not deal adequately with the farm question. The next day

Mr. Hoover made the fateful announcement that he would call the special session, thus yielding to Borah on a matter which he had cause to regret a thousand times if not for the remainder of his life.

Well satisfied over his efforts with Hoover, Borah went on to his engagements in Baltimore, Boston, and Utica. It is unnecessary to discuss the content of these last speeches, although it might be noted that in his Boston speech he expressed his unwavering faith in the tariff.

This Boston speech was one of his best, despite the fact that Borah was angry about two items in the arrangements for the meeting: first, that he was not to speak until 10:30 p.m. and second, that the meeting would be an hour old at that time. At first he said he would not speak at all, but would go to Salem where he was wanted at a rally. Finally, he agreed to stay in Boston and talk for a few minutes at the meeting. He ate a light supper, sat around and refused to talk, lay down and sent his pants out to be pressed. He invariably ate little and talked little before a speech. His "few minutes" of speaking ran to eighty minutes. He finished at twelve o'clock with the audience clamoring for more and men and women frantically rushing forward to grasp his hand. "Bob" Washburn, who president at the meeting, and who, according to Richard Washburn Child, introduced Borah with "something between the technique of Cicero and the Swiss bell ringers" said he had never seen such a spectacle as the demonstration for Borah at the conclusion of his address. Borah returned to his hotel. He was now willing to talk, saying that he never could sleep for about two hours after an effort of that kind, that it took him that long to let off steam.

After the election, Hoover fittingly expressed his appreciation to Borah for his aid. The Senator was congratulated by President Coolidge, by Will Hays, and by practically every one of consequence in the Republican party. Hays was of the opinion that Borah's speeches "exerted a greater influence upon the electorate than was ever before exercised by a human voice in a political campaign." "What a brave old lion you are! How splendidly you waged the battle!" wrote William Allen White. If he had been somewhat mercurial, or as one friend put it, a bit childish about speaking in Minneapolis and Boston, that was simply a little display of temperament to which any prima donna was justly entitled.

Just before the election, Mrs. Henry W. Peabody, the great Prohibition crusader of Massachusetts, wrote Borah that there was no doubt of Hoover's election and that Borah had won it for him. She said that Borah, not Hoover and the Republican politicians, had led in the campaign and that the women had followed him. She explained that many Republican newspapers were wet and the party organizations in a number of states were wet, and she was afraid they would dominate Hoover. She asked Borah to see that they did not. The Senator replied that Hoover was all right on the Eighteenth Amendment. "I have had many talks with him and I have never reached any other conclusion after leaving him."

In the middle of October, Ludwell Denny in the Washington *News* observed that Hoover was piling up a tremendous debt to Borah which had its origin in Borah's decisive support of Hoover before Coolidge, Mellon, and other wheel horses in the Republican organization had endorsed him. The situation might be very unpleasant for Hoover because Borah owed him absolutely nothing and wanted absolutely nothing for himself. There was nothing, he said, which Hoover could give Borah except the close political friendship of two equals. He wisely observed that the two men were utterly unlike in temperament "except for the extreme individualism they share." His conclusion was that Hoover's political debt to Borah was too big to result in anything but "the closest friendship or the bitterest enmity." [12]

[12] Washington *Daily News*, October 13, 1928.

CHAPTER XXII

BORAH AND HOOVER

"I HOPE they won't fool you out of the Senate into the Secretary of State's Office," said William Allen White in a letter to Borah immediately after the election. "You would be in the devil's own fix. I don't think you and Hoover could hit it off."

Colonel Robins says he went to Florida to see President-elect Hoover while he was at J. C. Penney's estate. He found that Hoover was not unappreciative of what Borah had done for him but that he did not realize how materially Borah had aided him. Robins wanted Hoover to offer Borah the Secretaryship of State and he strongly urged Hoover to make that gesture. At the same time the Colonel was advising Borah not to accept the offer, if it was made, telling him that he would be much more useful and independent in the Senate.

Some newspaper men wrote that Hoover never did offer Borah the Secretaryship of State, but he did. On January 19, 1929, the President-elect had the Senator for lunch. When the Senator returned to his office, he dictated, as was his custom, the substance of the conversation with Mr. Hoover. The President-elect said he had been thinking about the State Department post a great deal and that Borah had been mentioned for it. The Senator was about to make a remark, but the President-elect said before the Senator could reply that he would like to have him at the head of his Cabinet. He added that, while he should like to have him take the post, he would regard his going out of the Senate as a loss to the country. He stated that the decision rested with Borah. The Senator replied immediately: "I presume my name has been associated with the Secretaryship of State because of my activities in the campaign. I did not go into the campaign with that in mind and I have not had any thoughts along that line either before or since the campaign. Secondly, I haven't the financial means to be Secretary of State. The financial obligations and the social obligations are both beyond my reach in that respect. Thirdly, I do not feel that I ought to give up my work in the Senate. And lastly, we might not always be able to agree upon foreign matters; and in case we did not agree, of course, I should have to either surrender or get out, neither of which I would want to do but the latter of which I would, of course, do if necessary." He and Hoover then discussed other men for the place, including Messrs. Morrow and Stimson. Mr. Morrow was Borah's first choice and he had the impression he was the President-elect's first choice also, although the latter expressed some doubt of the advisability of taking Morrow away from his post as Ambassador to Mexico. Mr. Hoover gave Mr. Stimson a very high rating and Borah considered him well qualified for the place.

The Senator entertains no doubt that Mr. Hoover wanted him to feel that he appreciated his work in the campaign and decided that one way to express that appreciation was to offer him the highest place in the Cabinet. He believes that Mr. Hoover was sincere in this. He is equally convinced that Mr. Hoover did not prefer him for Secretary of State. "In this his judgment was sound," declares the Senator. In fact, he is convinced that he could not have held the place for more than a month or two.

Gossip had it that Mr. Hoover later offered the Senator the post of Attorney General. Indeed, there seems to have been more certainty among newspaper men about this than about the State Department offer. The Chicago *Tribune* said that Borah had declined the attorney-generalship, having concluded that "it is better to skin the Attorney-General than be one." [1] But at no time, either directly or indirectly, did Mr. Hoover offer the attorney-generalship to Borah. However, the President-elect did consult with Borah about the office, and Borah very strongly urged him to name a dry man for the post, stating that the people had indicated that they did not want a wet President and that they certainly would not want a wet Attorney-General. The Senator recommended W. D. Mitchell very highly, and Mr. Hoover was satisfied with him. When he hesitated because he was a Democrat, Borah stated that there would be a few grunts and growls on that account but that they would not be suffi-

[1] Chicago *Tribune,* February 23, 1929.

cient to cause any Senator to vote against Mitchell's confirmation.

THE Republican party declared in the campaign of 1928 that the agricultural problem was the most immediate and important economic problem before the American people, and the party proposed, among other things, to revise the tariff on farm commodities, to enact a law insuring better protection to the farmer in the marketing of his produce, and to create a board with authority to deal with the surplus problem. During the campaign, Hoover, at Borah's insistence, promised the farmers a special session of Congress. Borah made it his business to see that both the party and the President-elect kept faith with the farmer. From time to time he gave interviews on the promises to the farmer and the necessity for the special session. He quoted Jefferson: "I trust the good sense of our country will see that its greatest prosperity depends upon a due balance between agriculture, manufacturing and commerce." The Senator labeled this as "true then, true now, true at all times." [2]

Late in March a farmer of North Dakota wrote Borah that President Hoover was not going to do anything to give the farmer equality. Borah replied: "I believe . . . that you are in error in the views which you express with reference to President Hoover."

The special session was called for the middle of April, and Hoover's presidential honeymoon took its place in American history as the shortest on record. The debenture plan for agricultural relief spoiled it all. Under this proposal an exporter of a farm commodity, wheat, for example, would be given debenture certificates valued, say, at 30 cents for each bushel of wheat exported. These debentures would be receivable for the payment of import duties and would be negotiable. What was proposed, therefore, was an export bounty for the farmer. Although Borah had opposed the McNary-Haugen measure, he favored the debenture plan because it did not have the constitutional objections he saw in the equalization fee and because it would not require the farmer to pay for his own relief.

[2] New York *American,* March 3, 1929.

A Federal Judge who was a member of Congress in 1929 says that when he was at the White House with a colleague the President told them that during the campaign he had been sure that he and Borah agreed on farm relief, but that now Borah had come out for the debenture. The Congressmen started to express their disapproval of Borah, but the President stopped them by saying that Borah was always right on moral and ethical questions and right three-fifths of the time on economic questions.

But on Capitol Hill regular Republicans were disgusted with Borah. Senator Fess (May 9) said that Senator Borah, having led the President to call the special session for the farmer, should by every rule of the game now support the President by voting against the export debenture scheme. "I am sure," said Mr. Borah, "that Mr. Hoover did not assume for a moment that by my support I was changing my views upon public questions or surrendering the right to form them." Then, without looking too straight at Mr. Fess: "Only a base class of intellectual slaves would entertain or promulgate such an idea."

The White House may have taken Borah's support of the debenture calmly, the "regulars" in the Senate with only a show of resentment, but Republican editors made the atmosphere blue. The Cincinnati *Times-Star* had some respect for Norris and other Senators who had refused to support Hoover in 1928. At least, it felt that it had done its duty when it expressed its contempt for them during the campaign. But Borah's offense was much greater than theirs. The principal speaker for Hoover, the man who had almost forced him to agree to call the extra session and who "did not have the courtesy to permit Mr. Hoover" to announce that the session would be called, now "whips out his oratorical dagger . . . and declares that he is stabbing for the good of the farmer." The editorial concluded: "Senator Borah serves only that he may later betray." [3]

Of course, less partisan editors pointed out that Borah owed Mr. Hoover nothing and that Mr. Hoover owed Senator Borah much, that it was absurd to expect the Senator to follow the President blindly on the matter of farm relief. The

[3] The Cincinnati *Times-Star,* May 12, 1929.

idea that the two had reached any understanding concerning specific methods of farm relief during the campaign was strongly questioned and it was asserted that in those days the candidate had a much better conception of Borah's program for the farmer than Borah had of his. Even in New England, where the "anti-Borah rash" started to break out before the special session of Congress was called, "Bob" Washburn was saying that Borah was consistent in advocating the debenture which he had favored now for two or three years.[4] Might it not be said that the President was deserting Borah rather than that Borah was deserting the President? At any rate, Borah was not deserting the farmer.

As the session proceeded with tariff legislation, Borah saw that a general revision was planned, not simply revision for the benefit of agriculture. The House passed a bill on May 28 which entirely ignored the President's recommendation of a limited revision, a bill which practically ignored the farmer. Borah proposed a resolution to limit tariff legislation in the Senate to the relief of agriculture (June 13).

The Washington *Post* characterized this as a resolution to kill the Republican party, as calculated to stir up war between the industrial East and the agricultural West. It stated that the passage of the resolution would amount to a revision of President Hoover's message to Congress in which he had, the *Post* admitted, laid stress upon the needs of agriculture and recommended only limited revision in certain other cases. The *Post* admitted also that the tariff bill which had already passed the House favored the industrial East and went far beyond the limited revision asked for. Yet it was certain that the Borah resolution should not pass. It "would make the Senator from Idaho the master of the Republican party during the brief period preceding its annihilation by internal explosion."[5] The President was doubtless strongly inclined to favor the resolution, but for some such reasons as those suggested by the *Post* he hesitated to declare for it. It was defeated in the Senate 39 to 38 (June 17). The next day the White House let it be known that the President was opposed to general tariff revision.

[4] *Transcript,* July 22, 1929.
[5] Washington *Post,* June 15, 1929.

With a regular old-time industrial tariff bill before the Senate, carrying, with the endorsement of the President, the provision that "the President shall investigate the differences in conditions of competition in the principal market or markets of the United States between domestic articles and like or similar competitive imported articles," the Senator directed his efforts chiefly against the flexible tariff provision (September 26). What relief has been given to consumers under the flexible tariff enacted in 1922? he asked. "The Tariff Commission made a reduction of the duty on bob-white quail; that was one of the five reductions which they made." While they reduced the duty on quail, "they increased the duty on straw hats."

"They reduced the duty upon paint brush handles, a matter of tremendous moment to the great mass of the people of the United States. . . As an offset the Commission increased the duty on pig iron . . . which simply added profits to already exorbitant profits. . . The Commission reduced the duty on cresylic acid and increased the duty on plate glass. They increased the duty on wheat, and at the same time reduced the duty on mill feed, which is the exterior or the hull of the wheat kernel. They reduced the duty on phenol, a chemical commodity, there being already practically no imports into this country. There is the list of reductions after nearly seven years of activity."

But he was opposed to the flexible tariff provision on constitutional grounds also. "The only thing Congress can delegate is the simple duty of ascertaining whether this or that particular fact is true, but when they attempt to delegate power to exercise judgment, or to reflect upon a proposition, or to determine a policy, and to write that into a rule that will become the law of the land, that is power which, in my judgment, it is far from the power of the Congress to delegate; that is legislating, that is law making, something we cannot delegate."

But did not the Supreme Court in the Hampton case (276 U.S. 394) sustain the constitutionality of the flexible provision of the tariff act of 1922? "With all due respect to the Supreme Court of the United States," answered the Senator, "that decision was a great surprise, I will say, to me. But if it establishes the law in that case it only enjoins upon us more definitely the proposition of guarding our rights as a law-making body."

Some Senators said the flexible provision was necessary. The one from Idaho replied : "Necessity has no proper place in our vocabulary when we are exercising the constitutional powers of this Government. We must either find the authority in the Constitution or we must halt and go back to the people and ask the people if they themselves want to delegate that power. Upon no other principle can a republican government long endure."

Mr. James M. Beck, a member of the House at this time, wrote the Senator that of all his able speeches he regarded this as his greatest. He said that it read, as few printed speeches do, with much of the fire of its oral delivery. On October 2, the Senate voted with Borah against the flexible tariff, 47 to 42, but as the bill was finally enacted nearly a year later it carried a flexible provision.

In this same speech Borah spoke again for the farmer. "The real fight here is between the agricultural interests and the industrial interests. We feel that we are fighting for equality ; that that equality is constantly removed by the fact that duties are substantially increased upon the things we have to buy, even though they may be increased to some extent upon the things we have to sell. The most important question to the country, the one thing which will be fought out here until the snow falls is whether these industrial schedules are justified ; whether they shall be maintained, or increased or diminished."

Then he tried to force the President to take a stand, asking from the floor of the Senate that "he advise this body and advise the country, as he did with reference to the flexible tariff provision, whether he approves of the industrial schedules in this bill. Does he approve of the duty upon cement, upon pig iron, upon commodities which increase the profits of the steel corporations ? Does he approve of the duty upon shoes ? Secondly, is he satisfied with the duties which have been levied upon agricultural products ? And, finally, will he advise us whether he is satisfied that this bill meets the pledges and the promises which he made in the last campaign? . . . Will he say to agriculture, 'You have received all you were promised'?"

Borah's constant advocacy of justice for the farmer in the matter of the tariff brought a letter of mild protest from his old friend Governor E. C. Stokes of New Jersey stating a fear that agricultural products would be increased in price. "My God," replied the Senator, "I wish I could believe that your fears are well justified. . . The disparity between the manufacturer and the farmer, with reference to protection, is pronounced and unmistakable and it is that disparity which I am interested in eliminating."

To Ray McKaig he repeated the exclamation he had used in his letter to the Governor and said: "If we only thought as much of the farmer this September as we did last September!"

At the time this correspondence was being exchanged Borah was very busy with his farm-bloc colleagues (Norris, Howell, La Follette, Nye, and ten others) devising means of defeating the worst features of industrial protection in the Hawley-Smoot tariff and of winning some benefits for the farmer. The majority of the Democrats, led by Senator Simmons, coöperated with Borah and his farm bloc. As early as September 5, Borah had said after a talk with the Democratic leader: "We are agreed upon procedure. . . We have a complete understanding as we go along." Two months later Senator Simmons confirmed Borah's statement, characterizing the coalition as one that resulted from a union of minds. It was this coalition which had made it possible for Borah's resolution to confine tariff revision to agricultural schedules to come so near passing on June 17. In the fall the combination held the majority on a number of significant tariff votes. For example, it defeated Mr. Hoover's great hope — the flexible provision — on October 2 and succeeded in inserting on October 19 a provision for the issuance of export debentures in the discretion of the Farm Board. So powerful had the coalition become that, on November 9, Senator Smoot expressed his wish that the Senate take a recess for ten days during which time the coalition should examine the amendments proposed and report to the Senate whatever amendments they might agree upon. But the coalition wanted the discussion continued in the Senate and it was continued until the special session adjourned on November 22. A number of the Republican leaders considered the bill practically dead at that time.

When Congress met in regular session in December, the tariff discussion was resumed. The coalition resumed its activity also, although there were signs of its disintegration as the session continued. Nearly all of the Democratic members of the coalition deserted the independent Republicans on the sugar-bounty issue. Borah, ever interested in encouraging the beet-sugar industry, could not find any help for that industry in ordinary tariff protection. In a Senate speech of January 14, 1930, he made the point that the chief beneficiaries of a tariff on sugar were the Filipinos, a large part of whose annual output of 600,000 tons (with every prospect of a great increase in production) was admitted to the United States free of duty. He made another point — that the preferential given to Cuban sugar was simply a bounty for American capital which controlled at least four-fifths of the sugar production on that island. The Senator had given considerable study to the question of a sugar bounty for producers in the United States and he wanted to follow the precedent of the McKinley bill (1890) which granted producers a bounty of two cents per pound. The Howell sugar bounty amendment met his desires in part, but as only five Democrats joined the independent Republicans in voting for the amendment, it was defeated by a vote of 22 to 54 (January 17).

But on some other questions of tariff legislation the coalition continued to function fairly well. The day before the vote was taken on the Howell Amendment they had won on a motion to reduce the tariff on sugar by a vote of 48 to 38. On January 24, Borah's amendment placing hides, leather, and shoes on the free list was adopted for the time being by a vote of 46 to 28. Also, temporarily, the coalition had its way with cement, crude aluminum, and certain other commodities. The coalition did not always win, but it greatly annoyed regular Republicans both in Congress and in private life. The stock-market crash had come and the dark cloud of the economic depression was settling down upon the country. Senators who were fighting the Hawley-Smoot tariff were told by many good Americans that if they had not caused the halt in prosperity they were certainly prolonging it. The Los Angeles *Times,* hating communists, Hiram Johnson, and Borah, and loving Herbert Hoover, was of the opinion that the coalition opposing the tariff bill had no other object than the personal glorification of its members unless it had the object of disrupting the Republican party. As for Borah, "the country at large will not soon forget his assaults upon the policies of a President in whom the nation has full confidence." [6]

But the New York *World* said that the tariff deadlock was caused by the fact that the President had abdicated leadership when he refused to announce his stand on the Borah resolution (the resolution of June 13, 1929, to limit tariff revision to agricultural schedules) until the day after the resolution was defeated. The *World* was convinced that calling the coalition bad names would not break the deadlock and that charging them with interfering with the country's business would not do it. The thing that would do it would be a declaration by the President of what kind of tariff he and his party were pledged to enact. "If he wishes results he must cease to speak in riddles." [7]

As the Senate was taking the final vote on a hide, leather, and shoe duty on March 20, 1930, an incident occurred which epitomizes the tariff struggle as the Senator from Idaho has always seen it. Senators from the northwest were in a quandary because they wanted the tariff on hides but their constituents would more than pay for it in the tariff on leather and shoes. Borah voted for the duty. The vote stood 35 to 35 when Joseph Grundy, until quite recently one of the most potent of tariff lobbyists, now Senator from Pennsylvania, entered the chamber. He voted for the duty and looked immensely pleased. This genial gentleman had only a few months before publicly characterized a number of the western states as "backward" and he still had his private opinions of their Senators. Seated directly behind him was Borah, whose mobile features registered a firm resolve.

[6] As quoted in the Lewiston *Weekly Tribune,* March 6, 1930.
[7] New York *World,* February 20, 1930.

When Grundy cast his vote, the whole history of tariff legislation seemed to pass through Borah's mind — the farmer and stock man could always have their little protection if they would vote for a double or treble portion for the manufacturer. He arose and changed his vote, thus delivering a body blow to Grundy. He would not have been human had he not smiled grimly when he took his seat.[8]

The months dragged on. The coalition did not hang together well in the last period of the contest, thus losing a great deal of ground it had gained in the earlier stages of the tariff marathon. The Hawley-Smoot bill, much more pleasing to the East then to the West, much more satisfactory to Senator Grundy than to the Senators who had taken the lead in the coalition, finally passed the Senate on June 13, 1930, and the House on the next day. Borah led the insurgents against it to the last, insisting that the debenture which had been eliminated from the bill was the one provision that would give the farmers relief. He used the word "iniquities" in characterizing the bill and stated that the flexible provision would not be used to reduce them in number or degree. He concluded with the statement that the Republican party had broken its pledge to put the farming industry on a "basis of economic equality with other industry." In the Senate the vote was 44 to 42, Borah voting with 30 Democrats, 10 Republican insurgents, and the Farm-Labor member against the bill. Against the advice of many economists the President signed the measure, thus definitely taking his place with Grundy and Smoot.

What did the farmer think of Borah's efforts on his behalf? A. S. Goss, Master of the Washington State Grange, gave his estimate in a letter to an Idaho Granger September 9, 1930:

"Few people realize what this fight has cost Senator Borah. When President Hoover first called Congress into special session, the Senator was his most intimate adviser and was recognized as his spokesman on the Floor of the Senate. This is a most powerful position and one to be guarded and preserved at almost any cost. I was in Washington when President Hoover was formulating the policy which resulted in his denouncing the debenture and was in daily touch with

[8] Minneapolis *Tribune*, March 21, 1930.

Senator Borah. I was with him in his office, I was with him in his home, and conferred with him frequently at the Capitol, and never once did he show any signs of yielding to the great pressure upon him, but without a question and unwaveringly he stood by what he believed to be for the best interests of the American farmer. He knew this would cost him the powerful position which he occupied in the Senate, but he did not hesitate.

"Later, when the opportunity presented itself to gain administrative favor in the handling of the tariff measure, Senator Borah again led the fight for justice for agriculture and demanded that the Republican Party keep its pledges made to agriculture.

"Throughout those days every manner of condemnation and abuse were heaped upon Senator Borah and those who followed him. They were called insurgents, obstructionists, mal-contents, demagogues, sons of wild jackasses, and every name which a hostile press could devise, but they stayed steadily with the fight, and all but won a complete victory. As it was, the final defeat of their plans was by no means overwhelming and it is due to their influence that agriculture and the common people got anything like a square deal."

It is desirable to say a word more about Borah and the tariff. He believes in the protective system. He believes that its benefits should be extended to all classes. It is because he believes Republican tariffs have failed to distribute these benefits to the farmers that he has usually voted against them. Many economists, letting pass the question of the merits of the protective system, say that it would be impossible to enact a tariff law which would equally benefit all classes.

After the Hawley-Smoot tariff had been enacted, Borah continued to advocate the debenture scheme as an aid to the farmers. He was much irritated in 1931 with the East and with the Administration for what he regarded as their failure to appreciate the extent to which the farmer was hit by the depression and for the failure of the President to call a special session of Congress for relief legislation in the summer of that year.

Of the ill-fated Farm Board, created in 1929 and designed

to promote the effective merchandising of agricultural commodities, control surpluses, etc., he wrote an Oregon farmer in 1931 that he could not tolerate the proposal of a wheat-acreage reduction. "Fully one-third of the human race is hungry," he said, "and I utterly reject the doctrine of the over-production of food stuffs while that is true. . . When wheat was $1.20 a bushel, the Farm Board encouraged the farmer to hold his wheat. Anyone acquainted with . . . world conditions at that time would have known that that was a suicidal policy. Had they been willing to accept the debenture plan, and in connection with the debenture plan, to have adopted a policy of working off our wheat and holding as best we could our foreign markets conditions would have been fairly good, notwithstanding the general depression. Other people stepped in and took our markets. It is now proposed that the cotton growers shall plough up every third row of their cotton. This seems to me like the dying paroxysm of a bankrupt policy." This, he said, would mean the ultimate ruin of our agricultural markets. In April, 1932, he cried out against the big salaries paid by the Farm Board. "I get so out of patience with these damn grafters who stick their fingers in everything that goes, that I can not well express myself," he wrote Ray McKaig.

THERE was practically no opposition to Borah in Idaho in 1930. It seems that the organization men as well as the people generally had decided that the State should give him a life membership in the Senate. The Democratic Lewiston *Tribune* came out with an editorial, "The Democratic Party Can Honor Itself," by putting no candidate in the field against Borah. "In this country, all over the world, the name of Senator Borah is synonymous with unwavering courage, lofty patriotism, high ideals, thoughtful and sympathetic concern for all who may be oppressed." [9] For organization purposes the Democratic party did put up a candidate but it might just as well have not done so. Borah was given all the votes at the Republican state convention except those of Franklin County whose delegates explained that they would not support him because he had not voted for higher duties

[9] Lewiston *Weekly Tribune,* April 10, 1930.

on sugar. Later the Republican leaders in that county assured him that he would receive his customary majority in that section. William Green called upon labor in Idaho to see to it that Borah won an overwhelming victory.

The Idaho election figures in 1930 were significant. For Governor: Democrat 73,896, Republican 58,002; for Congressmen: Democrats 45,660, Republicans 80,869; for Senator: Democrat 36,162, Republican 94,938.

In the campaign of this year Borah made a few statements in aid of Senator Schall in Minnesota and Pinchot in Pennsylvania, the latter advising Borah that his threat to investigate the use of power companies' money in campaigns had been very helpful to him. The Idaho Senator was particularly active on behalf of Senator Norris in Nebraska and gave quiet encouragement to the campaign of Thomas Walsh (Democrat) in Montana. Claude Bowers had written Borah that he certainly hoped that the Administration was not trying to marshal forces to defeat Walsh, that such action would be a melancholy reflection upon it. Borah replied that he was interesting himself in that situation.

WHILE the significant part Borah played in conducting foreign relations during the period he was Chairman of the Foreign Relations Committee has already been discussed, the visit of Premier Laval to the United States in October, 1931, throws so much light upon the Borah-Hoover relationship that it calls for additional comment. With the Hoover war-debt moratorium in effect and with England off the gold standard, President Hoover invited Premier Laval to come to Washington to discuss the gold standard and the intergovernmental debts.

The night before M. Laval arrived, the President called Borah to the White House alone. The President spoke in appreciation of Laval's frankness and directness, but he said he was not certain as to the subjects the Premier would introduce for discussion. The President mentioned the dominant rôle of France in Europe and stated that the settlement of affairs on that continent was almost entirely in the hands of France. He spoke of reparations and war debts and the Polish Corridor and expressed the opinion that there could be no disarmament without the settlement of some or all of these questions.

The Senator stated that from what he could gather it seemed to him that M. Laval had very little to offer, that it was quite unlikely that he would be willing to discuss reduction in reparations or the Polish Corridor. It seemed to him, therefore, that we could offer France nothing.

The President said these were European questions and he did not see how we could say much about them. Borah agreed that they were European questions, but stated that France was in control of the situation and that we could say to her that unless she had a program for dealing with it we could see no basis for reducing the war debts.

The President said that if we went into those matters the French idea of a security pact would arise. The Senator said that that should not be a subject for discussion, that it could be disposed of in one sentence — "You can not have it." The President said he agreed with the Senator, for the past ten years had convinced him that we wanted no commitments in Europe. He stated further that it was his opinion that we should not cancel the debts.

"There is just one chance in ten thousand that they will cut reparations," said Borah, "and less than one chance in ten thousand that they will settle the Polish Corridor question, so we have about one chance in ten thousand of ever having to consider the question of reduction of debts. But so far as I am concerned, if they would cut reparations to a proper basis and settle the Polish Corridor, I would be willing to make some contribution on the debts." He concluded by again stating his opinion that Laval would have little or nothing to offer and was simply on an expedition of exploration.[10]

While the President and the Premier were conferring (October 23), a score of French newspaper men who had accompanied the Premier asked for and received an interview at Senator Borah's office. "I suppose I have likely started something," wrote the Senator to a friend immediately after the interview, "but I can not but believe that frank discus-

[10] Dictated by Senator Borah the day after his conference with the President (October 22, 1931).

sions are necessary." The Senator certainly did start something. Berlin and Budapest were almost beside themselves with joy. Warsaw was enraged. Paris gnashed its teeth. The rank and file in France called Borah a swine ; the more cultured damned him deeper with their term "naïve." He raised a bumper crop of cheers and jeers in his own country. The jeers may still be harvested from the files of conservative newspapers (but not from all of them), the cheers from less conventional publications in the East and from nearly all the papers of every variety a few hundred miles removed from the Atlantic seaboard. His correspondence files were filled with letters about the incident. Many letters of congratulation came from responsible persons who resided 2000 miles east of Boise.

What had he done ? Well, he had answered some questions which the French correspondents had asked him. He had, at their request, answered them frankly. He said that the Polish Corridor should be returned to Germany and that the former boundaries of Hungary should be restored. "I do not think that you are going to get any disarmament in Europe so long as certain conditions which arise out of the Versailles Treaty continue to exist." There will have to be some changes in the Versailles Treaty, he said. "That is just my opinion, 3000 miles away."

"The question of using force for a peace as a peace proposition has never appealed to me at all." He said that force might bring peace but it would never bring justice and contentment. Of course he was opposed to our signing any security pact with France or any other nation.

How about the debts ? "If reparations had in the first place been confined to direct damages, they could have been justified, and France would have had damages for her injuries, and Belgium would have had and that could have been well justified." At this time "I have in mind cancelation of reparations in their entirety, and cancelation of international debts in their entirety." As for moratoriums, the time is past for them.

This was the interview, dealing with subjects upon which the President and the Senator had but two days before expressed substantial accord, which was characterized by Administration newspapers as "childish, naïve, simple-minded, ill-timed, raucous, mischievous, tactless, indiscreet, and immature." It is doubtful whether the President was half as much vexed by the interview as were his partisan supporters. To be sure, the Senator had "stolen the show." As the Louisville *Courier-Journal* somewhat whimsically put it: as the world audience was eagerly awaiting an act by Hoover and Laval "the majestic notes of the overture died away, the lights went down, the curtain rose – and there stood Senator Borah bowing in the spotlight!" [11] But on this point two observations are pertinent: first, the Senator had not asked for the show and, second, anyone's taste is exceedingly bad who infers that the President had wanted to stage a show at the White House. Finally, might it not have been a good thing for the French people to learn in this dramatic way, as they would not in any other, just what a leading spokesman for the American people thought? In any case, is it wrong for a public man to express himself frankly on public questions when urged to do so?

At a dinner for Premier Laval at the residence of the Secretary of State, the Premier and Borah had a most friendly conversation which lasted for about an hour and a half. The Premier very earnestly told the Senator that France wanted peace and disarmament but that if the United States would join in a security pact, agreeing to join in punishing all aggressors, it would bring peace to the world and France would disarm to reasonable limits.

"Do you see any chance anywhere in the future of a revision in respect to the Treaty of Versailles?" asked the Senator. The Premier said he could not speak for all time, but could see no chance for revision. The Senator asked: "Do you see any chance for disarmament until the Treaty is revised?" The Premier replied that there could be disarmament if they could get the security pact, a pact which, as the Senator understood it, would make inviolate and eternal the Versailles Treaty.

At this point Secretary Stimson asked the Premier about the attitude of France toward Germany, if there was any hope of escape from the feelings and fears which had obtained in

[11] *Literary Digest*, November 7, 1931.

the past. The Premier did not give a direct answer to this question, but spoke generally and at length of the three times France had been invaded by Germany and of the recent efforts to bring the two nations together economically. It was in the course of these explanations that he said, in effect : If you Americans will quit lending money to Germany and quit encouraging Germany, we can take care of Germany and we can bring about an adjustment, or settlement, which ought to obtain. Senator David A. Reed and Borah walked away from the party together, agreeing that the outlook was discouraging.[12]

THERE was much greater difference of opinion between the President and the Senator relative to the fitness of nominees for the Supreme Bench than there was over international affairs. When Chief Justice Taft resigned, the President immediately named Mr. Hughes for that exalted post. A gentleman of some consequence in New York wired Borah that "the ability to point to the record of a negative vote will in my opinion become an asset of which you may be proud." But Borah's mind was made up before this. He was opposed to the confirmation of Mr. Hughes not because he questioned his integrity, nor yet because he questioned his ability. On the contrary, he freely acknowledged these qualities in the great leader of the American bar.

Why, then, did he oppose him ? He opposed him because he disapproved of his economic views. The little civics book tells us that the judges are concerned only with interpreting the law and the implication is that their economic views make no difference. Borah knows what everyone with even a fragmentary knowledge of our Supreme Court knows — that the Court is not just a legal tribunal, but that it takes unto itself the deciding of great social and economic questions. It decides that states may not limit the hours which bakers may be employed but may limit the hours miners may be employed. It decides what limits legislative bodies may put upon the financial returns of public-utility companies and how such companies may be valued for rate-making purposes.

12 Dictated by Senator Borah two days after the dinner (October 26, 1931).

Senator Borah was of the opinion that Mr. Hughes, as demonstrated by his record as counsel before the Court, "feels that practically no restraint ought to be placed upon the vast corporate interests of the United States ; that he will go to the Bench as Chief Justice carrying with him the conviction that these efforts at restraint are unwise and that after all we must leave, in a large measure, the course of these vast interests to their own discretion and to their own judgment." He said we were entering "upon an era when the greatest undetermined question before us is determining the relationship of these vast corporate interests to the millions of people in the United States who must pay them toll year by year. Could there be any more profound question, touching the interest of every man, woman, and child in the United States for years and years to come, than the question of how much the oil people, the transportation people, and all others dealing with those questions shall charge . . . for their service ?" He believed that Mr. Hughes' "how much" as counsel had been too much and that as Chief Justice he would continue in the same view. In short, he considered that Mr. Hughes gave the rights of property first and too high a place and he was unwilling to give him the opportunity to read these views into the American economic fabric from the Supreme Bench.[13]

"The fight against Hughes," wired a distinguished liberal minister of New York City, "is the greatest thing that has happened in many years. Congratulations on your brave and enlightened leadership." The number of votes Borah and his co-workers were able to muster against Mr. Hughes (the vote was 52 for and 26 against) really amazed the country. Borah was of the opinion that his group could have defeated the confirmation of Hughes had certain material they received after the committee had reported been available prior to that date.

"What a bloody mess you made of things," someone wrote Borah. "Better take your orders from Mr. Hoover."

On the other hand, President Hoover might have taken a tip from the Senator. But he did not. About two months later he nominated Federal District Judge John J. Parker

[13] *Record,* February 11, 1930, pp. 3448 ff.

for Associate Justice of the Supreme Court. Borah instituted inquiries in North Carolina, Parker's State, as to his career as lawyer and judge. He was satisfied as to Parker's ability and standing, but he opposed him as he had opposed Hughes because of his social and economic philosophy. One of the high points in the objection to Parker was that he had sustained the "yellow dog" contract, an agreement of employment wherein the employee promises his employer not to join a trade union.[14] Just before the vote was taken on Judge Parker Borah made a short brilliant speech in which he denounced the charge that those who were opposing Parker were undermining the Supreme Court. He showed that Calhoun, Clay, Ewing, and Webster had opposed Taney's confirmation as Chief Justice, and rightly, because they did not like his interpretation of the Constitution, that Lincoln had opposed the Dred Scott decision because he differed with the judges on their interpretation of that instrument. The Senator exposed the absurdity of the claim, if an exposure was needed, that Senators should not consider the philosophy of nominees for the supreme Court.[15]

"It is very easy," wrote Borah during the debate on Parker, "when matters are pending here which involve the rights of labor for people to say that those who support the cause are demagogues and political cowards. If these same people would devote their rare intellectual attainments to ascertaining just what the question is and whether or not it is right, they might make a great saving of adjectives and epithets."

Judge Parker failed of confirmation on May 7, 1930, by a vote of 39 to 41. William Green immediately wrote Borah: "I can appreciate the fact that it requires unusual courage to espouse the cause of the masses of the people as against power and privilege. . . Your championship of human rights in this great struggle has endeared you to the hearts and minds of the working people of our country and of their loyal friends."

The Negroes were opposed to the confirmation of Parker because, although a Republican, he held essentially the same ideas as the southern Democrats regarding the place of the

[14] *Ibid.*, April 28 and 29, 1930, pp. 7930 ff.
[15] *Ibid.*, May 7, pp. 8486–8587.

Negro. It was stated at the time that the Negro protest had a great deal to do with the failure of the Senate to confirm Parker. Without a doubt it was a factor, but the New York *World* pointed out that of the seventeen Republicans who voted against Parker only two or three could be considered as having voted on the Negro issue; all of the others were regular progressives fighting to liberalize the Supreme Court. If the race question had been the issue, it is fair to assume that nearly all of the southern Senators would have voted for Parker. Actually nine voted for him and nine against him.[16]

When Justice Holmes resigned early in 1932, Borah immediately got in touch with people in New York and asked them to back Judge Benjamin Cardozo as his successor. They said they would be very glad to do so, but they did not want to move unless they could be fairly sure of success. The Senator replied that they could not be sure; that the President alone was responsible for the nomination; and that they ought to be willing to take the chance. They agreed to proceed.

The Senator went to see the President. The President had not thought of Cardozo but had thought of six or seven other men the name of only one of whom the Senator recalled three years later. The Senator told the President that if he were in his place he would not lose a moment's time in naming Judge Cardozo, for this outstanding man was eminently qualified for the place.

On the Sunday preceding the Monday on which the nomination was made, the President sent for Borah. He handed him a list, in order of his preference, of names of men he was considering for the nomination. At the top of the list was a man who was a judge in the Southwest. The Senator remembers his name because he recalls that he was the President's first choice. At the bottom of the list was the name of Judge Benjamin Cardozo. The Senator smiled, and said, "Your list is all right, but you handed it to me upside down." The President said that there were already two men from New York on the Supreme Bench. The Senator replied that he was naming a man to succeed the immortal Holmes and that geography should have nothing to do with the selection.

[16] New York *World*, May 8, 1930.

The President had no objection to Cardozo because he was a Democrat nor did he object on the ground of race, but he stated that the latter objection had been made. He had been advised that there should not be two Jews on the Bench. Borah replied that he would not give a moment's consideration to this objection. "Anyone who raises the question of race is unfit to advise you concerning so important a matter," he added.

But could we get Judge Cardozo through the Senate? asked the President. The Senator said he was positive that the Senate would not spend fifteen minutes in confirming the appointment; in fact, he was willing to guarantee favorable action. The President was impressed with this declaration, and told the Senator that if he sent in the name of Cardozo he would expect him to take care of it.[17] The Senator replied that there would be no occasion for taking care of Judge Cardozo. And so the baffled President, in the tragic winter of 1932, won the practically unanimous acclaim of his countrymen for naming Judge Cardozo to succeed Justice Holmes.

In an editorial for the *World's Work* of June, 1929, Borah vigorously attacked the call money plan as a method of promoting stock gambling. "Abolish the daily settlement plan of the New York Stock Exchange," he urged, "and substitute the fortnightly or weekly clearings of the European exchanges, and a certain and definite curb on Wall Street gambling and sudden money panics will be in the process of achievement. . . The daily settlement plan makes possible perilous confusion and frantic stampedes when anything in the nature of a panic is in the air. With daily clearings the public can rush in at any moment and buy insanely; just so it can sell in a frenzy of fear, whereupon the cost of call money can jump from six per cent to thirty per cent and back again to six per cent in a few hours. . .

". . . With American speculation in a dozen American exchanges what it is today, the whole world can be subjected to a demoralizing money stringency with thirty per cent call

[17] Dictated by Senator Borah the day after the conference with the President (February 15, 1932). Amplified in discussion with the Senator.

money under the daily settlement rule that now prevails. It would seem to be time for the Federal Reserve Board in Washington to comment on this fact and make some public declaration — even though it might stir up many of the spectacular leaders of bull operations to further denunciation of the Board for interference with their glorious gambling drives.

The Senator also called attention to the fact that six billion dollars had been drawn from legitimate business operations for use on the Exchange. He concluded that unless drastic limitation was put upon the call-money system a world-wide smash would come. His warnings were not heeded and they were probably too late. Even so, he was one of the few public men who seemed to realize the grave dangers of stock-market prosperity.

Borah's warning was not appreciated. Indeed, when the November crash came, many very reputable business men had an entirely different explanation of the "lack of confidence" throughout the country — Congress had caused it by its delay in completing the task of making a tariff. Borah then suggested that the stock exchange might well be investigated. Perhaps Mr. Hoover did not believe that Congress had caused the crash, but as the depression continued he seemed to have some fear that Congresses might be obstacles to recovery. At least the President made efforts to prevent any extra session to deal with the question of relief, and his "superlative impudence" in this matter triumphed over Senator Borah and others who wanted a special session in the summer of 1931.

The big fight between Administration forces and Borah came over the question of relief for sufferers, particularly drought sufferers, on February 2, 1931. The Administration was willing to give relief, but it was opposed to voting direct relief for individuals. The Senate had already passed a measure calling for $25,000,000 for direct relief and members of the House had given out interviews condemning the scheme, saying it was unprecedented. Full of earnestness and passion, Borah arose in the Senate and accused them of intellectual dishonesty. He showed that relief had often been granted in such cases. He stated, amid applause on the floor and in the galleries, that he was ready to fight to keep

Congress in session "until the hungry are fed, until the sick are taken care of, until the Government of the United States has met its obligation to its diseased and hungry citizens." [18] Nearly two weeks later the Senator was on his feet again on the same subject. This time he questioned the accuracy of a report issued by the President's representative who had made a hurried tour of inspection through the stricken regions. The report stated that the Red Cross had the situation well in hand. The Senator said that was just an opinion, just the sort of thing they had been hearing for some time. He then read what the representative of the *Christian Science Monitor* had to say after his visit to the same areas. This observer held that the Red Cross had not adequately relieved suffering. He read from other sources which substantiated the claim the *Monitor* representative had made.[19]

"I reject utterly the doctrine that the government owes nothing to its citizens," he wrote in a letter a few days later. "When the citizen is overtaken by an act of God, such as the drought, a government that would not aid him would be a disgrace to the map of the world." Borah was told that all his utterances about the obligations of the government to its citizens were defeating the efforts of the Red Cross to raise money for the sufferers ; that it was causing people to get false hopes of what was going to be done for them ; and that government aid would ruin the spirit of the people. One critic wrote Borah that he should pay some attention to public opinion and enclosed an editorial from the New York *Sun*. Borah asked another critic how much he had contributed to the Red Cross. "Five dollars, and thank God for Mellon and Hoover," was the reply.

But with all the criticism he received, Borah retained a sense of humor. Speaking at the Progressive Conference in Washington on March 11, 1931, he referred to Alexander Hamilton as "one of the two greatest Secretaries of the Treasury we have had." Catching this dig at Mr. Mellon, the audience laughed. Whereupon Borah stated that he might have been referring to Albert Gallatin.

His frontal attacks on the Administration for its opposi-

[18] *Record*, February 2, 1931, p. 3760.
[19] *Ibid.*, February 14, 1931, p. 4890.

tion to any appropriation for the purpose of feeding the people, his criticisms of unduly optimistic statements about good times being just around the corner, and his advocacy of a special session of Congress for 1931 placed him miles away from the Administration. In fact, their differences were such that a White House invitation to lunch in March was not only regarded as newsworthy but as meriting large headlines in some newspapers. The President and the Senator talked for two hours, but neither was willing to report the conversation.

The Senator continued to say during 1931 that the government should grant direct relief where private agencies were unable to give it, and in February, 1932, there was a repetition of the fight of the year before for such relief. In the debate over the La Follette-Costigan relief bill, Borah dramatically denounced as slanderers of their countrymen any Senators or administrative officials who said that direct relief granted to American men and women in distress would ruin their fibre and soon make us a nation of dole gatherers.[20] (Here was Borah's faith in the people again.) The bill was defeated, and on February 18 the Chicago *Tribune* ran an editorial on the "Defeat of the Beggar States."

As has been stated, Borah had no hope that the depression would end soon. He came to this conclusion early in 1931. His solution for it, as proposed in 1932, was "that unless the armaments of the world are reduced, so that that burden will be lightened upon the people ; unless reparations are settled, so that Europe can regain economic recovery; and unless silver is restored to the place which it occupied prior to 1925, so that nearly one-half of the human family may have means by which to transact business, and, to some extent, restore their purchasing power, there can not, in my judgment, be any ready return to prosperity." [21] At other times the Senator indicated his willingness to cancel the allied war debts to this country in return for their cancelation of reparations and for trade concessions.

Perhaps the chief item in Borah's program for domestic recovery was currency expansion. In the spring and summer

[20] *Ibid.*, February 10, 1932.
[21] *Ibid.*, May 5, 1932.

of 1932, he supported the Glass bill, designed to accomplish that purpose to a limited degree. On July 5, he stated: "Congress should not adjourn until the problem of the expansion of the currency has been considered. We have sufficient gold in this country to justify upon a sound basis currency expansion to the extent of billions if necessary." He stated that if measures for expansion were not soon adopted Congress would later be compelled to devalue the dollar. Three days later, he offered the original Glass bill as an amendment to the Home-Loan Bank bill. He said: "I am not arguing for paper money or fiat money or attacking the gold standard, but I am of the opinion that the gold standard is sufficient if utilized to the end to which it should be utilized. Conservatism has come to be a cover for timidity. We have the power in our gold supply to do vastly more than we have been willing to do." This amendment, providing for about $1,000,000,000 of additional currency, was adopted by the Senate on July 11. The program of currency expansion, without departing from the gold standard, was a program which Borah repeatedly urged as a means of checking the fall in prices. It was a program for which he received no support from the Administration.

A minor domestic item on his recovery program was a reduction of salaries of all government employees who received as much as $2500 or $2000 a year. A significant domestic item was his *opposition* to a sales tax, either national or state. When the agitation for this tax was started in Idaho late in 1932, he wrote a friend a letter which is worthy of extended quotation. "The sales tax," he said, "violates the most fundamental law of taxation, that is, that taxes should be laid in accordance with ability to pay. This tax is laid in accordance with the necessities of the people and it strikes home with those who are the least able to pay. It can be passed on more perfectly and completely than any other tax, and you can well see how heavily it would bear upon those least able to meet their obligations.

"The one thing needed to restore prosperity is the restoration of purchasing power to the masses. It is not sufficient that a few be able to buy what they want, but in order that we may receive anything like a return to better days, there

Courtesy of Berryman and the Washington Star

must be a restoration of purchasing power to the great body of the people. This tax is in opposition to everything of that kind. . . In this particular instance we are reaching down to get hold of the pennies of the poor.

"It is argued that this tax is necessary to meet the present emergency. The trouble is, that with the tax once established, it will be practically impossible to get rid of it. It should be borne in mind that long before the present emergency arose, there was an effort upon the part of large interests to establish a sales tax in order to relieve their own taxes. . .

"I sincerely hope that before any such proposition becomes a law, it will be thoroughly discussed among the people of the State. We have the same proposition here [in Washington] and I presume in all probability it will succeed in passing, but not without opposition."

PROHIBITION remained one of the prime concerns of Senator Borah during President Hoover's term of office. Just before Mr. Hoover was inaugurated, Senator Reed of Missouri, about to retire to private life, and Senator Borah staged a debate on the Eighteenth Amendment. These two veterans, warm personal friends and usually on the same side on matters of foreign policy, were as far apart as the poles on Prohibition. No particular purpose was served by the debate, but Representatives and clerks who lined the walls of the Senate Chamber and the gentlemen of the press and the general public in the galleries were highly satisfied at having seen the two foremost debaters of the Senate have it out before one of them quit the Chamber.

On June 8, 1929, the Senator had an article on Prohibition in *Collier's* entitled "Speak Up or Shut Up." "No use skulking in the shadow of a blind pig," he wrote. "What is your offer in place of the Eighteenth Amendment?" On July 28, he had an article in the New York *Times* on the obligation of the states to help enforce that Amendment.

On December 24, 1929, Borah issued a statement to the press, the significant part of which read: "I am not deeply concerned about a report of the [Wickersham] Commission. The great facts that stand out with me are these: We have the law; the Supreme Court has construed it. There is no difficulty about the officers understanding it. But have we the officials who are willing to execute the law?" He concluded that there could be no adequate enforcement until the personnel had had a shaking up from top to bottom. Later he declared that practically open saloons were operating under the noses of district attorneys in other cities than New York and Chicago. For good measure he said that the Federal permit system under which industrial alcohol was released constituted a scandal.[22] Coming during the holiday season, these announcements received wide publicity. They were "poo-pooed" by good Hoover newspapers and the drys generally advised the Senator to be more restrained in his utterances and to "stand by the President."

On December 26 he had lunch with the President. The conversation was devoted exclusively to Prohibition enforcement. The President was of the opinion that they were making progress. He mentioned certain changes in the or-

22 Washington *News*, December 30, 1929.

Courtesy of the Hartford Times

ganization for enforcement, commenting particularly upon the removal of the enforcement division from the Treasury to the Justice Department. He hoped for help from a report the Commission would issue shortly. He stated that the personnel of enforcement was better than it had been, although he admitted that some changes would have to be made.

The Senator was very positive that the real trouble was with the personnel and he told the President that he would never get district attorneys who would enforce the law as long as he followed the long-established practice of nominating for district attorneyships men recommended by Senators in whose states appointments were to be made. He explained that it was politics for such Senators to trim and sidestep and to recommend district attorneys who would do the same. Borah recommended that the President make the nominations without regard to any party organization and in particular without regard to the wishes of an individual Senator in whose state an appointment was to be made.

The President made no comment on Senator Borah's suggestions as to appointment of district attorneys, but a day or two later he wrote the Senator to give him his plan more fully. The Senator gave his opinion that in choosing judges and other officers of the court, the President should nominate the men he wanted, paying no attention to the wishes of individual Senators. The Senate as a body, without benefit of "senatorial courtesy," would then confirm or reject the President's nominees.

"I believe the people would overwhelmingly support you," he continued, "in an *announced policy* [italics mine] that you would feel free to select men purely upon their fitness and regardless of organization or senatorial recommendations. I feel, furthermore, that if such a policy were announced, a good majority of the Senate would support the practice. Of course, if the matter came up as a test upon some particular appointment, the situation would be different. But if it came up as an announced policy and if the Senate understood that was to be the policy, I have no doubt as to what the result would be in the Senate.

"Everyone must realize that such a course has become absolutely indispensable to clean, efficient and able public service. In my opinion, it would make a change, the benefits of which cannot well be overestimated."

Then comes an elementary lesson on the Constitution. "You say that Senators might conscientiously feel there would be danger in placing such unlimited authority in the hands of the President. But how could they argue that? Nowhere in the Constitution . . . is there any provision, any plan, or implication of provision or plan, of the right of Senators from a state — and of course the right of organizations — to dominate appointments — that belongs to the President. The safeguard which the fathers contemplated is found in the consenting power of the Senate as a body — where only the fitness of the man can be successfully challenged, and that challenge would have to be in the open and the facts disclosed. All this vicious practice of organizations and Senators impressing their views on appointments is outside of the Constitution, beyond the law, and, in my judgment, too often results in crowding the public service with a vast number of political accidents, political incompetents, not to say corrupt officials.

"My idea, therefore, is to adopt the course which the President has a perfect right under the Constitution and the law to adopt, and if there is any challenge to it, let public opinion pass judgment.

"I want to say, Mr. President, that if this should meet with your judgment and approval, I assure you I will support you wholeheartedly and with whatever ability and influence I may have, both in the country and in the Senate. You are bound to be successful. . ."

But the President consulted with some other Senators and they told him that Borah's plan would cause a "young revolution" in the Senate. Furthermore, the President advised Borah that the matter of appointments was only one of the many angles to the problem of Prohibition enforcement. All things considered, he felt that he must drop the Borah idea of appointments.

"Great and dear friend of the long years," Colonel Robins was writing the Senator about the same time the Senator was discussing Prohibition with the President, "I covet for you the supreme leadership in the maintenance of the Constitution and the reëstablishment of American liberty in this generation. — In love and faith."

After the elections of 1930 had revealed a strong wet tendency, Borah declared that the only issue over the Eighteenth Amendment was now repeal or no repeal. When the Wickersham report came out a few months later, he stated that it did not help the situation and repeated his statement that the only issue was that of repeal. This aroused his indignation much less than had the light wine and beer and "leave the alcoholic content to be determined by the states" talk of previous years. Repeal was an honest constitutional issue, not a method of circumventing or nullifying the Amendment.

The country became completely engulfed in the depression. The political parties met and drafted their platform. The Republican convention wanted to endorse repeal but was afraid to do so ; consequently, it simply agreed to refer the matter to the people. The Democrats, having had the advantage of witnessing popular reaction to the Republican plank, decided that a straight repeal plank would make a good issue. Borah declared that there was no difference between the two planks, except that the Democrats spoke directly while the Republicans spoke indirectly. He was opposed to repeal and would support neither group in the campaign. Some people wanted him to run on a third ticket, but he soon decided not to do that either.

A Republican county chairman wrote Borah in October, 1932 : "Do you think you are giving the party the same support you would expect from the party if you were a candidate for reëlection at this time ?"

"Unequivocally, yes," replied Borah. "I have been in active politics for twenty-seven or -eight years and during that time I have never had one particle of support from the national committee and have never used one dollar of their money. The national party organization has never given me any support whatever. I recall distinctly that the first time I was a candidate for the Senate, William H. Taft came into the State, spoke at Boise and I was on the platform. Fred Dubois [Democratic candidate for the Senate] had ridden with him all day on the train, and that night Mr. Taft did not so much as mention my name." He went on to say that his support from the state organization had not been much better, but that he did not mind as he did not want support except from those who accepted his doctrine of Republicanism.

A chairman of a Republican league in the State said they might have to change Senators in 1936 if he did not support Hoover. Borah replied : "I am sorry . . . that after forty years of residence in this State . . . I have left so poor an impression with the people of my State that any of them would suppose that by such threats I would be moved in my position in regard to public matters. . .

"My position with reference to public questions in this campaign is the same as it was when I covered fourteen states of the Union in 1928. . . I am aware it is not consistent with some of the views of the President. Personally I am truly sorry that is so because it would be much more agreeable to me to be in harmony with the President. But I want to assure you now definitely and conclusively that I shall not change my position upon public questions and I am perfectly willing to take the political consequences. . ."

The national Republican organization continued to annoy the Senator with requests and entreaties that he come out for Hoover. One night they called him at Lewiston, Idaho, after he had gone to bed. A political supporter who was traveling with him answered the telephone and said to the Senator, "It's Sanders again." The Senator jumped up in bed and told his friend to say that if the Republican headquarters did not leave him alone he would deliver a speech that would make Senator Johnson's "It Might Have Been Worse" denunciation of Hoover read like a Sunday School pamphlet.

A man in New York wired Borah in September that Russia was to be recognized, the war debts were to be considered objectively, and tariff adjustments were to be made. You will be "in the most commanding position possible if you will hibernate until after election."

Borah hoped that Hoover would say something in his Des Moines speech he could take hold of and support, but neither in this speech nor in any other did the President satisfy the Senator. His only assistance to Hoover, which was quite indirect, was in his statement (October 26) that Smith's denunciation of the Prohibition forces in his Newark speech was one of the most effective utterances yet made for Mr. Hoover. At this time it was reported that Borah had said he would vote for Hoover. However, in response to a wire from the United Press at Salt Lake City, Borah replied that he did not recall having made such a statement. It seems, though, that he did finally decide to cast his vote for Mr. Hoover.

Senator Borah made his greatest contribution of the campaign period, but not in the interest of any candidate, in a speech at Minneapolis on August 3. What is the way out of the depression? He answered: an all-inclusive world conference in which the Versailles Treaty, disarmament, war debts, tariffs, and monetary problems must be settled. America could well afford to cancel the war debts in return for disarmament, tariff adjustments, and markets, he said. He was congratulated by many distinguished Americans and applauded in European countries. He traveled over Idaho, stressing these same ideas during the campaign, adding to them the need for scaling down farm mortgages. He paid very little attention to the fight for the presidency.

As far as the election was concerned, his efforts were limited to a sincere plea for the reëlection to the Senate of his colleague John Thomas. Thomas had written Borah in August that the only disturbing factor in Idaho politics was Hoover and "that is simply hell." Thomas went down with Hoover in November.

In conclusion, what of Borah's attitude toward Hoover from 1929 to 1932? Was he simply trying to annoy him? Did he enjoy playing upon his political ineptitudes? Did he hate him? Let the Senator answer this question. He does it very well in a letter he wrote in 1930:

"In your letter you say: 'Now, what I would like to know is this: Have you fallen out with the President.' I have not to my knowledge fallen out with the President. I have no personal feeling myself whatever. I am pursuing the course which I have pursued for twenty-four years and which I trust I will have the courage to pursue while I am in public life, and that is, recording my convictions upon public questions as they come along.

"Truly, Mr. Eriksson, what would you have a Senator do? As an illustration: One of the things about which much has been said in my differing with the President is that of the debenture. I was an advocate of the debenture long prior to Mr. Hoover's nomination or election to the Presidency. If you had been in my place would you have simply changed your position and voted not as you felt but as somebody else wanted you to vote?

"It so happens that I have not advocated a single proposition since the election of Mr. Hoover that I had not advocated prior to the election of Mr. Hoover. May I ask you a question therefore: What would you have a Senator do? Sincerely represent his views, however inadequate they may be, or act as an intellectual prostitute for some party organization?

"Take my position, for instance, with reference to the farmer and the tariff. If you care to read a speech of mine which I made sixteen years ago on this subject, you will find I have been advocating in this session what I so earnestly advocated at that time. I have no doubt as to the correctness of my position. I believe I am working in the interest of agriculture. Furthermore, I am advocating what I advocated in the campaign. And I am advocating what I thought the President advocated in the campaign.

"I might go on, but this letter is long enough, I think. But I am sure, Mr. Eriksson, you will get my view.

"There is an ideal Senate over in Italy, Mr. Eriksson. If any Senator expresses views unsatisfactory to the Prime Minister or if he records a vote unsatisfactory to him, he is either driven from public life or sent as a prisoner to one of the Islands which has been set apart to take care of Mussolini's enemies. That is the most ideal Senate, I suppose, in existence according to the views of a great many people. But I can not quite bring myself to conform my acts to that ideal. I am sure if you were in my place you would feel the same way. . ."

A striking story might be made of the rupture and enmity between Borah and Hoover, but like many striking stories it would not be altogether a true story. It is true that they were temperamentally different. It is also true that Hoover's lack of sympathy with progressive principles was a severe disappointment to Borah. The Senator found it necessary to differ strenuously with the President on the tariff, farm relief, unemployment relief, judicial appointments, the World Court, Prohibition, Andrew D. Mellon, high governmental expenditures, the creation of bureaus and commissions, silver and the currency, and the independence of the Philippines. On the other hand, he was a supporter of the President's disarmament program, he applauded his resistance to the "big navy" advocates, he approved his Latin American policy, and he reported favorably to the Senate scores of treaties proposed by the Administration. Perhaps there was more conflict than coöperation between the two men, but to state that there was constant enmity would be an egregious fallacy. Their differences were on issues. One might be tempted to say that such frequent and fundamental differences on issues must result in personal enmity. It frequently does, but if there is one trait of character that distinguishes William E. Borah from the great majority of his fellows, it is his desire and capacity to consider issues apart from the person or persons who advocate or oppose them, to work with men today and work against them tomorrow as issues come and go. If this unvarying rule of conduct brought to the Senator the enmity of the President the Senator is sorry, but if he had it all to do over again his course would be the same.

CHAPTER XXIII

THE NEW DEAL

"A GREAT individualist and moralist . . . goes down in defeat before a new day's forces," wrote Jay Franklin in *Vanity Fair* (June, 1933), in a very penetrating article on Senator Borah. With the Democratic victory in the Senate, which deprived him of his post as Chairman of the Committee on Foreign Relations, with the country swinging away from individualism toward collectivism and manifesting an impatience with constitutional restraints, with Prohibition repealed and with wars waged despite peace pacts, the "Lone Wolf of the Northwest" was regarded by Franklin as in a pitiable position. Presidents we may "repeal," but they may go, somewhat dazed, into a dignified retirement. A "rotten borough" Senator must stay on, a political Prometheus, seeing his policies nullified and his reputation destroyed. The writer was genuinely sorry for the honest, industrious, studious, sincere, and kindly Borah.

But the tragedy was not so great as the sorrowing writer pictured it. The rôle of the Senator under the New Deal proved to be about what it had been under all other deals. Somehow there was still a place for the man who supported an administration when he approved of a policy and opposed it when he disapproved a policy. That has been Senator Borah's program from the day Theodore Roosevelt denounced malefactors of great wealth until and after the day Franklin Roosevelt announced that the money changers had fled from the temple. But perhaps tragedy is found in the fact that Borah spoke little and lost the front page of the newspaper during the first months of the New Deal. No; the Senator had spent months in silence before, months in 1908 in which he had learned the functions of a Senator. Now he was content to be silent again until he had had time to learn what the New Deal was, and until a declaration would rise above mere partisan mouthing.

It is a matter of common knowledge that the banks of the country were in utter collapse when Roosevelt was inaugurated and that he immediately proclaimed a four-day bank holiday, put an embargo on gold, and called Congress into special session to deal with the crisis. On March 9, after forty minutes of discussion of a measure of which its members did not know the contents, the House passed the President's banking bill by acclamation. The bill then went to the Senate and many House Members went with it in the hope of learning from the Senate discussion the nature of the bill the House had just passed. The Senate debated the bill for three hours. Senator Borah secured a copy at 4:45 P.M. It was passed at 7:00, Borah and six other Senators voting against it. "Babe Ruth at last has signed up, but Senator Borah is still holding out," commented a wag.

"Why didn't you vote with them and thus place all of the responsibility on their doorstep?" a gentleman wrote from Idaho. "What about my constitutional oath?" the Senator inquired in turn.

In other letters he explained that he had voted against the bill because he was convinced beyond any doubt that it was unconstitutional and conferred autocratic powers upon the President. He was convinced, furthermore, that in some respects it was unjust and unwise – that it would destroy state banks and some national banks and centralize the banking system in New York. "Country banks are more important in many respects to the salvation of the country now than the large banks in the great centers," he advised a correspondent. He objected also to the measure because it did not guarantee bank deposits, a guarantee which was given in the banking bill passed later in the summer. Finally, even "if I had been in favor of the bill I would not have voted for it under such circumstances. I decline to be an intellectual slave, even when I am being lashed in the direction in which I want to go."

The economy measure, which authorized the President to use very wide discretion in lowering salaries and veterans' benefits, Borah opposed as an instrument of autocracy and as an unconstitutional delegation of legislative power.

THE monetary policies of the New Deal were more to the Senator's liking, although they were not in exact accord with his ideas.

Senator Borah approved, with certain reservations, the Thomas Amendment to the Emergency Agricultural Act. This "inflation" amendment authorized the President to arrange for the purchase in the open market of government obligations up to the value of three billion dollars, the purpose of such purchase being to raise prices and stimulate trade. If this should not have the desired effect, the President might issue United States notes up to three billion dollars, reduce the gold content of the dollar by as much as 50 per cent, and provide for the unlimited coinage of silver at a fixed ratio with gold. The Senator stood ready to vote for the amendment as a whole, but he hoped the provision relative to reducing the gold content of the dollar would be stricken out. He said that its effect would be deflationary rather than inflationary and that uncertainty as to the value of the dollar two or five years hence would prevent any revival in business and any improvement in prices. "I do not say that I would not vote under some circumstances to reduce the value of the gold in the dollar. But that is one of those things which, as Shakespeare said : 'If it were done, when 't is done, then 't were well it were done quickly.' We cannot . . . hang a sword of Damocles over the business world in the nature of deflation of the dollar and not have a deflationary effect upon business." He felt also, although he did not discuss this point at length, that there were constitutional objections to delegating to the President this power to reduce the gold content of the dollar.[1]

When the bill, including the section on reducing the gold content of the dollar, had passed, Borah was quite ready to join with the majority and pass the resolution canceling or "repudiating" the "gold clause" in contracts. "Gold coin of the present weight and fineness," to use the term of these contracts, referred to a gold dollar containing 23.22 grains of gold. The resolution provided that such contracts should be satisfied by payment in legal money, whatever it might be, at the time payment fell due. In other words, whatever Congress declares to be a legal dollar was declared to be a dollar in satisfaction of any contract regardless of the specification in a contract as to what constituted a dollar. As it

[1] *Record,* April 26, 1933, p. 2403.

turned out, this meant that dollars representing a weight of 15 5/21 grains of gold had to be accepted for the 23.22 grain dollars specified in the "gold clause" contracts.

Senator Borah defended the passage of the joint resolution canceling the gold clauses both on constitutional grounds and on grounds of policy. Referring to the clause of the Constitution reading, "The Congress shall have power . . . to coin money, regulate the value thereof, and of foreign coin," Senator Borah declared that "the Supreme Court has construed that provision of the Constitution to mean that the Congress has full and complete and plenary power over the entire subject of money." He cited cases to prove this contention, and concluded the constitutional argument with the statement that the power of Congress over money was not limited by contractual relations.

Mr. Glass: "Mr. President, does the Senator contend that it is competent for the Congress to declare that 12.9 grains of gold constitute 25.8 grains of gold?"

Mr. Borah: "No; I do not contend that, but I contend that Congress may declare that a dollar with 12.9 grains must be accepted in payment of a dollar of 25.8 grains. It may fix the value of the dollar, the value of money."

Considering the question from the standpoint of policy, the Senator admitted that the cancelation of the gold clause in government obligations amounted to repudiation and that holders of private bonds would suffer some. But he argued that these were simply a part of the loss bondholders must carry in the period of readjustment. He said that the world is today off the gold standard and that the United States must adjust her currency or lose still more in trade and commerce to nations which have adopted the managed-currency system. "Now, Mr. President," he concluded, "I concede that there is some harshness here. But we are dealing with a great national emergency. I would not legislate against the bondholder, but I would legislate in the interest of the Nation as a whole. If in doing so some detriment flows to the bondholder then I say . . . the bondholder was made for the country, not the country for the bondholder." [2]

Borah considered that the masses would benefit by the

[2] *Record*, June 3, 1933.

devaluation of the dollar, since the gold dollar of March, 1933 represented twice as many pounds of potatoes, wheat, and cotton as it had represented a few years before. As long ago as July 8, 1932, Borah had defined the "honest dollar" as "merely a dollar which will purchase the same quantity of commodities today as upon some agreed previous date. An honest dollar is a stable dollar."

On November 25, 1933, he defended the President against the criticisms of Alfred E. Smith, O. M. W. Sprague, James P. Warburg, and others. "I doubt if the critics of the President's monetary policy will succeed in winning public opinion away from the President unless they are prepared to offer an affirmative, constructive program. . . We had the gold standard for three and one-half years of the depression. We should have had the confidence which it is said now waits on a return of the gold standard. . . The only thing that is offered now by the critics of the President is a return to the gold standard and apparently the program which marked the gloomy days from October, 1929 to March 3, 1933. . ."

But on one phase of the monetary problem the President did not move fast enough for Borah. That was on the silver question. From 1890 to 1900 the Idaho attorney had been interested in silver as a commodity and as money. He had left his party on this issue in 1896 and 1898. The world-wide depression brought him back to the silver question. Over and over he spoke for silver. In October, 1930, he said that "an international agreement between the leading nations, fixing the ratio of silver and gold, should be urged, and that there are some reasonable grounds to believe it might be had. If such an agreement could be had it would lead at once to full use of silver in India, China, and other countries. Fully one-half of the human family wants to use silver and on any sound international agreement they would do so." [3]

In May, 1931, former President Coolidge made bold to say that silver had been cheapened by the increased use of machinery and invention in its production. The Senator stated that there was no over-production of silver; in fact, more silver was being consumed than was being produced.

[3] Lewiston *Weekly Tribune,* October 16, 1930.

What had happened, he said, was that an over-supply of silver had been brought about because governments had ceased coining silver money or had reduced the silver content of their coins, thus flooding the markets of the world with silver.[4]

From the Senator's numerous utterances on the silver question during the New Deal period we may take as an example his Senate speech of January 26, 1934, when the Senate had under consideration the Gold Reserve bill. He approved of this bill, which called for the "nationalization" of the gold supply, because he considered it a step in the right direction. Then he turned to the question of silver. "A large portion of the world which is without gold cannot use paper. They have no banking system. They have no checking system. . . They want silver. They have used silver for 2000 years. In the name of justice why not give it to them?" The nations of wealth have followed the practice of increasing the value of their holdings by decreasing the amount of money in circulation, he said. But they may follow this plan to their ruin, as the present depression indicates. One way out is to remonetize silver which will give the hundreds of millions in the Far East a medium of exchange, thus reviving the commerce of the world and increasing prices. "I undertake to say, Mr. President, that until we shall have restored the money of the Constitution, specifically written into the Constitution . . . until we shall give the people of the world a metallic basis for their currency, we shall not be in a position to expect any trade or commerce from that part of the world which has no metallic money, and we shall not restore the purchasing power of the masses."

The silver men in Congress put on an intensive campaign during the session in which this speech was made. They besieged the Treasury Department and the White House on behalf of the white metal. Borah had been reluctant to go to the White House on this mission because he was of the opinion that the President was not warmly favorable to silver. But one day his silver associates persuaded him to go along. Paul Mallon has it that the Senator, before dropping his hat, asked the President if he was ready to declare remonetization of silver to be a fixed policy. It was understood that the

[4] May 18, 1931.

President had said "yes." Silver Congressmen thereupon started to draft bills leading off with the expression, "It is hereby declared to be the fixed policy of Congress that silver," etc. Then the Congressmen learned that the Treasury Department had a bill : "It is the sense of Congress" that silver, etc. There is, of course, all the difference in the world between the "fixed policy of Congress" and "the sense of Congress." The silver men became angry. Borah said he thought they should have no silver legislation at all ; he preferred to go out and discuss the issue for six months, after which he thought they could get a real silver bill through Congress. This sort of thing from Borah had often worried Republican administrations.[5] It worried this Administration no less. A compromise bill, the Silver Purchase bill, was passed in June, 1934. It declared the policy of the United States to be to increase the proportion of silver to gold in our monetary stock until one-fourth the value of such stock should be in silver.

"We passed the so-called silver bill last evening," Borah wrote his friend Rockwell on June 12. "I left the Senate without any elation and a tinge of gloom. The bill was a compromise and, like all compromises on fundamental questions, it satisfies no one. Yet I do not feel resentful toward the President. I understand his position, and it was perhaps not right for me to expect more at this session. But, as I said to him, the stars in their course are fighting on our side, things will be different later."

"I SEE that Governor Roosevelt is taking up the question of refinancing farm mortgages," the Senator wrote in a letter in December, 1932. "He is getting at the heart of the question of farm relief." For more than a year the Senator had considered this the most pressing problem in the complex farm-relief question. The other problems as he saw them in December, 1932, were those of the currency and foreign markets. "Deal with the money problem, either by devaluation of the dollar or expansion of the currency," he wrote a friend. Prices must be raised or the value of the dollar must be lowered. Foreign markets could be restored to the

[5] Paul Mallon's column, May 15, 1934.

farmer if international debts were wiped out and disarmament accomplished. Propositions other than these three he considered only palliatives for the farmers' distress.

The Senator did not have a great deal to say while the Agricultural Adjustment bill was being put through the Senate. He was opposed to the efforts to improve the farmers' condition by crop reductions. This, he thought, would amount to giving up hope of foreign markets. Besides, he could not justify on ethical ground the economics of artificial scarcity. With one-half the world hungry, this man-made scarcity seemed to him a crime. He was, of course, in favor of the inflationary legislation which accompanied the bill ; he even spoke for additional inflation. He admitted that uncontrolled inflation would be disastrous, but he maintained that there was no good reason why a managed currency system should not be perfectly sound.[6] The section of the bill which gave him the greatest satisfaction and the section which he said would lead him to support it, regardless of its objectionable provisions, was the provision for refinancing farm mortgages, two billion dollars being allowed for this purpose.[7]

The Senate placed a provision in the bill to the effect that the farmer should be guaranteed the cost of production. With this and a number of other amendments it passed the Senate (April 28, 1933), Borah voting with the majority. In the conference agreement between the Senate and House this cost-of-production provision was dropped. Borah and several other Senators from agricultural states, including Frasier and Nye, who considered this provision the most significant part of the bill, as far as the "farm" section was concerned, voted against the adoption of the conference report.[8]

Leaving Washington for Idaho after the special session of Congress, the Senator continued to discuss the necessity of inflation if the farmer was to be saved, and the wickedness of reducing crops and slaughtering stock. In an interview for the *Statesman* he declared that the suspension of the anti-trust laws made it comparatively easy for the manufacturers

[6] *Record,* April 17, 1933, p. 1830.
[7] *Ibid.,* April 10, 1933, p. 1429.
[8] *Ibid.,* May 10, 1933, p. 3120.

to increase prices by agreement, but that the farmers could not get an increase by agreement.[9] Inflation was their only salvation. "If there is some other way, well and good. I care nothing for inflation except in the results it may bring in the way of increased prices. . .

"England . . . abandoned gold and went upon a managed currency basis some two years ago. She has controlled her currency with eminent success. . . It is not surprising that when the proposal was made by other countries to return to the gold standard she politely informed them the present system was satisfactory.

"I read in the papers that we have paid out . . . $110,000,000 to cotton farmers in payment for ploughing up their cotton. I read that millions more . . . are to be paid wheat farmers for reducing their acreage. We know that millions are being expended for pigs to be turned into a glutted market or used to fertilize acreages which are already producing more than we can market. . ." The Senator was of the opinion that this would not save the farmer. The next summer he gave small Idaho towns advertising in the metropolitan dailies by likening AAA plans to chinch bugs, boll weevils, and locusts which make scarce "the things for which millions are nightly praying." AAA promoters admitted it was an experiment. The Senator would replace it with his experiment — controlled inflation — which he believed would be more successful.

Senator Borah has continued his objections to farm relief by planned and purchased scarcity, although he voted for the AAA amendments in August, 1935. He continues to support measures for lightening the farmers' mortgage burden. Although, for constitutional reasons, he could not support the Frasier-Lemke bill of 1934, he took a leading part in securing the enactment of the farm-mortgage bill of 1935, which he considers constitutional. In addition, he still advocates a limited expansion of the currency as a means of improving prices.

THE National Recovery bill (June, 1933), in view of the spirit of Congress and administrative backing, was sure to be

[9] *Statesman*, September 24, 1933.

enacted into law. But it did not get through the Senate "without some semblance of the debate that it deserved," commented the Baltimore *Sun*.[10] "The serious-minded statesman," the subject of this biography, received the *Sun's* credit for exposing the bill.

On June 7, Senator Wagner presented his bill and made a rather detailed explanation of it. As soon as he sat down Senator Borah took the floor, not for a speech but for comments and questions. He and the Senator from New York held the center of attention in their running-fire debate for the better part of the two days the bill was under consideration. The Senator from Idaho concentrated his attack upon that provision of the bill which would suspend the anti-trust laws. "As I understand the measure," he said, "we are to have trusts and combines and monopolies, but we are not to call them such ; and we are to regulate them." (This was the same charge he had made in 1914 against the plan of Perkins and the other Progressive leaders for dealing with the trusts.) Mr. Wagner stated that the anti-trust laws had not prevented monopoly and a concentration of wealth and that this bill was designed "to prevent further monopoly."

"I accept the Senator's statement that he is trying to prevent monopoly," replied Borah, "but I am undertaking to say that he is accentuating and making possible greater concentration of wealth than could possibly take place under the Sherman anti-trust laws if reasonably enforced. My contention is that whatever may be the Senator's intention, he is giving monopoly something it has been fighting for these twenty-five years — the death of the anti-trust laws."

Senator Wagner explained that such laws were to be suspended only with reference to the provisions of the codes. "It is perfectly evident, then," countered Borah, "that the provisions of the codes are going to be combinations or contracts in restraint of trade, or it would not be necessary to suspend the anti-trust laws."

Senator Wagner replied : "Under the anti-trust laws as they stand today no group of smaller or larger industries can coöperate for the purpose of putting wages and hours of labor upon a proper basis." Borah answered this with the

[10] Baltimore *Sun*, June 10, 1933.

statement that agreements as to hours and wages would result in agreements as to prices.

Turning his attention to the small business man, Borah remarked that the plan seemed to be to protect him by suspending the anti-trust laws which only the larger business concerns wanted suspended! He stated that the codes would be written by the representatives of big business and that the Government would be practically powerless in its efforts to guarantee the smaller enterprises an opportunity to make themselves heard.

A few other Senators entered the discussion, objecting to the price-fixing possibilities under the proposed codes. Borah offered an amendment which provided that "such code or codes shall not permit combinations in restraint of trade, price fixing or other monopolistic practices." [11] Senator Wagner was willing to accept this amendment, since it did no more than give a statutory guarantee for his statement that "it is not contemplated that prices shall be fixed, because the fixation of prices is not in conformity with the preservation of fair competition." [12] On June 9, the bill, carrying the Borah amendment, passed the Senate, Cutting, La Follette, Norris, and other liberal Republicans, excepting Borah, voting for it.

When the bill came from conference Borah's amendment simply stipulated that the codes should not "permit monopolies or monopolistic practices." The Senator took this to mean that the sponsors of the measure did not consider combinations in restraint of trade and price fixing as monopolistic practices and that their plan was to permit the two practices which had been prohibited by his original amendment. Borah denounced the bill for its provisions which placed arbitrary powers in the hands of administrative officers, as well as for the opportunities it gave for price fixing. Despite the fact that all of the independent or liberal Republicans now joined Borah in opposing the measure, on June 13 the Senate adopted the conference report.

With the NRA in operation Borah soon got the scent of monopoly on its trail. When the petroleum agreement was

[11] *Record,* June 8, 1933, p. 5246.
[12] *Ibid.,* June 8, 1933, p. 5244.

in preparation, Secretary Harold L. Ickes took the precaution of having Mr. Nathan R. Margold, Chairman of the Petroleum Administrative Board, call the Senator's office. But the Chairman, although he made a number of attempts, was not able to get an appointment with Borah. When it was known that the proposed code was awaiting the signature of Secretary Ickes, Senator Borah criticized the agreement. The Secretary asked the Senator (December 21, 1933) for specific and detailed suggestions.

The Senator wrote him four pages (December 28), the keynote of which was: "It does not seem to me possible under this agreement to protect the consumers or to save from utter destruction the independents. It seems to me it would in effect be an approval of the combine and monopoly, and then withholding all power of control over the combine and monopoly." These were to be Borah's standing criticisms of the Recovery scheme – its failure to protect the consumer and the independent, or small, business.

For six months General Hugh S. Johnson had been busy explaining NRA to the country. He had threatened to "crack down" on Henry Ford and other industrialists, but when he had no particular individuals to threaten he belittled the critics of his policy with such picturesque designations as "witch doctors," "tom-tom beaters," and "corporals of disaster." When, at the end of 1933, Borah and Nye made their general charge of the existence of monopoly under NRA, the General had two new individuals to attack. He said they were out to kill the Recovery program and called them "dialecticians." He pounded the table and brought in something about the "angel of death." But about this time Mr. Eugene Grace of Bethlehem Steel was testifying that NRA had worked well for industry, thus giving some point to the Borah-Nye charge. Frank Kent reviewed this situation and concluded that the General was in danger of losing another bout.[13] David Lawrence, writing for the Cincinnati *Times-Star,* explained that the senatorial mind had one thing in common with the Canadian "mounties" – it gets its man.[14]

[13] Baltimore *Sun,* January 2, 1934.
[14] Cincinnati *Times-Star,* January 20, 1934.

In defending the rights of consumers and small business, Borah was quickly recognized in his proper character as spokesman for the masses, and these masses deluged him with letters. He answered these letters in a radio address, February 7, 1934 : ". . . Cotton towels have risen 87 per cent. . . Children's hosiery has risen 94 per cent. Who is responsible for that ? Men's wear, such as men's socks, have risen 67 per cent ; cheap shirts, 72 per cent ; overalls, 110 per cent. . . Who is responsible for this picking the meager pockets of the working man ? . . . I have a letter in my files from an elderly lady from the South who says : 'I am sending you a sample of knitting cotton which sold last spring — 1933 — for 50 cents a pound. Now I must pay 90 cents a pound.' And she asks, 'Who gets this large profit ?' Yes ; who does ? . . . I ask : Does the National Recovery Act and those who are administering it need any help to prevent this extortion ? Has the 'blue eagle' become a hawk ? Certainly not. What is happening is this. While the NRA is seeking to restore purchasing power, monopoly hovers around, soars down like a bird of prey upon the citizen. . ."

He quoted from a letter he had received from a western lumber company, giving exact figures from its records. The figures showed that lumber prices had doubled in one year's time in the 120 items handled by the company. "Balzac, the great French novelist," the Senator commented, "once said that money never loses an opportunity to be stupid. It seems to me that economic power never loses an opportunity to be stupid. These prices will in the end injure the lumber industry. People who want to build a home will not build a home ; they cannot build it. Farmers who want to improve their barns and granaries or build new ones will not do so. . ."

Then he quoted from letters of small business, of which the following letter is typical : "In almost every industry there are large units. These large units are made up of a number of concerns being merged together. In ninety-nine cases out of a hundred, where these mergers take place the concerns are over-capitalized. Now these concerns that are over-capitalized attempt to make a profit on the over-capitalization with the result that they have to get excessively high prices for their merchandise. Such concerns are not able to compete with small units except by price fixing. And if they can fix the prices for the entire industry, they will naturally fix them high enough for themselves to make a profit. And if the little man could get the business, he would make a profit out of all proportion to what he was entitled and what he would ask for if he were permitted to sell the goods in his own way. But the real trouble exists where one price is fixed in an industry — the larger units are usually the people who get all the business and the small units get nothing."

The Senator then told of a conversation he had had with "one of the prominent figures in one of the great industries in the country which is under a code. I do not feel justified in giving his name, but he made this statement: 'Senator, you must realize that the small business man is passing out. He does not belong in our modern industrial development. It is not in the interest [of progress] that a business should be conducted upon the theory that he must be retained. It is natural for us to sympathize with him, but the philosophy of the present constructive program is against him.'"

The salvation of the farmer, the consumer, and the small business man the Senator found in a restoration of the anti-trust laws. At the time he made this address, he had an amendment to the National Recovery Act pending for that purpose.

He delivered scores of addresses denouncing monopoly, particularly during the summer and fall of 1934. He easily held his place as the most devastating critic of NRA results until the "blue eagle" was caught in a chicken coop and carried by the poultryman to the chopping block, where nine Elderly Gentlemen severed his head from his body, doused the body into scalding water, and removed every feather.

"Dear Governor Lehman: Permit me to offer you my most sincere congratulations on your letter to the Mayor of New York. It was timely, it was patriotic, it was statesmanlike. It is distinctly a matter of congratulation to the whole country that the Governor of a great state in these days of wild grasping for power and the utter disregard of personal rights should say once and for all that such things are essentially unamerican."

Governor Lehman had just expressed his disapproval of Mayor LaGuardia's request to the Legislature for extraordinary power in New York City for several months for the purpose of reorganizing city departments and cutting down expenses. In congratulating (January 6, 1934) the Governor for opposing such grant of authority the Senator was whipping the National Administration over the shoulders of the Mayor of New York. Borah thought the time had come to speak out against what he conceived to be executive usurpation and autocracy. He found a convenient opportunity to do it in the Lehman-LaGuardia affair. This oblique attack upon the national Administration probably drew as much comment as a frontal attack would have drawn and was much more in keeping with Borah's disinclination to make personal attacks upon the President, upon any President.

The reciprocal tariff proposal which came before Congress in the spring of 1934 was but another manifestation of the tendency to increase executive power. It was stated that an emergency existed in foreign trade (which none disputed) and that the President should be given the authority to make tariff agreements or treaties, within very broad limits, with foreign powers. This proposal called forth one of the Senator's best constitutional arguments (May 17).

He stated that treaty-making was lodged by the Constitution in the President and the Senate combined, and that the same instrument gave the powers of taxation and the regulation of foreign commerce to Congress. How could Congress take the treaty power and give it to the President when the Constitution stipulated that the President and the Senate should exercise it? How could Congress give the powers over taxation and foreign commerce to the President when the Constitution provided that Congress itself should exercise them? But it was said by the advocates of this proposal that Congress could delegate the power to make tariff agreements because the Court had held that such delegation of power did not violate the Constitution as long as Congress fixed an intelligible principle which would guide the Executive in the exercise of the delegated power. Senator Borah admitted this, and regretted that the Court had been so liberal. But he claimed that there was no such intelligible principle fixed in this proposed grant of power; the President was to be given practically a free hand in making these tariff agreements.

"There has been a supposition undoubtedly entertained by many people that an emergency, somewhat like the midnight hags upon the blasted heath tormenting the soul of Macbeth, can call up power from the unknown deep of the Constitution that is desired for any particular occasion." The Senator tried once more to lay this superstition, quoting from the Minnesota Mortgage Moratorium case: "Emergency does not create power. Emergency does not increase granted power or remove or diminish the restrictions imposed upon power granted or reserved."

But his plea was always more than a lawyer's plea. We take a few sentences from his peroration. "We need something of the ancient faith, something of the ancient vision. You will remember, Mr. President, in the history of the American Revolution when the British forces were in possession of the Old Dominion, when the traitor Benedict Arnold was leading his marauding forces up and down the coast, when Tarleton was burning the homes and villages, that Mr. Nicholas, a distinguished citizen of Virginia, seconded by Patrick Henry, moved that a dictator be appointed for the Commonwealth. Thomas Jefferson was then Governor of Virginia. He had just narrowly escaped capture at the hands of the British forces. When this resolution came to his attention he said: 'The very thought alone was treason against mankind in general, as riveting forever the chains which bow down their necks by giving their oppressors proof (do not forget that) — by giving their oppressors proof, which they would have trumpeted throughout the universe, of the imbecility of republican government in times of pressing danger to shield us from harm.'

"What vision! What trust! What confidence! Of these things this Republic was built, and of these things alone will it be maintained."

It is not possible nor perhaps desirable to consider at

length Borah's attitude toward each New Deal measure. Through 1935 he voted on what are commonly regarded as 17 New Deal measures. He supported 11 and opposed 6. He voted for the inflation amendment, the invalidation of the "gold clause" in contracts, the Tennessee Valley project, the gold-reserve act, stock-exchange control, the silver-purchase act, social-security legislation, the labor-relations act, the AAA amendments, the holding-companies act, and the works-relief act. It goes without saying that he did not thoroughly approve of each act for which he voted. He voted for some of them because they were the best he could hope to get. His negative votes were cast on the economy act, NRA, the original AAA (because it did not guarantee the farmer the cost of production), cotton control, the reciprocal tariff, and the Guffey coal act. This is the record of the so-called Great Opposer on the New Deal.

The record of certain other Republican Senators is of interest. Frazier, La Follette, Norris, and Nye voted for the eleven measures which Borah supported. They joined Borah in opposing the original AAA and the NRA, although they had supported the latter measure when it first passed the Senate carrying the Borah amendment against monopolies (Borah had voted against it even with his amendment). Frazier, Nye, and La Follette voted with Borah against the economy act; Norris' vote is not recorded. The two Senators from North Dakota voted with Borah against the reciprocal tariff; Norris and La Follette voted for it. Frazier and Nye voted against four of the seventeen representative New Deal measures; La Follette and Norris voted against three. The late Senator Cutting voted with Borah on every New Deal measure. Senator Capper has the perfect New Deal score, excepting the fact that his vote is not recorded on the Senate motion to recede on the "cost of production" amendment to the AAA measure. In general, then, the progressive Senators who had given Hoover so much trouble were friendly to the New Deal, but Borah, both in terms of votes and in the vigor of his attacks on measures he could not support, was the least friendly.

His position on the New Deal, as on other public matters, was determined by his humanity to man, his conscience, and his Constitution. Relief measures, the social-security measure, stock-market and holding-company legislation, and inflation met his tests. In voting for the cancelation of the "gold clause" he stood with the five Justices of the Supreme Court who later sustained that resolution. He opposed the Frazier-Lemke Farm Mortgage Moratorium bill on the ground of unconstitutionality, thus taking the position unanimously adopted by the Supreme Court the following year. Had Borah been a Justice of the Supreme Court he would have voted with the minority of that Court to sustain AAA. His objections to it were on grounds of policy only.

His primary opposition to certain New Deal measures is well stated in his speech against the reciprocal-tariff legislation. It is that powers have been unconstitutionally delegated to the Executive. To the Senator this means much more than a simple violation of the Constitution. It is the admission of a failure of representative government, of democracy itself. The plea that emergency demands extraordinary powers for the Executive is simply the first tenet in that political philosophy of which the last is "democracy is a rotten carcass."

We do not prove that Senator Borah is a New Dealer because he has been courteous to President Franklin Roosevelt. He has been courteous to and considerate of all Presidents, even to Wilson at the very peak of the League of Nations fight. We can not prove that he has the new spirit because he has voted for New Deal measures about two-thirds of the time. When we consider that he is absolutely opposed to any delegation of power beyond the "intelligible principle" which the Supreme Court said was permissible in the Hampton case, and when we note that he thought the Court went too far in that case, it may become apparent that he is far from the New Dealers' ideal. At any rate, he still believes in a jealous, alert, and industrious Congress which should legislate much and delegate little.

In the summer and fall of 1934 Borah gave his time to Idaho, discussing, as was his custom, public affairs in general. His attacks on the New Deal were leveled principally at monopoly under NRA, but he did not hesitate to question, even in rural communities, the AAA crop-reduction program. Close friends summering in Maine wrote him to come to that state and help Senator Hale in his campaign for reëlection. Borah replied that he absolutely could not do so, that he was opposed to nearly everything Hale had stood for. In Indiana Senator Robinson was having his troubles. Borah was asked to help him. He replied that he would come to Indiana if they would be satisfied with "his kind of speeches." To this wire Borah received no answer.

He continued his speech-making in Idaho. At the little farming town of Genesee, on September 24, he attacked the Liberty League which was then getting under way. "I would suggest that the Liberty League broaden the scope of its crusade. Reading its platform, I discover that something has been inadvertently omitted. I do not find anything there which would insure economic freedom. . . There is a power in this country and now operating under the sanction of government, which visits daily every home in the land, presses down upon the inmates and takes in the way of arbitrary prices what it wills to take. The power to fix prices is the power to destroy, not only business, but human rights. Is the League interested in this problem?"

Borah supported the Republican candidates in Idaho for both state and national offices. His ardor in this matter was not noteworthy, but he went so far as to commend certain candidates by name, a form of endorsement which Idahoans had long since come to understand as representing Borah's "grade A" stamp of approval. At Idaho Falls, on November 1, he declared: "There is no record that equals the record of the Republican party in its leadership." But the Republicans were badly beaten in Idaho in 1934.

In 1933, word was being passed around in Idaho that Borah would not stand for reëlection in 1936. This rumor was due in part to the fact that Borah was undergoing a serious operation and in part to the fact that the wish is father to the thought. Ray McKaig wrote the Senator that he should stop this talk by announcing his intention of being a candidate. He told him that he should not take the defeat of certain other Senators who had served long terms as any indication of what the Idaho people would do for him. He said the Senator had never ceased to represent the people of Idaho and the people of the United States.

"Every measure has been studied carefully by you with the thought of the joker in the measure," he continued. "You have done more to prevent evil legislation than any man in the Senate. . .

"The other night at the Valley View Grange . . . they took a number of your franked letters on the trend of monopoly . . . and laid them right beside the Bible on the altar and everybody, as they went by, was called upon by the lecturer to take one. In all my life I have never seen any literature placed on the altar beside the Bible before that night."

At the state Republican platform convention in 1934, the delegates passed by a chorus of "ayes" a resolution "that the Republicans of Idaho express to Senator Borah their sincere appreciation of the great service he has done to the State and Nation, and pledge their unqualified support to return him to the Senate in 1936." [15]

It was rumored that certain Democratic leaders, carried to the point of audacity by the sweeping Democratic victory in 1934, were planning to retire Senator Borah two years hence. It is no secret that at least two Democratic Senators, Roosevelt Democrats at that, let it be known that they would come into Idaho and campaign for Borah in 1936 if Democratic leaders in Washington gave more than normal opposition to Borah in Idaho.

On December 1, 1934, the Senator wrote a friend in Lewiston, Idaho, as follows: "When I went home last July, I had fully made up my mind to retire at the end of my present term. I made the campaign with that idea in mind all the time. I felt I ought to give the people the best there was in me under circumstances when there was nothing selfish behind it. And I still entertain that desire. If I do not it will be because circumstances have arisen which would make it impossible for me to retire with any degree of self-respect. In other words, I do not propose to be bullied

[15] *Statesman,* September 2, 1934.

or kicked out or under circumstances which would seem to show I was afraid to make the fight. If they keep on, I suppose they will have a fight on their hands."

One may hazard a guess that the Senator could have made his peace with the Roosevelt Administration at any time he desired. But, as he would put it, he preferred two more years of absolute political freedom to eight years of political prostitution.

After the smashing defeat of the Republican party in the elections of November, 1934, Senator Borah declared it was high time for the party to become liberal. C. D. Hilles of New York thought the Republicans should stand pat and wrote a letter to that effect. Borah replied that the party should be reorganized. Chairman H. P. Fletcher of the National Committee said that he would not resign and nearly all of the members of the committee agreed that nothing should be done just then.[16] But Borah received bags of mail from the rank and file of the Republican party endorsing his stand. That was all he had expected anyhow. He knew that there would be no reorganization unless the people forced it.

In response to an invitation of the New York County Republican Committee he and Senator Nye spoke at a big meeting in New York on December 13. Borah stated again that the party should reorganize and that since the leaders would not help the only thing to do was for the people interested in reorganization to start in the counties and force it on the leaders. He said the party should go liberal. What is meant by a liberal? "I read in the dictionary this afternoon the definition of a liberal, and I accept it as being correct. It says: 'A liberal is one who is friendly to new ideas, one who looks with favor upon reform in the administration of government.' " What does this mean translated into policies? "As I see it," said the Senator, "the supreme question in politics . . . is how to protect and preserve the rights and liberties and economic privileges of the average man and woman in the United States." The basic answer to this question, he said, was to break monopoly.

It was suggested to the Senator that he was not offering a

[16] New York *Times*, December 2–4, 1934.

very concrete program. This he privately admitted. Why did he not offer one? He gave an interesting explanation in response to a letter from a warm and influential friend who had suggested that they get together and write the party principles for the new Republicans. The Senator wrote: "You may recall when Lord Randolph Churchill was making his great fight to reorganize and to democratize the old Tory party in England, which he finally succeeded in doing in a masterly way, they undertook to draw him out on his platform. He made his platform by attacking certain propositions of the so-called Liberals, or the Gladstone party, and by advocating from time to time certain public policies. But he always declined to put out any specific set of principles and declined it on the ground that, in the first place, he was not in position to have them enacted, and, in the second place, it would give not only the Liberals, but those within the Tory party who were opposed to him, an object of assault."

The Senator has continued to follow the example of Lord Randolph Churchill. He attacks the old guard Republicans generally and exercises his sharp-shooter on the Democrats occasionally. Adopt a liberal program with a strong plank on monopoly and nominate a liberal candidate, he says to the Republicans. Only with such a program and such a candidate can the Republicans, in his opinion, dislodge the Democrats with their monopolistic and bureaucratic tendencies.

CHAPTER XXIV

BORAH THE INSCRUTABLE?

NO MAN in public life is better known than the United States "Senator-at-Large" in the sense that every person who reads a newspaper, however casually, feels that he has some acquaintance with him. Yet practically everyone has a feeling of not understanding Borah. All concede that he is an interesting man, but the opinion is common that he is "as inscrutable as the Will of God." Yet it is possible to arrive at a fairly satisfactory understanding of him if we take into consideration certain backgrounds, attitudes, and characteristics.

Remember the father, William Nathan Borah, industrious, honest, stern, pious, yet tolerant and not with human sympathy and understanding. The Senator has often spoken of his father's influence upon him.

Recall that William Edgar was born in Lincoln's state and just two months after the martyr was laid away at Springfield. Lincoln the emancipator of the slaves, Lincoln the savior of the Union, Lincoln the *nationalist* was a saint in the Borah home. Reverence for Washington and those who made the Union almost matched the Borahs' reverence for sacred things.

Fairfield, Illinois, Lyons and Lawrence, Kansas, and Boise, Idaho, were the communities in which William E. Borah read and studied and thought himself into maturity, the maturity of self-confidence and self-reliance. "Rugged American individual," the frontier democrats, inordinately proud of their country, suspicious of foreign dynasties and convinced of the decadence of Old World civilization, were the products of such communities.

It is not possible to estimate the influence of this background upon the Senator; all agree that it was tremendous. A few might say we need go no further to understand Borah. At any rate, some of his characteristics and attitudes now to be reviewed seem very definitely to have their roots in that background.

Borah loves the common man. It would never occur to him to refer to the "forgotten man." It would never occur to him for the simple reason that he never forgets him. The common man is *the* man as far as Borah is concerned. He sees in the common man common sense, simplicity, directness, frankness, bluntness, sincerity, honesty, industry, charity, and patriotism. For the common man, governments were instituted among men and by all the rules of justice and humanity the common man should have a controlling voice in government. Borah might make such a declaration. One of the leading explanations of the Senator's hatred of war is that the common man has nothing to do with bringing it on, never wants it, and yet spills his blood and sacrifices his little treasure in it. Borah's chief objection to sales taxes is that the common man must pay more than his fair share. He has been a champion of the farmer not for reasons of geography only, but also because he is his ideal type of man. He has espoused the cause of the wage-earner for the same reason. And Borah will go on to the bottom of the social strata and plead the cause of the untouchables. He has often said that he instinctively takes the side of the "under dog," and he does this whether the "under dog" is an abused individual, a subject people, or an oppressed race.

Senator Borah has a rare combination of Americanism (Chs. XII and XIII). To those who loudly advertise their Americanism and try to force everyone else to conform to the same pattern, Americanism usually means a repudiation of the Declaration of Independence and the personal rights guaranteed in our constitutions. At the same time these people venerate the Federal Constitution (of which they have practically no knowledge). They hold the gravest fears of any kind of association with any foreign powers, and have the greatest suspicion of many types of people whom they indiscriminately lump together as communists. Borah's Americanism does not fit this pattern. He yields to no American in his respect for the Constitution, civil-rights provisions and all; neither does he yield to any in his admiration of the Declaration of Independence. He gives absolute pleasure to the fascist type of American in only one particular — in his belief that America should avoid any foreign political commitments, commitments in which a body of diplomats might assemble and announce the nature of the obligations of the United States under certain contingencies. Commitments of a purely legal nature or of a purely economic nature he is perfectly willing to make. He raised no objection when the United States accepted membership in the International Labor Organization, with headquarters at Geneva ; he has for a long time advocated the codification of international law, and he for a like period urged an international court of compulsory jurisdiction to apply that law. Repeatedly he has urged economic conferences. He goes into his particular shell of Americanism only when he sees a political commitment in the offing (and he is very suspicious of this) or when sanctions of force, military or economic, are proposed as instruments for the enforcement of peace. Recent developments seem to show that the Senator's horror of sanctions may be well grounded.

Borah's nationalism has a peculiar consistency. Many nationalists are at the same time imperialists. They would throttle the national aspirations of other peoples. Borah advocates nationalism for all peoples — Russians, Indians, Chinese, and the peoples of Central America. Imperialism under the cover of the Monroe Doctrine or under any other cover or disguise finds no defender in this nationalist.

Associated with Borah's nationalism is his faith in American democracy. America has her own type of democracy which includes not only political democracy but also civil liberty, without which democracy is impossible, and the possibility of economic liberty. We risk the impairment of our system by political associations and combinations with foreign powers, the Senator believes. His faith in our democratic system, as he understands it, is a faith continuous and triumphant. It has never wavered since he attended Tom's Prairie School. He freely admits that the people may make mistakes, but he says they will correct those mistakes. Besides, he is convinced that they will not make as many mistakes as an oligarchy.

If representative government were what the Senator conceives it to be and what he has by his own actions interpreted it to be, democracy would have some checks to its excesses this side of the supreme courts. Borah's type of representative government is that type which has been ornamented by such men as Burke, Madison, and Webster. The people's choice should not simply be an errand boy to parrot their whims, but he should represent them with his intelligence and conscience. He should not give the people a serpent if they should happen to mistake a serpent for a fish. The people should never attempt to dictate to their representative; their remedy is to elect a different one on the next election date if an incumbent proves unsatisfactory. These are the ideas of Burke and Borah. Borah has followed them in practice with few exceptions. In practice he has done another very significant thing — he has reported to the electorate on the issues which faced him as a Senator, giving these reports in the form of numerous addresses throughout the state and giving them in non-election years as well as in election years.

It is important to try to understand Borah's attitude toward the Constitution. Electing law as his profession, he gave it all of his fine qualities of mind and heart, but not his soul. He was a lawyer with a social conscience. Now after thirty years without a client, except the people of the United States, he still conducts himself very much as a lawyer, a constitutional lawyer, with a social conscience. The conscience in him causes the lawyer in him to insist upon a broad application of those provisions of the Constitution which guarantee and enlarge human rights. When he is engaged in emphasizing this aspect of the Constitution he is called a liberal or a dangerous radical, depending upon one's viewpoint. The lawyer in him causes the conscience in him to stop at the point where he fears the Constitution may be distorted (anti-lynch bills, for example). When this occurs he is called ridiculous, a hopeless reactionary, or a valiant defender of the Constitution, again depending upon one's viewpoint. Borah simply says that his oath compels him to follow the Constitution, as he understands it.

The law is majesty with the Senator. He has something of his common man's faith in the law. Of course, he rises far above the common man in his understanding of the difficulties of drafting a statute which will have the effect desired, but he shares something of the common faith in the efficacy of statutory commands and prohibitions. Monopoly is an evil calculated to reduce the people to economic slavery. Very well, abolish monopoly by statute. Intoxicating liquor ruins homes and the majority of the people seem to want the trade in it stopped. Very well, prohibit the trade by law. War is one of the great curses of mankind and the people of all nations profess to hate it. Then let us abolish it by a simple treaty agreement. This may be an over-simplification of the Senator's conception of the power of law, but he has many friends who understand this to be his view.

With the law on the books, it is the ethical and patriotic duty of every person to obey it, says the Senator. The joyous manner in which many people break the law and the failure of a government to enforce it may even cause the Senator to question the future of democracy for a brief moment. Few question the Senator's point that the citizen should obey all law. Many question the wisdom of laws which the citizens simply will not obey. There are those who believe that the Senator may not consider sufficiently the social and economic trends which laws may alter but not prevent.

Borah has always been a student. He has seldom given snap judgments. He has not always been quick to make up his mind. When a problem or issue has arisen, he has studied it carefully before arriving at a conclusion. Having arrived at the conclusion, he is sure of himself, and in explaining and defending his position on the floor of the Senate he accepts interruptions with unruffled good humor. It is sometimes said that he is mentally stubborn, that having made up his mind he will not change it. This, like many other charges, can not be proved or disproved. But it may be said that he regrets having voted for war in 1917. He insisted in 1921 that the war debts must be paid, and a few years later he said he might be willing to trade a part of them for disarmament, and still later he was willing to write them off for trade concessions. Considering what the pure isolationists (and Borah is not of this group) were saying during all these years, this represents considerable mental fluidity on the debt question. He ceased to advocate the silver issue after gold discoveries had served in part the purpose the free silver advocates wanted the white metal to serve. He returned to silver when he thought the world depression called for relief through additional currency and a restoration of the purchasing power in countries of the East. It is by no means impossible that the very people who make this charge of mental rigidity against the Senator may also charge him with inconsistency.

Borah is a man of courage. He has never run from a fight on an issue. His success as a lawyer alone demonstrates his courage, at least the fighting element of it. His political courage has been the subject of much comment. He started out by fighting the Republican machine in Idaho and continued with that fight until 1924, when the machine gave up. He has championed many unpopular causes: anti-profiteering during the war, the release of political prisoners after the war, and the recognition of Soviet Russia, among others. Some of his critics have suggested that he has been given too much credit for courage because with his state almost solidly behind him he could annoy Republican Presidents and advocate detestable causes with little fear of political retribution. It must be stated again that the Republican organization of Idaho fought Borah for at least eighteen years.

Yet one of the Senator's warmest friends says he is timid. What this friend means is that he is timid in putting himself forward for political advancement, advancement to the Presidency. He says that Borah shrinks from risking defeat. But Borah's reluctance to "throw his hat in the ring" has been due to his feeling that efforts to win the Presidency would weaken him as a Senator, not to his fear of defeat in seeking the nomination and election. It is due also to another factor — that he hates to bother with the organization work necessary to win the nomination.

The Senator's failure to oppose the Townsend plan during the first year of its agitation was taken by some as an indication of a lack of courage. Borah had the very highest regard for Dr. Townsend and his followers. He recognized them as the very type of honest, sincere folk who had always supported him. In the Senator's mind, the fact that the Townsend plan had been promptly denounced by nearly all of the economists and students of public affairs did not render it impossible. He has never made up his mind on a public question by counting the opinions of the authorities. He has respected those authorities, but he has never taken their opinions as conclusive evidence. The Senator felt that the plan of the California physician was one which conventional authorities would be likely to discard at once without adequate reflection. He wanted to hear it discussed for a time. He considered it seriously for months, and in the course of time it was rumored that he would presently announce his approval of the Townsend solution of the problem of old-age security. In September, 1935, Borah stated that the plan would cost less than one year of the depression and that if it was not constitutional, it could be made constitutional. (Both parts of this statement seem to be true.) But this is as near as the greatest hope of the Townsendites ever came to a public endorsement of their proposal. In an address in New York on January 28, 1936, the Senator declared that he had for years advocated old-age pensions. Regarding the Townsend plan, he said: "I do not think that is practicable, but I do think that we must provide an old-age pension of fifty or sixty dollars a month – and beyond that I am not prepared to go."

BORAH's political technique is almost entirely his own. He has no organization, much less a machine. His power of oratorical persuasion is such that he won his first election to the Senate in a state in which towns were few and scattered, almost single-handed against his own party's state organization. No Republican since Theodore Roosevelt has been able to influence as many people from the platform as has Borah. It was Borah more than any other individual who turned the people away from the League of Nations. It was Borah who from his place in the Senate forced the President against his will to call the Washington Conference. Borah is one of the few Senators who by sheer forensic power can change votes in the Senate Chamber. This writer is tempted to say that history will place him by the side of Webster as an orator.

One other significant feature of his technique must be restated. It is his publicity sense. Yet it is more than that. His ability to get publicity comes from more fundamental qualities. When he speaks he has something to say, he says it well, often dramatically, and he says it at the right time. Among the refinements of his publicity technique we may list the courtesy with which he treats the press and his natural friendliness with newspaper men. The facility with which he gets publicity may explain in part why he is sometimes called a "grand stand" player.

Borah is the Straddler Magnificent, it is said. May it not be suggested that this characterization arises from the fact that Borah judges each issue on its merits and takes his stand regardless of party platforms, Senate caucuses (or conferences), and Presidents? He may follow Republican leadership on one issue, Democratic leadership on another, and he may originate and champion an issue entirely independent of either party. This is not straddling, but it is so irritating to good party men who want to know where a man can be found at all times that they call it straddling.

There is more truth to the statement that the Senator is the Great Opposer. Genially, almost proudly, he admits it. "Some of my best service," he says, "has been in the things I have been able to prevent." At the top of this list he places his part in keeping the United States from accepting membership in the League of Nations. A large majority in the country or in Congress may be nearly ready to adopt a policy which they are sure will prove to be the salvation of the Republic. The voice of Borah will then be heard to say: "Hold on; let us examine this thing. In any case, what is the hurry?" Then he may find jokers in it, taking care to expose them with cool deliberation or with dramatic heat as the occasion may require. Or he may strip the mask from the thing, pointing in holy horror at its awful nakedness.

Yet let it be said again — for this is a most significant fact about Borah — that he opposes issues, not men. Men may go down with the issue Borah opposes, but the issue, not the men, is the object of his attack. If Borah has thwarted five or six Presidents it is not because he had any personal enmity toward them; it is simply because he disagreed with them on policies. The Senator says that he has no attitude toward

Presidents. This writer cannot accept that statement. He has an attitude, an attitude of unfailing courtesy, unless frank announcement of disagreement on public questions at times amounts to discourtesy.

But Senator Borah's reputation should no more rest on his opposition to measures than that of Justice Holmes should rest on his dissenting opinions. Borah has voted with the majority. He has often spoken for the majority. He has on a number of issues made majorities out of minorities. Consider the income-tax amendment, the amendment for direct election of Senators, the Prohibition Amendment, reclamation laws, homestead laws, farm-marketing laws, farm-mortgage laws, the Children's Bureau bill, the Department of Labor bill, the Norris-LaGuardia anti-injunction bill, the appointment of Justice Cardozo, the release of political prisoners, the Washington Conference, the Outlawry of War, and the recognition of Russia, to mention only a partial list of achievements in which Borah was the leader or one of the leaders. Among the lost causes which Borah has advocated and which are worthy of mention are the following: the debenture plan of agricultural relief, tariff revision for agriculture, 80 per cent tax on war profits, increases on income taxes for large incomes, the restoration of the anti-trust laws, and a government owned and controlled bank.

It is often said that Borah is inconsistent. He opposed the Woman Suffrage Amendment and advocated the Prohibition Amendment and defended his position on the ground of states' rights in both instances. He bitterly opposed the League of Nations and then immediately forced a Disarmament Conference and tried to get an economic conference as well. He defended Theodore Roosevelt's action in Panama and then condemned Coolidge's policy in Nicaragua. He did more than any other man to put Hoover in the White House and then he turned against him violently. These are but a few of the charges of inconsistency.

The reader is not to be bored again with the explanation of how Borah could take opposite positions on the Suffrage and Prohibition amendments and rest his case on states' rights (see Chapters X and XXI). Opposition to the League of Nations was chiefly on the ground that it would involve the United States in a political way with world affairs. Agreements to disarm need not carry any political commitments. In like manner, economic agreements may be made without entanglements. As for turning against Hoover, the Senator would deny this, absolutely. He would say that he could not support certain policies which Mr. Hoover advocated. He supported Hoover where he could agree with him, particularly on disarmament and on Latin-American policy. In the matter of defending Theodore Roosevelt's policy in Panama and at the same time opposing imperialism, let the inconsistency be recorded. Perhaps it should be recorded also on the soldiers' bonus to which the Senator was for a long time earnestly opposed but which he supported in 1935 and 1936. His resolution, in 1935, calling for an investigation of religious persecution in Mexico seems inconsistent with his earlier opposition against any interference with the domestic affairs of that country.

The Senator is about as consistent as any of the rest of us, with this difference — he makes little effort to establish a record for consistency. Suggest in conversation that his positions might not be consistent, and he may wave his hand and scoff at the term. Write him asking him to explain how such and such stands are consistent, and he may reply: "I lay no particular claim to consistency, indeed I do not know that consistency is a virtue of any particular worth." But he will never use this quotation: "With great souls consistency has nothing to do."

It is frequently said that William E. Borah never "goes through." He winds himself up grandly, in perfect form, and hurls a ball right over the plate. Strike one! He repeats the process for strike two. They wait for strike three. It does not come. It is not that he proceeds to walk his man after having two strikes against him. He simply throws no more balls — retires from the mound, so to speak. This is the conception many of Borah's critics, some of whom are his warm friends, have of him. In the light of the great issues he has opposed, successfully opposed, and in the light of the big issues he has espoused, a number of which he originated, why should he have this reputation? The answer is not simple. Borah is a student, a speaker, an orator, rather than an organizer and "fixer." He dislikes routine, dislikes committee work. A trail-blazing speech in the Senate may therefore be followed by inaction for some time. A great many of his speeches are educational in character and are made before the time is ripe for routine work on the subject. Yet when the time comes for this work, Borah is not exactly a shirker. He has often carried a good part of the drudgery in farm, labor, and silver legislation. But Borah's reputation is as the orator and constitutional lawyer of the Senate and he gets little credit for quiet work when he does it. Whether Borah gets down to routine or not, he seldom loses interest in a cause. There is no major issue of which this writer has knowledge which Borah championed or opposed in which he lost interest until the matter was settled. He may consider the time inopportune and say little on the subject for years, but the time will come when he will urge it again. He said little about the recognition of Russia from 1925 to 1929. Strong advocates of the Outlawry of War often became impatient with him for not striking more often. But the Senator had not lost interest ; he was only biding his time. Yet it may be said in all fairness, it seems, that Borah is sometimes slow and reluctant to press an issue through its committee-work stages.

BOLD indeed is the biographer who attempts to assign an active statesman his place in history. Kindliness, frankness, unselfishness, truth, honesty, independence, courage, justice, reverence, righteousness, and common decency — the major attributes of the character of William Edgar Borah — belong to all ages. But the man himself, his work and his influence, may be judged only by the relatively impartial tribunals of future generations. In one of his most notable addresses, that of November 19, 1919, the Senator said : "Time, and time alone, unerring and remorseless, will give us each our proper place in the affections of our countrymen and in the esteem and commendation of those who are to come after us."

INDEX

A

Adamic, Louis, cited, 81
Aldrich, Nelson W., misconceives Borah's character, 89, 132
American Problems (volume of Borah's speeches), cited, 242
Anti-lynching bill, 187
Anti-Saloon League, tactics in Idaho, 174 ff
Anti-trust laws
  the Sherman, 155
  the Clayton, 156
  see National Recovery Administration and Republican Party, reorganization of
Atlantic Monthly, The, 328
Austro-German Customs Union Case, 384

B

Bacon, Augustus O., says South does not violate the 15th Amendment, 413
Bailey, Joseph W., a leader in debate for income tax, 117
Bakhmeteff, Boris, 355
Baltimore *Evening Sun*, 400
Baltimore *Sun*, 298, 350, 477, 479
Baruch, Bernard M., 319
Beck, James M.,
  suggests that Borah is ideal man to trail Wilson against the League, 240
  recommends that Supreme Court be empowered to give advisory opinions, 375
  congratulates Borah on his flexible tariff speech, 438
Bee, The, 182
Beveridge, Albert J.
  Borah attacks his position on trusts, 163, 166-167
  supports Borah on League issue, 233, 245
  his *John Marshall*, 330
Boise, Idaho, character of the city, 1890-1900, 27-28
Boise *Sentinel*, 50
Bolshevism, 354, 358, 359
Borah, Charles F.
  favorite brother of William E., 3
  lawyer in New Orleans, 14-15
Borah, Charles F. (*continued*)
  wants to line up Louisiana delegates for his brother's nomination for President in 1916, 169
  pride in his brother, 208
Borah, Elizabeth West, mother of William E., 2-3
Borah, William E.
  ancestry of, 1
  parents, 2-7
  influence of parents, 2-3, 5-7
  early reading, 7
  religion, 7-10
  attends Tom's Prairie school, 10
  attends Enfield College, 10-11
  first political interests, 12
  first interest in law, 13
  wants to become an actor, 13
  regard for his family, 14-15
  attends school at Lyons, Kansas, 16
  attends University of Kansas, 16-19
  admitted to the bar and begins practice of law, 20-22
  locates in Boise, Idaho, 23
  early law practice in Idaho, 23-25
  the student and reader, 26-27
  Idaho friendships, 33-35, 38
  marries Miss Mamie McConnell, 35-36
  first public address in Idaho, 39-40
  defeated for City attorneyship of Boise, 40-41
  active in Idaho politics, 1890-1896, 41-47
  follows Bryan in 1896, 47-51
  candidate for Congress on the Silver Republican ticket, 51-52
  goes back to Republican party, 54
  defeated for Senate, 55-56
  supports Gooding for governor of Idaho in 1904, 57 ff
  answers Dubois' charges against the Mormons, 59 ff, 69 ff
  wins pre-convention fight for convention nomination of U. S.
  senator, 63 ff
  campaign for election to Senate, 68 ff
  prosecutes labor leader for murder in Cœur d'Alenes, 74 ff
  makes daring ride on a box car, 75
  saves a Negro from lynching, 77
  prosecutes Haywood for murder, not for being labor leader, 79 ff

Borah, William E. (*continued*)
indicted, tried, and acquitted in timber fraud case, 84 ff
timeliness of his election to Senate, 88-90
introduces bill to prohibit members of Congress from practicing before Federal courts, 91-93
defends disciplinary action taken against Negro troops at Brownsville, Texas, 94-95
makes "good" Republican speeches in 1908 and 1910, 95-96
asks that western states be treated fairly in conservation matters, 97-100
his work for reclamation, 100-103
his homestead laws, 103-106
opposes reciprocity with Canada, 106-107
the Borah licensing bill, 107-108
general interest in his constituents, 108 ff
near regular on the Payne-Aldrich tariff, 114-116
a leader in the income tax fight, 117-120
answers Governor Hughes' objection to income tax, 120-123
leads the movement for direct election of Senators, 124 ff
attacks Republican party for hypocrisy on Negro question, 126-128
opposes seating of Lorimer and Stephenson, 129-130
opposes recall of judges, 130-131
suggested for Supreme Court, 131
leads in proposing social legislation, 132-133
always a liberal of the Progressive Era, 133
supports Theodore Roosevelt for nomination in 1912, 136 ff
supports neither Taft nor Roosevelt for election, 141 ff
explains his Republicanism, 142 ff, 162-163
reëlected to the Senate, 149
attitude toward Wilson's domestic program, 154 ff
opposes "pork barrel" and corruption in public life, 158 ff
efforts to reorganize the Republican party, 161 ff
a presidential possibility for 1916, 167 ff
maker of harmony at Chicago, 1916, 171-172

Borah, William E. (*continued*)
not an early convert to Prohibition, 174
favors Webb-Kenyon Act, 175-176
favors Prohibition by constitutional amendment, 177 ff
advocates Woman Suffrage by state action and opposes Suffrage Amendment to Federal Constitution, 181 ff
defends right of Negroes to vote in South, 186
opposes anti-lynching law, Federal department of education, child labor amendment, etc., 187 ff
opposes repeal of Panama tolls exemption, 190-191
opposes settlement with Colombia, 191-193
criticizes Wilson's Mexican policy, 193-197
insists upon neutral rights, 1914-1917, 197 ff
votes for war with Germany, 201-202
opposes conscription and espionage laws, 204, 214
supports other war measures, 204 ff
considers retirement from the Senate, 208-209
refuses to repudiate non-Partisan League support, 209 ff
third election to Senate, 213
fights for release of political prisoners and civil rights in general, 215 ff
the original Irreconcilable, 223 ff
declines Wilson's invitation to dinner to discuss the League, 227-228
speeches against the League, 228 ff
he and other Irreconcilables force Lodge to adhere to the reservations, 246-248
opposes League at Republican convention and in campaign of 1920, 248 ff
retains Wilson's respect, 255-256
opposes treaty of peace with Germany, 259
opposes Fordney-McCumber tariff, 260-261
opposes confirmation of Taft as Chief Justice, 262
forces President Harding to call Disarmament Conference, 262 ff
denounces big navy propagandists, 272
advocates an agreement on the

Borah, William E. (*continued*)
freedom of the seas, 273-274
opposes further cancelation of war debts unless accompanied by disarmament, 274-278
agrees to debt cancelation if foreign markets are to be opened, 278-280
proposes international economic conference, 279
opposes seating of Newberry, Vare and Smith, 282-287
on Senate resolution calling for Denby's resignation, 287-288
recommends removal of Attorney-General Daugherty, 288-290
opposes confirmation of Warren as Attorney-General, 290-293
his "conscience fund" drive, 293-294
supports Coolidge on economy 295-297, 303
opposes soldiers' bonus, 297-299
refuses to accept nomination for Vice-Presidency, 300-301
fights for primary law in Idaho, 304-306
nominated by both Republicans and Progressives for Senate in 1924, 306-308
fourth election to the Senate, 310
contrasted with Lodge and Hughes, 311-314
conception of his duties as Chairman of the Committee on Foreign Relations, 314, 352-353
never went abroad, 316-318
as student of foreign affairs, 318-319
as a speaker, 320-325
his dealings with the press, 325-328
his reading habits, 328-330
use of his time, 331-332
his recreation, 332-335
defends Mexico, 336-339
approves of Morrow as Ambassador to Mexico, 339-340
champions the cause of Nicaragua, 342-346
favors repeal of Platt Amendment, 346-347
advocates square deal for China, 348-350
opposes coercive action against Japan for activities in Manchuria, 350
favors independence of Philippines, 350-352

Borah, William E. (*continued*)
advocates recognition of Soviet Russia, 354 ff
opposes World Court as constituted in 1923, 371
opposes it with Harding-Hughes reservations, 374 ff
opposes it with "Root formula," 382 ff
objects to force as sanction for outlawry of war, 388, 406-407
prepares (with Levinson) plan to outlaw war, 388-392
his resolution to outlaw war, 392-394
broadens Briand's proposal for outlawry, 397-400
urges Kellogg to act on outlawry, 400-402
position on farm relief, 1926-1928, 409-410, 421-422
attacks Prohibition referendums, 410 ff
insists that Republican party take a clear stand for Prohibition, 1928, 415 ff
helps bring Progressives back to Republican party, 417-419, 427-428
campaigns for Hoover, 419 ff
declines Secretaryship of State, 432-433
breaks with Hoover on the tariff, 434 ff
fifth election to the Senate, 444-445
interview with French newspaper correspondents, 446-448
opposes Hughes and Parker for the Supreme Court, 449-452
persuades Hoover to appoint Cardozo to Supreme Court, 452-453
predicts financial collapse, May, 1929, 453-454
differs with Hoover on relief measures, 454 ff
on Prohibition, 1929-1932, 458-463
refuses to support Hoover, 1932, 463 ff
does not support New Deal Emergency Banking Act and Economy Act, 469
supports New Deal monetary policies, 469-472
would restore silver, 472-474
opposes AAA, 475
votes for AAA amendments, 476
attacks NRA, 476 ff
denounces centralization of power and delegation of powers, 481-

Borah, William E. (*continued*)
483
summary of attitude on New Deal, 483-485
advocates reorganization of Republican Party, 485-489
possible influence of background upon, 490
attitude toward the common man, 491
unusual type of Americanism, 491-492
faith in American democracy, 492
conception of representative government, 492-493
position on the Constitution, 493
faith in law, 493-494
studious habits, 494-495
courage, 495-496
power as an orator, 496
sense for publicity, 496-497
the charge of straddling, 497, of opposing, 497-498
constructive record, 498
the question of his consistency, 498-499
the charge that he does not go through, 499-500
Borah, Mrs. William E. (Mamie McConnell)
marries Senator Borah, 35-36
sense of humor, 36-37
capacity for friendship, 37
kindliness, 37-38
Borah, William Nathan
settles in Wayne County, Ill., 2
religion of, 3-5
public spirit of, 5
stern qualities of, 6-7
similarities of father and son, 7
Borchard, Edwin, 319
Border Cities Star, 424
Boston *Herald*, 377, 412
Boston *Transcript*, 162, 168, 169, 187, 225, 234, 235, 310, 324, 436
Bowers, Claude G., 319, 445
Brandeis, Louis D., Borah opposes confirmation of, 157
Briand, Aristide, his original outlawry of war proposal, 396-398
Bridgeport *Post*, 412
Brooklyn *Citizen*, 207
Brooklyn *Eagle*, 327
Brownsville riot, 93 ff
Bryan, W. J.
Borah supports for President, 45 ff
advises bankers against making loans to belligerents, 198
says war debts will never be paid, 274
compared with Borah as an orator, 323
Buffalo *Express*, 226
Bullitt, William C., 367
Burke, Edmund, 329, 493
Burrell, E. A., urges Borah to support Woman Suffrage Amendment, 184-185
Butler, Nicholas Murray, urges U. S. Government to accept Briand's offer to outlaw war, 397, debates Borah on Prohibition, 415-417
Butler, William M., 417

C

Caldwell *News*, 100
Calles, President, 338
Cannon, Joseph, 101
Capital News, 146, 171, 302, 305, 308, 358, 359
Cardozo, Benjamin, appointed Associate Justice of the Supreme Court, 452-453
Chamberlain, G. A., 336
Charleston *News Courier*, 231
Chicago *Evening Post*, 374
Chicago *Record-Herald*, 129
Chicago *Tribune*, 106, 122, 219, 226, 234, 237, 258, 328, 350, 433, 456
Chicherin, George, 360
Child Labor Amendment, 188-189
Child, Richard Washburn, 430
China, 348 ff
Christian Advocate, 415
Christian Science Monitor, 125, 208, 327, 455
Churchill, Lord Randolph, 489
Churchill, Winston, 363
Cincinatti *Times-Star*, 435, 479
Civil Liberties union, 220
Civil rights, 214 ff
Clark, Champ, 104-105, 167
Clay, Henry, 418, 421
Cleveland *Press*, 359, 397
Cobb, Calvin, 28, 33, 64
Cobb, Frank I.
congratulates Borah on his fight for individual liberty, 216
aids in movement for disarmament, 269
Collier's Weekly, 343, 346, 459
Colombia, American settlement with, 191-193
Commercial Tribune, 228
Conservation, 97 ff

Coolidge, Calvin
refuses to attend anti-League meeting in Boston in 1919, 233
on resolution for removal of Denby, 287-288
on removal of Daugherty, 288-290
understands Borah, 291
on nomination of Warren for Attorney-General, 290-293
on economy, 295 ff
wants Borah to run for Vice President, 300-301
on outlawry of war, 395
declines to be a candidate in 1928, 417
congratulates Borah on 1928 campaign, 430
Cooper, Hugh L., 366
Crane, W. M., wants Republican Party to declare for League in 1920, 252
Cuba and the Platt Amendment, 316-317
Cummins, Albert B., a leader in debate for income tax, 117
Currency, expansion of, 470 ff
Current Opinion, 168
Cutting, Bronson, position on New Deal measures, 478, 484

D

Dallas *Morning News,* 215
Darrow, Clarence
defends Wm. D. Haywood, 80 ff
praises Borah's conduct at Haywood trial, 81
cited, 81
believes Borah innocent of fraud in timber cases, 85
Daugherty, Harry M., efforts to remove, 288-289
Davis, Jerome, 356, 367
Debs, Eugene V., 80, 217
Denby, Edwin, resolution for removal of, 287-288
Denny, Ludwell, quoted, 431
Denver *Times,* 101
Depression, 453 ff
Des Moines *Register,* 234
Dewey, John, 387
Disarmament, 262 ff
District attorneys, question of nonpolitical appointment of, 460-462
Doran, Thomas F., writes of fraternity prank played on Borah, 19
Dubois, Fred T.
leads Idaho free silver forces, 46 ff
fails of election to Senate in 1897, 52
becomes a Democrat, 55
brings Mormon question into Idaho politics, 58 ff
defeated for Senate by Borah, 71
supports Borah for Senate, 1918, 212-213
Durant, Will, 329

E

Eighteenth Amendment, *see* Prohibition
Enfield College, Borah and Wesley Jones attend, 11
Executive power, 481 ff

F

Fairfield *Press,* 5 6, 15
Farm bloc, 439 ff
Farm Board, 443 444
Farm relief
the debenture proposal, 434-436
proposal to limit tariff revision to agricultural schedule (1929), 436
farm v. industry, 438 ff
under New Deal, 474 ff
see conservation, homestead laws, and reclamation
Fifteenth Amendment, *see* Negro Suffrage
Fisher, Irving, 396
Fleming, D. F., cited, 239
Flexible tariff, 437-438
Fordney-McCumber tariff, 260
Frank, Glenn, 329
Frankfurter, Felix, 356
Franklin, Jay, quoted, 468
Frazier-Lemke Farm Mortgage Moratorium bill, 476, 485
Frazier, Lynn J., position on New Deal measures, 475, 484

G

Geneva Conferences, 272-273
Gilbert, Clinton W., cited, 200
Giornale d'Italia, Il, 280
Glass, Carter, opposes cancelation of "gold clause," 471
"Gold clause," repeal of, 470-471
Golden Trail, 109
Gompers, Samuel, 147-148, 357
Gooding, Frank,
Borah supports for governor, 62

Gooding, Frank (*continued*)
opposes convention nomination of Senators, 64 ff
alleged to have sought Non-Partisan League endorsement for Senate, 210
endorsed by Theodore Roosevelt, 210-211
Goodrich, James P., 357
Goss, A. S., praises Borah for fighting the farmers' battle, 442-443
Government economy, 295-296
Grand Rapids *Herald*, 192
Grand Rapids *Review*, 195
Green, William, congratulates Borah on his fight against the confirmation of Judge Parker, 451
Grundy, Joseph, 441
Gumberg, Alexander, 356

H

Hackett, C. W., 337
Haiti, 347
Hapgood, Norman, 220
Hard, William, cited, 324-325
Harding, Warren G.
asks Borah to make anti-League speeches in Ohio, 233
uncertain on League issue in campaign of 1920, 254
could not work with Borah, 258
opposes calling of Disarmament Conference, 266-267
recommends American adherence to World Court Protocol, 370-372
Harper's Magazine, 328
Hart, A. B., 329
Hart, John
friend and trusted political adviser of Borah, 34, 306-307
asks Borah to take leadership of Republican Party in the Senate, 315
Harvey, George, 167, 169
Hawley, James H.
friend of Borah, 33
prosecutes Wm. D. Haywood, 81
defends Borah in land fraud case, 86
candidate for governor, 96, 148
candidate for Senate, 160
says Borah should be President, 418
Hawley-Smoot tariff, 434 ff
Hay-Pauncefote treaty, 190
Hays, Will H.
with Borah in Indiana, 166
Hays, Will H. (*continued*)
asks Borah to coöperate with the Republican organization, 236
congratulates Borah on 1928 campaign, 430
Haywood, Wm. D., 78 ff, 81
Hearst's International, 220
Heyburn, Weldon B.
remains a regular Republican in 1896, 49
defeats Borah for Republican nomination to Senate in legislative caucus in 1903, 55-56
opposes convention nomination of Senators, 63-64
his character, 89-90
opposes tariff revision, 114
Hill, David Jayne, 319
Hilles, C. D., 488
Hitchcock, Gilbert M.
his resolution approving Wilson's note requesting belligerents to state peace terms, 224
leads Wilson Democrats for ratification of Versailles treaty, 240
Holmes, John Haynes, 387
Homestead laws, 103 ff
Hoover, Herbert
his weak pronouncement for outlawry of war, 403
satisfies Borah as a candidate in 1928, 408, 423, 425 ff
his "noble experiment" letter, 420
confers with Borah on party platform for 1928, 421
agrees to call special session of Congress if elected, 429-430
political debt to Borah, 431
expresses appreciation to Borah for assistance in campaign, 430
offers Borah Secretaryship of State, 432-433
consults with him about Attorney-Generalship, 433
calls special session of Congress in 1929, 434
opposes Borah's debenture plan, 435-436
fails to support Borah's resolution to limit tariff revision to agricultural schedule, 436
asks for flexible tariff, 437
confers with Borah on approaching visit of Premier Laval, 445-446
differs with Borah on problem of relief, 454 ff
differs with Borah on Prohibition enforcement, 459 ff

Howell, R. B.
  a member of the farm bloc, 439
  proposes sugar bounty amendment, 440
Howerth, J. W., gives estimate of Borah as a student at Enfield College, 11
Hughes, Charles Evans
  opposes Federal income tax amendment, 120
  compared with Borah, 313
  opposes recognition of Russia, 360
  recommends American adherence to the World Court Protocol, 370, 374
  campaigns for Hoover, 424
  appointed Chief Justice, 449-450

I

Ickes, Harold L., seeks Borah's advice on oil code, 479
Idaho
  its population and industry, 1890-1910, 28-32
  Borah's love for, 32-33
Idaho *Statesman*, 36, 39, 41, 42, 43, 46, 47, 48, 50-51, 54, 61, 62, 63, 64, 66, 67, 69, 71, 72, 101, 106, [illegible], 219-220, 241, 306, 421, 475-476, 487
Income tax, Federal, 117 ff
Indianapolis *News*, 166
Indianapolis *Star*, 228
Inman, S. G., 337
International Labor Organization, 492
Irrigation, 100 ff

J

Jefferson, Thomas, 32, 230, 244, 329, 483
Johnson, Hiram
  takes position with Borah against League, 236
  attack on Hoover, 464
Johnson, Hugh S.
  says Borah saved Northwest for Republicans in 1928, 426
  defends NRA, 479
Joliet *News*, 165
Jones Act, 351
Journal of Commerce, 361
Judges, recall of, 130-131

K

Kansas City *Times*, 421
Kellogg, Frank Billings
  fails to understand proposal to outlaw war, 399
  opposes outlawry, 400-401
  Borah persuades him to propose multilateral treaty outlawing war, 401
Kent, Frank, quoted, 479
Kerensky government, 354
Knox-Castrillo convention, 342
Knox, Frank
  favors national Prohibition, 180
  opposes settlement with Colombia, 192
Knox, Philander C.
  his resolution that Peace Conference should be concerned only with accomplishing the aims of the war, 230
  his interest in outlawry of war, 387

L

Labor, supports Borah for reëlection in 1912, 147-148
Labor Age, 301
Labor legislation, 132-133, 477 ff, 484
Labor union troubles in Idaho, 73 ff
La Follette, R. M., Jr.
  member of farm bloc, 439
  position on New Deal measures, 478, 481
La Follette, R. M., Sr.
  Borah assists in Senate campaign, 96
  presidential possibilities of, 1912, 136
  cited, 136
  compared with Borah, 168
  attempts to keep America out of European war, 197 ff, 200-201
  Borah's tribute to, 216, 230-231
  Progressive candidate for President, 1924, 301-303
Lasley, Mrs. A. M., sister of Borah, 14
Latané, J. H.
  cited, 276
  quoted, 399
Lausanne Conference, 278
Laval, Pierre, visit of to U. S., 445-449
Lawrence, David, quoted, 479
League of Nations
  contest over American membership in, 223 ff

League of Nations (*continued*)
relation to World Court, 371-372, 374-375, 378-379
League to Enforce Peace, 224 ff
Lehman, Herbert, 481-482
Lenin, Nicolai, 354
Levinson, Salmon O.
article on war in *New Republic*, 386
works with Borah on outlawry of war, 388 ff
Borah's tribute to, 406
Lewiston *Teller*, 41
Lewiston *Tribune*, 46, 47, 48, 49, 57, 59, 66, 67, 69, 70, 98, 137, 147, 149, 175
Lewiston *Weekly Tribune*, 444, 472
Liberty, 221-222
Liberty League, 486
Literary Digest, 447-448
Lincoln, Abraham, 5, 65, 230, 490
Lippmann, Walter, 319
Litvinoff, Maxim, 366
Lodge, Henry Cabot
criticized by George Wharton Pepper for timid opposition to League, 231
his round-robin resolution, 232
confers with Reservationists, 245 ff
against League in 1920, 252
compared with Borah, 311-312
his *George Washington*, 329
opposes recognition of Russia, 360
Longworth, Mrs. Alice, cited, 140
London *Daily News*, 275
London *Spectator*, 278
Lorimer, William, 129
Los Angeles *Times*, 441
Louisville *Courier-Journal*, 428
Lynchburg *News*, 182

M

MacDonald, Ramsey, congratulates Borah on his address on the world situation, 280
McAdoo, William G., 417
McConnell, William J., 35, 46, 48
McCumber, Porter J., 240
McDonald, James G., 356
McKaig, Ray
urges Borah to support Woman Suffrage Amendment, 184
organizes Idaho Progressives for Borah, 1924, 307
tries to line up Progressives for Borah for President in 1928, 417-419
McKaig, Ray (*continued*)
on Borah's Minneapolis speech, 426-427
encourages Borah to run for Senate in 1936, 486-487
McNary-Haugen bill, 409-410, 421-422
Madison, James, 329, 388, 493
Mallon, Paul, 473
Manchuria, 365
Marbury, William L., 182
Marshall, Thomas R., quoted, 324
Meadows *Eagle*, 102
Mellon, Andrew W.
proposes lowering of taxes, 261
slow to support Hoover in 1928, 431
Borah's sly reference to, 455
Memphis *Commercial Appeal*, 259
Mexico, relations of United States with, 1911-1917, 193 ff, 336 ff
Mills, Walter, cited, 198
Minneapolis *Tribune*, 441-442
Mitchell, W. D., 433
Monopoly, under NRA, 477 ff *see* Republican Party, reorganization of
Monroe Doctrine, 194, 224, 229, 337, 347, 404
Montgomery *Advertiser*, 185-186
Mormons
number in Idaho, 29
Borah appreciates, 32
Borah fights for political rights of, 41
in campaigns of 1904 and 1906, 58 ff
Morrison, C. C., 383, 387, 403
Morrow, Dwight, 339-341, 432
Munsey, Frank A., 216

N

Nation, 328, 348
Nation (London), 274
National Recovery Administration, 476 ff
Navy, building program for, 263 ff
Nearing, Scott, 356
Negro
Republican discrimination against in the South, 186-187
and the nomination of Judge Parker for the Supreme Court, 451-452
Negro Suffrage, 413-415
Neutrality, 197 ff
Newark *News*, 227, 310
New Deal, 468 ff

New Republic, 314, 328, 386
New York *American*, 328, 434
New York *Herald*, 216
New York *Post*, 138-139, 232, 426
New York Stock Exchange, 453-454
New York *Sun*, 130, 138, 383, 423
New York *Times*, 82, 183, 198, 226, 328, 337, 342, 347, 360, 365, 366, 371, 381, 397, 402, 459, 488
New York *Tribune*, 228
New York *World*, 216, 269, 285, 290, 308, 313, 328, 361, 441, 452
Nicaragua, American relations with, 342 ff
Nineteenth Amendment, *see* Woman Suffrage
Non-Partisan League
  opposes profiteering, 205
  supports Borah for Senate, 209 ff
Norris, George
  opposes arming merchant ships, 200
  votes against declaring war on Germany, 201
  a member of farm bloc, 439
  position on New Deal measures, 478, 484
Nye, Gerald P.
  a member of the farm bloc, 439
  position on New Deal measures, 475, 484
  speaks at Republican rally in New York, 488

O

Oil scandals, 287, 289, 293-294
Outlawry of War, 386 ff
  The William Edgar Borah Foundation for the, 406
Overman, Lee S., expresses appreciation for Borah's help on war measures, 206-207

P

Pact for the Renunciation of War
  and Russian recognition, 361,
  and World Court, 382-383, 386 ff
Panama Canal, tolls question, 190-191
Parker, John J., fails of confirmation as Associate Justice of the Supreme Court, 450-452
Payne-Aldrich Tariff, 114 ff
Pearson, Drew, and Brown, Constantine, cited, 400
Perishable Agricultural Commodities bill, 107-108
Perkins, George W., 163 ff, 172
Permanent Court of International Justice, *see* World Court
Philadelphia *Public Ledger*, 234, 257, 266, 267, 268
Philadelphia *Record*, 279-280
Philippines, 350 ff
Phillips, H. I., quoted, 421
Pinchot, Gifford
  West opposes policies of, 97-98
  makes trouble for President Taft, 135
Polish Corridor, 446, 447
Populist party, 42 ff
"Pork barrel," 158-159
Portland *Oregonian*, 85, 86, 102, 264
Primary election law, contest for in Idaho, 1922, 304 ff
Progressive era, the, Borah goes to Senate at beginning of, 89, 113
Progressive party
  in 1912, 135 ff
  in 1916, 171
  in 1924, 301-303, 307-308
Progressive Senators
  on Payne-Aldrich tariff, 114-115
  on income tax, 117
  on measures in general, 150-151
Progressives in 1928, 417 ff
Prohibition
  the contest in Idaho, 174 ff
  the national amendment, 180
  referendums on, 410 ff
  Borah-Butler debate on, 415-417
  in campaign of 1928, 419 ff
  in the Hoover administration, 458-463
  in the campaign of 1932, 463-464
Pueblo *Chieftain*, 128

R

Reciprocity with Canada, 105-106
Reed, James A.
  denounces Norris for opposing war with Germany, 201
  an Irreconcilable Democrat, 233
  compared to Borah as a debator, 324-325
  debates Borah on Prohibition, 459
Republican party, fight for reorganization of, 161 ff, 485 ff, *see* Progressive party
Rinard, Mrs. Mattie, sister of William E. Borah, 3, 14
Robins, Raymond
  on appointment of Morrow as Ambassador to Mexico, 339-341
  advises Borah on Russia, 356, 360

Robins, Raymond (*continued*)
Borah's choice for Ambassador to Russia, 367
works with Borah and Levinson on outlawry of war, 387 ff
in campaign of 1928, 424-425
urges Hoover to offer Borah place in Cabinet, 432
encourages Borah to continue Prohibition fight, 462
Rockwell, Irvin E., 364
Roosevelt, Franklin D.
on recognition of Russia, 365-366
Borah defends monetary policies of, 472
confers with "Silver Senators," 473-474
farm relief program of, 474 ff
Borah's courtesy to, 485
Roosevelt, Theodore
sends special prosecutor to Idaho to try Borah, 86
removes officers who had secured Borah's indictment, 87
Borah friendly with despite disagreements, 88
candidate for President, 1912, 136 ff
reported to have favored the nomination of Borah for President in 1916, 169
reported to have said Borah was right in staying with Republicans in 1912, 167
Borah defends in Panama affair, 191-193
opposes League to Enforce Peace, 225
Lodge confers with on League issue, 239
Root, Elihu
praises Borah's speech on income tax, 118
opposes Webb-Kenyon Act, 175
his compromise plank on the League in 1920, 252
urges delay on disarmament, 266
advises Borah on treaty to outlaw war, 404
Root formula, the, 382 ff
Round Table, 379-380
Rowell, Chester, cited, 316
Ruhr, French occupation of, 275
Russo-Japanese crisis of 1932, 365
Russia, recognition of, 354 ff

S

Sales tax, 457-458
Salmon *Herald,* 235
Salt Lake *Telegram,* 122
Salt Lake *Tribune,* 147
San Francisco *Argonaut,* 147
San Francisco *Chronicle,* 316
Schreiner, George A., 318
Seas, Freedom of, 273-274
Senators
direct election of, 124 ff
excessive campaign expenditures of, 182 ff
Shantung, 348
Shaw, G. B., remark about Borah, 317
Ship subsidy, 261
Shotwell, James T., 387, 398 cited, 396
Silver, 44 ff, 473 ff
the New Deal and, 473 ff
Simmons, F. M., a Democratic leader against the Hawley-Smoot tariff, 439
Simonds, Frank, cited, 314
Slemp, C. Bascom, 300, 423
Smith, Alfred E.
acceptance speech, 424
Borah's reference to, 425, 428
Smith, Frank L., 285-287
Smoot, Reed
seat in Senate contested, 58
conversation with Borah over candidate for Vice-Presidency in 1928, 423-424
see Hawley-Smoot tariff
Soldiers' bonus, 258-259, 297-299
Soviet Propaganda, 358, 360
Spargo, John, 356
Spokane *Chronicle,* 181
Spokesman-Review, 75, 102, 106, 302
Spreckles, Rudolph, 417
Springfield *Republican,* 157, 169, 293
Stearns, Frank W., 417
Stephenson, Isaac, 129-130
Steunenberg, Frank, 74, 78
Stimson, Henry M., 432, 448
Stokes, E. C.
congratulates Borah on a war speech, 208
praises Borah for his position on Russia, 355
fears rise in agricultural prices, 439
Stryker, Lloyd P., 330
Sullivan, Mark, quoted, 267, 298-299
Swope, Herbert Bayard, 319

T

Taft, William H.
heads League to Enforce Peace, 224
Borah opposes his appointment as

Taft, William H. (*continued*)
Chief Justice, 262
Tammany Hall, 425, 428
Tariff Commission, 437
Tariff
farm bloc Republicans and Democratic coalition against (1929-1930), 439 ff
reciprocal, 482 ff
see Payne-Aldrich, Fordney-McCumber, and Hawley-Smoot
Temps, Le, 280
Third Internationale, 360
Thomas, John, 465
Thomas, Norman, 356
Thompson, William Hale, 380
Time, 375, 385
Towner-Sterling bill, 188
Townsend Plan, 495-496
Treaty of Versailles, 237 ff, 447, 448
Trotsky, Leon, 354

U

Unemployed, relief of, 454-456
Unity, 371-372
Untermyer, Samuel, 93

V

Vanity Fair, 468
Vare, William S., 285-287
Villard, Oswald Garrison, 319
Volstead Act, *see* Prohibition

W

Wagner, Robert F., explains and defends NIRA, 475-476
Wallace *Miner,* 309
Walsh, Thomas, compared to Borah as a debater, 324-325
War debts, 274 ff, 447
War measures, 204 ff
War profiteers, 204-206
War, resolution to outlaw, 392-394
Warren, Charles B., failure of confirmation of, 290-292
Washburn, R. M.
cited, 311
quoted, 324
arranges Borah-Butler Prohibition debate, 416
on Borah's Boston speech in 1928, 430
defends Borah as consistent, 436
Washington, George, 229, 230, 242, 490
Washington Conference, 262 ff
Washington *Herald,* 274
Washington *News,* 365
Washington *Post,* 94, 209, 436
Washington *Star,* 267
Washington *Times,* 324
Webster, Daniel, 92, 418, 493
Wells, H. G., cited, 167
White, William Allen
a classmate of Borah at the University of Kansas, 16
gives impression of Borah as a student, 18-19
his editorial, "What's the Matter with Kansas," 52
persuades President Theodore Roosevelt to send special prosecutor to Idaho to try Borah, 85-86
pleased with the work of the Washington Conference, 272
a Senate possibility, 423
says Hoover is interested in Progressive program, 408
congratulates Borah on his efforts in 1928, 430
Wickersham Commission, 459, 462
Willebrant, Mabel, wires Borah to denounce Smith's stand on Prohibition, 424
Williams, John Sharp
ridicules La Follette's opposition to war with Germany, 201
praises Borah, 207
Williams, James T., Jr., opposes League, 234, 239, 240
Wilson, Henry Lane, 194
Wilson, Luther B., 356
Wilson, Woodrow
cited, 153-154
his domestic legislation, 154 ff
on Panama tolls question, 190-191
on Mexican crisis, 193-194
on neutrality, 197 ff
cited, 205-206
appreciates Borah's support, 206-207
would support Borah for reëlection if Borah needed aid, 212
always respected Borah, 255-256
Wise, Rabbi Steven, supports Borah for reëlection in 1912, 147
Woman Suffrage, 180 ff, 413, 416
Wood River *Weekly Times,* 210
World Court, 369 ff
World's Work, 453

DATE DUE